Inside the
Spanish-American War

Inside the Spanish-American War

A History Based on First-Person Accounts

JAMES M. MCCAFFREY

McFarland & Company, Inc., Publishers
Jefferson, North Carolina

The present work is a reprint of the illustrated case bound edition of Inside the Spanish-American War: A History Based on First-Person Accounts, *first published in 2009 by McFarland.*

LIBRARY OF CONGRESS CATALOGUING-IN-PUBLICATION DATA

McCaffrey, James M., 1946–
Inside the Spanish-American War : a history based on first-person accounts / James M. McCaffrey.
    p.   cm.
Includes bibliographical references and index.

ISBN 978-1-4766-8179-5
softcover : acid free paper ∞

1. Spanish-American War, 1898.   2. Spanish-American War, 1898 — Campaigns.   I. Title.
E715.M367   2020
973.8'9092273 — dc22   2008045664

British Library cataloguing data are available

© 2009 James M. McCaffrey. All rights reserved

No part of this book may be reproduced or transmitted in any form or by any means, electronic or mechanical, including photocopying or recording, or by any information storage and retrieval system, without permission in writing from the publisher.

Cover image: Colonel Roosevelt and his Rough Riders, Battle of San Juan, Library of Congress.

Printed in the United States of America

*McFarland & Company, Inc., Publishers
Box 611, Jefferson, North Carolina 28640
www.mcfarlandpub.com*

Table of Contents

Preface 1

1. From Cuban Revolution to American War with Spain 3
2. Dewey's Battle for Manila Bay 8
3. Mobilizing for War 20
4. Naval Blockade of Cuba 49
5. Fifth Corps' Baptism of Fire 75
6. Heavy Fighting in Cuba 91
7. Naval Battle Forces Surrender 110
8. Eighth Corps to Manila 129
9. The Philippines Campaign 142
10. The Puerto Rico Campaign 158
11. Coming Home 174
12. Epilogue 186

Chapter Notes 193
Bibliography 209
Index 221

Preface

THE UNITED STATES WENT TO WAR with Spain in 1898, and for the first time in more than fifty years American combat troops fought major campaigns outside the borders of their country. Many books have been written about this war in the century that has now elapsed. Both participants and historians have investigated such issues as whether the reasons for the war were justified and what the outcome of the war meant for the future of the country and the world. Did the United States altruistically enter into this conflict only to aid Cuban independence, or were other reasons more important? Did the situation in Cuba simply offer an excuse for the United States to join the European countries in establishing overseas dependencies—if not outright colonies? Was this war something to distract Americans from the economic doldrums of the mid–1890s? Did victory over Spain give American political and military leaders an optimistically unrealistic view of their place in the new century? Were the acquisitions of the Philippines, Puerto Rico, and Guam from Spain as much of a boon to the American economy as pre-war businessmen might have predicted? Did victory ensure acceptance as a world power by the older nations of the world? Eminent scholars have debated these and many other questions, and it is not the aim of this book to plow the same ground.

This work, like those above, also seeks answers to various questions. For example, how did America's young men react to the call for volunteers to fight Spain? And what about those who chose to stay home? How did the new soldiers adapt to military regimentation? Did they, as most soldiers throughout time seemed to do, complain about army food, inexperienced officers, and countless other things? What were their opinions of their Spanish enemy, and how well did they get along with their Cuban and Filipino allies?

This book presents a narrative look at the conflict from the points of view of the American soldiers, sailors, and Marines who participated in it and the news correspondents in the field who witnessed and reported it. Many officers, from high-ranking generals to the lowliest second lieutenants, along with a handful of enlisted men found diverse publishing outlets anxious to give the reading public descriptions of the war from the men who fought it. Some men, such as Admiral George Dewey and Major General William Shafter, put down their thoughts in books, while other, lesser, lights found the pages of popular magazines like *Harper's* and *Century* or hometown newspapers to be acceptable venues for their contributions. And in an age of increasing telephonic, as well as telegraphic, capabilities, news correspondents traveled with the troops and were able to file eye-witness stories almost instantaneously. Thus there is a considerable amount of material available that allows one to look into the day-to-day existence of the American warrior of 1898.

CHAPTER 1

From Cuban Revolution to American War with Spain

THE CUBAN REVOLUTION WAS a long time coming. Cuba, the first important Spanish colony in the Western Hemisphere, was, by the 1890s, one of the last. During the first quarter of the nineteenth century Mexico and all of the other mainland colonies had gained their independence. Now only Cuba and nearby Puerto Rico were still bound by colonial ties to Spain. Cubans had grown more and more restive in recent years, and had in fact waged a ten-year struggle for independence that had ended in 1878 with unfulfilled promises of autonomy for their country. Late in February 1895, Havana-born lawyer-poet José Martí led a group of dissidents in the eastern part of the island colony to openly proclaim another revolution.[1]

When the new Spanish governor-general Valeriano Weyler y Nicolau stepped ashore at Havana on February 10, 1896, the Cuban populace did not have long to wait to see how he intended to fulfill his assignment to bring the revolution to a close. Recognizing that a guerrilla movement is only successful if it has the support of the populace, Weyler determined to deny this support to Martí's followers. He quickly issued orders that all of the people living in certain areas of eastern Cuba must leave their home villages and relocate to central reconcentration camps under Spanish military control. With the civilians thus under direct military observation they would not be able to provide the rebels with recruits, food, or even accurate information about Spanish military plans in the area. While this plan has much to recommend it on a purely strategic level its implementation was atrocious.

The camps were overcrowded breeding grounds for all sorts of epidemic diseases. The rebels added to the misery of the inhabitants by not allowing food and other supplies to go into the camps. Tens of thousands of Cuban civilians—estimates range from 100,000 to an unlikely high of 400,000—died of disease and malnutrition in these camps. In Matanzas, for example, the normal mortality rate was six per day. By November 1897, however, this rate had skyrocketed to more than eighty. The situation was even more devastating elsewhere. The normal death rate of seventeen per month in Santa Clara shot up to 550 per month.[2]

These conditions began to be known to Americans in large part due to a circulation war between two New York newspapers. William Randolph Hearst's *New York Journal* and Joseph Pulitzer's *New York World* led the way in what came to be known as "yellow journalism." Their aim was to sell newspapers, and realizing that nothing sells papers like scandals or disasters of one sort or another, they quickly assigned reporters to cover the horrible reconcentration camps and other Spanish "misdeeds." Nor did some of the reporters let the truth stand in the way of a good story. General Weyler soon earned the sobriquet "Butcher" Weyler.[3]

As the situation in Cuba became more volatile, U.S. President William McKinley decided to send an American warship, the U.S.S. *Maine*, to Cuba to be on hand in case it became necessary to evacuate endangered Americans. The *Maine*, a second-class battleship barely two years old, arrived in Havana Harbor on the morning of January 25, 1898. The *Maine* was a good choice for such a mission. She boasted four big ten-inch guns in two protected turrets as well as six six-inch guns, seven fast-firing six-pounders, and eight rapid-fire one pounders. In case of ship-to-ship confrontations, the *Maine* also carried four torpedo tubes. At 324 feet in length, this battleship was more than suited for a show-the-flag mission. Americans in Havana might logically draw comfort from its visit, and anyone who might have meant them harm might decide not to risk retribution from its big guns.[4]

The weather in Havana was unseasonably hot and sultry on the evening of February 15. Captain Charles D. Sigsbee, commanding the *Maine*, had some official correspondence to catch up on — Assistant Secretary of the Navy Theodore Roosevelt wanted his opinion on the advisability of continuing to equip cruisers and battleships with torpedo tubes — but it was too hot to work in his uniform. He removed his uniform coat and donned a lightweight civilian coat only to find in a pocket a letter to his wife that a friend had written to her the previous April, and that he had still not mailed to her. He would have to write an apologetic letter home as soon as he finished his report to Roosevelt. He heard the Marine bugler signal the end of another day with the mournful notes of "Taps" at ten minutes after nine o'clock and knew that most of the 354-man crew had turned in. A few officers strolled on deck, smoking their last cigars of the day, while the men on guard duty remained at their posts. Then, at about 9:40, as Captain Sigsbee was finishing up his paperwork, an explosion, followed seconds later by a second enormous blast, tore through the forward portion of the ship. Within only minutes the once-proud *Maine* settled into the mud of Havana harbor.[5]

Sigsbee, with naval experience stretching back to the Civil War, immediately reacted to what he assumed was an enemy attack of some kind by issuing orders to repel boarders. His executive officer also thought that someone was shooting at the ship, and the *Maine*'s navigator jumped up from his table in the officers' mess and exclaimed, "We have been torpedoed." Another officer had pulled his chair close enough to the port side rail to put his feet up on it as he relaxed at the end of the day. When he heard the explosions he turned and looked forward. "I saw the whole starboard side of the deck and everything above it as far aft as the after end of the superstructure spring up in the air," he recalled. The Marine sergeant of the guard was blown completely off the ship and into the water some fifteen or twenty feet away. An off-duty Marine had slung his hammock topside to enjoy the breeze and avoid the stifling heat in his regular quarters. He had not quite gotten to sleep when the blast hurled him bodily through an awning and onto the hard steel deck.[6]

The officers on deck or in their quarters were more fortunate than most of the crewmen. Hardly anyone below decks in the forward part of the ship got out alive. Those who were not killed outright or suffered grievous wounds found that the blasts had so mangled the ship's ladders as to render them useless. The quickly rising level of the inrushing water drowned some of those who were not otherwise injured. A bosun's mate, just about to go to sleep in the topmost of three hammocks in a forward compartment, was blown "somewhere in a hot place," he recalled. "Wherever that was I don't know. I got burned on my arms and legs, and I got a mouthful of ashes.... The next thing I was ... way under the water somewhere with a lot of wreckage on top of me that was sinking me down." He was one of the lucky ones. He fought his way to the surface where a Spanish rescue boat picked him up. Only two sailors from the berth deck, located directly over the explosion, survived, and Captain Sigsbee later recalled seeing dents in the ceiling where the force of the blast had thrown the bodies of two men. Dozens of crewmen suffered injuries of various degrees of severity, and eight of these men ultimately succumbed to their wounds. Only sixteen enlisted crewmen came through the explosion completely unscathed.[7]

The scene on the waterfront, so placid only minutes before, soon became one of mass confusion. The blast was so powerful that it knocked out the electric lights throughout the city, and the concussion jostled other ships in the harbor amidst flying debris from the *Maine*. A couple of American tobacco dealers were enjoying the night air aboard the *City of Washington* when they heard the explosions. "I looked around," one later recorded, "and I saw the bow of the *Maine* rise a little, go a little out of the water." As debris from the blast rained down all around him he saw "the whole boat lifted out [of the water], I should judge about two feet. As she lifted out, the bow went right down...." His companion thought that the ship rose even more than that, perhaps nine or ten feet, before settling. Another passenger rushed to a porthole upon hearing the *Maine* explode and saw "an immense flash shoot up in the air with a horrible, grinding, hissing noise that might have been an earthquake or a cyclone. Débris of all kinds and a large number of bodies were thrown upward." A half mile away, at the dock at Regla, the captain of the *Deva* felt the concussion of the first blast in his ship and rushed on deck in time to see clouds and debris over 150 feet in the air above the *Maine*.[8]

Nothing could be done for those men trapped in the flooded wreckage of the forward portion of the ship, but rescue efforts began immediately for those who had been thrown overboard and into the water. Sailors aboard the *Alfonso XII* and the *City of Washington* quickly lowered boats to save as many men as they could, although flying pieces of the wrecked ship had destroyed two of the *Washington*'s small boats. Politics had no place in the water surrounding the wreckage as Spaniards and Americans alike worked desperately to reach as many of the survivors as they could and get them to makeshift hospitals aboard neighboring ships or to facilities ashore.[9]

Captain Sigsbee oversaw rescue efforts as much as he could from his crippled vessel until finally he, too, abandoned ship. There was some concern that the fire might reach the magazine holding ammunition for the ten-inch guns. If these shells began exploding from the heat there was no way of telling how much additional damage might be done to anyone or anything nearby. Finally, with the highest deck on the ship nearly awash, Captain Sigsbee, following time-honored naval tradition, was the last man to leave his stricken ship.

The captain's gig took Sigsbee, and some other officers, to the *City of Washington*, whose commander offered him temporary quarters. From his cabin there he composed a message to the Secretary of the Navy. After stating the bare outline of facts surrounding the disaster, and recognizing that sensationalist newspapers would undoubtedly use the incident to incite fervid anti–Spanish feeling, he urged that no one jump to conclusions about the possible cause of the explosion. "Public opinion should be suspended," he wrote, "until further report." It would be unwise to affix blame before a thorough investigation could be conducted. George Bronson Rea, a news correspondent who happened to be at the right place at the right time, carried the message ashore to the telegraph office. It was about 11 P.M.[10]

Government officials, from the Navy Department to the White House, heeded the captain's warning. They continuously assured reporters that there was, as yet, no reason to believe that the explosion was anything other than an accident. No evidence had been uncovered to suggest anything more sinister. Captain Sigsbee's plea for restraint fell upon deaf ears at the offices of both the *New York Journal* and the *New York World*, however. The *Journal* assured its readers that the Spanish had been behind the sinking of the American warship, and even

Wreckage of the USS *Maine* sticks above the waters of Havana Bay (U.S. Army Military History Institute).

carried a huge illustration depicting a mine immediately beneath the ship with electrical wires running onto shore where Spanish soldiers could — and according to the *Journal* did — detonate it from a safe distance. Many Americans began clamoring for war to avenge the loss of the men of the *Maine*. In New Orleans, an editorial in the *Times-Democrat* castigated what it perceived as President McKinley's lack of backbone in not immediately asking Congress to declare war on Spain. The jingoistic writer was anxious for such a war and did not really care under what pretext it began. He favored war even if "it should develop that the Spanish authorities had nothing to do with the treacherous design, if treacherous design it were."[11]

There were journalists, although apparently very few, who kept cooler heads in the face of all the excitement. E. L. Godkin labeled the excesses of Hearst and Pulitzer as "disgraceful." He accused them of "gross misrepresentation of facts, deliberate invention of tales calculated to excite the public, and wanton recklessness in the construction of headlines which outdid even these inventions." The *New York Tribune* responded to all the war fever by coolly reminding its readers that as horrible as was the loss of life aboard the *Maine*, going to war would undoubtedly lead to an even longer casualty list. Such voices of reason were drowned out by the screaming headlines in other papers.[12]

In the meantime, after more than a month of scrupulously examining the evidence, the members of the Navy board investigating the sinking of the *Maine* finally finished their work. First of all, their report exonerated everyone aboard the ship of any possible negligence that might have led to the explosion. That left only some external cause, and that is exactly what the board found. It declared that the explosion was the result an external explosive mine, but the board stopped short of blaming the Spanish. It was unable to decide who had set off the destructive device, only that it had been external to the hull of the battleship. In spite of this disclaimer, most Americans now believed that Spanish treachery was to blame.

Popular outcry swept President McKinley, basically a man of peace, toward war. On Monday, April 11, 1898, McKinley asked Congress to grant him the power to use military and naval force to end the hostilities in Cuba — a thinly veiled request for a declaration of war. Such a momentous step as plunging the nation into war was not one that the legislators regarded lightly. A little over a week later, in the early morning hours of April 19, Congress gave the President the authorization he had sought, and the next day he ordered the U.S. Navy to blockade the major ports of Cuba.[13]

Spain reacted indignantly, and quite understandably, to developments in Washington. After having made what they felt were all the concessions politically possible, Spanish diplomats now faced the very real possibility that American troops would step into their colonial affair with Cuba anyway. Spain declared war on the United States on April 23. The U.S. Congress reciprocated by declaring that a state of war had existed between the two countries since April 21.

CHAPTER 2

Dewey's Battle for Manila Bay

HALFWAY AROUND THE WORLD from Cuba, meanwhile, Commodore George Dewey's little squadron bided its time at Hong Kong, waiting for the Spanish and American diplomats to either resolve their difficulties peaceably or to make the ultimate decision to go to war. There was much work to do and an unknown amount of time in which to do it. In addition to his flagship, the six-year-old protected cruiser *Olympia*, he had two other, smaller protected cruisers at his disposal, the *Raleigh*, also launched in 1892, and the fourteen-year-old *Boston*. The gunboats *Monocacy*, *Petrel* and *Concord* rounded out his squadron. Not all of them were battle ready. The *Olympia* had been in Asiatic waters for three years and was due to be replaced by the protected cruiser *Baltimore*, currently in Honolulu, so it could proceed to California for an overhaul. The *Monocacy* was an old paddle-wheeler that had long since seen its prime days as a warship, and Dewey decided to leave it at Shanghai with a skeleton crew.[1]

Ammunition was in short supply in the Asiatic Squadron. Before Dewey's arrival on station the ships lacked even their regular peacetime allotment of powder and shells. The *Concord* had brought thirty-five tons of munitions when it joined the squadron on February 9, but even with that increase there was still a serious deficiency. Officials in San Francisco filled the old *Mohican* with another thirty-seven tons and dispatched it to Honolulu where the cargo was hurriedly transferred to the *Baltimore*. That ship, then, instead of replacing the *Olympia*, hurriedly steamed westward as an *addition* to Dewey's force.[2]

When war began, if it began, Britain would likely declare its neutrality, and one effect of such a declaration was that Dewey, representing a belligerent nation, would only be able to buy enough coal for his ships to reach the United States. As a precaution, therefore, Dewey purchased the freighter *Nanshan* and the liner *Zafiro* from their British owners as supply ships. The *Nanshan* was full of 3,000 tons of good Welsh coal when he bought it, and the *Zafiro* was soon filled with another 600 tons of coal as well as 600 tons of other stores. The civilian crews of both ships, including their officers, volunteered to stay on and share whatever excitement was in store for their ships' new owner. Dewey eagerly accepted the offer, appointing only one Navy officer and four men to augment each ship's complement.[3]

Dewey first received word that war was to be the course on April 23, and not from Washington, but from British officials in Hong Kong. For many of the Americans this news meant that what they had been preparing for was finally at hand. No one shrank from the new responsibility. In fact, Captain Frank Wildes, commander of the *Boston*, was due to rotate back to the United States, and even though Commander B. P. Lamberton, his replacement, had already arrived, Dewey granted the outgoing commander's request that he be allowed to remain in command of his ship for the impending combat. Lamberton would serve Dewey as his chief of staff. Others also volunteered to extend their tours of duty so they might not miss the action.[4]

Britain announced its neutrality immediately, and in order to preserve the spirit, as well as the letter of this decision, declared on April 23 that all American and Spanish ships must leave the crown colony by 4 P.M. on the 25th. Several American officers had become friends with their British counterparts, and as they prepared to sail there were many fond farewells. So completely had the reports of Manila's stout defenses circulated, however, that none of Her Majesty's officers were willing to wager on the friendly Americans—even at heavy odds. The consensus seemed to be that the yanks were "a fine set of fellows, but unhappily we shall never see them again."[5]

The anxiously awaited *Baltimore* had arrived at Hong Kong on April 22, much to Dewey's relief. Its ten 6- and 8-inch guns were a welcome augmentation to the already available firepower. Work crews immediately swarmed over the newcomer as it moved into a previously prepared dry dock. While some sailors laboriously scraped the barnacles from the ship's hull or loaded coal and other provisions aboard, others were at work covering its bright white paint with slate gray that would make it less conspicuous at sea. The crewmen on the other American ships in port had spent the better part of the previous three days applying the same camouflage to them. The work on the *Baltimore* was complete by the next morning, but the captain of the recently arrived *Raleigh* was still waiting for some repair parts from a machine shop on shore. Since there was little reason for most of his ships to remain in Hong Kong, Dewey sent them away on the afternoon of the 24th, while the *Olympia*, the *Baltimore*, and the *Raleigh* followed the next morning. As his ships, wearing their somber gray paint of war, glided through the harbor toward the sea the crews of British men-o-war anchored nearby gave them a hearty sendoff, and three small boats full of American civilian well-wishers accompanied the fleet out of the harbor.

Dewey was not quite ready to head for the Philippines, so he led his ships to the Chinese port of Mirs, only about thirty miles down the coast from Hong Kong and still about six hundred miles from Manila. Chinese authorities were not as concerned with the propriety of strictly maintaining neutrality as had been the British at Hong Kong. They did not order the Americans to leave, and, as one American officer aboard the *Petrel* observed, they "would not have been able to make us leave" if they had issued such an order.[6]

Here Dewey awaited *official* notice that his country had gone to war, and he oversaw the distribution of the *Baltimore*'s supply of extra ammunition to the rest of the ships. It did not take long following his arrival at Mirs for new orders to arrive. "War has commenced between the United States and Spain," the cable read. "Proceed at once to Philippine Islands. Commence operations particularly against the Spanish fleet. You must capture vessels or destroy. Use utmost endeavor."[7]

Dewey spent the next two days waiting for the *Raleigh*'s machine parts from Hong Kong and for the arrival from Manila of American consul O. F. Williams with late information on Spanish defenses there. Williams arrived on the morning of April 27, and although he was not trained in gathering militarily valuable information, he had done his best. Dewey learned from him, and other sources, that the enemy had approximately forty armed vessels in Manila Bay. Most of them, fortunately for the Americans, were small gunboats more suited for river operations than for the open seas engagement that seemed to be shaping up. The Spanish did have half a dozen cruisers, although one of them was a completely unarmored wooden ship. There were also several shore batteries scattered along the coast at Manila, the nearby naval station at Cavite, and at a few points overlooking the entrance into Manila Bay. The day before his departure from Manila, Williams informed Dewey, the Spanish *Isla de Mindinao* had arrived in port with a load of even more munitions. Not only did the Spanish defenders receive more heavy guns, but the cargo also included a number of underwater mines, which were undoubtedly destined to bolster the defenses at the mouth of the bay.[8]

The *Raleigh*'s parts arrived on the same tug that had brought Consul Williams down from Hong Kong, so by two o'clock that afternoon, on a calm sea and under a clear sky, Dewey's little squadron, in two parallel lines, set its course for the Philippines. The *Olympia* led the line of warships with the *Baltimore, Raleigh, Petrel, Concord,* and *Boston* in that order. The revenue cutter *Hugh McCulloch*, hurriedly added to Dewey's command while it was returning to the west coast of the United States from a Mediterranean cruise, led the *Nanshan* and the *Zafiro* about a half mile to the right of the main battle line. The cumulative firepower available was ten 8-inch guns, twenty-three 6-inch guns, twenty 5-inch guns, and dozens of guns of smaller caliber.[9]

As the American ships plowed through the South China Sea the crews were not sure exactly where they were bound, but they knew that combat was imminent and they busily stripped their vessels for action. They hung heavy anchor chains around the gun positions that were most exposed to enemy fire to protect the gunners from flying shrapnel. And since even a well-protected gun crew is worthless if it cannot use its weapon, they wrapped additional chains around the ammunition hoists that brought shot and shell from deep within the ships. They spread splinter nets to reduce the likelihood of injury from secondary projectiles. On some of the ships the lifeboats were wrapped in canvas to contain any wood splinters that might be created when enemy fire hit them. On others the boats were lowered halfway down to the water so as to save precious time if the crew had to abandon ship. Over the side went wooden tables, chairs, wall panels, gratings, and anything else that might burn during a battle. Battle damage itself was difficult enough to deal with without the blinding, choking smoke of fire.[10]

In the sick bays the medical officers carefully laid out the surgical instruments they would need to treat the expected wounded. They positioned anesthetics, tourniquets, antiseptic solutions for washing wounds, ligatures, and other supplies within easy reach of the operating tables. Prior to leaving the Chinese coast they had instructed all the men on the basics of first aid, such as how and where to apply tourniquets and how to carry an injured man on a litter to the sick bay. To make scalp wounds easier to clean and treat the officers and men had their hair clipped very short.[11]

An old petty officer on board the *Olympia*, a man who had served in the Union Army during the Civil War before beginning a long stint in the Navy, hung around on deck apparently trying to muster up the courage to address the commodore. Dewey took notice and finally asked the man what was on his mind. The sailor came to attention and saluted as he began speaking. "I hope, sir, ye don't intend to fight on the 3d of May," he said. When Dewey pressed him for a reason he replied, "Well, ye see, sir, the last time I fought on the 3d of May I got licked," referring to the Battle of Chancellorsville in 1863. Dewey, perhaps struggling to conceal a smile, allayed his fears by promising not to fight on May 3, "but when we do fight," he assured him, "you'll have a different kind of May anniversary to think about."[12]

The first night out, about midnight, Dewey ordered an alarm sounded to see how long it took his crew to tumble out of their bunks and reach their battle stations in case of a real emergency. Standing on the bridge, with watch in hand, he was pleased to see that the *Olympia* had gone from a state of quiet slumber to battle ready status in just seven minutes.[13]

The next day copies of a proclamation from the governor-general of the Philippines to his loyal subjects appeared on the bulletin boards of the American ships. It announced the existence of a state of war between Spain and the United States and called on the people to protect their homeland from the approaching Americans. The enemy crews, according to this broadside, were made up of "foreigners, possessing neither instructions nor discipline," and were bent on all manner of mayhem, including robbery and kidnapping. "Perhaps in comparison with some foreign navies," a disgusted Dewey later noted, "we lacked the etiquette of discipline, which is immaterial if the spirit of discipline exists. We had the spirit — efficient, dependable, and intelligent." The men, 80 percent of whom were native born, were also incensed by the governor-general's accusations. It was only then that they learned that they were bound for the Philippines, and "no such cheers have ever before floated over the China Sea as then went up from each ship of the squadron, assuring each commander that he need not count alone on the skill and obedience, but upon the eagerness and enthusiasm of the men behind the guns."[14]

As the squadron steamed onward at a steady eight knots, Spanish officials in Manila tried to decide how best to defend their city. A great wall surrounded the old part of the city, and it was upon or adjacent to this wall that most of the city's defensive artillery had been situated. These guns ranged in size and quality from modern 9.5-inch rifled guns — bigger than anything Dewey had on any of his ships — to obsolete muzzle-loading cannons, some of which still used flintlocks as firing mechanisms. These latter pieces were almost useless in the face of Dewey's modern naval armament.[15]

Several miles south of Manila, as the shoreline gently curves to the southwest, a narrow peninsula juts out into the water. Shaped like a giant lobster claw reaching for the city, it was the site of the Cavite naval arsenal, and any plan to defend Manila should also include fortifications here. Accordingly, the Spanish had erected a modern earthwork on Sangley Point, one of the lobster's "pincers," in which they had emplaced six modern 5.9-inch rifled cannons. The arsenal itself was on the other "pincer" and was further protected by three old British-made 6.3-inch muzzle-loading rifles.[16]

Dewey's Spanish counterpart, Admiral Patricio Montojo y Pasarón, was also busy. He was well aware of Dewey's location and of his probable orders, and he planned to dispute the Americans' entrance into Manila Bay with closely placed shore batteries and numerous underwater mines. The bay's geography lent itself to a very stiff defense against any outsiders. Two islands lay in the mouth of the bay, Corregidor, shaped like some giant meerschaum pipe, near the north shore and the much smaller Caballo just south of the larger island. Each island rose several hundred feet above the sea, and both were ideal places for the deployment of heavy cannon. The locations of these islands forced all traffic into or out of the bay to use one of two main channels. Narrow Boca Chica ran north of Corregidor, and three-mile wide Boca Grande passed between Caballo and the mainland to the south. Within this wider and deeper channel was another small island known as El Fraile.

Several batteries of guns, a hodgepodge of up to date breech loading rifled cannons and antiquated muzzle-loading smoothbores overlooked the channels. The muzzle-loaders, however, while powerful enough to hole the unarmored sides of Dewey's ships, took so long to reload that unless the first shots were effective the ships would likely be out of range before a second shot could be fired. Montojo decided to meet Dewey at Subic Bay, about thirty-five miles north of Manila along the west coast of the island of Luzon. Having made that decision, he left Manila on April 25 with several cruisers and a lightly armed dispatch boat.

Montojo had, some weeks previously, sent four 5.9-inch rifles to Subic Bay to be emplaced on Isla Grande, but when he and his squadron arrived he found the guns still lying on the ground, unmounted and of no use to anyone. Only about a third of the underwater mines were in place, and, the admiral now learned, the Americans had already left the China coast and were undoubtedly heading for Luzon. There was no more time to improve the defenses. Disgusted with the lack of preparation he found and disenchanted with the prospect of having to fight the Americans without adequate help from shore batteries or mines, Montojo called his ship captains to a strategy meeting on April 28. The almost unanimous decision was to abandon Subic Bay.

Montojo still had several options. He could avoid an immediate fight altogether and simply leave the Philippines. Dewey would likely follow after him until conditions favored victory, and he turned to face the Americans. Another possibility was to put to sea and intercept Dewey before he reached the Philippines. In either case, however, such an open seas battle would deprive the Spaniard of the comforting support of shore-based artillery.

Instead it was back to Manila on April 29. Montojo could, as he had earlier considered, try to block the entrance into Manila Bay, but his shortage of mines and modern artillery precluded this. He could anchor his fleet right under the batteries of Manila itself where he would have the comfort of the shore batteries backing him up, but this meant that American shells that overshot their marks would put innocent civilians at risk. Finally, he settled on placing his fleet in the shallow waters off Cavite, within range of the artillery at Sangley Point. The relatively shallow water there also meant that in the event that American gunfire sank any of his ships, fewer of his men would perish from drowning than if they were in deeper water.

Admiral Montojo anchored his ships in about twenty-five feet of water in Cañacao Bay near the guns of the Cavite Arsenal. The obsolete *Castilla* was particularly vulnerable so he sent to Manila for sand-filled lighters to be anchored alongside it to absorb American shells. The *Don Antonio de Ulloa* likewise was unable to maneuver under its own power and was anchored in a fixed position so that its starboard guns could be brought into play.

As sunlight lightened the seas around them on April 30, the American seamen realized they were approaching the island of Luzon. Even before it was light enough to see the shoreline their noses picked up the distinctive odor of tropical jungle. Dewey knew that he could not steam straight for Manila Bay without first investigating Subic Bay, because Spanish ships there could fall upon his supply line with potentially devastating results. To preclude such a possibility, he signaled the *Boston* and the *Concord* to separate themselves from the rest of the squadron, put on full steam, and reconnoiter Subic Bay. A little later, concerned that these two ships might be overpowered if a large Spanish fleet was there, he also dispatched the *Baltimore* on the same mission.

By late afternoon, the squadron caught up with the three scout ships near the entrance to Subic Bay. They reported to the commodore that they had seen no sign of significant enemy activity. Upon hearing this news Dewey turned to Commander Lamberton and said, "Now we have them." He soon ordered the entire squadron to stop while the captains of the ships came aboard the *Olympia* for final instructions. The meeting was short and to the point. There was no need to engage in discussion or issue written orders. "We shall enter Manila Bay to-night," Dewey informed his subordinates, "and you will follow the motions and movements of the flagship, which will lead."[17]

Dewey prescribed a leisurely pace for the voyage from Subic to Manila. There was still plenty of daylight, and he did not want to arrive at the entrance to Manila Bay until well after dark, thereby making it more difficult for Spanish artillerists to pinpoint his ships. The ships cruised southward about three or four miles off the coast. As the skies darkened, so too did the ships. Dewey ordered all lights extinguished on every ship except for a single light at the stern. This light, shielded from view on three sides, was only visible to the rear and would serve to guide the ship behind it.

Spanish gunners would find it difficult to see the darkened American ships at night, but darkness also masked the locations of any mines, which Consul Williams had reported were present. Dewey, however, had serious doubts as to the presence, much less the lethality, of mines in the channels into Manila Bay. He knew that the depth of water in Boca Grande was such that only highly trained and experienced men could place mines effectively there, and he did not believe such men existed in the Spanish service. Should this assumption be in error, he calculated that the warm salt water of the tropics would rapidly render any such mines inoperable anyway.[18]

By midnight on April 30, the time had come for the American fleet to test the vigilance of Spanish gunners on Caballo and El Fraile. The moon only occasionally peaked from behind dark storm clouds. The best course into the bay was also one that exposed the ships to the potential fire from both Spanish islands. Lieutenant William Winder, Dewey's nephew and an officer on the *Baltimore*, asked him if he might take temporary command of the collier *Zafiro* and with it lead the procession into the bay. He pointed out that the coal ship drew more water than any of the other ships so if, contrary to the commodore's belief, Spanish mines were present in the channel and the coal ship made it through, then the other ships would also pass safely over them. And if a mine exploded under the *Zafiro* it would at least result in the loss of a noncombatant vessel rather than one of the cruisers. It was a dangerous undertaking, but it also represented a chance, as Winder honestly pointed out to the commodore, for fame. Dewey appreciated the younger man's offer, and his candor, but determined to have his flagship take the lead position. He ordered the gun crews to stand vigilantly by their pieces to return fire if necessary.[19]

In spite of the fact that the Spaniards knew that Dewey was in the vicinity and would undoubtedly attempt to enter Manila Bay, security measures at the entrance to the bay were surprisingly lax. The Spaniards neglected measures that seemed almost too obvious to deserve comment. As the American ships slid through the waves, for example, there was no challenge from patrolling picket boats, although small craft that could have been fitted out for this purpose were quite numerous. Nor did the defenders attempt to illuminate the area with searchlights. Perhaps they figured that no one would be foolhardy enough to try to enter a mined channel at night. If so, it was a serious miscalculation.

The American sailors were keyed up as their ships moved as noiselessly as possible between the islands at the entrance to the bay. "Each man of us," recalled one sailor, "took a tooth grip of the lower lip and had no idea of how many seconds lay between him and kingdom come." A junior officer aboard the *Baltimore*, a man not known for the use of profanity, softly swore a string of oaths that a bystander characterized as "the most extravagant and outlandish" he could imagine. Another man repeatedly sang the opening bars of a popular song until those within hearing thought they would go mad. Gunners stood vigilantly by their pieces and others stood by at their assigned battle stations, ready to treat wounded, put out fires, or shovel more coal into the furnaces to increase speed. Even though what appeared to be a few signal rockets arched into the air from shore there was no fire from the Spanish batteries. The *Olympia* passed El Fraile and turned into the bay. The last ship in the line, the *McCulloch*, was not yet out of the danger zone when sparks in its stack ignited soot and fire shot upward in what one observer described as looking like a "bonfire at election time." Finally, the Spanish gunners responded.[20]

With the flames temporarily marking the *McCulloch* as a target, gun crews on El Fraile opened up with their 4.7-inch guns. The *McCulloch*'s gunners at last had an outlet for their pent up energy and quickly answered the enemy with their six-pounder guns. Ahead, crewmen on the *Raleigh*, the *Concord* and the *Boston* also joined in with much heavier ordnance that lighted up the area around them for brief moments. Within minutes it was all over. The enemy battery had only fired three ineffectual shots before a big American shell destroyed it. Dewey had gotten into Manila Bay without any of his ships suffering so much as a scratch, but he lost one man. In the engine room of the *McCulloch* stifling heat and the stress of imminent combat proved too much for that ship's Chief Engineer Frank B. Randall, and he succumbed to a heart attack.[21]

Once in the bay, Dewey reduced the speed of his squadron to four knots and ordered the *McCulloch* and the two coal ships to move up in a parallel line to the left of the rest of the ships while he waited for daylight. The crewmen remained at their battle stations through the night, but their officers allowed them to get what sleep they could lying on the decks. Very few of the men had been in combat before, and they dealt with their pre-battle anxieties, if they had them, privately. By all accounts there were no outward displays of fear, only a determination by each man to do his duty as well as he could. An officer on the *Petrel* turned in for some badly needed sleep but was bothered a bit by what the future might hold. "The deck above my head was distant about two feet," he later recalled, "and I thought how very flat I would be squashed out against that deck if a torpedo exploded under the ship.... I can even now remember that the last thing in my mind before I went to sleep was how I would look if anybody saw me flattened out against that deck."[22]

As the first tinge of light colored the eastern sky the commodore's next problem was to locate Admiral Montojo's fleet. The most obvious place to find it was under the guns of Manila, but when Dewey got close enough to the city to see what was there he found a fair number of ships, but none of them were warships. Steering south toward Cavite he found the enemy fleet there and immediately began final preparations to engage it. The *McCulloch*, with its engines and boilers above the waterline, was particularly vulnerable to enemy fire so Dewey detached it and ordered its captain to take up a position where it would be out of immediate danger of enemy guns and could oversee the two colliers.

Throughout the little fleet watertight doors were shut to localize the effect of any breech of the hull below the waterline. Cooks extinguished their cooking fires to prevent their spread in case an enemy shell penetrated into the galleys. Air ventilators were likewise sealed shut to deny draft to any fire that might break out. These wise precautions also had the unpleasant side effect of making the working spaces below decks almost unbearable because of the heat. Coal heavers and ammunition passers stripped to their shoes and drawers to cope with temperatures that, according to some accounts soared to 116 degrees.[23]

By five o'clock, darkness had receded enough to reveal the small American squadron to observers in Manila. Within a few minutes, Spaniards manning the shore batteries scrambled to their pieces and opened fire on the invaders. The *Concord* and the *Boston* each responded with a couple of shots, but the Spanish aim was so poor that many sailors sighed with relief. There had been considerable scuttlebutt within the squadron about Manila's heavily armed defenses. When this threat proved empty one of the men reflected that the Spanish defenses were of no more concern than "so many children's sand forts at Coney Island." Dewey decided not to waste any more ammunition on them. He was there, after all, to defeat Montojo's fleet, and at 5:15 the Spanish ships, along with their supporting shore batteries, at Cavite opened fire. Signal flags aboard the *Olympia* encouraged the men of the small fleet to "Remember the *Maine!*"[24]

Shortly after the ineffectual fire from the shore batteries began, nervous Spaniards electrically detonated two mines. They exploded well ahead of the line of American ships but surprised Dewey. "They seem to have mines after all," he remarked, and although their premature use caused no harm he must have wondered how many others were about and whether the men assigned to set them off would be less rash as the battle progressed.[25]

Since the two sides were still too far apart for the Spanish fire to be effective, and since Dewey was ever mindful of the fact that he could not afford to waste ammunition, he ordered his commanders to hold their fire until they saw the *Olympia* begin firing. That ship then led its consorts forward in a single line that angled a little east of where the enemy ships lay, placing Montojo's squadron off the starboard bows of the Americans. This gave the Spanish gunners a relatively small target, but allowed the American ships to employ their starboard batteries whenever Dewey gave the order. Finally, twenty-five minutes later, the *Olympia* had closed to about two and a half miles, and Dewey turned toward the ship's commander, Captain Charles Gridley, beside him on the bridge and coolly told him, "You may fire when you are ready, Gridley." The words were barely out of the commodore's mouth when 150 pounds of powder detonated in the breech of an 8-inch gun in the forward turret and sent a 250-pound projectile on its way toward the Spanish fleet. As the flagship ran up pennants signaling the other ships to "Fire as convenient," the *Baltimore*, the *Raleigh*, the *Petrel*, the *Concord*, and the *Boston* all immediately joined the fray. The battle for Manila Bay was on.[26]

When the *Olympia* reached a point that the maps indicated was the shallowest water in which to operate safely it turned to the west. The rest of the ships followed course, and now, closed up to only two-hundred yard intervals, brought their portside batteries into action as they steamed slowly past the Spaniards. When the *Olympia* had passed well by the last Spanish ship the helmsman turned back again toward the east for a second run. All the other ships followed suit and were soon able to bring their starboard batteries back into play.

Many of the Spanish gunners concentrated their fire on the lead ship in the American squadron, the *Olympia*, and the *Baltimore*, second largest and immediately behind the flagship in the line of battle. Likewise, Montojo's flagship, the *Reina Cristina*, and the almost equally large *Castilla* drew American fire like a magnet. The noise of battle was deafening, and palls of gun smoke soon hung over the opposing ships. The American gunners worked like madmen to put as much fire as possible onto their targets. An officer on the *Petrel* accurately observed that their speed of fire hindered their accuracy, but Admiral Montojo was impressed by the "numberless projectiles" coming his way.[27]

Back and forth steamed Dewey's squadron, constantly pouring fire toward the enemy positions while Spanish guns replied at a somewhat slower rate. The massive clouds of gun smoke that accompanied every discharge of the big guns soon made accurate observation of the enemy difficult. Nevertheless, the American gunners were certain that their shots were striking home with a high degree of accuracy. Not everyone on the American ships was as confident as those actively involved. A man with a panoramic view of the battle from the revenue cutter *McCulloch* grew increasingly concerned as the battle unfolded before him. "Never," he observed, "did spectators watch a more desperate game; for from the continual rain of shot we saw poured into our ships it seemed certain that there would be heavy loss of life, and some of our ships probably crippled or sunk, before the fight was over." An officer who had climbed to a spot on the mast of the *Petrel* to measure ranges to the enemy ships, "could see that the Spanish ships were hit many times, especially the *Christina* and *Castilla*; but then it seemed to me," he continued, "that our ships were hit many times also, and from the way they cut away [shattered life] boats from the *Raleigh* and from other signs, I concluded the *Raleigh* was suffering severely. I could see projectiles falling in the water on all sides of all our ships." One of these enemy shells, in fact, hit the water near Dewey's flagship and then skipped completely over the bow of the vessel. Had the Spanish gunner increased the elevation of his piece just a fraction he might have changed the outcome of the battle.[28]

The Spanish sailors fought with commendable bravery, firing fast and furiously at the enemy ships. Just like the Americans, they had to deal with the deafening noise and the choking smoke of battle. Another aspect of the fighting that was not as apparent as on Dewey's ships was the mounting list of casualties as the American shells wrought havoc. A shell exploded in the forecastle of the *Reina Cristina*, shattering the forward mast and killing and wounding the crews of four rapid-fire guns and the helmsman on the bridge. Likewise, throughout Montojo's squadron, American fire dismounted Spanish guns and cut bloody swaths through the crews.[29]

Spanish gunfire, although not as accurate as that of the Americans, was not without effect. As Dewey's battle line passed from west to east a large shell, perhaps from one of the shore batteries, struck the *Baltimore*'s upper deck. It then caromed upward and tore through the engine room's steel skylight combing before slamming into the curved recoil cylinder of a 6-inch gun on the opposite side of the ship. The projectile, moving slower now, spun around the shield and across to the starboard side of the ship where a steel ventilator finally halted its erratic flight. Although the material damage to the ship was noticeable, human losses were slight. The enemy missile had exploded a couple of three-pounder shells near an American gun of that caliber, wounding two officers and six enlisted men.[30]

At about seven o'clock, in an effort to change the tide of battle, Montojo's flagship, the *Reina Cristina*, lifted anchor and made for the *Olympia*. Virtually the entire American line of battle then shifted its fire toward this new threat. In very short order Montojo found his steering gear shot away and his mizzenmast brought down. Another shell exploded in the officers' cabin, which had been converted to a hospital, killing or re-wounding all of the patients there and splattering the room with blood. An aft ammunition storage room was hit, and the resulting fire filled that part of the ship with smoke.[31]

Montojo realized that he had made a major tactical mistake and ordered his ship, now being steered by hand, to return to its anchorage. By now, however, the American gunners could smell victory. As the Spanish captain turned his broadside toward the enemy ships a big shell pierced the *Reina Cristina*'s superheater, releasing clouds of deadly, scalding steam. Time after time American shells slammed into the crippled Spanish flagship as it turned away and tried to limp back to the relative protection of its consorts. One large shell entered squarely through the stern and killed the ship's captain, Don Luis Cadarso, and sixty of his crew. Admiral Montojo found his flagship so badly pummeled that he now found it necessary to transfer his flag to the *Isla de Cuba*, while the *Reina Cristina*'s few remaining uninjured crewmen carried out orders to flood its magazines and scuttle it.[32]

Shortly after the *Reina Christina*'s ill-fated sortie two Spanish torpedo boats emerged from behind Sangley Point and made straight for the *Olympia*. These small vessels possessed a potential for lethality far out of proportion to their size. The Americans could not allow them to get close enough to put a torpedo or two into the *Olympia* or the *Baltimore*, the two largest American ships. The secondary batteries of both ships now turned their attention to this new menace and loosed a veritable hail of gunfire. One of the shots that hit the lead craft apparently either detonated one of its torpedoes or blew up its steam boiler, and it quickly sank. The captain of the other boat, obviously sensing a similar fate for his vessel, turned back for the beach. When Americans were able to examine this boat after the battle they found it riddled with holes and spattered with blood.[33]

At 7:30, Dewey received a status report from Captain Gridley that greatly concerned him. It stated that the *Olympia* only had an average of fifteen rounds of ammunition left for each of its 5-inch guns. With no ready resupply available within thousands of miles this presented a very real problem. These remaining rounds could be fired away in a matter of a few minutes and then what? The Spanish ships had been hit, as indeed had the American ships, but the extent of damage was not evident. If the other ships in his squadron were similarly short of ammunition, Dewey might have no other recourse but to retreat entirely away from the Philippines until he could replenish his ordnance supplies. He signaled the other ships to withdraw from the battle immediately so he could confer with their commanders. Thus, after five passes along the face of the Spanish position, the American ships headed back out into the bay so Dewey could confer with his captains.

The men at the guns and in the engine rooms and other duty stations had no idea of the reported ammunition shortage. Some were dismayed that they were withdrawing from the battle because they believed that they were winning. A news reporter on the *Olympia* told an inquisitive gun captain that the commodore had decided to stop and feed the men breakfast. "For God's sake," the man exclaimed, "don't let us stop now. To hell with breakfast."[34]

The break in the fighting gave both opposing commanders time to evaluate the course of the battle thus far. Dewey was pleasantly surprised to learn that the message regarding *Olympia*'s ammunition had somehow gotten garbled. The true state of affairs was not that it was reduced to just fifteen 5-inch rounds, but that each of the 5-inch guns on board had only *expended* fifteen rounds! He also found that none of the other ships in his command were short on ammunition and that American casualties had been unbelievably light. Four of the six American ships had been hit by Spanish gunfire, but American casualties were almost nonexistent. The recoil of a gun crushed the fingers of boatswain's mate on the *Olympia*, and a few other men had similar injuries, but the only wounds directly attributable to enemy fire were those on the *Baltimore*. Close calls included that experienced by a junior officer on the *Baltimore*. An enemy shot skimmed so low over his head that, even though he had not been hit, he was certain that his cap had been. As he removed it to inspect for damage another shot whisked it from his hand and into the sea.[35]

Admiral Montojo also used the lull in the battle to evaluate the condition of his ships and men, and the reports he received from his commanders were not very uplifting. His flagship was a burning wreck, the *Castilla* was aflame, and all of his other ships had been hit repeatedly. Some were so badly damaged as to be unable to continue the battle. While the American sailors were enjoying breakfast, therefore, Montojo ordered all his ships that could do so to sail south, into Bacoor Bay behind Sangley Point.

Dewey, meanwhile, having taken the time to see that his ships' crews had a chance to eat a hot breakfast, and with no more worries about an ammunition shortage, returned to the task at hand at about 11:15. By that time, the battle was all but over already. As the *Baltimore* led the *Raleigh* and the *Olympia* in this renewed attack, only the shore batteries on Sangley Point and the sailors on board the *Don Antonio de Ulloa* returned American fire. To make matters even more one-sided, the guns in the shore batteries were placed such that they could not be depressed low enough to hit any targets within two thousand yards, and that is precisely where the American ships lay. The land battery continued to fire, but all its shells sailed harmlessly over the American ships. The crew of the *Ulloa* fought gamely on, but with no real hope of victory—or even survival—in the face of the combined fire of the American ships. After silencing the shore batteries the *Baltimore* and *Olympia* turned their full attention to the crippled Spanish vessel while the *Raleigh* rounded Sangley Point and subjected it to a murderous crossfire. Finally, the brave Spaniards could take no more and abandoned their ship to swim for shore.[36]

About an hour after the resumption of the battle, someone on board the *Petrel* spotted a white flag of surrender at Cavite, and the battle drew to a close. Dewey ordered the *Petrel*, which was the only ship he had that had a light enough draft, into Cañacao Bay to make sure that none of the Spanish ships were capable of resuming the fight. The captain of the *Petrel* sent his executive officer, Lieutenant Edward M. Hughes, and seven sailors in a whaleboat to complete the destruction of the *Don Juan de Austria*, the *Isla de Cuba*, the *Isla de Luzon*, the *General Lezo*, the *Coreo*, and *the Marqués del Duero* already scuttled in the shallow waters of Bacoor Bay. Even though these men were no longer under enemy fire they faced the very real danger of exploding magazines aboard the Spanish ships. Nevertheless, they went about their work methodically. At one point, Lieutenant Hughes realized that in order to reach one of the enemy ships he and his party would be temporarily out of sight of the *Petrel*. He therefore stationed a sailor with a rifle and a signal flag on an elevated point of land from which the man could see both the whaleboat and the *Petrel*. Should anything go wrong he could instantly communicate with the gunboat. When Hughes and his men had finished setting fires aboard the *Don Juan de Austria, Isla de Cuba, Isla de Luzon, General Lezo, Correo,* and *Marques de Duero* they returned to pick up their signalman. They found him casually enjoying a smoke while a Spanish prisoner stood by with the signal flag.[37]

The battle for Manila Bay had been an extremely lopsided victory for the Americans. Three of the Spanish ships had sunk and the *Petrel*'s crew had set fire to six others. Admiral Montojo also suffered heavy personnel losses. On his flagship alone 130 men died and 80 more suffered wounds, while in the rest of his fleet 31 others paid the ultimate price and 130 more were wounded. Dewey's losses were almost nothing. None of his ships suffered appreciable damage, and only nine men were wounded.[38]

Of much interest for future battles was the level of accuracy of American naval gunfire and the effects of varying degrees of armor against these shells. The American ships fired almost 6,000 shots toward the Spanish fleet, but fewer than 150 struck their targets. This two-and-a-half percent accuracy was of great concern and may probably be attributed to the fact that the gun crews, in their haste to deliver ordnance on the targets, were firing too fast to allow for precise range finding. Fortunately, Spanish marksmanship was even worse. One grizzled American gunner, viewing the wreckage before him and unaware of his own squadron's poor shooting percentage, said: "God was pointing our guns, and maybe the devil was aiming the Spanish." It was also determined that the iron and steel plating on the sides of the Spanish ships was so thin that heavy American shells passed completely through the ships without exploding.[39]

Dewey, meanwhile, after a quick survey of the battle damage on his own and the Spanish ships, moved his squadron up to Manila. He let Spanish authorities there know that if they were foolish enough to open their big shore batteries against him he would have his ships destroy the city. Governor-General Basilio Augustín reluctantly agreed to this demand, but when Dewey next requested permission to use the telegraph cable that connected Manila to Hong Kong so he could transmit his battle report back to Washington Augustín refused. Dewey responded immediately by ordering one of his ships, the *Zafiro* to dredge up the cable and cut it. If the cable were to be unavailable to the Americans, it would be unavailable to everyone.

It was a few days before Dewey composed his report of the battle for Washington officials, but he tersely recorded the day's events in his diary: "Reached Manila at daylight. Immediately engaged the Spanish ships and batteries at Cavite. Destroyed eight of the former including the *Reina Christina* and *Castilla*. Anchored at noon off Manila." With no telegraph cable available, Dewey sent his dispatches by ship to Hong Kong, from whence they were transmitted to the United States. He finally sent the *McCulloch* with his reports, but not until May 5. In the meantime, sketchy reports had reached Washington by way of other nations' observers, and President McKinley was jubilant, although he admitted that he had to consult a globe to determine just where the Philippines lay. "I could not have told where those darned islands were," he said, "within 2,000 miles!" Dewey's official reports did not reach Washington until

May 7, and when they did there was a tremendous outpouring of patriotic celebration. Some began to push Commodore Dewey's name forward as the next president. McKinley immediately nominated him for promotion to the rank of rear admiral, and Congress appropriated $10,000 for bronze medals to be presented to each of Dewey's men and a special presentation sword for the new admiral.[40]

The motion picture industry was in its infancy, and as soon as word reached the United States of Dewey's victory, audiences clamored for movies that actually showed American sailors and soldiers in combat. The immense weight of the movie cameras of the day, along with all of their related paraphernalia, made such on-the-spot movies almost impossible. It did not take long, however, for some filmmakers to give the public what it wanted, and audiences were soon thrilled to witness the Battle of Manila Bay. The "battle" they saw, however, was a fake. A couple of enterprising businessmen had purchased photographs, printed on heavy stock, of American and Spanish ships. Then they filled a large canvas-covered frame with about an inch of water, positioned the photographs therein, and rolled camera. To add "realism," one of them blew cigar smoke in front of the camera to simulate the smoke and haze of naval combat.[41]

Commodore Dewey's naval victory in Manila Bay brought with it problems, some immediate and obvious and others that developed over time. The most prominent difficulty, of course, was what to do next. The American warships might well have been able to compel the surrender of the city of Manila, but they did not have enough manpower aboard to occupy the city effectively. Solving this problem required that the Army raise and train additional ground troops and transport them to the Philippines.

While Dewey, and the rest of the world, waited for all of this to transpire he initiated a blockade of the city of Manila. His ships stopped every vessel attempting to enter Manila Bay to determine its nationality and intent. If it was a merchant ship carrying a load of coal for sale in the city it was allowed to enter the bay, but Dewey purchased its cargo, at the current market price, for his ships. Commercial ships laden with anything else were turned away. Foreign warships were allowed to enter and were assigned specific anchorages that were out of the way in case Dewey found it necessary to bombard the city.

One of the most unusual circumstances of this blockade was the arrival of a Spanish gunboat on May 12. The *Callao* had steamed from one of the smaller islands of the Philippine archipelago, an island that apparently was not in regular communication with the outside world. Not only did the ship's captain not know of the American victory almost two weeks earlier, but he was also completely ignorant that his country had gone to war with the United States a week before that. The *Callao* was quickly captured and joined Dewey's rapidly expanding collection of captured vessels.[42]

In addition to the usual problems facing Admiral Dewey while maintaining a blockade of a hostile port were the difficulties that soon arose between United States forces and those of Filipino revolutionaries. The Philippines, like Cuba, had been a Spanish colony for centuries, and many Filipinos, like the Cubans, had tired of this status by the 1890s. A growing nationalist feeling soon found an outlet in the formation of a revolutionary Filipino Army and the beginnings of small-scale military operations against Spanish outposts near Manila in 1896. The uprising spread rather quickly, and an insurrectionist named Emilio Aguinaldo y Famy soon began to make a name for himself.[43]

Soon after Dewey's victory, Aguinaldo proclaimed himself dictator and went about acquiring arms and men for his cause. Even with the influx of several thousand Filipino deserters from the Spanish militia, however, his force was still not strong enough to overwhelm the defenders of the capital city.

CHAPTER 3

Mobilizing for War

BY THE SPRING OF 1898, there were perhaps as many as 175,000 Spanish troops in Cuba, although the high rate of sickness reduced the effective strength to around 80,000. The existence of a state of war found the United States with an Army of only about 28,000 officers and men, and it would have been folly to match such an under-strength force against the Spaniards in Cuba. The small size of the Army was not unusual. Americans had long had a fear of a standing Army in peacetime. And if emergency circumstances arose that dictated the need for a larger force the men of the various state militias could be called on to step forward.[1]

As the nineteenth century drew to a close these militias—in most instances referred to as the National Guard—were often little more than social clubs for a state's elite. The week or two set aside for summer training seemed more like a long round of grand reviews, parades, and evening dances than anything of real military value. The men with commissions greatly enjoyed being addressed by the titles of their military ranks. Up and coming businessmen and local politicians used their Guard affiliations to make connections that would help them in their decidedly unmilitary private careers. A Mississippi guardsman during this time aptly characterized many units when he spoke of his own as being "a company of good fellows, friends who enjoyed each other's society." Needless to say, regular Army officers had rather low opinions of the ability of most Guard units to perform well in any kind of national emergency.[2]

Still the very nature of the social makeup of the National Guard units in many states meant that it formed a rather influential lobbying force whenever Congress considered any legislation having to do with things military. As the crisis over Cuba deepened, high-ranking Army officers began calculating their manpower needs in the event of war. They believed that the regulars would do the bulk of any fighting that became necessary but also estimated that 50,000 volunteers might be needed to man coastal defenses in the United States and stand by as a ready reserve force. This secondary role for the National Guard was entirely unsatisfactory to its leading spokesmen. The pressure they brought to bear on Congress meant that the proposed expansion of the regular Army probably would not get enough votes for congressional passage without some consolation prize for the citizen-soldiers.

The national mood following the loss of the *Maine*, fostered in part by the fomentations of sensationalist newspapers, saw regular Army enlistments increase precipitously. Enlistments, which had been averaging somewhere between 700 and 1,000 men per month prior to the emergency of early 1898, suddenly spurted to over 9,000 in May and an equal number in

June. In fact, had there been enough officers available to detach to recruiting efforts the rate of enlistment might have been even greater. As it was, the Army increased its number of special regimental recruiting stations from only one in April to 126 in May. Many young men likewise anticipated the call for militia volunteers and sought to join those units.[3]

Some of these early volunteers undoubtedly had their dreams of performing daring deeds brought down a notch when, upon reporting to their respective armories for outfitting, they found how short of uniforms and equipment many of the state units were. An Oregon man, for example, joined a local National Guard company shortly after the loss of the *Maine*, and when he reported to receive his military equipment he drew a heavy blue wool coat and pants previously worn by someone much smaller than himself. "Putting them on," he later wrote, "I felt like a dam fool. Yet I issued into the street as a full blown hero, dog[g]ed by a pack of worshipful small boys." When he reported for drill he realized that he was not the only member of the company whose appearance was somewhat less than that of a bandbox soldier. "To tell the truth," he observed, "we were anything but models of military bearing. In the first place, our postures were bad, with a tendency to stoop, our blue uniforms were as ugly as a horse-tram driver's without being comfortable, our felt hats sat awkwardly on the mops of hair then in fashion among our youth. However, we did our best." A New Yorker had a similar awakening. He was convinced that the previous owner of his blouse, or jacket, had been a man of truly gargantuan proportions, "a mere fragment of whose clothing would have outfitted me inside and out, with a Sunday suit left over. The turned-back sleeves reached my elbows; the blouse folded around so that its buttons were at all times under my arms, and it reached to my knees like a frock coat." He was certain that anyone seeing him dressed in this oversized garment would think he was nothing more than the regimental mascot. A Massachusetts man described his state's militia equipment as being good for nothing beyond "eye service." In other words, the men had enough in the way of uniforms and basic gear to make an impressive parade appearance, but very little else.[4]

Not everyone relished the idea of having to answer to military discipline and sought other opportunities to win martial fame. Men all over the country, following the example that had been widespread during the Civil War, began to solicit recruits without having any formal authority to do so. They believed that if they could raise several hundred to a thousand eager young men they would, as a matter of course, receive commissions appropriate to the sizes of their commands. It soon seemed to some that there would not be enough men in the entire country to give all of the would-be Napoleons their desired ranks. An editorial comment in a Houston newspaper summed it up: "What a vast volunteer force this country could quickly put in the field if only colonels and majors were wanted." A Missouri editor made light of the fact that an inordinately large number of men were volunteering for non-combatant service in the bands. "One county," he wrote, "has organized three brass bands. The Dons could hardly stand an attack of American country bands massed in a hollow square all playing a 'Hot Time in the Old Town Tonight.'" Famed Army scout and Indian fighter William F. "Buffalo Bill" Cody was among those with pretensions to high rank. He proposed recruiting a force of 30,000 Indian warriors and leading them to victory in Cuba. Former outlaw Frank James wanted to lead a cowboy company. Martha A. Shute of Colorado also wanted to raise a cavalry troop, but its membership was to be restricted only to women. Needless to say the War Department declined all of these well-intentioned and patriotic offers.[5]

The anticipated influx of citizen-soldiers led to no little amount of rivalry, perhaps even resentment, on the part of the regular soldiers. One regular officer, although writing after the war had ended summed it up thus: "Fighting is a scientific trade. It would be no more absurd to give an idiot a tambourine and call him a musician — he would be an idiot all the

Tennessee volunteers arriving at camp to begin their training (U.S. Army Military History Institute).

same. So with the clerk, the laborer, the hod-carrier, the teacher; he remains the same in spite of all the polished arms, resplendent uniforms, and pompous titles bestowed upon him. He remains just what he was before, until he learns his new trade and becomes a soldier by acquisition of the necessary knowledge and experience to practice his new calling."[6]

By early April, it seemed only a matter of time, and probably not a very long time at that, until a state of war officially existed between the United States and Spain. On the 15th, Secretary of War Russell Alger finally issued orders to consolidate the Army at a handful of locations in the southeastern United States, from which they could stage to Cuba or Puerto Rico. The infantry was to report to New Orleans, Mobile, and Tampa, while the cavalry and most of the artillery received orders to report to the national park on the grounds of the Civil War battlefield of Chickamauga, in northern Georgia. The regulars responded immediately. In fact, Colonel Andrew Burt seemed to have anticipated the contents of the movement orders because his Twenty-fifth U.S. Infantry Regiment arrived at Chickamauga on April 14th.

The proposed consolidation of troops was extremely important because nobody could be certain that the U.S. Army would be able to conduct successfully a sustained, large-scale war. American forces had not been called upon to wage such warfare since 1865. In the intervening thirty-three years the Army had not only shrunk to an inadequate size, but its combat experiences had almost all been in skirmishes with the Indians where at most a company of soldiers had been employed. Very seldom did an entire regiment ever act together, much less a brigade or division. The enlisted men could probably make the necessary adjustments fairly quickly, but it would take some time to acclimate the officers to the different scale of warfare they now faced.

The federal government had established a National Military Park in northern Georgia in 1890 on the site of the ferocious two-day Battle of Chickamauga, fought in 1863. The 7,000-acre park, in addition to commemorating the battle, contained enough open terrain that later day military units might find it suitable ground on which to practice large-scale maneuvers. Thirty-five years after the battle, one of its survivors, Brigadier General Henry V. Boynton was head of the Park Commission and endorsed it as a rendezvous point for troops headed to Cuba and Puerto Rico. It was soon officially designated Camp George H. Thomas, after the heroic Union general who had made such a name for himself there.[7]

Camp Thomas, only a few miles south of Chattanooga, had much to recommend itself for the uses at hand. More than half of the land was covered in oak trees, although to say that it was heavily forested would be incorrect. Park workers had removed most of the underbrush, leaving groves of trees in which the men could camp comfortably in the shade. The park also offered enough open ground to permit the various units plenty of drill ground.

Camp Thomas was not large enough to hold all of the troops being raised for the war, and the transportation headaches incidental to moving all those soldiers to any one campsite would have been overwhelming. On May 18, therefore, the government leased some land about seven miles outside Washington, D.C. The site, named in honor of the secretary of war, was only about one-fifth the size of Camp Thomas and contained a mixture of rolling pastures and woodlands. Troops began arriving almost immediately, and by the end of May, Camp Alger was home to over 18,000 soldiers.[8]

The first official step toward increasing the size of the Army for this latest national crisis was the enabling legislation that emerged from the Congress, with National Guard support almost a month earlier, on April 22, 1898. This "Act to provide for temporarily increasing the military establishment of the United States in time of war" allowed the President to call for and accept volunteers between the ages of eighteen and forty-five for two-year enlistments. It is ironic that national guard officers were so instrumental in getting the service of guardsmen accepted, but that national guard *units* could not enter federal service. The Constitution is very clear on the uses of the militia. It may be used only "to execute the Laws of the Union, suppress insurrections and repel Invasions." Additionally, the Militia Act of 1792 was still in effect and it stated that the militiamen could not serve for more than three months at a time. So since foreign service was expressly forbidden, and since no one could accurately predict how long the war would last, the guardsmen had to enlist as individuals. If enough men from any existing unit offered themselves, however, they would serve together as a unit and would be able to elect their own company officers.[9]

President McKinley wasted little time. On April 23, he issued a call for 125,000 men. This number was dictated not by projected military necessity but by the fact that, with approximately 114,000 National Guardsmen on the rolls of the various state organizations, all of those who wished to volunteer could do so. Each state and territory, based upon its population was to contribute a portion of the necessary force, and it was to consist of not only infantry, but also cavalry, and light and heavy artillery. Wyoming Senator Francis E. Warren, hoping to wrangle a colonel's commission for his friend Judge Jay Torrey, and apparently skeptical that Wyoming's quota of troops under the proposed bill would not have enough such slots, introduced an amendment to the Volunteer Army Bill that provided for additional units raised at large. This gave the men in the less populous states in the West a chance to participate fully. Therefore, the bill, as signed, allowed for the mustering in of up to 3,000 more men. Secretary of War Alger quickly determined that these additional troops would form three regiments of volunteer cavalry and that they were "to be composed exclusively of frontiersmen possessing special qualifications as horsemen and marksmen." A recruiting notice for one of these new regiments stated these requirements rather more colorfully. According to the *Santa Fe New Mexican*, each prospective recruit "must be a good shot, be able to ride anything in the line of horseflesh, [be] a rough and ready fighter, and above all must absolutely have no understanding of the word fear."[10]

For all except these latter three regiments existing militia, or national guard, units would have preference "as far as their numbers will permit, for the reason that they are armed, equipped and drilled." The national guard units were indeed "armed, equipped and drilled," but most of them were under-strength, their arms were obsolete, much of their equipment was missing or in disrepair, and their level of competence as measured by regular drill was highly uneven from state to state. Those who believed, as some did, that these volunteers could simply spring forth to the recruiting offices and be on their way to Cuba with the next outgoing tide were sadly mistaken.

The U.S. Army had recently adopted a new rifle known by the names of its two principal Norwegian inventors. The Krag-Jorgensen was a modern bolt-action repeater capable of firing six .30 caliber bullets without reloading. The Krag was accurate, had a comfortable amount of recoil, and fired ammunition made with modern smokeless powder. It made the regular U.S. soldier the equal of any soldier in the world with regard to his personal weapon. The National Guardsmen, however, still carried the now-obsolete Springfield rifle, the basic design of which had been derived at the end of the Civil War. At that time there had been hundreds of thousands of muzzle-loading rifles on hand, and the most cost-efficient method of modernization had been to modify these guns to load from the breech, or rear, of the barrel. Modifications had occurred in the intervening years, but by 1898 it was still a single-shot, .45 caliber rifle whose cartridges contained black powder. These cartridges produced prodigious amounts of smoke with every discharge, both hiding the enemy from the shooter and revealing to the enemy the position of the shooter. And the recoil was punishing. A New York volunteer said that a man firing this rifle felt as if someone had thrown a brick at his shoulder. A 120-pound, teenaged Iowa bugler insisted that he had to shoot sitting down. "Every time I would fire," he claimed, "the recoil would turn me over."[11]

Throughout the country the initial reaction to the call for volunteers was overwhelming. Here was a chance for young men to earn martial glory. Many had heard their fathers' war stories and did not want to let the chance pass by to experience their own. Others probably planned to use military service as a stepping-stone to elected office. They had seen how Civil War veterans often touted their war service to get votes. In fact, almost every president since the Civil War had served therein. Some — at least those who believed an Iowa editor — believed that war service was absolutely essential, especially if they harbored political aspirations. "Peace never makes men great," according to this man. "It is war, conflict, terrible war, terrific war, that makes men. Peace decays, repose destroys, ease kills. Better a thousand times your boy or lover should die with a bayonet thrust than that his energies and talent should go into decay for want of exercise. This war may be his opportunity." A reporter for a North Carolina newspaper expressed a widespread concern when he wrote of "the fear that the war will be ended before the North Carolina soldiers get a whack at the enemy."[12]

Bursts of patriotic feelings sometimes manifested themselves in rather extravagant claims of military prowess. Florida's quota, for example, was for one regiment of infantry — about a thousand men. Nevertheless, at least three different Floridians each announced plans to raise 1,000-man regiments of *cavalry*. A Mississippian indicated that the other forty-four states could rest easy since "Mississippi single-handed and alone, would be enough for Spain in a short while." Not to be outdone, Texan James R. Carnahan offered the services of 100,000 Knights of Pythias to the war effort. Even this offer, however, pales in comparison to Minnesota Governor David M. Clough's offer. When a New York newspaper reporter asked him how many men of his state would answer the call for volunteers, he referred to the voting rolls for the last national election. He found that 341,762 Minnesota men had voted in 1896 and told the reporter that therefore he felt certain that 341,762 Minnesota men would volunteer for military service.[13]

Not all of the nation's National Guardsmen were anxious to go to war, and in fact the response was surprisingly disappointing in some locales. Recruiters for the Third Mississippi Infantry Regiment, for example, had to travel all the way to Chicago to fill their last 300 slots. Perhaps the thing that dampened the martial ardor of many guardsmen was the requirement that they enlist for two years. They feared the impact that a two-year absence from the business world would have on their personal finances. In Texas, an officer of the elite Houston Light Guard explained that "the majority of our company are [sic] not in a position to make the sacrifice that would be entailed ... particularly when no emergency seems to present itself." He went on to declare that the young businessmen who composed the Light Guard took "a philosophical view of the situation; that is, that their services are not actually needed, and that there are hundreds of idle men in the State, with no obligations attaching to them, and who are only too glad to fill [our] places." Ultimately, only twenty-one members of this organization came forward, and they formed the nucleus of Company A of the First Texas Infantry Volunteers.[14]

An enforced absence from the business world was not the only reason that some guardsmen were reluctant to volunteer. Many expressed concern that they would have to serve under other officers than those with whom they were already familiar. In Nebraska, a contingent of 200 civilians from Nuckolls County delivered a petition to the governor urging him to let their county's volunteers choose their own officers. They were too late. Officers had already been appointed, but the concerned citizens soon learned that their boys had wholeheartedly endorsed the selections.[15]

As concerned as many of the volunteers were that civil authorities would appoint officers over them from other national guard units, they were often even more afraid that their chosen officers would be replaced by regular Army men who would then "lord it over a regiment of gentlemen." Although the President legally could only appoint one regular Army officer per volunteer regiment, even this was too much for some of the prideful militiamen. When told that he might have to have a regular Army officer somewhere in the command structure over him, a proud member of the fabled Seventh New York dug in his heels and refused to volunteer. "To fight for my country as a volunteer in the regiment that I love would be a glorious pleasure," he stated, "but to serve in the Regular Army and do chores for some West Pointer.... Well, I would rather be excused." In fact, the members of this regiment held an election and voted not to participate in the war at all lest their unit be swallowed up by the regular Army. In another New York regiment only 40 percent of the officers and men volunteered, and among those opting to remain at home was the regiment's commanding officer. A Houstonian wrote that he could "imagine nothing more galling and humiliating than a gentleman serving under such conditions."[16]

The captain of a Texas company wired the state adjutant general that the men under his command would enlist, but not in either the regular or the volunteer U.S. Army. The adjutant general, his patience obviously worn thin by this sort of quibbling, responded by informing the captain that "the army of the United States is composed of the regular army and the volunteer army. The President has called for volunteers to organize the volunteer army and consequently your proposition to volunteer and yet not to enlist in either army is absurd." He made it clear that if this company, or any other unit for that matter, would not comply with every aspect of the call for volunteers, it was to disband and turn in all state property in its possession—rifles, uniforms, tents, etc.—so that other, less choosy, recruits could be equipped. Likewise, a North Carolina captain volunteered his company, but only for duty within the United States. "We need no conditional volunteers," was the response he received from his adjutant general as that officer struck his company from the regimental list. A similar situation obtained in Louisiana where only a handful of the enlisted men in the Fourth Battalion joined their officers in volunteering.[17]

Members of understrength Guard units discovered that the requirement that each man pass a physical examination before being accepted for federal service further thinned their ranks. Not everyone who came forward to offer his services, and perhaps his life, to his country was physically able to stand up to the rigors of active campaigning. Army physicians administered "very rigorous and exacting" physical examinations to all prospective soldiers. The doctors were to pay careful attention to any condition that would disqualify a man from service. They were to look for scars or other evidence of deep penetrating wounds, ascertain when, if ever, the recruit had been vaccinated and were to make note of his height, weight, complexion, circumference of chest, hair and eye color, and tattoos or other "indelible or permanent marks" on his body.[18]

Rumors circulated that the examiners would not accept smokers for service, so quite a number of volunteers did their best to give up the habit immediately. Others heard that the doctors would declare ineligible for service any men with corns on their feet, so out came the straight razors for some hurried do-it-yourself podiatric surgery. Men whose weight exceeded the regulation weight did everything they could to lose the unwanted pounds. One man lost seven pounds in one day by not eating anything and by spending a considerable amount of time in a hot Turkish bath. Conversely, some men discovered that they were too light and gorged themselves on cheese, bananas, or anything else that promised quick weight gain.[19]

Under normal conditions, the physical exams usually took about fifteen minutes per man. But with a large number of recruits to be looked at and only a small number of Army medical personnel to administer the exams, they sometimes processed some thirty to thirty-five men per hour. In Illinois, a five-doctor team examined recruits in the Senate chambers of the state capitol building and managed to look at between 800 and 950 recruits per eight-hour shift. Even though one soldier from the Prairie State claimed that "plenty of old men, so crooked in their knees until they looked like a weather beaten shingle, toothless, as stiff as a poker, blind in one eye, and bald headed passed" these exams, the doctors still turned up a significant percentage of men unfit for service, and not because they smoked or had corns. Some men who failed their exams, desperate to take part in the great adventure before them, simply offered themselves up as recruits in companies that had not yet presented themselves for examination and hoped they would somehow pass a second time through. In some instances men were weeded out because they had various foot problems that had the potential of causing them great difficulty in marching long distances. One recruit, with an obviously deformed foot, had another man take his place at the doctor's examination. Then, when the stand-in proved healthy, they switched places again and the unqualified man was soon wearing the blue uniform of one of Uncle Sam's finest. Examining doctors rejected other men because they did not have all of their molars in good working order. The thinking apparently was that men without good teeth would not be able to chew tough Army rations adequately and would therefore likely develop stomach problems from too much unchewed food. A Louisiana volunteer colonel observed that examining physicians had his men "exercise their arms, hands, fingers, and legs and wound up causing them to hop across the room, first on one foot and then on the other." A New York recruit remarked sarcastically that such tests of physical dexterity, consisting of a "group of naked enlistees who were jumping up and down as if practicing to stomp the Spaniards to death," were merely to determine "if our hearts were in the right place." The physicians also paid particular attention to men who wore glasses. One volunteer, noting the doctor's skepticism about his ability to see, assured him that his eyesight was good enough for him to have become "a bit better than a good pool shark" who had once run thirty-five balls. Perhaps he did not realize that most of the fighting would be at distances considerably greater than the length of a pool cue. And when the barely literate volunteer from Indiana was turned away, he complained: "I did'nt [sic] come here to teach school, I came here to fight."[20]

Examining surgeons found a surprisingly high percentage of recruits unfit for service. Of the 102,000 men applying for admission to the regular Army during May, June, and July of 1898, only 25,000 passed the physical, and similar rates must surely have obtained among the volunteers. Among those whom the physicians turned down for service were men who seemed to their comrades to be in the best of health, such as the heavy-weight prize fighter who unsuccessfully sought to join an Alabama unit. Volunteers who had their hopes of military excitement dashed by some physical disqualification were sometimes reduced to tears. Others used political connections to change the results. One such man, a lieutenant in a Massachusetts regiment, was able to wrangle a second exam, and this time he passed. Then, because his company commander had also failed his physical and was not as well connected politically, the lieutenant found himself elevated to captain and command of his company. In another instance, the captain of an Alabama company failed his physical, but it was the men of the company who pressured the government to accept him anyway by refusing to serve unless he, too, was accepted for service.[21]

The numbers of disqualified Guardsmen caused their officers real problems, because for the Guard units to be able to retain their own officers and unit designations they had to be up to full strength before federal mustering officers would accept them. The number of men in most National Guard regiments, however, was below even the peacetime requirement. Therefore even if an entire unit volunteered and passed the physical examinations it would still have to seek raw recruits before the mustering officers would accept it.

Whether recruiting to make up for previously understrength units or to fill the vacancies left by men who had failed their physicals, militia officers worked tirelessly to bring their companies up to full strength, and thereby protect their commissions. Many expressed shock at the caliber of men who answered their invitations to enlist. Many did not come from the same high social class as the reluctant Guardsmen, and one officer seemed almost horrified to have to record what a motley crowd presented itself for induction. "Here a militia man in his natty uniform looking an ideal soldier, on one hand a young man of the better class in neat well fitting clothing, straw hat and polished shoes; on the other hand a rough brawny recruit picked up from off the levees or out of the slums, with ragged and dirty clothing, frequently without a coat and appearing in soiled and tattered undershirt and shoes held together with strings." Not only were these volunteers not of the aristocratic class that originally had joined the ranks of the militia, but it was necessary, he continued, "to not only feed and quarter them, but some of them actually had to be furnished clothing."[22]

College students were among the many young men who were eager to answer their government's call, and this should come as no surprise. These were young men who were old enough to bear up under the physical requirements of war but too young to admit their own mortality. When Missouri's governor received his state's quota, he needed to look no farther than the campus of the University of Missouri to fulfill at least part of the requirement. Students there had formed a cadet corps, complete with band, and had begun drilling as soon as war seemed imminent. They were quickly mustered in as Company I of the Fifth Missouri Infantry, and their band took over those chores for the entire regiment. Likewise, students at Washington University in St. Louis, calling themselves the "University Rifles," answered a later call for volunteers from the Show-Me State. The entire senior class at Mississippi A & M College — all fourteen members— dropped out of school to enlist. The chancellor of the University of Nebraska, recognizing that this same fervor gripped many of the students at his institution, granted diplomas early to those seniors anxious to enlist. Nine seniors at Texas A & M University telegraphed the governor to inform him of their willingness to serve in any capacity he might dictate. At the same time a company of students formed on the campus of the rival University of Texas and began to drill in anticipation of a second call for volunteers— so long as it did not come until the end of the current semester. The president of Virginia's all-black Hampton Institute personally assured Secretary of War Alger that his student body could provide enough young men anxious to do their part for their country to form an entire company.[23]

Within the civilian populace, veterans of America's bloodiest war were usually on hand to offer their best wishes to this later generation's soldiers. These men, often wearing blue or gray coats bedecked with medals so there could be no misunderstanding as to their status in the community, formed honor guards for the departing volunteers. Many (some estimates suggest over 100,000) even tried to enlist, but since even the youngest of these men was in his fifties War Department authorities politely turned down most such requests. Many others remembered how horrible their war had been and were not as anxious to experience it again. They were often perfectly willing to fight if it meant repelling a Spanish invasion of the United States, but they had trouble equating the Cuban revolution with a threat to their country's security. A Texan who had once worn the gray of the Confederacy put his sentiments into verse:

> I know that public sentiment is growing rife
> You can hear the way the people talk, you can hear the drum and fife.
> But I'll tell you how I feel about the going off to war
> I'd a little rather stay right here and stand and shoot from taw.
>
> Brass buttons, plumes and soldier clothes are very fine, I know
> But when they march you off to fight, no telling where you'll go.
> I've 'done and seen' our own folks fight a-during of the war
> And you bet your life if the Spanish come I'll stay and shoot from taw.
>
> You'll never catch this chick again-a-going to the front
> I'll let the younger soldier boys go out and bear the brunt.
> I've reached that interesting age beyond the conscript law
> And rather than enlist again I'd go straight to Ark-an-sas!

An ex–Confederate in Charleston, South Carolina, put a different spin on the situation when a friend asked him if he was going to volunteer to fight the Spaniards. He told his friend that if he did he could probably explain his motivations to his surviving comrades-in-arms. But if he was killed in battle he would have a very difficult time in the afterlife explaining to Confederates there, who had died wearing gray uniforms, the circumstances under which he died wearing a blue one. Their judgment, he was certain, would be "Deserted, by God!"[24]

One of the more unusual volunteer units to form was a light artillery battery from New York City. John Jacob Astor, one of the country's wealthiest citizens, let government authorities know that he was willing to underwrite the cost of outfitting such a battery. Since Mr. Astor did not have the requisite training to command such a unit, the War Department sent First Lieutenant Peyton March to New York to recruit the required number of men. March called on Mr. Henry Ely, who managed Astor's estate, to ask where the battery's guns were located. March was stunned to find that there were no guns but that, in March's words, "the Astor Light Battery was simply a checkbook." Ely informed the young officer, however, to spend whatever was necessary to acquire the proper ordnance and men.

The existence of almost limitless funds certainly eased the difficulty of Lieutenant March's task, but it did not guarantee success. The U.S. government had bought up every serviceable piece of artillery in the country and had obligated every private manufacturer for at least the next three months. One such manufacturer, however, alerted March to the existence of a battery of 3-inch Hotchkiss mountain guns in Paris. They were soon on the way to New York.

The next obstacle was clothing. The overworked Quartermaster's Department could make no promises as to when the newly enrolled artillerymen could be uniformed, so once again Lieutenant March let Astor's checkbook speak for him. He arranged with John Wanamaker to deliver 100 custom-tailored uniforms in just four days. He also located and purchased a supply of British khaki uniforms, complete with pith helmets. Within six weeks of March's first contact with the Astor estate, he and his fully equipped battery were on a transport ship headed for the Philippines.[25]

Sentiment regarding the war was mixed in the African-American community. Not all black Americans supported the war. After all, they reasoned, why should they volunteer to go off somewhere and fight for the political freedom of another group of oppressed, dark-skinned people when they did not enjoy complete freedom themselves. It had only been a couple of years since the Supreme Court had ruled in favor of a Louisiana state law that required separate rail cars for black and white riders. This decision reverberated through society until it was used to justify segregation in virtually all public places. African-Americans, opined a Kansas newspaper editor, are "under the impression that there are Spaniards nearer home than Spain or Cuba." Such concerns were given added poignancy by the likes of the white officer of a South Carolina regiment. "We are South Carolinians and white men," he lectured his troops, "and no earthly power can force our boys to lift their hats to one of these negro officers. If I hear of one of the South Carolina boys saluting a negro I will kick him out of the company. We have enlisted to fight for our country and not to practice social equality with an inferior race whom our fathers held in bondage."[26]

Black Americans had served honorably in most of the country's armed conflicts, and many of them sought to continue the tradition in 1898. As a black newspaper editor stated: "The American Negro is strictly an American and can be trusted to defend the American flag against all comers." By demonstrating to their white neighbors that they were willing to fight for their country, many blacks hoped that they would be regarded more for what they did than for the color of their skin. In this same vein, a black trooper in the Ninth U.S. Cavalry, in a letter to the editor of the Cleveland *Gazette,* asked: "Is America any better than Spain? Has she not subjects in her very midst who are murdered daily without a trial or judge or jury? Has she not subjects in her own borders whose children are half-fed and half-clothed, because their father's skin is black...? Yet," he continued, "the Negro is loyal to his country's flag." Unfortunately, President McKinley's call for volunteers gave first preference to members of existing National Guard units, and black militia units were rare.[27]

Illinois had an all-black Guard battalion, but when its officers tendered its service to Governor John Tanner in response to the president's request for soldiers he declined. Acceptance of this battalion would have necessitated combining it with two white battalions to form a regiment, and he did not believe this was feasible. There would be too much friction, too much opposition from white Illinoisans. Upset black leaders in Chicago held a public meeting to discuss this affront and vowed to remember the governor's decision at the polls the following November. A similar situation prevailed in Virginia, where Governor J. Hoge Tyler passed over that state's existing black battalions when accepting volunteers for federal service. An obvious exception to the practice of ignoring the proffered services of African-Americans was in Massachusetts. There an all-black company was mustered in as part of that state's Second Massachusetts Volunteer Infantry Regiment with little or no public outcry. The only way for most African-American men to enlist under the first call for volunteers was to go into one of the four all-black regular Army regiments—the Ninth and Tenth U.S. Cavalry or the Twenty-fourth and Twenty-fifth U.S. Infantry.[28]

Governors selected assembly sites for the volunteers from their respective states. They were usually in or near large cities with good rail connections, often the state capitals. As the eager young soldiers began to arrive, many of them found that their housing for the near future would be somewhat less than that to which most of them had been accustomed. In many instances, state fair grounds served as campsites. They usually covered large enough expanses to hold the large number of recruits expected. Permanent buildings that could be converted readily into barracks were not numerous at such sites, and few if any, of the volunteer units arrived in camp with anything approaching the requisite amount of tentage.

An obvious choice for secure housing was the livestock barns at those camps situated on fair grounds. Three men could usually occupy a single stall fairly comfortably. Of course their level of comfort depended to a large degree upon how much effort had been expended in cleaning out the stalls before their arrival. A Minnesota volunteer assured his mother that the stable he shared with two other men was "certainly as clean as could be wished," but not everyone was as lucky. When the men of the Second Louisiana Volunteers arrived at their campgrounds they found that the men of the First Louisiana had already occupied the tents that were available, and they would have to make do with the stables nearby. The regimental commander informed his company first sergeants that he would need a certain number of men for a detail. The sergeants quickly called their companies together and selected the men with the best military bearing for this, their first, military duty. The non-coms apparently did not know that they were selecting men to clean out the stables, and chose the men with the most complete uniforms. After all, it was a military task, and they wanted their most military-looking men to have the first crack at it, whatever it might turn out to be. There is no record of how "military" these men looked when their work was over, but the regiment recorded some of its first desertions that night.[29]

An eighteen-year-old Texan found it quite difficult to adjust to the sleeping arrangements in camp. Although he certainly had not expected the state to supply him with a fine feather bed upon which to slumber, the ground was hard, and he often felt tree roots or rocks poking him when he turned in for the night. He partially eased his discomfort by laying his blanket on the ground to absorb some of the sharp edges, but then he was not warm enough to be comfortable. "After a little experience," he wrote, "I have come to the conclusion that the best way to do is; lay on your blanket an hour, then cover one hour, and doing this way you will soon find out that by the time you feel like you was laying on a 'board' with nails sticking up in it, it will be time to lay on [the blanket] again. And so on; you will get used to wakeing [sic] up every hour as regular as clock work."[30]

The assembly camps took on a carnival atmosphere during this early stage of the war, before the shooting started. Every weekend saw hundreds, if not thousands, of civilians trooping out to the campsites to look up a son or brother. Sometimes the local streetcar line put on extra cars to take care of the increased traffic. Other visitors used their own teams and buggies, bicycles, and whatever other form of transportation presented itself. A Nebraska newspaper described the scene at Camp Alvin Saunders at Lincoln: "The camp is simply overrun with visitors. They come in every way imaginable. The traction company is running cars every fifteen minutes. The roads are black with cyclists and all kinds of vehicles." At a dress parade at this same camp in early May an estimated 25,000 civilians showed up to watch, and fully one-third of them had come from someplace other than Lincoln.[31]

Not everyone could visit one of the camps, however, and perhaps they did not have to. Thomas Edison and other early promoters saw the attraction of military-themed movies. Edison cameramen were quick to visit camps in the United States and film such ordinary routines as soldiers washing dishes or tending to their own personal hygiene. These were among the films—most of them running less than a minute—that vaudeville patrons rushed to see in the spring of 1898. Edison and his competitors also soon had other works before audiences that showed the burials of the victims of the *Maine* explosion, the wreckage of the battleship *Maine*, a transport ship full of soldiers leaving a dock. Battle scenes were created with the assistance of blank-firing New Jersey national guardsmen who never left their home state.

Not every man who had originally entered his name on his company's rolls stayed around to see the glory of war. Some had signed up in the excitement, but upon more sober reflection decided that Army life was not for them. When the other men learned that some of their fainter-hearted brethren wanted out they jeered them, calling them "traitors," "skunks," and even "Spaniards." Occasionally their chastisements exceeded these verbal attacks. Some Ohio volunteers took one unfortunate, tied his hands and feet together, and proceeded to beat his buttocks. In another company from the same state, a "defector" had all of his hair shorn off and was ridden out of camp on a rail.[32]

In other cases the patriotism of the individuals never wavered, but they just did not fit in with the other men, who sometimes found interesting ways of pressuring them to leave the service. A volunteer cavalryman from South Dakota complained about one such recruit. "There is one man in the company," he wrote in a letter home, "that dont know anything hardly, he hasn't any time in him and he cant take two steps alike and besides that he thinks he knows every thing." The men in the company decided to figure out some way to prevent this unpopular fellow from accompanying them to their camp, so they proceeded to "treat" the unwary man to as many drinks as he could hold. Then, when he was so drunk that he could no longer stand, they dumped him in an out of the way alley where he would miss the train while sleeping it off. Some cavalry volunteers camped in Texas incorporated a more elaborate scheme to rid themselves of a recruit who was extremely naïve, gullible, and probably not very intelligent. They decided that they would all be happier if this man discontinued his association with them, and they cooked up a scheme to make it happen. Several of them approached him with a "special mission." After praising his patriotism and courage they told him that Spaniards had crossed the Rio Grande from Mexico and were headed for San Antonio, and that he was the one man among them brave enough to face up to this threat and protect the camp. Then they posted him under a tree outside of camp with three candles. "If one regiment of Spaniards attacks you light one candle," they instructed. "If the attack is made by two regiments, then light two; if three regiments come upon you in the night, light all three of them, and may God have mercy on your soul. We are sorry that we cannot give you a gun." The dull-witted recruit manfully accepted this grim responsibility and set out for his post. Giving the man several hours in the dark to reflect upon his mission, about twenty of the pranksters left camp about midnight and "attacked" the man's post from the direction of Mexico. Try as he might, he just could not bring himself to die for his country and left—never to be seen in uniform again.[33]

But the idyllic existence of these camps of assembly had to come to an end. When enough recruits finally had passed their physical exams to bring their respective companies and regiments up to the requisite manpower levels officers of the regular Army swore them into federal service. "All and each of you," ran the oath, "do solemnly swear that you will bear true faith and allegiance to the United States of America, and that you will serve them honestly and faithfully against all their enemies whomsoever, and that you will obey the President of the United States, and the orders of the officers appointed over you, according to the rules and articles of war, so help you God."[34]

The swearing in ceremony was often accompanied by the presentation of a flag or flags, although in some instances this was done as soon as a local company headed for the state rendezvous. Sometimes it was the Stars and Stripes, at others it was a state flag. Regardless of the description of the flag the rituals usually involved emotional presentation speeches by a lady or ladies of the community. In Southern states this was an opportunity not only to remember the valor of local Confederate veterans but to remind everyone of the unity of the country against the current enemy. "More than thirty-five years ago," said one woman as she presented a state flag to the men of the First Alabama Volunteers,

> the devoted women of the South placed in the hands of their husbands and brothers the "Stars and Bars," under which the Confederate soldier earned sad but glorious military fame and honor, in a brilliant but hopeless contest against the "Stars and Stripes." The same heroic devotion which animated our fathers in what they believed was a righteous cause against "Old Glory," prompts their sons of to day to shoulder their guns and march forth to uphold the honor of that same flag whose starry folds now wave over a united people.

Regardless of geographical section the presenter enjoined the eager recruits to do nothing that would dishonor the flag they received that day. An officer usually accepted the flag on behalf of the men and made a short acceptance speech in which he invariably promised that the flag would shortly wave victoriously over the vanquished foe. A Houston company received a *Cuban* flag from a representative of the Texas Cuban League. "I present it," intoned the delegate, "with assurance that it will be a passport to the heart of every loyal Cuban and that in their memory will be enshrined the name of the Emmett Rifles, who at their country's call promptly and patriotically volunteered to fight and die if need be in humanity's cause."[35]

And then it was time to leave the reception camps and start moving toward even larger camps closer to the proposed scenes of action. That meant places like Camp Thomas and Camp Alger for troops destined for Cuba and Puerto Rico and the west coast for those bound for the Philippines. The trip to camp, for most men, was probably the best time of their entire military service, "a prodigiously pleasant excursion," an Alabama volunteer called it. Friends, relatives, and the merely curious crowded the railway stations to see the boys off, and crowds of cheering civilians showered the would-be warriors with flowers and edible delicacies all along the various routes. The best part might have been the willingness with which many young women showered kisses on the departing warriors. An Oregon volunteer claimed to have been thus favored by sixty-seven girls, although one of his companions noted that not every man was exactly smothered with this show of affection. The girls, he noted, "cleverly avoided the fellows who did not look kissable, the few weathered older fellows with drooping mustaches well dyed with soup, coffee and chewing tobacco." Among the common mediums of trade for such female indulgences were the shining brass buttons from the men's uniforms or pieces of hardtack with soldiers' names and addresses inscribed on them in ink. A soldier bestowing such favors on his feminine admirers could usually count on receiving their names and addresses in return. A New Yorker remembered that a man could pretty much guarantee receiving a kiss in exchange for his hat badge, and a Massachusetts man coyly

Brand new soldiers taking the oath of service (Library of Congress).

mentioned receiving "other feminine favors." More tangible trade items included hat pins — a Nebraska volunteer collected 387 of them while on the way to the west coast — ribbons, and stick pins.[36]

Amid the high-spirited leave taking there were many damp eyes among the mothers and sisters in the crowds. Singing was an important part of the departures, and the songs sung ranged from the raucous and popular "There'll Be a Hot Time in the Old Town Tonight" to the more reflective "God Be with You Till We Meet Again." The song an Iowa woman chose to sing as the local company was boarding the trains, however, has to take the prize for perhaps the most emotionally deflating of all. It was an old Civil War song called "Goodbye, Dear Mother! You Will Never Press Me to Your Heart Again."[37]

As the trains carrying the men to Chickamauga, or San Francisco, or any of the other camps rolled through the cities and towns along the way the inhabitants loaded the soldiers down with good wishes and good things to eat. The edibles included individual sandwiches, fresh fruit, box lunches, picnic baskets, and whole chickens. As a trainload of Texas volunteers stopped briefly in Houston on its way east, citizens passed picnic baskets through the car windows to the delighted men inside. Each basket contained enough fried chicken, sandwiches, boiled eggs, biscuits, pickles and cakes to feed six men. One of the Texans informed his diary that there were enough such baskets for every man on board to receive one, and that some got two.[38]

For the men of one New England regiment, the Sixth Massachusetts, the trip south stirred memories of their namesake regiment's trip in the same direction in 1861. In the earlier war, the men received advance notice that when they marched through Baltimore they might expect a less than friendly welcome from the predominantly secessionist citizenry there. In fact, that regiment had had to fight its way through showers of oaths, brickbats, and occasional gunshots. It was different in 1898. The citizens of Baltimore took this opportunity to atone for the behavior of that earlier crowd. This time they pelted the soldiers with flowers and cigarettes and cigars, although some of the flower-throwers later sheepishly confessed that they had been part of the hostile crowds so long ago.[39]

The festive mood continued as the young volunteers adopted mascots to take with them to war. Some of the choices were rather unremarkable, such as the Skye terrier that accompanied one of the troops of the First U.S. Volunteer Cavalry — soon to be known as the Rough Riders — or the bull terrier that members of a Fifth Missouri company named "Frank." Barnyard animals were not unknown as company pets. A Massachusetts company kept a goat, whose temperament was not unlike that of some of the men. Whenever the company marched away from the camp the goat faithfully followed, but when it came time to return the men had to forcibly drag her along. Another company in the same regiment somehow acquired a razor back hog *after* the men reached Camp Thomas. "He lived in the company street," recalled a Bay Stater, "and was as familiar with the men as a well-trained dog." Masquerading as man's best friend was not enough, however, as the pig later wound up as part of their Thanksgiving meal. A Missouri company christened its white pig mascot "Rosa O'Grady" and at some point she mysteriously disappeared. But her fate soon became known. She had found her way, perhaps with some human help, into the camp of a neighboring regiment where she had, according to one man, "presided at a feast ... in the character of the feastee." The troops from the southwest seemed to have the most unusual mascots. One of these companies kept a large, brown bear that, according to a Massachusetts soldier who observed it, was "the most orderly member of the command." New Mexicans coming east to join the Rough Riders brought a golden eagle with them that they named "Teddy" after their regimental lieutenant colonel, Theodore Roosevelt. A saloon keeper in Prescott, Arizona, was so impressed by the fighting spirit of the local lads as they, too, prepared to join the Rough Riders — and perhaps also in gratitude for the amount of business they had brought his establishment — donated "Josephine," a young mountain lion. Some of the members of this company also tried to entice an attractive young girl to come along with them as their train made a stopover in El Paso. She apparently gave it serious consideration, but the company officers decided that a mountain lion was one thing but a human "mascot" was something else altogether and quashed the idea. Nevertheless, men of the Eighth Ohio discovered two black teenagers riding the rails beneath their cars and "adopted" them into the regiment, and the men of the Tenth Pennsylvania Volunteers took two adolescent boys with them all the way to Manila where, sadly, one of them succumbed to typhoid.[40]

Recruits often commented on the landscape through which they traveled. A Nebraska man, headed for San Francisco and then on to the Philippines, was sure that, along with everyone else on his train, he must soon have "a neck several inches longer from looking at the sights." His journey was a long one, however, and he soon found the scenery quite boring. "Of all the lost, forsaken, starved, burned, good for no man land," he wrote, "the country along the Wyoming railroad takes the Bakery."[41]

Arrival at the large camps sometimes uncovered new difficulties. At Camp Thomas the Chickamauga River flowed along one side of the camp and was a major source of the camp's drinking, bathing, and cooking water. Officials soon realized that relying on the river would lead to some logistical problems with thousands of men all trying to make use of it, so Army engineers built a pump house on the Chickamauga that could pump almost two million gallons per day, and they constructed an elevated 17,000-gallon reservoir such that it could distribute water by gravitational force to all parts of the camp through a network of water pipes lying on top of the ground. Installing the pipes in such an arrangement was the quickest way to begin bringing water to the various regiments, but it meant that the summer sun rapidly heated the pipes to the point that the water flowing through them was too warm to be very refreshing. Park employees also drilled thirty-six new wells to augment the nine that already existed.[42]

The men at Camp Alger, members of the Second Army Corps, never did have enough water for all necessary uses. By late June, about forty wells had been dug, but that still only made enough water available for drinking and cooking. Soldiers who wanted a bath had to march seven miles to the Potomac River.

Railroad magnate Henry Flagler had induced government officials to build a camp at Miami, which at that time was a Flagler company town of about 1,500 to 2,000 souls. The arrival of 7,500 troops quickly overwhelmed the local infrastructure, and water supply became a serious problem. Polluted drinking water was only one of the reasons that soldiers soon dubbed their surroundings "Camp Hell."

As the number of arriving troops at Camp Thomas increased, so too did the economy of the nearby towns. Almost overnight, the sleepy little railroad town of Lytle, Georgia, grew to include a large Army bakery, a medical supply depot, a quartermaster's depot, and several storehouses as well as new hotels, restaurants, freight offices, gambling houses, and photographers. The number of fly-by-night establishments designed to separate the soldiers from their meager paychecks also increased. An Ohio volunteer asserted that the boom town indeed contained "all the penny-catch schemes known to the fakir's art." Regimental stores within the camp sold beer and other refreshments, and as many as 600 licensed peddlers moved through the camp selling pies, cakes, milk, and other delicacies. Even Chattanooga merchants shared in the economic boom accompanying the encampment. Only a few miles from camp via a good macadam road, the city proved very enticing to the soldiers, and many of them readily spent as much time and money as they could there. The sight of drunken soldiers collapsed in the street soon became almost commonplace. An Army doctor passing through town looked out of his hotel room window one morning and counted more than a dozen such men, and he was certain that there were hundreds of others scattered across town in the same condition. While citizens of the city were undoubtedly appalled at such exhibitions, merchants and city fathers welcomed the estimated $15,000 to $20,000 that the men spent there every day.[43]

Many of the young men in the camps were away from home for the first time, and sought diversions that they had been denied at home. One of these was certainly alcohol. There was a considerable amount of illicit distilling in the neighborhoods of many of the camps, and when the local moonshiners realized what a great market had been dropped into their laps they immediately found ways to profit from it. Word of mouth circulated quickly through Camp Thomas, for example, that if a thirsty man left an empty canteen and a twenty-five-cent piece at a particular place and then walked away for a while, he would return to find his money gone but his canteen filled with "Georgia Brew" or "Tennessee Pine Top." Of course, the degree of quality control that was a part of the manufacture of these libations was sketchy at best. An Ohio officer at Camp Alger was sure that the local brew was "a decoction that must have been compounded by the Alchemist of Hades. If a fellow got a good drink of the vile mixture inside his system, in ten minutes he became a raving maniac ... and no man who had dallied with the seductive potation once was ever stirred with an insatiable ambition to wrestle with it a second time." A Midwestern soldier characterized "moonshine whiskey" as "about the worst mixture that ever tickled a palate. It was prepared in such a way that a man could drink a quantity of it but would not feel the effects of the over indulgence for several hours. Take several drinks in the middle of the day and towards evening he would begin to feel queer, and couldn't find the tent he lived in, wander around a while, begin to feel sick, wabble and stagger a few moments and then he would give up in despair, 'Don't care if I ever get home,' and generally landed in the guard house, waking up in the morning he would reach out a foot or so feeling for his head and wonder what it all meant." Nevertheless, according to a New York volunteer, "not to have a bottle of whisky was simply open confession of abject poverty or poor bringing up."[44]

Thirsty soldiers did not always have to depend on drinking beverages of such questionable antecedence. Commercially prepared brews were available in some of the regimental canteens, and some soldiers were not above larceny to get possession of some of it. Three carloads of Pabst and Schlitz beer arrived at Camp Hamilton, Kentucky, for the enjoyment of the men of the Twelfth New York volunteers in the fall of 1898. For some reason it was not immediately unloaded and the cars were shuttled onto a side track that ran behind the camping area assigned to the Third Kentucky and the 160th Indiana. These troops were unable to let such a golden opportunity pass and raided the cars that night. They surreptitiously unloaded all of the kegs of beer from one car and half of those in another, along with 250 cases of bottled beer. They now faced the problem of where to hide so much beer. They buried it in holes dug beneath their tents. They weighted down kegs and hid them in the cool waters of a creek. Indeed, there was beer everywhere — except where it was supposed to be. Since the New Yorkers' canteen had not officially taken delivery of the beer, the two breweries faced a considerable financial embarrassment. They demanded payment from somebody. An investigation was apparently unable to detect the wholesale burglary and ordered the unhappy New Yorkers to pay for the stolen beer.[45]

The combination of armed men with free time and easily obtainable alcohol sometimes led to less innocent consequences. A few days before the Rough Riders departed San Antonio for Tampa in late May, a band concert was held in their honor at the campground. One of the pieces on the program was called "The Cavalry Charge," and at a designated point one of the band members raised a pistol loaded with blanks and fired several shots for dramatic effect. Mixed among the audience were quite a number of Rough Riders who, perhaps, had been imbibing before the show, and they now decided to "help" the embattled bandsman by drawing their revolvers and blasting away. Near panic ensued as terrified civilians scrambled to get away. No one reported any injuries, so one San Antonio newspaper might have been correct when it reported that the soldiers were also shooting blanks as part of a big prank.[46]

Drinking was not the only amusement available to the men at Camp Thomas. Organizations such as the Women's Christian Temperance Union, the Young Ladies Soldier Relief Society, and the Red Cross actively tried to steer the men into other off-duty pastimes. They made non-alcoholic refreshments available, as well as reading and writing material.

The transition to military life was a shock to some of the recruits. The individualistic volunteers often found that one of the things they had the most trouble adjusting to was taking orders without questioning either their source or substance. After all, sometimes the man issuing the orders was a newly-minted volunteer officer who might have been their neighbor in civilian life. "It was so easy," recalled one such soldier, "to ... enter into a discussion as to the necessity of carrying out [an] order or to point out the benefits [of] putting [it] off until tomorrow ... but we soon overcame this handicap."[47]

Because the volunteer regiments were drawn from individual states there was a fair amount of regional rivalry, some of it good-natured and some of it not, among the troops. An Iowa soldier rated his fellow westerners as "nice chaps" but had very little use for the men he met from New York and Maine and did not credit the Mississippians with more than "a

In what is certainly a posed picture, Indiana volunteers reach eagerly for food. One man, second from the left, wears what resembles a U.S. Marine cap, but civilian necktie and suspenders. Perhaps he was just visiting the camp and worked himself into the picture (U.S. Army Military History Institute).

lick of sense." Likewise, a Minnesota volunteer expressed his surprised disappointment at the arrival in camp of some Pennsylvanians "about whom so much has been said."[48]

Most of the new soldiers seemed to settle into whatever routine was prescribed for them. The daily schedule varied somewhat from camp to camp but generally followed that of the regular Army. The recruits could expect to hear the bugler welcoming them to the new day by blowing "Reveille" between 5:00 and 5:30 in the morning. After roll call and perhaps putting their quarters in order the men went to breakfast at about 6:30 or 7:00. After a couple of hours of drill and an hour or so of instructional lectures they were ready for lunch at noon. Two more hours of drill in the afternoon rounded out the day for most men, although guard duty and other details required their services on what was usually a rotating basis. A Kentuckian complained that "we have hardly a minute which we might call our own," and he was certain that "any section hand has a better time than we do." After the evening meal the men paraded once again for roll call, and they then had the evening hours to themselves. By 10:00 or 11:00 in the evening most men had turned in, and the bugler played "Taps" signifying that all lights were to be extinguished and all talking was to cease.[49]

The new soldiers also quickly found out how unimaginative Army food could be. The standard daily ration was in three basic groups: meat, bread, and vegetables. Each man was entitled to twenty ounces of fresh beef or mutton, however they might substitute varying quantities of pork, bacon, or salt beef as conditions dictated. The canned beef came in for a considerable amount of condemnation by the soldiers who ate it. A volunteer, unloading freight cars at a camp in Florida, discovered a delivery address in Yokohama, Japan, stamped on some of the wooden crates of canned beef, and he determined that these cans must have originally been intended for Japanese troops during their recent war with China. He was also convinced that the reason for China having lost that war "was because the Japanese let them captured those canned rations." What the Army called bacon, the soldiers called sowbelly. A disgruntled soldier has left a very colorful description of this particular part of the soldier's menu. "Sowbelly," he said with authority, "is exactly what its name implies, the belly of a very adult lady pig, faucets and all. It comes about two to three inches in thickness.... On one side is the meat; on the other, the leather. And no one but an old Army sergeant or a leather fancier can tell one from the other." In spite of this less-than-appetizing description, a Texas volunteer ate so much bacon, he later recorded, that he had nightmares of pigs seeking revenge by eating *him*. Likewise the normal bread ration was eighteen ounces of bread, hard or soft, or flour or corn meal from which the soldier could make his own bread. The hard bread, called hard tack, defied mastication. One of the volunteers was so disgusted with trying to bite into one that he confided in his nephew that he was going to have "a suit of mail made out [of] about 50 of them as I don't think a bullet will penetrate them + then if provisions should run out in Cuba I could simply eat my armor." A New York soldier was just as certain that hard tack "belongs in the ceramic group and is the best substitute for a durable bathroom tile yet discovered." Beans and potatoes made up the vegetable portion of the ration, although these were sometimes augmented or replaced by peas, rice, and hominy. An Ohio volunteer with a poetic bent recorded what was doubtless the sentiment of many of his fellows with regard to the food.

> Backward, turn backward O time in your flight;
> Feed me on grub again just for a night;
> I am so weary of sole leather steak,
> Petrified hard tack a sledge wouldn't break.
> Tomatoes and beans in a watery bath
> Sow belly as strong as Goliath of Gath.
> Weary of starving on what I can't eat,
> Chewing up rubber and calling it meat;
> Backward, turn backward, for weary I am,
> Give me a whack at my grandmother's jam.
> Let me drink milk that has never been skimmed;
> Let me eat butter whose hair has been trimmed;
> Let me have once more an old fashioned pie,
> Then I'll be ready to go south and die.[50]

Of course, those with a little pocket money patronized local establishments or the sutlers' stores that quickly sprang up in and around the camps. An Ohio officer described the peak business hours of these establishments after dark "when they were ablaze with the glory of gasoline lamps" and where the men could "exchange their good money for vile circus lemonade, or green apple pies, black cigars, and unripe bananas, after which they would wind up the banquet with a dish of ice cream containing all the elements of that toothsome delicacy except cream." Some soldiers apparently thought that it was not necessary for money to change hands. Recruits at Camp Alva Adams, in Denver, stole an entire wagonload of bananas from one sutler and a popcorn cart from another.[51]

Putting on a military uniform also seemed to have given some men the idea that it was acceptable for them to steal food from the civilian populace. Usually it was not done because of actual hunger, but more for the adventure of it. Of course this did not lessen the loss of those who had their hencoops raided. The Rough Riders were among the culprits. Every time the train carrying them from San Antonio to Tampa stopped some of them made use of the time to pillage the livestock in the immediate vicinity. The railroad station agent at Tallahassee was witness to the theft of his own pigs from a pen nearby, but a Rough Rider officer quickly assuaged him by ordering the guilty parties to put the captured animals off the train. "Those sonsofbitches ain't going to get away with no hogs of mine," the agent triumphantly crowed. In fact, however, many of the liberated pigs were swiftly grabbed up again before the train got underway.[52]

In one rather extreme example of men finding other ways to feed themselves a group of Louisiana officers discovered a professional cook in the ranks and assigned him to prepare their meals. This man was the nephew of a well known New Orleans chef and undoubtedly served his "clients" a menu that was much more palatable than fresh beef, hard bread, beans, and potatoes. In fact, he saw his military fortunes rise and fall based upon the food he served. If a course was particularly tasty, the head of the mess might compliment the cook by promoting him on the spot. If a dish somehow did not live up to the expectations of the diners, that same officer might *de*mote the cook. It was not unusual, according to one observer, for the cook's rank to vary from private up through corporal and sergeant to second lieutenant and back down again to private in the course of a single meal.[53]

Once the soldiers had received their uniforms and their full allotment of equipment, many of them hunted up the nearest photography gallery to have pictures made. That way the folks back home could see them in all of their martial glory. One news correspondent commented that "if the boys ... face the [Spanish] cannon so unflinchingly as they face the camera, they will all be heroes." The quality of these snapshots was not always the best. Sometimes the photographers who set up shop adjacent to the military camps were, like many of the other merchants in the vicinity, only anxious to turn a quick profit, and their work did not measure up to what many of the soldiers were used to seeing. An Indiana soldier paid the princely sum of ten cents to have his photograph taken, but the result was not up to his expectations. "It is not very good," he wrote when he sent it home from Camp Thomas, "but I guess you can tell who it is and get an idea how I look." An Illinois man was even less impressed when he described his experience with a photographer. "You will notice," he informed his sister, "that it, like everything else here, is Southern. Dirty, poorly finished and as poor a picture, generally, as I ever saw, but it is the best I could do." But a Missouri infantryman must have had the worst experience with having one's picture taken. He asked a visiting cavalryman if he could borrow his horse for his photograph. The mounted man readily assented, but then the unfortunate soldier decided that his picture would be much more impressive if, in addition to being on horseback, he was able to brandish a revolver so he borrowed one of those also. "Mr. Cow-boy," as the pistol's owner dubbed the soldier, played with the weapon until it went off, taking off one of his fingers and wounding an onlooker in the shoulder.[54]

The primary reason for assembling the thousands of soldiers at the various camps across the country was to prepare them for war service. Although the men learned to detest drilling, it was an absolutely essential part of their hoped for transformations from citizens to soldiers. The rawest recruits had to begin their instruction with the most basic lessons. They had to learn the proper method of how — and when — to stand at attention. They had to learn how to carry comfortably their canteens, haversacks, blanket rolls, and other such impedimenta. They had to learn the correct position of "Shoulder arms," and how to get from there to "Order arms" without dropping their rifles. When they had mastered these basic evolutions it was time to learn to move as part of a group — a company first, then a battalion, and on up to a regiment. All of this meant constant, repetitious, boring drill. The purpose of drill was to teach the men to act as part of a unit, not as undisciplined individuals. Just like everything else in life, some men took to it with gusto while others loathed every minute of it. Some could not see the usefulness of learning the manual of arms, or learning to march with precision with dozens of other men of the company. They just wanted to be let loose on the enemy. The amount of time actually spent in drilling varied over time and from place to place. Some soldiers believed that their officers were intent on "Drilling the life out of" them while others thought that the amount of drill required of them was entirely within the range of personal comfort.[55]

The troops were eager to reach the battlefront before the fighting was over. But as the time in the training camps dragged on, their officers sometimes sought to enhance their preparations for combat with target practice, long road marches, and sham battles. The amount of time required at the target range does not seem to have been handed down from higher authorities. Some regiments, indeed, spent no time at all there, and when it came time for a North Carolina regiment to occupy the rifle range about half of the men were sick, on detached duty, or in some other way indisposed and unable to participate. On the other hand, a New England regiment spent time at the range every day but Sunday for seven weeks. The skill exhibited by those who did make it to the range varied considerably. An Iowa volunteer related that he had hit barely one-fourth of the targets at 200 yards. A Massachusetts man described a target competition among the best shots in his division. Firing at 160 yards, the scores ranged from 68 percent to 80 percent. Nor were all of the "targets" made of wood and paper. One man wandered into the area downrange, perhaps looking for souvenirs left over from the Civil War battle. Either he did not know that a unit had taken up a firing position or he thought that he was out of their line of fire, but a bullet hit him in the head, wounding him severely. Another man, upon hearing of the mishap, wrote that the injured man "went behind the targets to get bullets—he only got one and that was all he needed."[56]

All the time in the world spent at the target range, however, could not prepare a soldier adequately for the time when his targets would be enemy soldiers and they would be firing back at him. Some officers, therefore, arranged for their men to participate in sham battles so that, even though they were shooting blanks, they might get some feel for the excitement and confusion of battle. On June 27, the Sixth Massachusetts, the Sixth Illinois, and the Eighth Ohio took up the line of march from Camp Alger to the Potomac River, about ten miles distant. The men camped near the site of the Civil War battle of Ball's Bluff and enjoyed the chance to bathe and relax in the cool river waters. Early the next morning the Massachusetts regiment left camp about an hour before the other two. The plan was for this unit to select a site somewhere along the route back to Camp Alger and deploy across it in such a way as to block the progress of the Midwesterners. The Ohio and Illinois troops dutifully formed into line of battle when they approached the "enemy" position and began blazing away with blank ammunition. The battle raged for about a half hour until the attackers finally prevailed and drove the defenders from their works. This exercise at least exposed the participants to the sounds of battle, but of course with no real bullets filling the air it was easy for them to get carried away. One of the attackers got so close to the Massachusetts line before he fired that the wadding of his blank cartridge severely wounded a man, taking a chunk out of his ear and burning his face with the powder gases. The major of the Ohio regiment also received a powder burn on the back of his neck, and one of his men suffered a saber cut on the hand.[57]

The novelty of military drill and ceremony wore off for most men in fairly short order as the boredom of camp routine became the order of the day. Many wrote home to family members telling them to discourage younger brothers or cousins from enlisting. An Iowa soldier at Camp Thomas rapidly tired of military routine or, as he called it, "this nigger life," and cautioned that "a man is a fool to enlist." Some decided that military life, at least as they had experienced it so far, was not what it had been cracked up to be and deserted. An Alabama

Wash day in camp finds this soldier busy with a bucket and a washboard (U.S. Army Military History Institute).

volunteer composed a poem that described not only his, but certainly many other men's views toward camp life.

> Singing ballads, playing cards,
> Eating sidemeat, running guards;
> Marching, drilling, exercising,
> Lying 'round philosophizing;
> Digging ditches, learning tactics,
> Standing guard until your back aches;
> Doing laundry, picking trash up;
> Cleaning camp and dishing hash up;
> Cooking pork and taking baths,
> Eating hardtack, cleaning paths;
> Getting yellow as a tanyard,
> Wondering when we'll meet the Spaniard;
> Getting letters from our folks,
> Snoozing, "boozing," cracking jokes;
> Thinking of the folks—if not them,
> Then of sweethearts—those who've got them;
> Reading papers, reading books,
> Fasting, grumbling, "cussing" cooks;
> Writing letters, cleaning tents up,
> In our trousers sewing rents up;
> Stewing, growling, fretting, fussing,
> Kicking, howling, working, "cussing";

> Drilling like old-time cadets,
> Smoking pipes and cigarettes;
> Telling stories, making wishes,
> Splitting wood and washing dishes;
> Turning in at sound of "taps,"
> Spouting verse and shooting "craps";
> Wanting fight with Spain's "conceitos,"
> Getting it with big mosquitoes;
> Taking quinine, sick or well,
> Castor oil and calomel;
> Running out to see the "dummies,"
> Calling one another "rummies";
> Getting up at five o'clock,
> Wanting fight and hearing talk;
> Thinking we are not in clover,
> Wondering when the war'll be over.[58]

Much of the discomfort afflicting the men in the camps was due to circumstances beyond their control—like Mother Nature. The heat and dust inherent at any summer gathering of thousands of men and animals was bad enough, but then when it rained it seemed to make things even worse. A Missouri officer thought that he had never witnessed rain like he did at Camp Thomas. "It does not begin in a gentle shower and get you accustomed to it," he wrote. "On the contrary, it just lets go all holds and comes flooding down in an unceasing torrent for hours at a time. If it holds up for a spell or a day, you may depend upon it that it is only getting ready for a renewal of hostilities." June and July were also particularly rainy at Tampa, where a large corral holding several hundred horses and mules was adjacent to, and slightly uphill from, a Florida regiment's campsite. Heavy rains that washed through the corral and into the company streets made life extremely uncomfortable.[59]

Nor was the weather the only natural phenomenon that caused the men discomfort, but mosquitoes, flies, lice, and other insects added to it. A Florida man was sure that the mosquitoes were armed with hammers and chisels in addition to their stingers, and related that many men awoke to what they thought was the morning bugle call only to discover that it was the incessant buzzing of these winged pests. During the day, flies took over to irritate the men. They were so thick at meal times that the men had to literally scrape them off their food. "When mess call sounds," related a Nebraska volunteer, "it is a scramble between the men and the flies to see which will get the food." Another man wrote his sisters that it was almost impossible to eat at all without ingesting "seven or eight flies."[60]

A New Hampshire officer commented on the fact that when a mule died within fifty yards of one of the camp's hospitals the troops made no effort to move it away for burial. In fact, the very word "burial" in this situation is a gross overstatement. The men dug a shallow hole and rolled the animal toward it. When it proved to be only deep enough for its head and legs, they merely mounded dirt up over its body and left. "The flies and smell," reported this officer, "would almost kill a person."[61]

A contributing factor to the huge insect population was the almost complete disregard of common hygiene exhibited in many camps. The men achieved personal cleanliness, what there was of it, by simply undressing, heating a bucket of water on the cook stove, and using its contents to try to scrub away varying degrees of sweat and dirt. Some men paid more attention to the importance of cleanliness than others. In one of the Massachusetts regiments at Camp Thomas orders were issued that each man would stand a weekly inspection—in the buff—by a surgeon to make sure that he was keeping himself clean. Not everyone took the regulation seriously and at the first such inspection a man was found, reported one of his comrades, "who had secreted on his person, a liberal amount of Georgia real estate." The cost of his disregard of the rule was quickly exacted. Eight non-commissioned officers stripped to the skin and escorted their "prisoner" through the camp to the nearest hydrant. Then with a growing number of fully-clad soldiers looking on, they plied soap and stable brooms until they judged their victim to be clean. This public exhibition ensured that no one else in the regiment ever again allowed himself to be found needing a bath.[62]

Although the young soldiers engaged in various physical sports in their spare time — baseball, foot races, etc.— one of the most popular pastimes was running the guards. This "sport" consisted of sneaking past the sentries and back into camp after overstaying a leave. Perhaps a man could slither through a hole in the fence surrounding the camp or have a comrade distract the guard while he snuck past him. But sometimes fortune favors the bold. While camped at San Antonio, a Rough Rider sergeant realized that he had lingered too long in the saloons in town and must now figure a way to avoid arrest when he returned to camp. He found several other soldiers from his regiment in various stages of inebriation, all with the same dilemma. As the group approached the camp gate the sergeant lined them up in some semblance of a military formation and strode purposefully past the sentinel on duty. When the guard ordered the men to halt their leader tore into him with a verbal tirade. How dare he interfere with a military working party on its way back into camp! The stunned and puzzled guard sheepishly waved them past without further question. It apparently did not occur to him to ask why a working party was out of camp so late — and without any visible picks, shovels, or other tools. Such antics as this became so rampant in some camps that officials issued orders to remind the men that they were training for serious business and that the sentinels should be the most respected soldiers in the Army. "Any man found trifling with a sentinel," one such circular read, "will be severely and summarily dealt with."[63]

The locations of the two largest training camps—Camp Thomas and Camp Alger—made sightseeing and souvenir hunting natural pastimes. Camp Alger was close to several Civil War battlefields and to the tourist attractions of the nation's capital. Camp Thomas could not help but evoke memories of the terrible carnage that had taken place there thirty-five years earlier, and there was still a fair amount of battle debris in the area. Fired lead bullets and iron shell fragments were plentiful, and uniform buttons and belt buckles also occasionally turned up, particularly after a heavy rain had washed away some of the top soil. Eager soldiers even unearthed unexploded artillery projectiles.[64]

And when they were not busy scouring the historical battlefield for souvenirs some of the men took the train up to Lookout Mountain, near Chattanooga, where they could enjoy a panoramic vista of considerable beauty. One such excursion, in mid–June, ended in tragedy. A number of the young soldiers decided to climb to the roofs of the cars to better enjoy the fresh air and sunshine. Unfortunately, an overhanging wire swept several of them off the train with fatal results for two of them.[65]

A majority of soldiers had never traveled very far from their homes, and some eagerly took advantage of every opportunity to see some of the country. An Indiana volunteer seemed particularly happy to have had this chance. "We camped for nine weeks upon one of the most picturesque battlefields of the 'civil war,' Chickamauga," he confided to a friend back home.

> We have seen the large elevators and ship building establishments of Newport News, Va. Also Fortress Monroe.... We had a glimpse of Jamestown one of the first settlements of the New World. Swam in the bay of the James River. Spent half a day on the U.S. Minnesota, the fastest cruiser in the world.... Passed thru Richmond, Va. the seat of the southern confederacy. Enjoyed a sail on the James River at the very point where the Monitor locked horns with the Merrimac in '63. Passed thru the great coal mining districts of West Virginia. We are now

camped in the heart of the Blue Grass region, one of the greatest racing and stock raising centers in the world. Who would not experience a few hardships to see where we have been?[66]

All of the activity at the training camps at least sufficed to lay the groundwork for the influx of volunteers into the Army, but it failed to address the understrength units of the regular force, so on April 26, Congress passed another act to provide for "the better organization of the line of the Army of the United States." This law enabled the President to authorize the various units in the field to recruit their companies up to full, war-time strength — which in infantry companies meant 106 men — and to add two more companies to each regiment, thus allowing for three four-company battalions in each. Military pay, never a very attractive inducement in peacetime, was increased by 20 percent while the war lasted. In this way, the overall authorized strength of the regular Army was allowed to reach almost 65,000 men.[67]

On May 11, Congress passed another military manpower bill that authorized the president to issue a second call for volunteers. McKinley was not quite as quick to act on this bill and waited for two weeks before asking that 75,000 more young men volunteer for service in the war against Spain. With the second call for volunteers the few black national guard units that existed brought increased pressure to bear upon their respective state governors to allow them to participate. Governor Tanner responded by authorizing the all-black Ninth Illinois Infantry Battalion to recruit two more African American battalions so it would be of regimental strength. The newly augmented unit became the Eighth Illinois Volunteer Infantry Regiment, and was accepted into federal service in July. Similar expansions saw the births of the Sixth Virginia Volunteer Infantry and the Third Alabama Volunteer Infantry, while black Kansans raised the Twenty-third Kansas Volunteer Infantry from scratch.[68]

Most of the volunteers faced enemies that were even more deadly than Spanish soldiers. By mid–July there were more than six hundred sick men from two brigades of the Second Army Corps stationed at Miami. At Camp Thomas the sick list exceeded 2,000 (and nearly tripled by mid–August). Still government officials did not appear to be too concerned since in the three largest camps the number of ailing men constituted only about six percent of the effective strength present. In fact, most of the men unavailable for duty at Camp Thomas at this time were nursing sore arms after having been vaccinated.[69]

Some illnesses, considered a century later to be fairly easily-controlled childhood diseases, wreaked havoc in the close quarters of the training camps. Measles and mumps, for example, each raced through the densely populated camps until they reached epidemic proportions. Bronchitis, and occasionally pneumonia, was also considered inevitable under such overcrowded conditions, as were diarrhea and dysentery. One doctor characterized these afflictions as "inseparable from the changed conditions of life for the recruit, both as regards his exposure to the weather and the character and cookery of his food." Much more dangerous than any of these to a man's health, however, was typhoid fever, often traced to polluted drinking water in the various camps and directly attributable for over 900 deaths throughout the Army.[70]

The situation at Camp Thomas was fairly typical. The occurrence of typhoid among the troops there led to several investigations — some official and others not — to isolate the source of the disease. The commander of a divisional hospital at Chickamauga was certain that the civilian population near the camp was suffering from typhoid before the soldiers even arrived there. The surgeon of the Twelfth New York Volunteers arrived at the same conclusion after making a sanitation inspection in mid–August. "The appearance of the inhabitants of the vicinity," he wrote, "seldom robust, almost uniformly thin and sallow, would seem to indicate that, on account of the water and other reasons, this is not a healthy locality. Typhoid fever is of common occurrence." General Boynton had a decidedly different opinion on the healthfulness of the neighborhood. He cited the most recent federal census to prove that there had been only very few fatal cases of typhoid in the surrounding area. Drawing upon the seven-year history of the park itself, he declared that there had not been a single case of typhoid among the hundreds of workers there.[71]

At the first inkling of trouble with the drinking water at Camp Thomas, maybe even before that, several sales agents were at the camp trying to interest the government in buying their water filtration and purification systems. One outspoken member of this class let it be known throughout the camp, in Chattanooga, and anywhere else he could command an audience, that the water situation would soon be the ruination of the Army. According to this man, the nearby fresh water springs, as well as the wells within the camp, were terribly polluted. Even the Chickamauga River could not escape pollutants from the camp. He also expressed concern for the civilians in the area. For if, as he gloomily predicted, the unsafe water at Camp Thomas brought disaster to the troops encamped there, the resultant epidemic would probably spread to nearby Chattanooga. He encouraged the city's concerned inhabitants to unite to raise $100,000 to provide a water filtration system for the camp. Another such salesman was temporarily at a loss to explain why his filters, when used at Camp Thomas, proved to be utterly worthless. He ultimately blamed the water itself and proceeded to distribute the results of some "scientific study" to support his claims. Independent chemical analyses of the available water, however, showed that after it was filtered it was of excellent quality.[72]

The reported problem with the drinking water soon attracted public attention. It seemed to many that the problem was being compounded by the use of the same suspect water in the hospitals. How, one might ask, could a man hope to recover from an illness brought on by drinking impure water if the only water available to him in the hospital was of the same low quality? Eventually, the Red Cross Society began shipping fresh water to Camp Thomas from New York for use in the camp's hospitals. After it had been in use for some time, someone finally ran a test on its purity and found it to be worse than the naturally occurring water in the camp.[73]

Perhaps it was the soldiers who were the cause of their own illness. Within two weeks of the first troops arriving at Camp Thomas, the camp commander issued an order stressing the importance of keeping the camps clean. He ordered regimental and battalion commanders to make daily inspections of their immediate camp areas to ensure their cleanliness. Brigade commanders were to carry out similar inspections every other day and division commanders once a week. The surgeon general was more specific in his instructions to Army medical personnel. He emphasized how important camp sanitation was to the overall health, and military effectiveness, of the troops. He enjoined his officers to make sure that the men prepared adequate sinks, or latrines, and maintained them properly. The contents of these pits were to be covered with earth, quicklime, or ashes three times per day to control the odors. When the level reached within two feet of the surface, the men were to abandon them and completely fill them in. Furthermore, the message went on: "Every man should be punished who fails to make use of the sinks." The regular troops followed these recommendations fairly well, and the incidence of disease within their ranks was appreciably less than among the volunteers.[74]

It was impossible to dig the sinks very deeply at Camp Thomas—twelve feet deep would have been ideal—because rock lay only a few feet below the surface. Consequently, they filled up rather quickly. Then, when it rained, the offal flooded out onto the ground and sometimes flowed through the camps. The shallowness of the sinks did not constitute an insurmountable problem. The soldiers would simply have to dig more of them. Unfortunately, they were not always very careful about selecting sites for these pits. A volunteer regiment from New York, for instance, located a sink a mere ten feet from its kitchen, virtually ensuring that the constantly swarming flies would have only a short flight to reach, and infect, the men's food. An Iowa sergeant, in fact, described trays of beef being delivered to his campsite at Camp Thomas "so covered with bluebottle flies the meat was scarcely visible." An Indiana regiment established a garbage pit for its kitchen refuse only twenty feet away from the men's dining tables, and its sinks were only thirty feet farther away. Further exacerbating these unhealthful conditions was the widespread habit among the volunteers of not using the sinks at all if they could simply wander a short distance into the trees near their camp and defecate there.[75]

The incidence of disease at Camp Alger was somewhat less than at Camp Thomas. One reason was that the fatigue parties were able to dig into the soil more easily, and their sinks were thus much deeper. There was still a fair number of men who chose to relieve themselves in the woods rather than at the appointed facilities, but officers were very vigilant about enforcing camp sanitation.

At Miami a fair proportion of the sick suffered because of the sewage that contaminated newly dug wells. Nor was the polluted water completely obvious to many of the soldiers as the source of their sickness. At Jacksonville, Florida, for instance, where almost 80 percent of the patients in the hospital suffered from typhoid fever, an inspector blamed the widespread patronage of civilian vendors in the camp who offered lemonade and other such drinks made from polluted water. General Boynton described the wares provided by "hucksters" at Camp Thomas as consisting of "indigestible pies, green fruits, pop, manufactured milk, and slop of every name and every deleterious nature." A concerned Philadelphia citizen complained to his congressmen of the sutlers at Camp Alger where "there were 200 booths breeding filth and selling to our soldiers green fruit and all sorts of deleterious food and drink."[76]

Making the problem of widespread sickness worse was the relative lack of qualified medical personnel in the Army. Some soldiers were convinced that going to the hospital would only decrease their chances of survival because the medical personnel was either ignorant, uncaring, or both. An Indiana soldier at Camp Thomas was convinced that "if a person has a pain in their toe they give him a Pill or if he has Fever a Pill. They dont care now what becomes of a person." An Ohio man wrote, "A man suffering with diarrhea or indigestion gets a pill from the same bottle as the man with a sprained ankle or weak back," and characterized the Army medical department as "the biggest farce in the army." In peacetime, a handful of Hospital Corps enlisted men were usually enough to assist a doctor at most posts. These men, after passing an examination and after serving a sufficient time in grade, could advance from private through acting hospital steward to hospital steward. If one regiment garrisoned a post, its hospital was entitled to the services of two hospital stewards, one acting hospital steward, and eight Medical Corps privates. The size of the Medical Corps was sufficient in early 1898 to attend to the health needs of the Regular Army. However, when the various regiments prepared to leave their posts for the training camps, most of their medical support stayed behind at the permanent posts. Only 250 of the Army's 791 non-commissioned members of the Hospital Corps accompanied the troops toward Cuba. Then, when the volunteers began to pour into the training camps they rapidly overtaxed the available medical facilities. The volunteer regiments, although authorized a full complement of commissioned and non-commissioned medical staff, rarely arrived with anything more than one or two medical officers. One such officer watched the influx of soldiers without enough hospital corpsmen and commented that there were "plenty of broom handles, as it were, but no brooms."[77]

In order to make up for the shortage, the government sought to hire contract doctors

Funeral procession bears the body of an Illinois volunteer who died in a stateside camp (U.S. Army Military History Institute).

and nurses from the civilian sector. Between 600 and 700 doctors were thus hired, but in the rush of events none of them faced any kind of competency examination until late October. When only slightly more than 500 male civilian nurses signed Army contracts it became necessary to hire female nurses to meet the Army's needs. The employment of female nurses met a mixed reaction from Army doctors. One stated that women tended to coddle patients under their care and that therefore "the female nurse should never be employed in military hospitals." The Chief Surgeon of the U.S. Volunteers took an entirely different position. He saw women's tendency to "coddle" as of great benefit to sick and wounded soldiers. "Nursing is woman's special sphere," he remarked. "It is her natural calling. She is a born nurse. She is endowed with all the qualifications, mentally and physically, to take care of the sick. Her sweet smile and gentle touch are often of more benefit to the patient than the medicine she administers." Overcoming the resistance of many in the military, Congress authorized the employment of female nurses on a contract basis during the war. An influential female physician, Dr. Anita Newcomb McGee, offered the services of the Daughters of the American Revolution (DAR), of which she was vice president general, to screen and hire applicants. Upon acceptance of this offer Daughters all across the country set up local screening committees to process candidates.[78]

Many women wanted to serve but lacked the requisite training. Dr. McGee looked at three qualities when determining the fitness of an aspirant to be an Army nurse. First, of course, was technical proficiency. The woman had to be the product of a reputable nursing school and must have written endorsements from doctors testifying to her qualifications. If, however, she lacked similar confirmation from the superintendent of her nursing school her

Some of the nuns and other female nurses (U.S. Army Military History Institute).

application was summarily rejected. Second, the would-be Army nurses had to present certification of their good moral character. A member in good standing of the DAR was, of course, the best source of such a testimonial, but, failing that, any woman of known standing in the community could vouch for the applicant. The third thing that Dr. McGee's organization looked for was evidence of good physical health. It certainly did not want to hire nurses who would soon become patients themselves. This requirement necessitated a physician's certification. Approximately 5,000 female nurses applied for positions with the Army, but only 20 percent passed the DAR's muster.[79]

Among the female nurses recruited in this fashion were Roman Catholic nuns from various orders. Holy Cross nuns in central Illinois offered Governor John Tanner the use of their two small hospitals for convalescent local troops. Likewise, the Daughters of Charity offered their hospitals in Washington, Indianapolis, and Philadelphia to the government, and Baltimore's Sisters of Mercy made their hospital available for the use of Maryland's troops. And when letters went out to the different nursing orders asking for the assignment of nuns "to serve God and their Government" more than 200 responded. The nuns, just like their civilian counterparts, signed contracts for their services, and they often referred to themselves as "Army nuns."[80]

Very few of the women nurses accompanied troops overseas. There were more than enough sick soldiers for them to tend in the hospitals of the stateside camps. The work hours were long, and the primitive living conditions were often nothing more than leaky tents. One nun good-naturedly remembered her first night at Camp Thomas. "We certainly did look like soldiers, for we had no bedding, simply a blanket, one half under us, and the other over us, with one pillow."[81]

CHAPTER 4

Naval Blockade of Cuba

ALTHOUGH THE NAVY WAS probably more prepared for war than was its sister service there was still a certain amount of apprehension among naval planners. Was the American fleet powerful enough for the task at hand? After all, a respected publication of the time gave high marks to Spain's Navy. On paper, Admiral Pascual Cervera y Topete's squadron looked quite formidable. The new cruiser *Cristóbal Colón*, for example, was supposed to be armed with 10-inch guns. Unfortunately for Cervera, however, these guns were so poorly constructed that they were not accepted, and the Italian manufacturer could not promise replacements for six to eight months. The 5.5-inch guns on three of his cruisers were also defective, and much of the ammunition for these guns was unreliable. The cruiser *Vizcaya* had to sail without having a chance to have its bottom scraped free from a nine-months' assortment of barnacles, thereby drastically reducing its steaming speed. Cervera, in fact, thought this ship to be "nothing more than a buoy" in its present condition, "only a boil in the body of the fleet." An American naval officer later summed up the situation thus: "Spain was without the primal necessities of a fleet: without guns, without ammunition, without engineers, without coal, and even with the ships short of bread."[1]

The Spanish admiral, meanwhile, persistently sought to have his orders changed in the face of what he considered a disastrous defeat in the making. To illustrate his point he mentioned that on his flagship a few days before, while his crewmen manned the rail for saluting, a rope railing gave way and three sailors tumbled overboard. A replacement rope had been requested through regular supply channels before the mishap — seven weeks before — and still had not arrived. If something as uncomplicated as a length of rope was so difficult to obtain in a timely fashion, what hope was there that the much more important issue of faulty guns and ammunition could be resolved?[2]

Cervera believed that the situation in Cuba was irretrievable. The determination shown by the Cuban rebels, along with the daily increasing American sympathy for their cause, made the loss of that island colony certain. Sending warships to dispute this would not only lead to the loss of the ships, but would lay the Canary Islands and the Spanish coast itself open to enemy naval bombardment. Cervera was not unpatriotic, having already spent forty-six years in the service of his country, and would follow orders even when the end result was disaster.[3]

Commodore Dewey's American squadron, meanwhile, was too far away to take part in any fleet actions in or around Cuba, and in fact was more valuable where it was so he could keep an eye on the Spanish ships in the Philippines. There were a few ships on the west coast, including the powerful U.S.S. *Oregon*. Its 13-inch guns were as big as any other ship in the fleet and bigger than any of the guns on the Spanish ships. If the *Oregon* could reach Caribbean waters before any clash with Admiral Cervera's squadron the weight of its guns might make a critical difference in the outcome. The difficulty to be overcome was a logistical one. With no Panama Canal to shorten the voyage, the *Oregon* would have to steam down the western coastlines of both North and South America, through the treacherous Straits of Magellan, and then on up the eastern coast of South America in order to reach the scene of the expected action. It would have to cover a distance of some 14,000 miles.

War with Spain was not yet a certainty when Captain Charles E. Clark received orders to sail the *Oregon* from its home port of San Francisco with all possible speed to Callao, Peru, some 4,000 miles away. Perhaps by the time he reached there the naval board of inquiry looking into the sinking of the *Maine* would have arrived at some conclusion as to whom to blame. If the board judged Spain to be culpable and war was imminent, the powerful *Oregon* would be that much closer to Cuba. If, on the other hand, the board exonerated Spain and found, perhaps, that the *Maine* went down as a result of some accident, then the officers and crew of the *Oregon* would have gained some valuable sea experience and could then steam back home.

For the next two days crew members hurriedly stowed coal, ammunition, and all other supplies necessary for a six-month cruise aboard the battleship and puzzled over their destination. Most guessed that it would either be Cuba or the Philippines. Finally, on March 19, the *Oregon* cleared the Golden Gate and began its fateful voyage.

Captain Clark, who had begun his service to his country as a seventeen-year-old midshipman at the Naval Academy almost forty years earlier, was a stickler for preparedness and had his crewmen drilled daily. They practiced clearing the ship for action, the gunners went over their gun drills until they felt they could perform them in their sleep, the damage control parties practiced chores they all hoped they would never have to carry out in reality. At the end of the hectic day, however, the ship's band played popular tunes for the enjoyment of all aboard.[4]

As the ship moved into the tropics the supply of fresh water on board became critical. This was not only the water that the crew used for drinking and bathing, but it was also the water that the engine room crew used to produce steam for the ship's two engines. The ship's chief engineer informed the captain that although the engines could use salt water for a while, its corrosive effect would shorten the lives of the heat exchanger tubes inside the boilers. The other option was to continue to use fresh water in the boilers and severely restrict water usage by the men. It was not an easy decision. The health and well-being of the men on board was important, but so too was the ability to crowd on speed if necessary, and corroded boilers would make this much more difficult. Clark called the crew together and explained the situation to them. They agreed that they could exist with less fresh water than usual if it meant that they could get to the scene of the fighting in time to participate in it.[5]

As the ship prepared to cross the equator, all non-essential regular duties ceased so that the crew could observe an age-old naval tradition—a visit from "King Neptune." The day before—March 30—a member of the crew, wearing an outlandish costume, seemed to come onto the ship from the very depths of the ocean itself. This was one of Neptune's representatives who came aboard to inform the officers and crew that on the next day Neptune and his court would pay an official visit to make sure that all on board had earned the right to enter into his domain. The next morning, Neptune appeared with a retinue of about twenty similarly costumed men and went up on the quarterdeck. From there he welcomed the captain and asked to be introduced to any crewmembers who had never crossed the equator— and quite a large percentage of the crew fell into that category. Captain Clark, in turn, welcomed the king and his court to the ship and fairly well turned it over to them for the rest of the day. The crew assembled aft and anyone who was too slow to report or who seemed reluctant to participate in this humorous affair found himself pummeled by some of Neptune's men who wielded big padded clubs.

The ceremony itself consisted of initiating the newcomers with a "shave." Neptune's helpers prepared the initiate for his shave. The enthusiastic barbers first lathered their customers' faces using a ship's paintbrush as an applicator. The lather itself consisted of flour, molasses, salt water, vinegar, tar, cylinder oil, strands of rope string, and anything else that was offensive to the nose, taste, or touch. It was not by accident that much of this concoction wound up in the unfortunate sailor's mouth. As the victim choked and sputtered the "barbers" proceeded to shave him with a three-foot-long barrel stave "razor." Upon completion of the shave Neptune's helpers tipped the chair over backwards dumping its unfortunate occupant onto a chute that delivered him into a big canvas water tank on the deck twenty feet below, where a half a dozen of Neptune's minions made sure that he spent a considerable amount of time under water. Every time he surfaced they plied their padded clubs and ducked him again. Finally, he was allowed to escape before the next victim appeared. He had earned the right to cross the equator, and he would never again have to submit to this particular form of "torture." In fact, crew members who had gone through this process later received ornate proclamations certifying their worthiness as sailors.[6]

The many new men on the ship greatly outnumbered the old "salts," so, apparently at the suggestion of Captain Clark, they turned the tables on their more experienced shipmates. Men who had undergone such initiations much earlier in their naval careers now found themselves victimized once again. Nor were officers exempt. Even the captain received a good-natured ducking.[7]

After this brief respite, the big battleship continued its mission and finally reached Callao at 5 A.M. on April 4. There was little rest for the men, however, as they had to load coal and clean and adjust as much mechanical equipment as possible. While in Callao the vigilance of the *Oregon*'s crew remained at a high level. Rumors abounded that some Spanish-sympathizing Peruvians meant to see that the visiting American warship met the same fate as the *Maine*. Clark doubled the sentries on board and stationed Marines in the fighting tops. Other Marines set up a perimeter watch as they constantly patrolled in the ship's steam cutters with orders to prevent any vessel from approaching within 500 yards of the *Oregon*, in case someone ashore decided to make good on these threats.[8]

There was no word yet from the naval board of inquiry, but Clark did receive information that the Spanish torpedo boat *Temerario* was somewhere off the eastern coast of South America. Its destination or purpose could only be guessed at, but Captain Clark made a momentous decision. If he received orders for Cuban waters and he encountered the Spanish craft while navigating the treacherous waters at the southern tip of South America, he meant to sink it whether war had been announced or not![9]

While at Callao, orders arrived instructing Clark to proceed to the Caribbean, and the next day, after loading 1,000 tons of coal in the bunkers and another 100 tons packed in canvas bags on the deck, the *Oregon* departed under cover of a fog bank. The diplomatic situation was growing more tense by the day, and the daily routine aboard ship reflected a heightened sense of readiness. Gun drills and small arms practice became regular parts of each day. As boxes and barrels became empty they were thrown overboard to give the gunners even more practice. The gunners kept the big guns loaded when not engaged in practice, and at night they slept near their pieces with every light above the waterline extinguished.[10]

The weather deteriorated as the ship neared the Straits of Magellan. Still the *Oregon* resolutely plunged through the swells. A veteran fireman on board noted in his diary that he had never seen "a ship take such seas before," and postulated that "if she was any thing else but a battle ship a sea like some of these would crush her like an egg." Another crewman, with the soul of a poet, remembered watching in awe from the top of an 8-inch gun turret as the seawater broke over the ship. "The big waves," he wrote, "used to go rushing over the bows and thundering down the deck, racing aft they would strike the 13 inch turret and break into masses of spray, which the stiff south winds caught and threw back over the whole length of the ship, while the forecastle would be a mass of swirling, foaming water, seething and boiling around the turret and other obstructions."[11]

Late on the afternoon of April 16, there was a momentary break in the weather, and Captain Clark pushed hard to reach a safe anchorage within the Straits of Magellan before nightfall. Unfortunately, dark overtook him before he reached his hoped-for haven. There was not much likelihood of a collision with another ship in these waters at night, but the gale force winds and the waves could push an unwary captain's vessel onto rocks in almost any direction, so Clark ordered anchors run out. Some on board must have held their breath as the anchor chains rapidly disappeared into the water. Finally, however, at a depth of over 300 feet, the anchors hit the sea floor. As the storm raged on "the good ship Oregon held on well," noted a lieutenant, "as if aware that she was destined to render her country distinguished service."[12]

With the cold wind and rain lashing the ship, every hatch was battened down to keep out the weather. Unfortunately, this also prevented the circulation of fresh air below decks, and the crew quarters became almost unbearably stuffy. Adding to the danger were the frequent fires in the coal bunkers due to spontaneous combustion of coal dust. One such fire burned all the paint off a common bulkhead between the coal and a powder magazine before it was discovered.[13]

The next day the weather abated somewhat, after a morning snowstorm, and the *Oregon* reached Punta Arenas, Chile, that night. The next morning while the Marines again provided security around the ship, the sailors busied themselves in replenishing the *Oregon*'s coal supplies as swiftly as possible. The Scottish agent from whom Captain Clark obtained the coal proved true to his stereotype as he frequently stopped the loading process so that the coal buckets might be weighed. He wanted to make sure that, since he was selling the coal by weight, he received credit, and hence pay, for every ounce. It finally reached a point where one of the crewmen turned the tables on him. "Here!" the sailor sang out as a coal bucket reached the deck, "Lower again for another weigh! There's a fly on the edge of that bucket!"[14]

Those sailors not directly concerned with the coaling operation and not members of gun crews, enjoyed a brief respite from sea duty and had a little time to go ashore and to enjoy the magnificent scenery around them. The town itself, a former Chilean penal colony with no telegraph contact to the outside world, was not very large, and the many prefabricated dwellings of corrugated iron did not lend it much in the way of architectural interest. Still, the visiting sailors bought souvenirs that the local Indians had fashioned from various animal skins.[15]

A smaller American gunboat, the *Marietta*, met up with the *Oregon* at Punta Arenas on April 18, and together they cleared port for Rio de Janeiro three days later. The *Marietta* took the lead as the ships steamed northward up the coast, bypassing both Montevideo and Buenos Aires. At night, both ships ran without lights except for a small light on the stern of the leading vessel. After more than a week at sea the *Oregon* moved ahead of the smaller ship and steamed ahead to Rio, where it arrived on the afternoon of April 30. It was there that Captain

Clark and his crew finally learned that war had indeed been declared between the United States and Spain. The crewmen seemed almost relieved at the news. They immediately sent ashore for enough red ribbon for each man to fashion himself a cap band with applied brass letters spelling out "Remember the Maine." The ship's band played patriotic tunes while the sailors and Marines whooped with enthusiasm. As one Marine confided to his diary: "Every one on this ship is crasie [sic] to get at the Spaniard."[16]

Along with the news that his nation was now at war, Clark also received a further caution about the *Temerario*. It had apparently cleared Montevideo and was thought now to be heading his way. Clark worried over this piece of information, even though international law protected the *Oregon* while it remained in this neutral port. "If the torpedo boat should arrive and had an ordinarily enterprising commander," he recalled, "I felt he would not hesitate to violate the rights of a neutral port, if by so doing he could put one of our four first-class battleships out of action." If the *Temerario* arrived in port its commander would presumably anchor it near the *Oregon* since that was the section of the harbor normally reserved for visiting warships. The resulting proximity of the two enemy vessels, however, might give the Spaniards an opportunity for mischief that Clark would not be able to foil. In order to minimize the chance of this occurring he ordered his ship to move about two miles up the bay. That way, if the torpedo boat made any attempt to come closer to the American, Clark would regard it as a hostile act, an act in violation of Brazilian neutrality, and immediately open fire on it. Brazilian officials concurred with Clark's disposition of his ship and promised to make sure that if the *Temerario* arrived that it moor in the farthest reaches of the bay.[17]

While America's biggest battleship ploughed its way up the east coast of South America headed for the Caribbean, Navy leaders began to implement a blockade of select Cuban ports. Acting Rear Admiral William T. Sampson had his squadron at Key West underway for Havana on April 22, within four hours of having received orders to proceed. Within a few days his ships had closed the ports of Havana, Matanzas, Cárdenas, Mariel, Cabañas, and Cienfuegos. Unfortunately, Sampson faced the same problem that had bedeviled the Navy at the start of the Civil War; he did not have enough ships available to closely patrol all of the possible points of entry into Cuba.[18]

The purpose of any such blockade, of course, is to deny any and all outside support for the enemy. The United States did not want the Spanish soldiers on the island to be able to receive reinforcements or supplies from the mother country or anywhere else. The blockaders had to remain alert for any such incoming traffic, and they also had to be ready in case Spain sent its own warships to break the blockade. In fact, the first military engagements of the Spanish-American War came about as a result of the blockade.

The blockaders did not waste any time in carrying out their orders. The *Nashville* intercepted the Spanish steamer *Buenaventura* on April 22 as it passed north of Cuba. It was carrying a load of lumber from Pascagoula, Mississippi to Spain, and its captain was unaware of the existence of the American blockade. The anxiety level within the American fleet increased perceptibly the next day, however, when the crews of the *Marblehead*, the *Cincinnati*, and the *New York* spotted a large ship approaching. They believed it might be the cruiser *Alfonso XII* with over a thousand Spanish troops aboard. The unknown ship began firing its cannons as the Americans closed in, but lookouts quickly determined that these shots were blanks being fired as a salute to Admiral Sampson. As the ships drew nearer to one another the Americans were able to identify the stranger as an Italian warship bound for Havana.[19]

On April 27, four full days before Commodore Dewey's overwhelming triumph in the Philippines, Admiral Sampson in the *New York* led the protected cruiser *Cincinnati* and the monitor *Puritan* in a bombardment of some shore batteries near Matanzas. The excitement was such that four of the six patients in the *New York*'s sickbay rose from their beds and reported to their regular battle stations. They did not want to miss out on any action. It was only after being ordered back to bed twice that they obeyed. The duel only lasted about twenty minutes, and although one of the *Puritan*'s 12-inch shells knocked out one of the enemy guns, the smoke that wreathed the ships made it almost impossible to gauge the effect, if any, of the 300 shots fired by the Americans. Sampson's chief of staff later characterized the day's action as only a relatively insignificant incident but one that the sensationalist press inflated beyond its actual importance. The Spaniards apparently recognized early in the fight that the ships were too far away for their shore batteries to reach and only fired a dozen or so rounds. These results were rather less spectacular than those obtained by Dewey a few days later, but the war had certainly begun.[20]

While the comic opera surrounding the whereabouts of Cervera's squadron played itself out in early May, the Army decided on a very small-scale operation to bring succor to the Cuban insurgents. On May 10, a large crowd gathered on the docks at Tampa, Florida, to see the old side-wheeler *Gussie* off on its mission to deliver a supply of badly needed munitions to General Pedro Díaz in Pinar del Río Province in western Cuba. There were also quite a number of passengers on board. Captain Joseph H. Dorst of the Fourth U.S. Cavalry was in command of the operation and had two companies from the First U.S. Infantry Regiment on board to provide security for the landing. There were also three Cuban guides and several news correspondents along to cover whatever story might develop.

The plan was for the *Gussie* to proceed to the northern coast of Cuba, west of Havana near Mariel, where Captain Dorst would meet up with rebel elements and land his supplies. By the time he arrived in the agreed upon vicinity two days later, he had picked up an additional escort of two chartered boats full of reporters and several curious blockading vessels. So much for the element of surprise! Dorst, nevertheless, had a mission to accomplish and was determined to carry it out. When the little flotilla reached a small bay at Point Abolitas he ordered two boats lowered and sent the Cuban guides and forty soldiers toward shore to reconnoiter and contact the rebels. A hail of bullets greeted the American infantrymen as they became the first American troops to set foot on Cuban soil during this war. They returned fire while the Cuban scouts tried to make contact with their comrades. After a short time, one of the scouts returned to report that not only were there no friendly Cubans in the vicinity, but that they had landed within two miles of a Spanish fort whose garrison numbered approximately 2,000. The infantrymen began retreating toward their boats, and as they broke out of the brush and onto the beach, the *Manning* and the *Wasp* opened a covering fire on the Spaniards. The only American casualty in this first land skirmish of the war was James F. J. Archibald, a reporter for the *San Francisco Post*, who suffered a slight wound to his left arm.[21]

The *Gussie* cruised back and forth off the northern coast of Cuba for a couple more days but was never able to make contact with the insurgents. Finally, Dorst ordered the ship to return to Tampa with the cargo undelivered. On a second attempt, Dorst was able to land his supplies at Port Bañes on the northeast coast of Cuba, on May 26–27, but after that the Army played little part in the war for some time.[22]

Also on May 26, the *Oregon* dropped anchor at Key West, Florida. It had traveled approximately 14,000 miles in sixty-eight days.

The blockaders of 1898 had to deal with a problem that had not existed for their predecessors of the 1860s. Cuba was connected to the rest of the world by a number of underwater telegraph cables, and for the blockade to be completely effective some measure had to be found to keep the Spaniards in Cuba from using them to communicate with their home government. The only such cable on the northern side of the island connected Havana to the

American cable station at Key West, so it was not necessary to disturb it. Others, however, radiated out from Santiago, Guantánamo, and Cienfuegos to Jamaica, Haiti, and other Caribbean islands. One early attempt to silence these cables was at the southern port of Cienfuegos.

Commander B. H. McCalla was the senior officer of the little blockading squadron off Cienfuegos. It consisted of his own cruiser *Marblehead*, the gunboat *Nashville*, the converted yacht *Eagle*, the revenue cutter *Windom*, and the collier *Saturn*. On the evening of May 10, McCalla ordered preparations for severing the telegraph lines that connected Cienfuegos with the outside world. He selected Lieutenant Cameron Winslow from the *Nashville* to command the effort and Lieutenant E. A. Anderson of the *Marblehead* to assist him. Winslow's prior experience in *installing* such cables undoubtedly led to his selection, but cutting them presented an entirely new consideration. What tools would be needed for this unusual work? "Cable cutting was something new to all of us," recalled one of the sailors who took part. "To tell the truth," he continued, "I didn't have the faintest idea of the work. To be prepared for all emergencies we equipped ourselves with every possible tool that suggested itself to us, and thus we took along chisels, axes, hammers, saws, etc."[23]

The two officers immediately set to work planning their sortie. The cable-cutters would do their work from two sailing launches, one each from the *Marblehead* and the *Nashville*, and the two ships would also each furnish a steam launch full of Marines to provide covering fire for the working parties if it became necessary. Lieutenant Winslow found no shortage of volunteers when he set out to man his small force. He took twelve sailors in each of the sailing launches to man the oars, a coxswain to steer, and a blacksmith and a carpenter's mate to cut through the heavy cables. He ordered rifles distributed to half of the men and pistols to the other half, with a few extra rifles and an ample supply of ammunition added. The crews of each of the steam launches consisted of a coxswain, two seamen, a fireman, and a coal passer. A Marine sergeant and a half dozen riflemen completed each contingent. A one-pounder Hotchkiss rapid-fire cannon mounted near the bow provided additional firepower aboard the *Marblehead*'s steam launch. Two Colt machineguns augmented the armament of the Marines aboard the *Nashville*'s cutter.

The next morning McCalla gave final instructions to Winslow. All he had to do was cut the cables and drag their ends into deep water to prevent the Spaniards from fishing up the severed ends and splicing them back together. Of course, no one on board the American vessels was absolutely sure just what the Spanish soldiers on shore would be doing while this operation was taking place. The cable house, at which point the cables came ashore, was only twenty or thirty feet from the water's edge. Between it and the lighthouse, some three hundred yards westward along the shore, were well-camouflaged Spanish trenches. So dense was the undergrowth that the Americans could not determine how many enemy soldiers might be present or if they had any machineguns or field artillery. In fact, had they not chanced to spy some soldiers digging to improve their positions they might not have known of the Spanish presence at all.

Lieutenant Winslow told his men to dress comfortably for the work ahead. The only restrictions were that he did not want anyone to wear white clothing — because it was so easy for Spanish riflemen to see — and he did not want anyone to go barefoot — in case they wound up going ashore across the sharp coral heads. The end result was a decidedly unmilitary looking group of men as they climbed into the boats shortly after 6 A.M. and waited for the signal to proceed.

The *Marblehead* and the *Nashville* steamed in to within 1,400 yards of shore and began a methodic bombardment of the cable house and the surrounding terrain, including the Spanish earthworks. Just before seven the two steam cutters, each towing a launch, moved out from behind the protective bulk of the *Nashville* and headed toward the cable house. About a quarter mile from the beach the cutters cast loose their towlines and let the lighter-draft launches proceed under oar power. Lieutenants Winslow and Anderson kept a vigilant watch for the submarine cables, but the water was still too deep to reveal them. Finally, when the working parties had reached a point only a hundred feet from land, sailors aboard the *Marblehead*'s boat spotted the cable that connected with Santiago about twenty feet down on the ocean floor. The *Nashville*'s boat quickly pulled over to assist, and together the crews hooked it with grapnels and laboriously began hauling it aboard.

The cable was not a simple wire. Instead seven twisted copper wires, insulated with gutta percha formed the central conductor. And since the gutta percha was subject to attack from shipworms it was then encased in lead. Twenty-six iron wires, each about a quarter inch in diameter, wound around the lead, and jute braiding formed the outermost wrapping. The whole thing was two inches thick, and a ten-foot section of it weighed sixty pounds. "So far as the cutting of the cable was concerned," Lieutenant Winslow later wrote, "it was equivalent to cutting through a bar of iron about as thick as a man's wrist." Nevertheless, the seamen from the *Marblehead* manhandled the cable up onto rollers at both ends of their boat. Soon the other boat had accomplished the same thing and, with the help of a towline from one of the steam cutters, under ran the cable southward for about a hundred and fifty feet.[24]

Now the actual work of severing the cable began on both boats. The dangerous work would be fruitless unless it was done in such a way as to permanently deny telegraphic messages to or from Cienfuegos. Of all the tools that the men had brought along, the most effective proved to be the small hand-held hacksaws. The work was physically fatiguing, and the occasional whistle of Mauser bullets from shore added an unnerving element to it. Working in reliefs the men finally cut through the cable in twenty to thirty minutes. The sailors aboard the *Marblehead* launch coiled up a 150-foot section of the cable in the bottom of the boat. It would now be virtually impossible for the Spaniards to repair the cable. Still, the work was not finished. There was a second cable to deal with, one leading westward toward Batabano.

The *Nashville*'s launch now pulled to within sixty feet of the enemy shore. The range from the Spanish trenches was then about a hundred feet, but miraculously the work continued with no American casualties. Offshore, the gunners aboard the *Marblehead* and the *Nashville* redoubled their efforts to protect their crewmen. Naval shells passed so low over the boats that the men grappling for the cable instinctively ducked their heads while working. Spanish return fire was growing, and Winslow ordered those men not directly involved with raising the cable to pick up their rifles and do what they could to protect the boats. Nor were the Marines aboard the steam cutters idle. Finally, the sweating sailors, repeating the technique used on the first cable, succeeded in removing a one hundred-foot section of this telegraphic lifeline.

In the course of locating and cutting this cable the sailors also discovered a third, smaller cable that connected the cable house on the beach to Cienfuegos, six miles away. Lieutenant Winslow decided to have the men sever this one too since there were still no casualties among them, and figuring that this cable would not be as heavy to haul aboard or as time-consuming to cut. The men in the *Marblehead*'s launch soon snagged the cable and were at work hauling it aboard when the volume of fire from shore suddenly increased to a very dangerous level. It was no longer random rifle shots. The Spanish were now employing machine guns and some light field guns. The Marines in the steam launches worked the bolts of their Lee rifles with equal fervor, but the time had come to drop the third cable back into the water and head back to the ships. (A detachment from the battleship *Texas* successfully severed the third cable a few days later with no Spanish resistance.) Even with the covering fire of the *Marblehead*, the *Nashville*, and the revenue cutter *Windom* the cable cutters had to make their way back to the ships under a blistering fire. By the time these working parties returned to the safety of their ships, a little after 10 A.M., Marine Private Patrick Reagan was dead and another Marine lay wounded in the *Marblehead*'s steam cutter. Casualties were much greater in the *Marblehead*'s sailing launch, where five sailors fell wounded, one of them fatally. Seaman Robert Volz, struck by at least four bullets, was the only casualty aboard the *Nashville*'s launch, although Lieutenant Winslow and Washburn Maynard, the commander of the *Nashville*, were also hit.[25]

By this time, Captain Caspar Goodrich and several of his subordinate officers on board the auxiliary cruiser *St. Louis* were also discussing what a great service it would be to be able to disrupt Puerto Rican cable traffic. Of course, locating the cable in the first place required some educated guessing. Maps showing these lines were schematic in nature, perhaps indicating that a cable ran from the vicinity of one port to another. Where it came ashore the installers might have had to thread it along the sea floor between coral heads or other obstructions. But in deep water, where surface weather conditions would be unlikely to affect it, these expensive cables would probably lie in as straight a line as possible between the two ports. That left two possibilities for locating the cables. The searchers could come in close enough to shore where they could actually see the cable lying in shallow water, or they could lay offshore and plot the most likely route of the cable in the deeper water. The former method was the more efficient, but it would necessarily bring the erstwhile cable-cutters under the guns of Spaniards ashore.

The crewmen of the *St. Louis* made their first attempt on May 13, as they sought to sever the cable connecting San Juan, Puerto Rico, with St. Thomas. The guns of the forts near the harbor mouth made it too difficult to try for the cable near San Juan. Diagrams, however, indicated that the cable was likely close in to the northern shore of the island as it headed eastward so the *St. Louis* made its attempt about eight miles east of San Juan. The water was too deep to actually see the bottom, but the boat dragged its grapnel across the sea floor where it was most likely to snag the cable. Eventually, as the resistance on the cable increased, the boat stopped its forward progress while the men hauled the grapnel toward the surface. Before they retrieved it, however, the tension suddenly went to zero. When they recovered the grapnel they saw that whatever it had grabbed had been so heavy as to straighten out its prongs until it looked like an umbrella that had been turned inside out by a gale force wind. They noticed traces of gutta percha insulation on the grapnel and therefore calculated that they had in fact snagged the elusive cable and that the sudden release in tension occurred when the cable snapped in two.

In light of this apparent success, Admiral Sampson gave Captain Goodrich permission to continue such work wherever he thought it would be successful. He also assigned the tugboat *Wompatuck* to help out. Three nights later the little tug steamed in close to the mouth of Santiago harbor. As quietly as possible the men began paying out the grapnel, hoping to hook the cable leading to Jamaica, raise it up, cut it, and be out of the area well before dawn the next morning. They had barely begun to work when a Spanish patrol boat headed out of the channel toward them, and they had to abandon their plans and return to the *St. Louis*, far off shore. Two nights later they were again unsuccessful.[26]

Ships of the blockading squadron on the northern side of the island also tangled with the enemy in early May, this time in the harbor at Cárdenas. Commander Chapman Todd, of the gunboat *Wilmington*, arrived to take charge of the blockade there on May 11. The presence of three Spanish gunboats in the harbor worried Todd because of the possibility that they might dash out under cover of darkness and sink one of the blockaders on station. He lost no time in planning a pre-emptive attack. His first concern was getting his vessel, which drew ten feet of water, into the shallow waters of the bay. He and his Cuban pilot studied his maritime charts and found what appeared to be a deep enough channel. By noon the *Wilmington*, along with the torpedo boat *Winslow* and the revenue cutter *Hudson*, had successfully navigated the channel, and Todd now spread his little flotilla to cover as much of the bay as possible to prevent any of the gunboats from making a run for the open sea.

Cautiously the three American ships glided through the shallow water and closed on the town. There were plenty of ships along the wharves, but it was impossible to pick out which of them, if any, were the enemy gunboats. Todd ordered Lieutenant John B. Bernadou to take the *Winslow*, which drew only six feet of water, in closer to reconnoiter. Upon doing so, Bernadou noticed several red buoys in his path. He soon realized that these were range markers for Spanish guns.

As the American torpedo boat approached to within about 1,200 yards of the docks a puff of smoke appeared near shore, and almost immediately a great geyser of water erupted close to the *Winslow*. It did not take long for the Spanish gunners to improve their accuracy. Only a week earlier, one of the *Winslow*'s young officers, Worth Bagley, had complained about the lack of excitement. "A war only comes once in a generation," he had disconsolately written his mother, "and it will be very hard if I can get no chance to do some unusual service." He soon found himself in the middle of all the action he could have desired. Within five minutes the fire of moored Spanish gunboats and several shore batteries had served notice to the interloper. The Spanish artillerists knew their job. A shot quickly penetrated the thin, quarter-inch armor of the *Winslow*'s bow, sailed through the captain's quarters and exploded in a paint locker. Work parties instantly went to work to extinguish the resulting flames as their vessel continued forward. There was no let up in the Spanish fire. Another round exploded near the conning tower, driving a shard of shrapnel into Lieutenant Bernadou's groin. Other shots quickly disabled the small craft's steering, pierced a forward boiler, and knocked one of the engines out of commission. The American sailors worked their four one-pounder rapid fire guns courageously, but with all of its steering gear shot away the *Winslow* had to get away from this fire if it or its crewmen were to survive.[27]

Lieutenant Bernadou, still mobile despite his painful injury, hailed the *Hudson* for a tow out of range of the Spanish guns. His ship had been riddled by gunfire, but he was the only casualty aboard so far. Then, as the *Hudson* passed a towline to the crippled *Winslow*, a Spanish shell exploded in the midst of a group of sailors. The ensign who had craved action, two firemen, an oiler, and a cabin cook were killed and others mangled by the shrapnel. The *Hudson* finally was able to pull the *Winslow* out of harm's way, and the *Wilmington* was able to sink two of the enemy gunboats. This was real war![28]

Such encounters with Spanish gunboats already resident in Cuban waters were not the U.S. Navy's biggest worry. Of greater concern for the blockading vessels was the whereabouts of Admiral Cerveras, four armored cruisers and three torpedo-boat destroyers. All along the east coast of the United States, worried citizens heard rumors that the Spanish fleet was headed for New York City, or Philadelphia, or Baltimore. They bought bombardment insurance and removed valuables to safer inland locations. They begged the McKinley administration not to abandon them by sending the entire Navy off to blockade duty. Massachusetts officials proclaimed that forty-one of their cities and towns were vulnerable to enemy naval action and that 43 percent of the state's entire population lived in these threatened areas.[29]

The Navy did not have enough ships to send one to every port on the eastern seaboard to calm the fears of the residents there. The Army, however, did have on hand something in its inventory that could be used to protect against — or at least observe the approach of — enemy fleets — a hot air balloon. The Army's balloon, named *The Gen'l Myer* after the Army's first signal officer, had been built in France in 1893 and shipped to the United States in the hope that demonstration ascents might be made at Chicago's Columbian Exposition that year. By early 1898, varnished silk replaced the balloon's original skin of stretched, beaten animal intestines, called "goldbeater's skin," and it was at Fort Logan, Colorado, where the Army was using it to test various methods of air-to-ground communication and aerial photography.

In March, with hostilities appearing more and more unavoidable, the *Gen'l. Myer* was ordered eastward to New York City. From a position hundreds of feet above the nation's busiest seaport, an observer would be able to spot an enemy fleet when it was still well out to sea and alert those on the ground to commence active defensive measures. Houston attorney John Phillips proposed an interesting alternative using hot air balloons for offensive warfare. His plan called for the balloons to be anchored to the decks of rapid war ships where they could be inflated using the hot gases from the ships' stacks. Long cables would connect them to one another, thus forming a network of protection. Phillips postulated that these balloon ships could launch their aircraft while still a safe distance from enemy shores or fleets, preferably at night. The balloons would then rise to a great height and drift over the enemy positions. Each balloonist would then lower his armored basket, via block and tackle, until it was in position from which to "hurl explosives upon the enemy's ships or ports, while he remains secure from harm in his armored car, and his balloon above the clouds is beyond the possibility of puncture from guns below." Theoretically, this plan only required a handful of such balloon-equipped ships to rain destruction down upon an enemy of almost any size.[30]

No matter how feasible — or how outlandish — these schemes seemed at the time, one simple problem remained. The government did not have enough balloons or trained balloonists to implement them. And there were other logistical problems. Before any such aerial warfare could occur the many various support elements had to be in good working order. These included portable and semi-portable boilers, gas generators and compressors, almost a mile of cable, iron turnings and sulfuric acid in sufficient quantities to generate the necessary amounts of hydrogen, dozens and dozens of steel cylinders for holding the compressed gas, innumerable tools, and wagons and teams for transporting all of it.

Although Cervera's location and intentions remained a mystery to Admiral Sampson, he decided that he could not bring the enemy to battle by waiting on blockade duty at Havana. On May 4, therefore, he took two battleships, an armored cruiser, two ocean-going monitors, two unprotected cruisers, a torpedo boat, a collier, and an armored tug and headed east. Accompanying the ponderously moving little fleet were several privately chartered boats full of reporters. Sampson hoped to catch the Spanish ships at San Juan where an American victory, he believed, would be easier than if the two squadrons met upon the open seas. "Their ships are faster than ours," he observed, "and they will be able to engage or run away at pleasure. Should they risk an engagement, we should, with any kind of luck, be able to defeat them. If they run away, we can do next to nothing."[31]

The American squadron made anything but record time on its voyage eastward. Although Sampson's flagship, the *New York*, had a design speed of twenty-one knots and the *Iowa* and the *Indiana* could each steam at over fifteen knots, the monitors *Terror* and *Amphitrite* could barely make seven knots. Sampson therefore issued orders for the *Iowa* to take the *Amphitrite* in tow and for the *New York* to likewise assist the *Terror*. Mechanical breakdowns and broken tow lines slowed the little flotilla to an average speed of only seven knots.[32]

Late on the afternoon of May 11, Sampson took up temporary residence aboard the *Iowa* and began preparations for the final approach to San Juan, only fifty miles away. All unnecessary lights aboard the ships were extinguished; even the officers and sailors who usually went on deck for a late night smoke abstained for fear of giving away their ship's position by the glowing embers at the end of a cigar. The ships' bells, which usually tolled the time at regular intervals, were silent this night. Much as Commodore Dewey had done half a world away in the Philippines, Sampson planned to reach the enemy city just before dawn when he would have the element of surprise in his favor.[33]

By five o'clock on the morning of May 12, the dim early light of day revealed a tranquil picture as the city of San Juan slowly wakened. The men aboard the American ships were up early, and, unlike their fellows at Manila Bay, ate a good breakfast. Now, with the decks liberally sprinkled with gray sand to soak up blood from the expected casualties, they only awaited the signal to open fire on the enemy positions protecting the sleepy port. The light draft cruiser *Detroit* went ahead, according to plan, to verify the water's depth at the chart locations that Sampson had specified as his intended maneuver area. The tugboat *Wompatuck* followed to anchor a small boat that the other ships would use as a range marker.

The signal came about ten minutes later when the *Iowa* reached the *Wompatuck*'s boat and turned eastward across the mouth of the harbor. One of the *Iowa*'s small six-pounders barked, and within seconds its larger guns added their thunder. Following along in single file from the northwest were the *Indiana*, the *New York*, the *Amphitrite*, and the *Terror*. A reporter on a nearby press boat described the terrific concussion that followed the fire of the big 12- and 13-inch guns of the *Iowa* and the *Indiana*. "With every discharge of a great gun," he wrote, "the ship beneath it shivered under the recoil.... Even spectators who were two miles away ... felt the tremble of each discharge, as one feels an earthquake shock."[34]

In spite of the noise and smoke that so impressed onlookers, the American shots did not appear to be doing much damage ashore. The gunners had apparently calculated the range to the targets fairly accurately but had not adjusted for their elevations. Consequently, many of the shots fell harmlessly along the shoreline, well beneath the Spanish gun positions. Return fire from the shore was spirited but equally inaccurate, and after one pass to the eastward in front of the mouth of the harbor Sampson and led his squadron back out to sea. If Cervera was there, he would surely put on steam and give chase to the Americans.

Admiral Sampson had not intended for the lightly armed *Detroit* to take an active part in the bombardment after it led the other ships into position, but its captain, Commander J. H. Dayton, either misunderstood or purposely ignored this order. He posted his ship at a point only 1,500 yards from the enemy's heavy guns and took part fully. Sampson signaled Dayton to withdraw when he noticed the *Detroit*'s vulnerable position, but by that time the smoke of battle made signals difficult to see. "I expected to find her torn to pieces," Sampson said of the smaller ship, "but the precision and deliberation with which she maintained her fire convinced me that she was doing well."[35]

Not only were the officers and crew of the *Detroit* "doing well," but Dayton provided a bit of levity amidst the crashing gunfire around his ship. He had someone throw an empty sardine can overboard, and then he calmly emptied his revolver at it. He hit it five times before it slipped under the waves, and he undoubtedly hoped that his ship's guns were having the same effect on the Spaniards.[36]

When Sampson led his ships back in for a second attack on the forts he decided not to employ his smaller guns— those smaller than 8-inch — because they did not appear to be inflicting much damage, and their gun smoke only further obscured the vision of the gunners at the bigger pieces. This time there was a marked improvement in gunfire accuracy as rounds repeatedly struck the walls of the old Morro Castle guarding the harbor. The fire from the shore batteries also improved. A shell hit the *Iowa* just as it completed its second run past the targets. It smashed a whaleboat and scattered fragments among a group of spectators. Shell fragments wounded two sailors and a Marine. At almost the same instant another shell struck the *New York*, destroying a searchlight and two cutters and causing considerable damage among the crew of a portside 8-inch gun. One fragment struck Seaman Frank Widemark in the neck inflicting a mortal wound, and several other men in the vicinity suffered wounds of varying degrees of severity.[37]

Meanwhile, some of the rounds fired by the ships passed over the forts and into the town, causing civilian casualties. By the time the attackers had made three passes it was obvious that Cervera's ships were not present, and continued bombardment of the port served no measurable purpose since Sampson did not have enough men to put ashore and occupy the city even if it surrendered. At 7:45 he broke off the attack. The small flotilla stopped long enough to conduct funeral services for Seaman Widemark and Gunner John Erickson, who had succumbed to the heat inside the stifling after gun turret on the *Amphitrite*. After their burials at sea the long trip back to Key West commenced.

Sampson had nothing much to show for his efforts except some excellent target practice for his gun crews. This action did give him some idea of the strength and location of the enemy positions at San Juan so that when the time came to attack the port in earnest the American fleet would have that information. And, as Captain Robley D. Evans of the *Iowa* noted, it gave most of the American sailors their first taste of combat. "Our men," he said, "received just what they most needed — practical demonstration of the fact that it required a great many shots to seriously injure a modern ship, and that every shell fired was not going to kill each individual man who heard it screaming over his head."[38]

Sampson was disappointed in not finding the Spanish ships. He was certain that Cervera was nearby, and it was essential that he prevent him from reaching Havana. On the evening of June 14, off the northern coast of Santo Domingo, Sampson encountered the hospital ship *Solace*, recently from Key West, and received the surprising report that Cervera had returned to Spain. He halted his ships near Puerto Plata and sent the *Porter* into port to telegraph Washington for confirmation. If the rumor proved true, Sampson intended to reverse course back to Puerto Rico and capture San Juan.

It was several hours after midnight when the *Porter* returned to the other ships bringing with it, as Sampson noted, "a great budget of news." Far from having returned to Spain, the bulk of Cervera's squadron was even then at Curaçao, and one of his smaller ships was already at Martinique. This news took most of the pressure off the east coast and permitted the Navy Department to dispatch Commodore Winfield S. Schley's Flying Squadron southward where his ships could do the most good. Sampson, meanwhile, ordered the *New York* to steam ahead of the rest of his ships in order to reach Key West, and up-to-date information, as soon as possible.[39]

On May 18, the *New York* arrived at Key West, and found Schley already there. Unfortunately, Cervera had left Curaçao by that time and his *exact* location was again a mystery. The Naval War Board was certain, however, that the reason that the Spanish fleet had sailed west in the first place was to bring help to Havana. That meant that Cervera must either steer directly for that port or for Cienfuegos on the south coast, from which any supplies and reinforcements could move by railroad across the island to the capital. Sampson ordered Schley to set sail the next day with the *Brooklyn*, the *Massachusetts*, the *Texas*, and the *Scorpion* and try to reach Cienfuegos before Cervera did. Sampson would lead other ships to keep Havana under close watch, and several fast cruisers took up positions near San Juan, Puerto Rico and in other strategic areas so that as soon as one of them sighted the Spanish fleet it could send word back to Sampson.

Meanwhile, Spanish officials in Havana on May 19 learned of Cervera's arrival at Santiago de Cuba early that morning. A telegrapher with rebel sympathies immediately sent this information on to Key West. Cervera, at last, had been found! Navy Department officials in Washington wasted no time in ordering the fast cruisers *St. Paul* and *Minneapolis* to converge on Santiago to verify the report. Admiral Sampson also revised Commodore Schley's orders. On May 22, he sent instructions to his subordinate at Cienfuegos: "Spanish squadron probably at Santiago de Cuba — 4 ships and 3 torpedo boat destroyers. If you are satisfied that they are not at Cienfuegos, proceed with all dispatch, but cautiously, to Santiago de Cuba, and if the enemy is there blockade him in port." Where the Navy had been unable to prevent the Spanish ships from reaching Cuba, perhaps now it could make sure that they would never leave. With this accomplished, the Army could begin land operations in both Cuba and Puerto Rico without the threat of Spanish seaborne interference.[40]

Schley, however, was slow to act. He received Sampson's order on the morning of May 23, but at that time he was still not sure that Cervera had not slipped into Cienfuegos harbor before he got there! He had heard noises while still many miles out to sea that he believed were the shore batteries at Cienfuegos saluting the arrival of the Spanish fleet. His ship was far enough out from the port that he could not visually identify the ships in the harbor so he questioned the captain of the British merchant ship *Adula* as it left port. The word thus received was that Cervera had indeed gone into Santiago de Cuba on the 19th, but that he had only stayed until the next day. The British captain did not, apparently, report that he had actually seen any Spanish warships in the harbor when he left, but Schley inferred that they were there. Finally, word reached the blockading squadron from Cuban rebels on shore that Cervera was definitely *not* at Cienfuegos. At last convinced, Schley started his ships eastward that evening.

The Flying Squadron arrived about twenty miles south of Santiago on May 26, and found three American ships already patrolling the waters there. They had been there for a few days already, but in that time had made no visual sighting of any Spanish warships, due to the fact that the harbor is not directly observable from the sea. Nevertheless, within a few hours, Schley decided to sail back around the western end of the island and on to Key West for more coal. The three ships on station joined him, and Santiago was without even a single blockader for almost twenty-four hours.

Secretary of the Navy John Long was extremely upset by Schley's decision to leave his post before finding out for sure whether the enemy was there or not. He thought that the commodore's announced shortage of coal might not have been the real reason for his actions. He believed instead that Schley had insufficient reserves "of that unswerving steadiness of purpose and nerve which is the essence of supreme command." Both Secretary Long and Admiral Sampson ordered Schley to turn around and return to Santiago, verify the presence or absence of Cervera's squadron, and, assuming that the enemy ships were indeed there, erect an immediate naval blockade.[41]

Sampson was worried. It did not seem to make sense to him that Cervera would not try to leave Santiago. He hoped that Schley would reach there in time to prevent that, but even if he did it would be difficult to establish an effective blockade with the number of ships at his disposal. Some would certainly be low on coal before long, and that would necessitate a reduction in the blockading force while they made the round trip to Key West. If the Americans could manage to sink an old ship or two full of stone or coal in the mouth of the channel it would certainly make it easier to keep Cervera bottled up, and Sampson began discussing such a plan with his chief of staff. Early on May 27, he signaled three other high ranking subordinates to come aboard his flagship to get their thoughts on the idea. Captain G. A. Converse of the *Montgomery* suggested using the collier *Merrimac* for this duty. It was already in the vicinity of Santiago, and its ballast of coal would not only help it sink more quickly but make it that much more difficult to be removed. Sampson immediately agreed and decided that the plan was too important to commit to writing. He therefore dispatched Captain W. Folger in the *New Orleans* to go to Schley and explain it to him personally. If Cervera escaped Santiago before Schley arrived there, the Flying Squadron was to give chase.[42]

Even as the American officers planned on a way to bottle up Cervera, naval planning was also under way in Spain. New Minister of Marine Ramón Auñón sent orders to Rear Admiral Manuel Cámara to sail his flagship, the armored cruiser *Emperador Carlos V*, along with the cruisers *Rápido*, *Patriota*, and *Meteoro* toward North America. He was to attack Charleston, South Carolina, or such other coastal targets as promised good results, and raid northward along the Atlantic coast. The hope was that, in addition to causing as much damage as possible, the civilian hysteria that such a foray would generate would force Washington to dispatch some of Sampson's ships in pursuit. With the blockade of Santiago thus weakened Admiral Cervera would have a better chance of escaping to the open seas. Cámara, meanwhile, could swing back toward the West Indies and aim for San Juan de Puerto Rico, Havana, or, in the event that Cervera had not sortied, Santiago.

Commodore Schley, meanwhile, finally arrived back on station on the evening of May 28. Early the next morning, officers aboard the *Iowa* thought they spotted something in the water at the mouth of the channel. Straining to make it out through their binoculars, they finally determined that it was the *Cristóbal Colón*, passively guarding the entrance to the harbor. They immediately flagged this information to Schley and continued peering toward the enemy. In a few minutes they made out two more Spanish ships slightly farther up the channel, and again relayed this fact to the flagship. Gun crews on the *Iowa*, meanwhile, cleared for action and waited for orders to open fire, but those orders did not come.[43]

A couple of days earlier, with Admiral Cervera safely ensconced, or perhaps imprisoned, in Santiago harbor, President McKinley sat down again with his primary military advisers. They jointly agreed to discard previous plans to attack Havana. Instead, the initial focus of land operations against the Spaniards would be at Santiago and Puerto Rico. Sampson's ships could only reach the harbor by entering into a narrow, twisting inlet, less than a quarter of a mile wide, with very high bluffs on each side. The Spaniards had placed artillery on these heights, and numerous other gun positions studded both sides of the channel. And just in case enemy ships survived the fire from these shore batteries, there were a dozen command-detonated underwater mines. It was virtually suicidal for Sampson to attempt to enter the harbor. Plans were afoot to land a large contingent of Army troops nearby whose job would be to reduce the land batteries guarding the channel. Then Sampson could leisurely remove any mines and proceed into the harbor. Major General William Shafter would lead the expedition against Santiago from Tampa as soon as enough shipping became available to transport and protect a 25,000-man force.[44]

On May 29, General Shafter, in Tampa, received orders to get his men onto the transport ships as soon as possible. The Navy would escort his force to the vicinity of Santiago where he would select a landing site either east or west of the entrance to the harbor. As soon as he had landed, he was to "move to the high ground and bluffs overlooking the harbor or into the interior, and cover the Navy as it sends its men in small boats to remove torpedoes, or, with the aid of the Navy, capture or destroy the Spanish fleet now reported to be in Santiago harbor.... When will you sail?"[45]

The success of this operation depended to a great extent on how well the Army and the Navy cooperated with one another, and in this there was to be some disappointment. Each service, of course, had the long-range goal of bringing the war to a successful conclusion, but they differed on how best to achieve that goal. The Navy assumed that the Army was being deployed to knock out the shore batteries and other naval obstructions at the mouth of the harbor inlet. Ships could then enter the harbor and capture or destroy Cervera's ships. The Army, on the other hand, although realizing the importance of neutralizing Cervera's squadron, also knew that it was important to dispose of the Spanish garrison at Santiago. It would be an interesting campaign.

There was no longer any doubt as to the whereabouts of the Spanish squadron, and for the next couple of days the men on the blockading ships kept a close watch on the Spanish ships, looking for any indication that the enemy was preparing to offer battle. All they saw, however, were ships gently riding at anchor with awnings spread and apparently not a care in the world among the crews. They knew, however, that the Spaniards were just as vigilantly watching for signs of American hostile intentions. Finally, a little before noon on May 31, signal officers aboard the American ships read the signal flags aboard the *Brooklyn* that spelled out the following message: "The *Massachusetts*, *New Orleans*, and *Iowa* will go in after dinner to a distance of seven thousand yards and fire at *Cristóbal Colón* with 8- and 12- and 13-inch guns. Speed about ten knots."[46]

Two hours later the three ships set out to carry out these orders. The *Massachusetts*, with Commodore Schley aboard, led the small procession, followed by the *New Orleans* and then the *Iowa*. When the ships turned parallel to the shore, the *Massachusetts* opened with a 13-inch shot that splashed harmlessly into the sea well short of the Spanish ship. The gunners adjusted the range upward by elevating their muzzles. By the time the *Iowa* commenced firing, its gunnery officers had increased their estimate of the range to 9,000 yards. Still they failed to reach the *Colón*.

Schley issued orders for the ships to venture no closer to the shore, so when they turned and began their second pass they increased the range of their guns even further. Gunners aboard the *Iowa* fired their last shots with an estimated range of 11,000 yards. One of these shells finally hit within about forty feet of the *Colón*, but Schley had seen enough and called off any further action. None of the ships involved on either side suffered any damage, and the Spanish ships soon retired into the harbor and out of sight of the Americans.[47]

Admiral Sampson, who no longer had any need to blockade Havana or any other Cuban port, arrived off Santiago early on the morning of June 1. He immediately signaled the American ships already there to come in closer as he tightened the noose on Cervera.

Cervera's situation, meanwhile, was anything but reassuring. He had originally steamed into Santiago harbor hoping to find plentiful supplies of coal for his squadron's depleted bunkers, but in this he was disappointed. Then, when Commodore Schley inexplicably abandoned the blockade after his initial arrival, Cervera contemplated taking his squadron to sea again. A meeting with his subordinates on the proper course to follow, however, revealed a consensus opposed to leaving. Another meeting, on June 8, similarly discouraged a proposed nighttime breakout. Cervera then seemed resigned to remaining bottled up by the American blockaders. And by then the blockading fleet had reached truly powerful proportions. In addition to the battleships *Oregon*, *Massachusetts*, *Iowa*, and *Texas* were the armored cruisers *New York* and *Brooklyn*, the protected cruiser *New Orleans*, the unprotected cruiser *Marblehead*, the auxiliary cruiser *Harvard*, the torpedo boat *Porter*, and the colliers *Sterling* and *Merrimac*.[48]

Of course, it was imperative for the sake of the Shafter's operation that Cervera stay where he was, so Sampson was anxious to implement the plan to sink the collier *Merrimac* in the channel. He chose the *Merrimac* for this dubious honor because its cantankerous engines and age made it the most expendable of his ships. He did not, however, select the *Merrimac*'s captain, Commander J. M. Miller, to carry out the dangerous task despite that officer's vigorous protests. Miller even openly questioned the admiral's right to remove him from a command that the Navy Department, and not the admiral, had bestowed upon him. Sampson finally convinced him of the efficacy of his decision. Lieutenant Richmond P. Hobson got the nod even though he was not a line officer, but a naval constructor. Sampson had already asked Hobson to look into finding a way to sink the *Merrimac* as quickly as possible in the desired location. Having come up with a good plan, Hobson now actively sought the chance to put it into practice, citing the value of his technical knowledge to place explosive charges in the most advantageous positions for scuttling the craft.[49]

A call for volunteer crewmen was then broadcast through the fleet, and the result was overwhelming as officers and men, tired of boring blockade duty and anxious for action, eagerly stepped forward. The scene aboard the *Texas* was typical. Captain John W. "Jack" Philip addressed his 300-man crew: "The 'Merrimac' will be ready for the attempt to-night, but will not go in before morning, or an hour or so before daylight. The Admiral [Sampson] is anxious to give each ship an opportunity of sharing the glory, or the misfortune: before I say any more, permit me to state that every man putting his foot on the deck of the 'Merrimac' to-night will take his life right in his hand." Then, after a short pause, he asked, "Who will represent the 'Texas?'" Every man, with a yell, thrust his hand into the air in response.[50]

Hobson had the final say on who would go, and, not surprisingly, selected most of his men from among the *Merrimac*'s regular crew. He wanted men who could deal effectively with any problems that might arise with regard to the normal functioning of the ship.[51]

Of course, the Spanish defenders could not be counted upon to sit idly by while an American ship steamed into the channel and sank itself. Hobson suggested that, once the *Merrimac* was ready, that he hoist a Spanish flag on it and have the blockading ships "chase" it toward the entrance. Done at night, the enemy would not be as likely to discern the true identity of the ship and open fire on it. If the defenders did not buy into the ruse and started shooting at the *Merrimac*, the blockaders could then turn their powerful search lights onto the enemy batteries, thereby making it difficult for them to see their target and making it easier for the American gunners to see theirs. After some discussion, however, someone pointed out that no "true" Spanish ship would attempt to enter the dangerous waters around the mouth of the channel at night, whether there was a blockading force there or not, and such an attempt to fool the Spaniards would more than likely fail.[52]

There was very little time to prepare the *Merrimac* or to train the scratch crew because meteorological conditions dictated that the predawn hours of June 2 offered the greatest chance of success. On that date there would be an hour and fifteen minutes between moonset and daybreak and the tide would be at flood stage, presenting a narrow window of opportunity. If, for any reason, the attempt had to be postponed for a day this propitious period of near total darkness would only last for thirty minutes. And on June 4, the moon did not set until *after* daybreak.[53]

The next problem was to decide how best to sink the collier. It was not simply a matter of opening the seacocks and letting water in for that would take too long. It had to be done quickly, before the Spaniards had a chance to react and tow it away from the center of the channel. One plan that Hobson considered was to detach six of the bottom plates, allowing water to rush in. First, workmen would have to cut all the rivet heads on the insides of these plates, depending upon the water pressure from beneath the vessel to hold them in place temporarily. Then, over each of them, they would rig up a nine-inch diameter vertical pipe that they would brace at the deck level and then fill with black powder. When detonated, these makeshift "cannons" would blow the plates away from the hull with considerable force. The problem with this plan, however, was that it would take two to three days to make the necessary preparations and that time was not available if the attempt was to take advantage of pre-dawn darkness.[54]

Hobson was not deterred. He quickly shifted to another plan. He would place ten electrically-detonated explosive charges, or torpedoes, at strategic points well below the waterline on the port side of the ship. He calculated that if all ten of them detonated as planned, the ship would sink in a mere seventy-five seconds. Gunners from the *New York* got to work building these devices, packing seventy-eight pounds of brown prismatic powder around a four-pound trigger charge of black powder in each one. A mixture of pitch and tallow would waterproof each torpedo. Paraffin might have been more efficient, but none was available, and there was no time to send back to Key West for some. Unfortunately, Hobson was unable to locate an electrical detonating machine anywhere within the fleet, and he could only come up with enough batteries for six of the ten charges.[55]

Nevertheless, work crews toiled frantically to get the vessel ready. Although the *Massachusetts* was already alongside receiving coal, the *Merrimac* still had 2,300 tons of coal aboard and much salvageable equipment. There was not time to unload all the coal — and its weight would help sink the *Merrimac* faster anyway — but the sailors worked feverishly to move as much of it as they could away from the port side bulkheads. That was where the charges were being placed, and Hobson did not want coal piled up to cushion the blasts or to hinder the inrushing waters. Workmen also flooded 700 tons of seawater into the *Merrimac* as additional ballast.[56]

Finally the time came to begin the operation, but a delay caused the *Merrimac* to still be in the open sea at dawn of June 2. Admiral Sampson had paid a farewell call to the men of the doomed ship, and upon leaving, the propeller of his launch fouled a line on the *Merrimac*. It was 4 A.M. before it was cleared, but Hobson began to make the run into the channel despite the delay. The admiral, however, signaled Hobson to abort the mission because of the fast approaching dawn. He was afraid that the Spanish shore batteries would be able to stop the *Merrimac* before it even got into the channel. It would be better to wait one more day. Perhaps Hobson could use the extra time to work on his temperamental torpedoes, only six of which seemed to be in working order.[57]

The strain of waiting and the physical fatigue incident to preparing for the mission began to take a toll. One of the crewmen, held over from the crew of the *Merrimac*, was exhausted and unable to continue, so the call went out to the nearby *Iowa* for a volunteer to replace him. All six hundred officers and men volunteered for this suicide mission, but only one could be accepted. Captain Robley Evans faced a dilemma. How was he to select just one man from among his eager crew? "I was naturally anxious," he later wrote, "to send a man who would die reflecting credit on the ship. I had no idea that any one would ever come out of the scrape alive." Somehow, Evans narrowed the selection down to two men, one selected by him and one by his executive officer. He informed both men that whomever he selected likely would not come back from the dangerous mission ahead, but neither of them asked to be excused. In fact, one of the men offered the other fifty dollars — not an inconsiderable sum in those days — to voluntarily drop out of the selection process. The other man refused and the choice then rested on the tossing of a coin. Coxswain John Edward Murphy — the man who had turned down the offer of money — won the toss. The unhappy loser now offered Murphy $150 to switch places with him, but again Murphy refused.[58]

Hobson and his small crew, their nerves on edge, waited anxiously through the long day. The extra time allowed the crew to come up with enough batteries to rig the other four charges, but in testing the circuits they found that three of the charges were still inoperable. They would have to make do with seven.

Finally, it was time. Hobson and his crew stripped down to their woolen underwear or trunks, socks, a life preserver, and a pistol belt with a revolver and thirty-two rounds of ammunition. It was about 1:30 on the morning of June 3 when the *Merrimac*, accompanied part of the way by a launch from the *New York*, headed slowly in the general direction of the channel. It cruised back and forth for over an hour, waiting for the moon to set, before finally implementing the plan. That plan called for the engineer to shut down the engine before actually entering the channel and allow the ship's momentum to carry it forward. Then, with the speed reduced to about four and a half knots, and when Hobson judged that he had reached the narrowest part of the channel, the helmsman would turn the wheel hard, bringing the bow around to starboard, while others ran out the bow and stern anchors to further slow the ship. Then in a carefully choreographed sequence crewmen opened the seacocks and detonated the torpedoes. The movement of the ship at this point would be such as to force water into the holes thus opened up and hasten its sinking. The 333-foot long *Merrimac* would, if all went as planned, sink astride the channel where it was only about 400 feet wide and seal the Spanish squadron in the harbor. Hobson and his crew would, in the mean time, make their escape in a small boat.[59]

At first, everything went precisely as planned. No sleepy Spanish sentry atop the bluffs sounded the alarm as the *Merrimac* glided slowly toward the mouth of the inlet. But this good fortune did not last. With only about 400 yards to go, someone on a Spanish picket boat noticed the intruder and opened fire. It was 3:20 A.M. when the *Merrimac* entered the channel, but at a greater speed than the plan called for. When things started going wrong they went wrong in a hurry. Shore batteries soon entered the fray. One of the Spanish cruisers and a torpedo boat joined in with their guns and even launched four torpedoes. Other Spaniards began setting off underwater mines hoping to stop the American ship before it got any farther, but only one of them did any damage. A sailor aboard the *Texas* described what it looked like from off shore:

> At first we could distinguish the separate flashes from different guns, but almost immediately it became impossible to tell one from another. It was a steady rainpour, one combined solid sheet of fire, with seemingly not a single break in it; looked something like mammoth sheet lightning, only it did not come and go as does lightning, but was one continuous steady glare which made the harbor entrance resemble somewhat a monster furnace door thrown open with all the fires of hell raging within.[60]

Attempting to make the best of a bad situation that was rapidly getting worse, Hobson ordered the torpedoes detonated and the prearranged hard turn to the right, but his bad luck continued. Enemy fire had already shot away the *Merrimac*'s steering gear in three different places. Not only did the big collier continue moving forward at such a speed as to render the anchors useless, but only two of the torpedoes functioned properly, enemy fire having disabled the batteries for all the others, and although the *Merrimac* did finally go down, its momentum had carried it past the channel's bottleneck and into a wider part of the channel where it did little to obstruct navigation. As the ship slowly settled, Spanish fire continued unabated.

Shells exploded and sent shards of hot steel in all directions. Machine gun and rifle bullets clattered against the sides of the vessel without letup. In an effort to make the smallest of targets of themselves Hobson and his men lay flat on the deck. "It seemed to me," recalled one man, "like all one roar and flash, and as though the heavens had opened, and it was raining fire. The Spanish batteries were within a ship's length, and by the light from the flash of their guns and exploding shells we could plainly distinguish objects from one end of the ship to the other." Hobson "waited to see one man's leg, another man's shoulder, the top of another's head, taken off. I looked for my own body to be cut in two diagonally, from the left hip upward, and wondered for a moment what the sensation would be." Amazingly, his premonition did not come true. None of the men were hit.[61]

Escape, however, was impossible. The men had been too busy to cut their catamaran loose from the deck of the *Merrimac* before it went down, so they now found themselves clinging to their partially submerged escape vessel. The deafening fire finally stopped, and the Spanish pushed out from shore in small boats to capture anyone who might have survived the firestorm. The Americans were able to escape detection amid the wreckage in the dark, but when the sun rose about an hour later, and the searchers did not have to rely on the glimmer of lanterns, the game was up. Hobson hailed a passing steam launch, which immediately pulled closer to the wreckage of the *Merrimac*. An officer on board ordered the men to swim toward him one at a time and surrender their weapons while half a dozen Spanish riflemen in the bow kept the others in their sights. Hobson was the first to comply, but the rest of the waiting sailors used the time to unbuckle their pistol belts and let them sink to the ocean floor rather than turn them over to their captors. As the Americans were hauled shivering and covered with coal dust and oil from their sunken ship out of the water they found themselves face to face with none other than Admiral Cervera. He praised their courage, and in spite of the failure of their mission, Hobson and his crewmen became overnight heroes in the United States.[62]

Later in the day a Spanish tugboat under a flag of truce approached Sampson's flagship with information on the fate of the *Merrimac*'s last crew. The Spanish captain praised the bravery of the Americans and assured Admiral Sampson that they were all uninjured and receiving humane treatment. They had asked him to bring back some of their clothing, and Sampson also insisted on sending a modest amount of money along for them to use to purchase food, medicine, or any other necessities.

With the *Merrimac* sunk too far into the channel to obstruct Cervera's warships, Admiral Sampson looked for other methods to keep his opposite number bottled up. He decided to move one of his battleships in close to the channel at night and beam its powerful searchlight directly into the harbor opening while a second capital ship took up a support position nearby. This guard ship stayed completely darkened. He chose the *Iowa* as the first ship to make this experiment, and when its captain inquired just how close he should take his ship the admiral replied that he wanted the men on board to be able to see even a rowboat if it crossed from one side of the channel to the other. Such a move had the obvious intent of making it impossible for any Spanish ships to slip out of the channel under cover of darkness—there would be no darkness. There were also considerable risks to the American ship involved. It was possible that one of the fast Spanish torpedo boats might be able to break out of the channel and send its deadly torpedoes at whatever battleship was on searchlight duty at the time. The torpedo boat would almost certainly be blown out of the water by the concentrated fire of the American ships, but if it could inflict a mortal injury to one of Sampson's capital ships in the process it would upset the balance of power in the immediate area. Such a thing did not happen, and the *Iowa* rotated search light duty with the battleships *Oregon* and *Massachusetts*, while the *Indiana* and *Texas* took turns as guard ships with their broadsides facing up the channel. The light ships rotated every two hours because of the wear and tear on the lights and on the nerves of the men.[63]

It was obvious that things were now at an impasse. Sampson did not wish to risk any of his ships in the twisting channel that led into Santiago Bay. Nor did Cervera wish to challenge the heavy guns of the American fleet by leaving his current anchorage. The element necessary to tip the balance in the favor of the United States was an Army operation to reduce the Spanish defenses near the mouth of the inlet. With these positions neutralized, Sampson could then bring his ships up the channel and cooperate with the Army in capturing or destroying the Spanish squadron.

Hour after hour and day after day the blockading sailors kept a watchful eye on the entrance to the harbor. Not only was this extremely boring, but the ships constantly consumed fuel while remaining on station, and meant a return all the way back to Key West for replenishment. These trips were staggered so as never to leave the blockade too weak, but it was immediately obvious that if there were some point on the Cuban coast itself where these functions could be attended to it would add greatly to the overall efficiency of the blockade. Navy Department planners quickly realized that Guantánamo Bay, only forty miles east of Santiago, was ideal. Its harbor was large and relatively sheltered.

Naval authorities had already foreseen the need of a battalion-sized unit of Marines to secure such sites and handle other problems that were too much for the various ships' normal detachments and authorized the formation of such a unit. Lieutenant Colonel Robert W. Huntington commanded the Marine Barracks in Brooklyn, and had begun forming this provisional unit about a week before the formal declaration of war. He organized the battalion into six companies. Five of them served as infantry while the sixth manned the battalion's four rapid-firing 3-inch landing guns. Huntington's ad hoc command constituted more than 20 percent of the manpower of the entire Marine Corps. Nevertheless, the battalion reached Key West on April 24.[64]

Almost a third of the men had only been in uniform since the first of the year so Colonel Huntington had ordered target practice en route, both to keep them occupied and to bring them a little closer to combat readiness. This phase of the men's training, however, was only marginally better than none at all. Each Marine rifleman received only ten rounds of ammunition to fire, and each of the four artillery crews fired only one round.[65]

Telegraphic orders from Washington sent the battalion aboard the *Panther* on June 7. The Marines were heading for action at last. Even as they were getting underway again, the *Marblehead* and the converted merchant ship *Yankee* carefully nosed into Guantánamo Bay, threw shells at a Spanish artillery battery near Cayo del Toro, and drove the Spanish gunboat *Sandoval* back up the bay toward the town of Caimanera.

By the time the Marines reached Guantánamo early on June 10, the battleship *Oregon*, the monitor *Yosemite*, the torpedo boat *Porter*, and the gunboat *Dolphin* had also arrived. A landing party of forty Marines from the *Oregon* and twenty from the *Marblehead* went ashore to locate a campsite for Colonel Huntington's battalion, and the *Panther* began disembarking troops early in the afternoon. The landing went smoothly, but getting all the necessary supplies ashore proved to be another matter. Due to intra-service rivalry, Commander G. C. Reiter of the *Panther* refused to put his crew to work unloading stores. Then, to make matters worse, Reiter decided that he needed to keep most of the small arms ammunition stowed in the hold so his ship would ride better. Commander McCalla, captain of the *Marblehead* and senior officer present, blew up. "Sir," he lectured Reiter, "Break out immediately and land with the crew of the *Panther*, 50,000 rounds of ... ammunition. In future, do not require Colonel Huntington to break out or land his stores with members of his command. Use your own officers and men for this purpose, and supply the Commanding Officer of Marines promptly with anything he may desire." The sailors soon manhandled ashore Col. Huntington's necessary supplies, and, in gratitude, he named his new hilltop camp after the *Marblehead*'s skipper.[66]

While the battalion erected its tents and laid out its camp on a hill overlooking the bay, a Spanish force initiated a probe of the area. Even though Marine scouts had gone out, many of the Americans were unaware of the near proximity of the enemy, and the attack caught them bathing, carrying water, and generally attending to camp chores. They quickly regained their composure and drove off the attackers.

The next day Huntington sent out two small patrols under First Lieutenant Wendall C. Neville (a future Commandant of the Marine Corps) and Second Lieutenant Melville J. Shaw. They saw no sign of the enemy all day. Then, early in the evening, Lieutenant Neville's patrol stopped for a light supper. It was then that the Spaniards opened up on his men from nearby heights. Neville quickly got his men into line and attacked in the direction of the enemy fire. The Spaniards were difficult to spot in the darkening jungle, particularly since many of them had attached sprigs of foliage to their clothing as camouflage. Still the Marines saw two enemy soldiers fall before it grew too dark to continue fighting.

At about 9 P.M., another party of enemy troops appeared on a small island about a mile northeast of the Marine camp, but they were too far away to inflict any damage on the Americans. Colonel Huntington nevertheless detailed about a dozen of his men to shell the island with their 3-inch gun just to let the Spaniards know that their presence had not gone unnoticed. By the time the gunners got the range, however, the enemy had gone. They had other plans in mind.

Camp McCalla soon came under rifle fire from the nearby jungle. Although this did not take the Marines completely by surprise, some of them were bathing in the waters of the bay below the camp. When the Mausers began popping, they came out of the water, grabbed their rifles, and scampered up the hill to join the skirmish line that Colonel Huntington was forming below the brow of the hill. They must have presented an interesting sight; some of them fully uniformed and outfitted, others in various stages of undress, and still others dripping from their interrupted salt water baths. The Marines fired a volley blindly into the surrounding brush, and when there was no immediate return fire Huntington ordered them to assault down the hill. A newspaper correspondent noted wryly that "there was no fun in this for naked men but they held their places and charged with the others." But, alas, the enemy had melted back into the jungle, and the Americans climbed back up to their camp.[67]

This night saw the death of the first American officer on Cuban soil during the war. Ensign John B. Gibbs was a medical doctor assigned to the U.S.S. *Oregon*, and, since the Marine Corps has always relied on the Navy for medical service, he had accompanied the landing party ashore. Gibbs was not a career Navy man. In fact, at age 39, he probably could have avoided military service altogether with no risk to his reputation. When war broke out, however, he left his flourishing medical practice in New York and, partially through the intercession of his friend Assistant Secretary of the Navy Theodore Roosevelt, received a commission in the Navy.

It was after midnight when Dr. Gibbs decided to leave the hospital tent and make his way to a safer location to avoid the growing intensity of Spanish rifle fire peppering the camp. As he and two Marine privates stepped out into the open, they encountered others seeking safety, journalist Stephen Crane among them. Crane later wrote that the enemy fire was so intense that he soon employed the "more congenial occupation of lying flat and feeling the hot hiss of the bullets trying to cut my hair. For the moment," he wrote, "I was no longer a cynic. I was a child who, in a fit of ignorance, had jumped into the vat of war." Unlike his friend, Dr. Gibbs, Crane survived his baptism of fire without a scratch. The doctor fell, mortally wounded in the head.[68]

As the fire increased the Marines signaled the *Marblehead* to turn its powerful searchlight on the area. The illumination revealed a group of enemy soldiers only 200 yards from the camp. A few well-placed shots from the *Marblehead*'s 6-inch guns sent them scrambling, and Commander McCalla sent more of his ship's contingent of Marines ashore as a further reinforcement.

The next morning, McCalla anxiously awaited further word from shore about the night's action. He learned of the death of Ensign Gibbs and two enlisted Marines, but what bothered him more was that there were still forty Marines who had not returned from their reconnaissance patrols. He did not know whether they were dead, alive, or perhaps prisoners of the Spaniards. Marine Lieutenant Cyrus Radford, commander of the forty-one-man ship's guard aboard the *Texas*, shared McCalla's concern and asked Captain Philip if he could take his men ashore to help strengthen the American position. Philip readily assented and had the men take two Colt's machineguns with them.

Chaplain Harry Jones also secured permission to go ashore and was about to follow Lieutenant Radford down the ladder to a waiting boat when the lieutenant stopped him. He rather curtly informed the chaplain that he would just be in the Marines' way and that he should stay aboard the battleship. When Jones told him he was going ashore to minister to the wounded and help bury the dead, Radford was adamant. "You had better give us a chance to get wounded or killed before you come," he said. Jones pointed out to him that men had already been killed and wounded in Camp McCalla and they were the Marines to whom he intended to offer his services. Radford had forgotten about these earlier casualties in the excitement of the moment and sheepishly apologized. "I thought you were coming over to bury some of us," he ruefully remarked.[69]

The funeral service that Chaplain Jones conducted for Ensign Gibbs and the two Marines was unlike any he had experienced before. Marines wrapped the three bodies in blankets and carried them on stretchers to the freshly dug graves. Colonel Huntington accompanied the chaplain, as did a Navy surgeon and as many men as could be spared from securing the camp. The service had barely begun when Spanish rifle shots marred the solemnity of the proceedings. Jones thought at first that someone was whistling, which seemed rather inappropriate. He turned to Colonel Huntington to see if he had been the one whistling. "No," responded Huntington stoically, "I did not whistle: that was a Mauser bullet: we are attacked." With that, and with little urging from another officer, Jones made his way into a nearby trench. Even his untrained ears now recognized the escalating sounds of gunshots.

From the relative safety of the trench, Jones looked back toward the burial site and saw Colonel Huntington still standing there, calmly issuing orders to his subordinates. Taking some comfort from the colonel's example, Jones left the trench to go on with the service. He had scarcely commenced when three Marines with a Colt machine gun set it up right next to him and began blazing away. Almost simultaneously some other men set up one of their 3-inch guns on the other side of him and began shelling the enemy. Although the chaplain's back was to the enemy he was encouraged by the efforts being taken to protect him. "Not a bullet passed by me during the Committal Service," he recalled, "but as I closed my eyes, asking God to bless the men of that camp, I heard them whistling around me like so many bees." He was undoubtedly glad to finish the service and leave such an exposed area.[70]

Men in the camp heard scattered shooting throughout the night and well into the next day as they waited anxiously for the return of the patrolling Marines. When Lieutenant Neville led them back into the camp the next day they were a disheveled, tired, thirsty, mosquito-bitten lot. And there were casualties.

Lieutenant Neville had sent Sergeant Charles H. Smith and Private Brown out as a listening post near midnight while he reconnoitered in another direction. The two enlisted Marines soon ran into more trouble than they were prepared to handle. They came under fire from three sides and tried desperately to make their way through the darkness and back to the relative safety of Camp McCalla. When Sergeant Smith clambered over a slight elevation his silhouette momentarily became visible to an alert Spanish sniper. As he fell with a Mauser bullet in him he urged Brown to save himself. The private, in the best tradition of the American fighting man, refused to leave the wounded man until he had carried him to a position somewhat sheltered from additional Spanish sniper fire. Brown then made it back into camp, but Sergeant Smith did not survive the night.[71]

Two other Marines died during the night. They were apparently both out, as had been Sergeant Smith, on a two-man reconnaissance. Their comrades recovered their bodies the next day and were horrified at the conditions of the bodies. It looked as if the Spaniards had used the dead Marines for target practice. One had twenty-one bullet holes in his face, and the other had fifteen.[72]

Such an adverse beginning for the Marines in Cuba caused Colonel Huntington to have second thoughts on the advisability of trying to establish a presence in the midst of such seemingly overwhelming numbers of enemy troops. But when he proposed that the Navy should re-embark his battalion, Commander McCalla launched into a tirade of opposition. "Leave this camp?" he stormed. "No sir, that camp is named for me.... My family would suffer." McCalla seemed to rue the dishonor that might attach to his family name by a withdrawal more than the effect of more Marine casualties ashore. "You were put there," he reminded the colonel, "to hold the hill and you'll stay there! If you are killed," he magnanimously added, "I'll come out and get your dead body."[73]

The Marines stayed ashore, but it was obvious that they could not accomplish their task of preventing land-based Spanish troops from harassing the American ships in the harbor without some vigorous offensive action. The key to limiting the effectiveness of Spanish forces in the area around Camp McCalla appeared to be the ready availability of fresh water. The Spaniards' nearest source of drinking water was a well in the nearby village of Cuzco, and if the Marines could capture or destroy it the enemy troops would be unable to operate in strength.

On the morning of June 14, Colonel Huntington sent Captain George Elliott with Company C and Captain William F. Spicer with Company D to neutralize Cuzco Well. A fifty-man company of Cuban troops accompanied the Americans to guide them through the unfamiliar countryside. The Spaniards had six companies of the Sixth Barcelona Regiment stationed at Cuzco so the extra firepower of the Cuban auxiliaries was welcome. The Marines were not accustomed to the rigors of marching in the type of terrain of eastern Cuba. The steep hills and the brutal tropical sun caused almost two dozen of them to fall out of the line of march exhausted.[74]

The village of Cuzco was in a small valley opening onto the sea a couple of miles east of Camp McCalla, and as soon as the Marines and Cubans appeared on the surrounding hills the Spaniards opened fire upon them. Second Lieutenant Louis J. Magill took most of Company C and a handful of Cubans and moved around to the inland side of the village, the closed end of the valley, to prevent the enemy from escaping in that direction. The defenders allowed the Americans the tactical advantage of the high ground, relying on the walls of their blockhouse to protect them. They apparently had not factored in the possibility of naval bombardment however. The *Dolphin* steamed along offshore paralleling the infantry's advance and soon added its fire to the musketry ashore.

As the fire fight progressed the Marines more than held their own. Spanish rifle fire proved particularly ineffective. In fact, the greatest threat to Marine lives soon became the artillery fire of the *Dolphin*, some of whose shells were overshooting the enemy and falling within Lieutenant Magill's position. Quick thinking Sergeant John H. Quick pulled out his blue handkerchief, attached it to a stick, and jumped up amid the maelstrom of shot and shell and began waving his makeshift signal flag vigorously at the friendly ship. Showing no outward concern about the Mauser bullets snapping past him, Sergeant Quick waited for the Navy signalman on the ship to acknowledge his message before he ducked back under cover. He did not want to risk having his message not received, or received but not understood, so that he would have to rise up and send it again. The shellfire from offshore quickly stopped.[75]

Without the worry of friendly fire casualties, the Marine riflemen and their Cuban allies settled down to the task at hand. By the middle of the afternoon the fighting was over. The Spaniards had abandoned their blockhouse and taken to the surrounding hills. They had lost approximately sixty men killed and 150 wounded, and the Marines took one officer and seventeen men prisoner. On the other side of the ledger, two Cubans died, and two Cubans and three Marines were wounded. The victorious Marines filled in the well and destroyed a signal station at Cuzco before returning to camp. Colonel Huntington praised the performance of the Cuban soldiers, saying that they "were of the greatest assistance." With no reliable source of drinking water any closer than the village of Caimanera, ten miles away, the Spaniards would cause no more trouble for the Marines around Guantánamo.[76]

With the immediate area around Camp McCalla thus secure, the *Marblehead*, the *Suwanee*, and the *Texas* steamed farther into the bay to try to destroy the fortifications at Caimanera. The three ships threw shells for three hours without apparent effect, but by that time the Spanish garrison decided to abandon this position for the relative safety of Santiago. The *Texas* sent one last 6-inch shell at the trainload of troops as it escaped.[77]

The entire area around Guantánamo Bay was now secure, and at relatively small cost to the Americans. That cost, however, could have been much higher. Both the *Texas* and the *Marblehead* encountered sub-surface contact mines that had enough explosives in them to have sunk either ship. "But," Captain Philip of the *Texas* said, "owing to Divine care neither of them exploded." These mines had been in the water so long that salt corrosion and barnacle buildup had so encrusted the firing mechanisms as to prevent them from detonating.[78]

While the Navy waited on the Army to complete its plans for landing troops in Cuba, routine blockade duty continued. The crushing tedium was occasionally broken with some small excitement or other. A few days after Hobson's heroics Admiral Sampson decided to test the strength of the Spanish shore batteries against his ships. He had witnessed, albeit from a predawn distance, the damage they seemed to have inflicted on the *Merrimac*, but he intended this time for his ships to shoot back. Early on Monday morning, June 6, two roughly parallel lines of American ships steamed toward the enemy defenses. Sampson's armored cruiser *New York*, led the right hand procession, followed at 400-yard intervals by the gunboat *Yankee*, the protected cruiser *New Orleans*, and the battleships *Oregon* and *Iowa*. These ships were to attack the gun positions to the east of Morro Castle. Sampson put the castle itself off limits because Lieutenant Hobson and his men were imprisoned in it. The armored cruiser *Brooklyn* led the other column, consisting of the gunboat *Marblehead* and the battleships *Texas* and *Massachusetts*. These vessels targeted the Estrella fortifications just inside the harbor entrance. When the *New York* and *Brooklyn* reached a point estimated at 5,000 yards from the harbor's mouth they turned right and left respectively, leading their consorts roughly parallel to the Cuban coast. Shortly after 7:30, with the range now fixed at 4,000 yards, firing commenced and was immediately answered from shore.

The firing was so rapid and so intense that one Spaniard thought "it resembled one prolonged thunder. In fact," he continued, "I had no idea that any firing could be as terrific as that of those ... ships." After about three hours, the ships retired to their blockading positions. For all the noise and smoke — and an estimated 8,000 rounds fired by the ships — Spanish losses were relatively light. The *Reina Mercedes*, which by this time had transferred most of its guns to various land batteries, received numerous hits. Commander Emilio de Acosta y Eyermann and five sailors were killed and several others wounded. A couple of soldiers were also wounded, but there was no damage to the gun emplacements. Damage by return fire was also insignificant, although one Spanish shell pierced the *Texas* and killed one man and wounded four others. ("Daisy," the *Texas*' pet dog, also died during the exchange and was buried at sea.[79])

Where were Admiral Cámara and his four cruisers? They had not yet left Spain. The *Carlos V*, built only three years earlier, had still not completed its full complement of sea trials. Nor had all of its armament been installed. Cámara was still waiting on workmen to complete the installation of his four 3.94-inch guns.[80]

In the meantime, however, the minister of marine had changed his mind about the best use of these ships. On June 15, he ordered Cámara to sail east instead of west. He was to take four cruisers, four destroyers, and the auxiliary vessels needed to escort two transports of troops to the Philippines. He was to proceed through the Strait of Gibraltar at night and be far enough into the Mediterranean by daylight the next morning to avoid observation from shore. He would then proceed through the Suez Canal and on to the Philippines.[81]

CHAPTER 5

Fifth Corps' Baptism of Fire

By the end of April, the War Department decided to mass regular infantry, cavalry, and artillery regiments at Tampa, Florida, for an immediate attack on Spanish positions in Cuba. The attack order was postponed almost immediately, but the consolidation continued apace. Within a week eight regiments of infantry, one of cavalry, and eight batteries of field artillery had arrived.[1]

Tampa's proximity to the expected seat of war was about the only thing that recommended it for the site of such a camp. The heat, the sand, and the rapidly overtaxed water and sewage systems soon made life less than exhilarating for the men in the blue wool uniforms. An Englishman in one of the regular regiments observed that Tampa consisted mostly of "sand, and then sand, and lastly sand. When the sun flames out in the hot season you can cook an egg in the sand. It happened to be the hot season when I arrived." A reporter described it as looking very much like a "city chiefly composed of derelict wooden houses drifting on an ocean of sand." One of his well-traveled associates was even more damning in his characterization of the town. "It is," he wrote, "a huddled collection of generally insignificant buildings standing in an arid desert of sand, and to me it suggested ... a wretched, verdureless town in southern Siberia, colloquially known to Russian Army officers as 'the Devil's Sandbox.'"[2]

Nevertheless, by the middle of May volunteer regiments were arriving at the rate of three to five per day. There were soon more soldiers in Tampa than civilians, and the Army established satellite camps in nearby Ybor City and in Lakeland and Jacksonville.[3]

General Shafter and other high-ranking officers, along with members of the press corps, foreign military observers, and others, took rooms at the magnificent Tampa Bay Hotel. They were able to find respite from the sun on the wide, cool verandas, but the hotel might just as well have been a foreign country for most of the enlisted men. Some might have walked through the posh reception areas wondering what it must be like to actually have a room there. Others, if they could afford it, ventured into the dining rooms to treat themselves to something much better than Army rations. One such man decided that, rather than gambling his money away on payday as so many of his comrades were doing, he would use part of his ready cash to dine like a true gentleman. After enjoying his meal he sat down at a piano in the lobby and began to pick out a few tunes. "Someone," he recalled, "tipped me a dollar — perhaps to stop. At any rate I decided to quit while I was ahead."[4]

Original plans for the gathering of troops at Tampa had been that they would stay there only long enough to replenish any lack of supplies before sailing for Cuba. The men were eager

Men of the 8th U.S. Infantry pack up in preparation to move toward the seat of war (Library of Congress).

to face the enemy, and the camp was rife with rumors. When a dark-skinned man was seen taking photographs about Tampa and the camps, some questioned his motives. Then, when a local Cuban cigar-maker voiced his concerns about the man, Army authorities arrested him on suspicion of spying. An officer versed in photography accompanied the accused man into a darkroom and watched carefully as he developed the pictures that were in his camera. The first picture to emerge from the chemical bath was of two Cuban girls sitting on a step. This was followed by one showing a boy on a bicycle, then one of the inside of a saloon's dining area, and other equally innocuous shots. Upon his release from custody the man, himself a Cuban cigar-maker, went looking for the one who had slandered him.[5]

With invasion plans postponed, and after the temporary excitement surrounding the "spy," the soldiers fell into a routine of drill and other military duties, but many of them still found time to look for diversions. Nor did they have to look very far. Almost immediately, enterprising vendors descended on Tampa as they had on Camp Alger, Camp Thomas, and all the other camps, and set up stores catering to the bored soldiers' every earthly desire. The proprietors of "Noah's Ark," for example, made cool beverages available to anyone with ready cash. "Pie factories and beer saloons multiplied and increased," recalled a volunteer officer, and led to a "partially successful effort to relieve us of as much pay as was consistent within the pale of the law." Others sold baby alligators to the men, many of whom promptly boxed them up and sent them home to unsuspecting family members.[6]

Perhaps the most colorful of the volunteer regiments camped at Tampa was that of the Rough Riders. Many of these men were rough-and-tumble characters, and even those who were not seemed to revel in the reputation. A New Jersey volunteer stationed at Tampa thought that the Rough Riders were "the toughest set of men I ever met. Many of them are outlaws and I might venture to state that 70 percent of them are 'man killers' of some note in one part or another of the wild and wooly West. They drink, gamble and raise the devil generally. Their language is beyond description and they are always fighting and ready to shoot at the first chance that offers. They all carry 45-calibre six-shooters and knives and when they get in Tampa on a good time they make things howl." The various antics of the Rough Riders may have been in fun, but the results were sometimes far from innocent. A couple of these cavalrymen, along with three mule packers, sought admittance one night in June to one Alice May's bawdy house. When the proprietress turned them away because of their advanced states of inebriation, they took matters into their own hands and tried to shoot their way in. One of the Rough Riders took a bullet in the shoulder in the ensuing gunplay, and Alice May was wounded in the leg.[7]

While drunken soldiers shooting up whorehouses was bad enough, there was at least one instance of such behavior that was much worse. On the night of June 6, a number of inebriated Ohio volunteers decided on a demeaning form of amusement that soon turned dangerous. One of the men approached a black woman and her two-year-old son. He snatched the child away from the mother and proceeded to spank him, much to the drunken delight of his comrades. Then he held the child at arm's length while the other soldiers fired toward him. It is unclear whether they meant to actually hit the child or to see how near they could come without hitting him. At any rate, after one of the bullets tore through the toddler's clothing, they had had their fun and returned him to his hysterical mother. This incident was the spark that set off the smoldering rage of the soldiers of the all-black Twenty-fourth and Twenty-fifth U.S. Infantry Regiments. They had routinely been denied service in local saloons, cafes, and brothels, and this latest racial insult pushed them to the breaking point. Many of them grabbed up pistols and began firing indiscriminately at the targets of their rage. Only the mobilization of the Second Georgia Volunteers as riot police brought the incident to an end. By the next morning over two dozen black regulars and an untold number of Georgians had been conveyed to an Army hospital near Atlanta with serious wounds.[8]

It was one thing, and a relatively easy thing at that, for the Secretary of War or the Commanding General to issue orders to General Shafter to immediately embark for Cuba and quite another to see them carried out. Tampa was one vast scene of chaos. Tons of supplies arrived regularly by rail, but in most cases the bills of lading did not accompany the shipments so there was no way to know what each car contained. By early June there were over 300 rail cars parked on sidings in Tampa and on tracks many miles away. The only way to determine what each of these cars held was for officers to open them and do a visual inspection of the contents. As an example of the inefficiency this system fostered was the fact that at a time when many of the soldiers at Tampa desperately needed clothing to replace what was worn out, fifteen cars loaded with brand new uniforms rested on a siding twenty-five miles away. Within a couple of weeks quartermaster troops were unloading seventy cars per day and finally catching up with the backlog.[9]

Meanwhile Secretary Alger bombarded General Shafter with telegrams urging him to get his expedition onto the ships and away. However, there was only a single railroad line from the camps at Tampa to the port facilities several miles away, and the congestion was almost beyond belief. Nevertheless, Shafter cabled Washington on the evening of June 7 that he would leave early the next morning with a force that included approximately 17,000 officers and men.[10]

There was no need for the general to enlighten his superiors as to the wild scramble he

Crowded dock at Tampa prior to shipping out for Cuba (U.S. Army Military History Institute).

had witnessed the day before as troops strove to board the limited number of ships available. It was common knowledge that not enough shipping was at hand to provide for all of the troops assembled at Tampa so the various regiments went to great lengths to avoid being left behind. The Sixth U.S. Infantry, for example, found that the Ninth U.S. had stolen the wagon train set aside for its transportation to the docks. The volunteer Seventy-first New York commandeered a train at bayonet point that had been reserved for the regular Thirteenth Infantry. The men of the First Volunteer Cavalry, the Rough Riders, lived up to their nickname in acquiring their transportation to the wharves. Arriving at the Tampa waterfront amid a crush of humanity, Colonels Leonard Wood and Theodore Roosevelt learned from a quartermaster officer that the *Yucatan*, just then heading in to the dock, was to be their transport, but that they should waste no time in boarding if they hoped to keep it for their regiment. Roosevelt turned, ran back to the regiment, and ordered it forward at the double quick. They arrived just as the ship was nudging up against the pier and hurried aboard. This same ship had been allotted to the Second Infantry and the Seventy-first New York, but the Rough Riders had gotten there first and the other regiments were left to shift for themselves. "Hell won't be worse crowded on the last day than this dock is now," observed one man.[11]

The shortage of shipping also meant that many important items had to be left behind. Among such equipment were ambulances. A few were shipped, but Army officials theorized that wounded soldiers could be transported to field hospitals in regular Army wagons instead of the more specialized ambulances. Then, when the wagons were no longer needed to transport human cargo they could revert back to their intended purpose of hauling food, ammunition, camp equipage, and whatever else was necessary.

Likewise, cavalry horses, with few exceptions, were left in Florida, meaning that the troopers would be living and fighting on foot, just like the infantry. "That almost took the starch out of the boys," remembered a Rough Rider sergeant, "as a cowboy is almost as helpless on foot as a fish is out of water." And since the cavalry regiments were not taking their horses with them they had to leave sufficient numbers of troops to tend to the animals, and that meant that roughly one-third of the men in the cavalry regiments would not be going to Cuba. One of the volunteers who was thus detailed as a hostler paid $50 to trade places with another man, who had apparently decided that going to war might not be such a good idea after all. Both men, however, were doomed to disappointment when Lieutenant Colonel Roosevelt said that he would not authorize any substitutions. "Two of my best friends," he explained to the crestfallen men, "are being left behind. All cannot go." At least one of the two, Hamilton Fish, *did* go, however, and was one of the first to be killed.[12]

In the midst of this sea of struggling humanity was Major J. E. Maxfield and his budding balloon corps. With the fear of a Spanish investment of the east coast having subsided, the aeronauts were ordered south from New York in May. This order found Maxfield far from having everything he thought he needed. He had ordered two more French balloons to augment the *Gen'l Myer* and one from a New York maker, but none of them had arrived yet. Some of the apparatus that had come east from Colorado was still undergoing repair, but material was sent south as soon as it became available. At Tampa, the balloonists fell victim to the same confusion and chaos that bedeviled the rest of the Army as its officers sought to locate and unload equipment packed in rail cars all over south Florida. Maxfield, after opening and searching through hundreds of boxcars, finally found most of the equipment he needed before time ran out. And now, with the Fifth Corps finally loading for Cuba, Maxfield discovered that quartermaster officers had not assigned him and his First Balloon Company of the Volunteer Signal Corps to *any* shipping. Only after the personal intercession by General Shafter did these signalmen finally begin loading their equipment onto the *Rio Grande*.

The men on the ships were anxious to get to Cuba and have a chance at the Spaniards, but for the huge majority of them this would be their first ocean voyage. Some, perhaps many, had misgivings about this mode of travel, but most of them kept any such anxieties to themselves. One who did not was renowned artist Frederic Remington, who was on his way to sketch the impending action for reproduction in American newspapers. He left little room for misunderstanding his qualms when he wrote: "Now it is so arranged in the world that I hate a ship in a compound, triple-expansion, forced-draught way.... Do anything to me, but do not have me entered on the list of a ship. It does not matter if I am to be the lordly proprietor of the finest yacht afloat, make me a feather in a sick chicken's tail on shore, and I will thank you."[13]

Finally, after spending all night aboard the crowded transports, the expedition started for the Gulf of Mexico on the afternoon of June 8. But it did not get very far. An American naval vessel reported the presence the night before of a Spanish armored cruiser and two destroyers in the St. Nicholas Channel along the northern coast of Cuba, and orders quickly emanated from Washington halting Shafter's expedition until the enemy ships could be definitely located and dealt with. The next day the auxiliary cruiser *Yankee* reported having sighted not three Spanish ships, but eight! And one of them was a large battleship. Admiral Sampson, on station off Santiago, received orders to dispatch two fast cruisers to the area of the ship sightings, and ships from Key West also joined the search. It certainly would not do to have these Spanish ships come upon Shafter's convoy in mid voyage and attack the virtually defenseless transports.

The large enemy warship turned out to be the British cruiser *Talbot* and the destroyers—

variously reported as being two or seven in number — were actually five *American* ships full of supplies for Admiral Sampson's blockading squadron. When Sampson discovered the true identity of this "ghost fleet" he saw no need to send his cruisers to escort the convoy from Tampa. The Navy Department was still reluctant to give Shafter's convoy the go-ahead signal, and instead ordered Sampson to determine beyond a doubt that all six of Cervera's ships were still in Santiago harbor. If one or two had gotten out they could wreak havoc with American war plans.[14]

While this reconnaissance was being carried out the men of the Fifth Corps stayed aboard their ships at Tampa. It would have been unwise to land them all because there was no place for them to camp closer than their original camps eight or nine miles away. And then, when it came time to re-embark, the same mad scramble would replay itself once again. The ships instead dropped anchor near shore, and the men were allowed to take turns on dry land while their officers waited for orders to start off again.

On some ships, at least, small groups of men went swimming as some of their fellow soldiers stood at the ships' rails with rifles — ready to discourage any sharks whose curiosity drew them to the thrashing, splashing swimmers. Other men stayed on board gambling away any money they happened to have.[15]

Finally, when all fears of the Spanish ghost squadron had been allayed, the eager soldiers left Tampa on June 14. The invasion force presented a truly inspiring scene early in its voyage. The twenty-nine transports and six support vessels started out traveling in three parallel columns about 800 yards apart and with each ship no closer than 300 yards to the one in front of or behind it. The dozen or so naval escorts shielded the convoy at the front and sides at a distance of about 1,600 yards. Before long, however, this precise alignment became deranged with the faster ships pulling far ahead of the others and then having to reduce speed to close up the formation. Newspaper reporter Richard Harding Davis, along to cover the story, reported that "it was a most happy-go-lucky expedition, run with real American optimism and readiness to take big chances, and with the spirit of a people who recklessly trust that it will come out all right in the end."[16]

Most of the enlisted men were unable to appreciate the grandeur of the movement or the "happy-go-lucky" enthusiasm. Some of them had remained cooped up below decks for the better part of two weeks, from the time they originally boarded at Tampa through the time spent chasing down the ghost squadron to their ultimate debarkation in Cuba. The converted troopships were overcrowded, dirty, and had poor ventilation. Carpenters had hastily constructed tiers of bunks out of rough, un-planed lumber, and they were so close together that any time a man wanted to turn over in his sleep he risked getting splinters from the bunk above his. They were stacked so close together that there was barely enough room for one man to pass down the aisles between them. A soldier on the overcrowded *Yucatan*, the ship carrying the Rough Riders, hung a sign over the side that read: "Standing Room only." It was not long before another wag added the words: "And Damn Little of That."[17]

Colonel Roosevelt, who of course as an officer had much better quarters than his men, nevertheless compared the lower hold of the *Yucatan* to the Black Hole of Calcutta. The civilian captain of the *Knickerbocker* was reported to have admitted the unseaworthiness of his vessel to a Massachusetts chaplain. "This boat," he disclosed, "is about as fit to carry troops as hell is to store gunpowder."[18]

En route to Cuba, Maxfield worried about the effect of heat and humidity on the fragile varnished silk of his balloon's envelope. Twice he ordered his men to unpack it and spread it out on the deck to check for damage. His fears were realized when they found several places where the varnish had begun to liquefy and the balloon was sticking to itself where it had been folded. These problems could be, and were, rather easily attended to, but the silk itself showed signs of rot in some areas.[19]

Major problems associated with the voyage were the quality of the drinking water and food, and the availability of toilet facilities. Several soldiers found the water so odoriferous as to be almost impossible to drink. A man on one ship reported that every water tank "had an odor as though there were dead rats" in it, while a soldier on another ship could only drink the water if he made coffee with it, "and even then it was almost unbearable." A New Yorker referred to the water on his ship as "barreled abomination" that "tasted like bilgewater."[20]

The soldiers received "travel rations" for their sea voyage. These consisted of canned meat and tomatoes, coffee, and bread. This unimaginative menu became even less palatable in light of the poor quality of the canned goods. On many of the ships, the crewmen did not let patriotism stand in the way of capitalism, and sold extra food to the hungry soldiers at prices that were even more exorbitant than the Tampa sutlers had charged. One ship's baker was said to have made $200 on the first day at sea in this manner.[21]

Even worse were the sanitation facilities. Typically these consisted of a couple of troughs three to six feet in length. Able to handle perhaps half a dozen men at a time, they were completely inadequate for the ships carrying—in many cases—more than a thousand soldiers. Men stood in long lines to use them, and sometimes they were unable to wait long enough. That happened often enough to cause very real health problems for others on the ship. "The deck was running with liquid filth," one man stated, "and this filtered through to the deck below, to drip on the poor devils who were compelled to eat and sleep there." When the ships finally arrived off Santiago on June 20, the men were more than anxious to get ashore.[22]

Admiral Sampson's chief of staff visited General Shafter on board the *Segurança* upon the convoy's arrival. Then, later that day, the Fifth Corps commander, Sampson, and General Calixto García all met on shore near Aserraderos, about eighteen miles west of the entrance to Santiago harbor. General García recommended that his American counterpart land his troops at Daiquirí, east of the entrance, near where a force of a thousand Cubans was ready to assist the landing by engaging Spanish troops in the area. Sampson's ships would bombard the shore at various points to further deceive the Spanish as to the real landing site, and after the Fifth Corps was safely ashore at Daiquirí, Navy ships would transport some 3,000 of García's troops from Asserraderos to Daiquirí where they would be of use to Shafter.

By this time, Shafter had decided that he would lead his men inland to attack the city of Santiago itself. This went against the desires of the Navy, who hoped that the land troops would dislodge the defenders from their gun positions overlooking the channel from the sea to the harbor. And even though Shafter dismissed the Navy plan as the "height of folly," Sampson believed that the general had embraced it.

Daiquirí, the agreed upon landing site, did not lend itself to an amphibious landing. Its beach was not protected from the ocean, and its only docking facilities were a small wooden structure and an iron pier built to facilitate the activities of an American owned mining operation in the area. The wooden dock only extended about twenty yards from shore, and the iron pier, running parallel to the shore, was too high out of the water to be of much use. It was designed for ships to anchor alongside it while ore cars from the iron mines rolled onto it and dumped their cargoes into the ships' holds.

Steep hills rose closely around the small village, and they were dotted with blockhouses and trenches and further defended by barbed wire entanglements. Nevertheless, the Spanish commander in eastern Cuba, Lieutenant General Arsenio Linares Pomba, was unable to ascertain ahead of time just where the Americans intended to come ashore. He had just under 10,000 men—about a third of whom were Cuban loyalists of doubtful value—to cover every conceivable location along thirty miles of coastline. He had deployed about 300 of his command at Daiquirí, along with some field artillery, but they did little to oppose the landing and by the time the first Americans waded ashore on the morning of June 22 the Spaniards were long gone.[23]

Of course the men on the warships could not know of this lack of Spanish resolve, and they prepared to lay down a covering fire to protect the landing. Steam launches towing strings of boats pulled alongside the transports and twenty to thirty soldiers scrambled over the sides and into each of these makeshift landing craft. By about 9:40 on the morning of June 22, the first wave was ready to head into shore, so the warships began their bombardment. Richard Harding Davis, on board the *Seguranca*, thought the scene strangely reminiscent of a boat race. All that was needed was for the starter to fire the signal gun. Many of the men in these boats, however, had a much less romantic view of their situation. The high level of anxiety normally incident to impending danger combined with the seasickness, brought about by the ceaselessly bobbing up and down of the small boats, to make them, at least temporarily, miserable.[24]

While the four ships shelled the shoreline at Daiquirí, the three others provided covering fire for a non-existent landing at Ensenada de los Altares, near Siboney, and two more did the same at Aquadores. A feint at Cabañas was much more detailed. There, while the Navy blasted the jungle, ten of the Army's troop transports, carrying Brigadier General Jacob F. Kent's infantry division, came in toward shore and lowered their small boats in an effort to deceive any Spanish coast-watchers into thinking that the invasion was going to occur right there while 500 Cubans actively demonstrated ashore.[25]

Soldiers, news correspondents, and foreign military attachés all lined the rails of the ships to watch the Navy go to work. Most had never before been so close to such a massive display of firepower. Their excitement and jubilation increased every time one of the shells appeared to hit home. The naval bombardment at Daiquirí turned out to be superfluous. The Spaniards were gone. The lack of enemy resistance was a godsend. If only a few hundred Spaniards had stayed behind they could have done considerable damage to the Fifth Corps even if they had used only their rifles. An Army officer, after having landed and gotten a look at the potential for defense, was amazed. He was certain that in the face of a stout Spanish resistance, "Shafter's army of 15,000 men would still be out on the water, except those who were floating in it. We couldn't have landed troops as fast as the Spaniards could have shot them."[26]

That this was a missed Spanish opportunity was lost on some of the Americans, but not all of them. A news correspondent talked with an Army major who had expressed his relief at not having to storm ashore under fire. They had both witnessed the naval bombardment, and to the untrained civilian the powerful guns of the fleet seemed quite enough to have destroyed any and all entrenched defenders ashore. He seemed to be having trouble understanding the depth of the major's feelings. The officer finally hit upon an example to show the reporter how difficult it is to hit an enemy that is well entrenched. First he asked the man if he was a good shot with a revolver. When the newsman responded in the affirmative, the officer said: "Then get a half-inch rope. Lay it on the ground, in a [groove] a half inch deep, so that the uppermost strands of the rope are just level with the ground. Next step off a hundred yards and try to hit that rope. Keep count of how many times you hit in a week's practice. That will give you some idea of how difficult it would be for the Navy to shell brave men out of those trenches."[27]

Getting the troops off the ships at Daiquirí was fraught with almost as much confusion as had been the process of getting them onto the ships back in Tampa. The ships carrying the troops brought along no landing craft. Indeed, such things did not even exist within the Army's inventory. It was up to the Navy to get the men ashore, and its efforts, although ultimately successful, were not routine. It had been more than a half century since American forces had staged an amphibious assault of any consequence onto a foreign shore. Back then, the Navy had used purpose-built landing boats. Off the coast of Cuba, however, such vessels were lacking. Instead, the ships of the blockading squadron contributed whatever small boats they could. These included a dozen steam launches, capable of carrying fifteen soldiers each; two sailing launches that could each move seventy men at a time; nine cutters with capacities of twenty-five passengers each; thirteen life boats that each held forty-five men; and thirteen other miscellaneous boats. It would require several round trips to land the entire Army.[28]

In spite of the Navy's artillery preparation, and even with the complete absence of return fire, some of the civilian ship captains of the chartered transports refused to risk their vessels too close to shore. Indeed some obstinately refused to come within four or five miles of the coast, and the *Knickerbocker* remained completely out of sight of the landing beaches until late in the afternoon. Nevertheless, with the able help of the Navy's steam launches and ships' boats, the landing got underway.[29]

General Shafter had specified that he wanted Brigadier General Henry W. Lawton's infantry division and the Gatling Gun battery to be the first troops to land. Brigadier General John C. Bates's independent brigade would follow as a ready reserve in case Lawton's men ran into trouble. The dismounted cavalry came next, followed, in order, by General Kent's infantry division, the lone mounted squadron of the Second U.S. Cavalry Regiment, and finally the field artillery. Of course, if the infantry ran into serious resistance on the beach, the artillery would go ashore to assist them.[30]

Vigilant defenders could have made things extremely difficult for the invaders as they worked their way through the heavy surf, but that did not happen. The only casualties during the operation occurred when two troopers of the Tenth Cavalry Regiment slipped while trying to swing onto the pier from their landing boat. Captain William "Bucky" O'Neill, of the Rough Riders, was nearby and saw the heavily laden soldiers plunge into the water. He immediately jumped in to try to save them, but it was no use. They both drowned. That these were the only fatalities was due more to good fortune than to anything else. One man described the scene, with boats jockeying for position, by noting that "to say confusion reigned would hardly express it."[31]

Shafter wanted every soldier going ashore to be self-sufficient for at least the first few days after landing. For example, he did not want to have these men, once they reached dry land, to suffer unnecessarily from the frequent tropical storms in case their tents did not get unloaded for the first day or so. Each man, therefore, carried his blanket, his rain poncho, and his shelter half rolled together into a horseshoe-shaped bundle that he carried slung over his shoulder. The commanding general also did not want his men to go hungry if the landing of food supplies was interrupted or did not go smoothly. Therefore each man also carried enough food to last him—at least theoretically—for three days. He also landed with a full canteen, which he could replenish from the abundant rivers and streams in the area. All of this, along with his weapon and a hundred rounds of ammunition, made up a considerable burden.[32]

Because of the uncertainty of what armed resistance—if any—awaited the American invasion Shafter allowed no news reporters to accompany the first landing wave. He did not want to have to worry about their safety at such a time. Richard Harding Davis, perhaps the dean of the press corps in Cuba, seemed almost personally affronted when he learned that this ban on reporters extended even to him. He confronted Shafter aboard the *Segurança* and somewhat haughtily informed him that he was no mere reporter but a "descriptive writer." "I do not care a damn what you are," the general blustered back. "I'll treat all of you alike." On the nearby *Yucatan*, carrying the Rough Riders, reporter Burr McIntosh was not so easily dissuaded. He planned to mingle with the debarking soldiers and get ashore with them. As the debarkation began, however, he saw that the soldiers were under too much scrutiny for this plan to have a chance to succeed. He quickly made up a bundle of spare clothing, cameras, and film and persuaded one of the soldiers to take it ashore for him. McIntosh then went to a cabin on the seaward side of the ship and let himself out through a window and into the water. He swam around the ship and headed for the beach. He was a strong swimmer, but the pull of the tide soon had him struggling. Finally he grabbed onto one of the boats carrying soldiers ashore and let it pull him along. An officer approached the dripping wet correspondent on the shore and, mindful of Shafter's edict, asked him how he got ashore. "Please, sir," McIntosh said respectfully, "I fell off the side of the boat. They tried to rescue me, but there were no loose ropes, so I had to swim in."[33]

By 6 P.M. Lawton's division, most of Bates's brigade, and about half of the dismounted cavalry were ashore, but getting these 6,000 men onto dry land was only part of the overall operation. Even though most of the cavalry units left their mounts in Florida, there were still a number of animals aboard. Two companies of the Second U.S. Cavalry brought their horses and most of the staff and field officers were mounted. In addition, a number of horses and mules were necessary to pull wagons and artillery pieces, and these now had to be landed. This presented more of a problem than had landing the men. First, each animal was fitted with a long halter rope and a blindfold. A soldier then led it to a large cargo door in the side of the ship, down near the water level. He passed the loose end of the lead rope to a waiting crewman in the rear of a small boat, and prodded the animal down a cleated gangplank that sloped into the water. When the horse or mule reached the water its natural instinct was to swim, and then the men in the rowboat headed for shore. When the boat and the trailing animal reached a certain point, about halfway to the beach, the sailor slipped off the long rope, removed the blindfold, and urged the horse or mule to continue in toward the beach, while he turned his boat back toward the ship to repeat the process. This method was not always successful. Near sunset a cavalry bugler on the beach noticed a number of horses being carried by the current toward some rocks. He quickly began sounding the call for a "right wheel." Some of the animals, the well-trained cavalry horses, responded with redoubled efforts and turned toward the shore and safety. Unfortunately, the draft animals swept on toward the rocks and their deaths. One cavalry officer later wrote to his wife that "sometimes they get nearly to shore, then turn around and swim to sea. Of course a great many of them are drowned, and the beach is covered with dead horses and mules." Among the equine casualties were at least fifty mules as well as Colonel Roosevelt's "Rain-in-the-Face."[34]

The men were happy to leave the close confines of shipboard life behind them and stretch their muscles on dry land once again. Cuba was so different! The lush tropical vegetation and the steep, hilly terrain were causes for much comment. But the people of the island were even more remarkable. The soldiers had read in the sensationalist American press of the heroic deeds of the underdog Cubans, fighting for freedom from cruel Spanish oppression, but their first sight of their "allies" up close was quite eye-opening. Upon encountering them, one American recorded: "There were probably two hundred of them dressed, in general, in a kind of ecru-colored linen, the raggedest uniforms conceivable. Of the straw hats they wore ... there is only one phrase that will do them justice, and that phrase is uniform nondescriptness. The shoes of the few who wore such articles were shapeless articles, made, seemingly, from sailcloth." Their weapons were also a hodge-podge, including obsolete U.S. Springfield rifles (also being carried by most of the American volunteer troops), new German-produced Mausers that they had captured from the Spanish, and many commercially produced American Winchesters, Marlins, and Remingtons.[35]

With most of the American troops ashore the movement inland toward Santiago was imminent. At Daiquirí, Major General Joseph Wheeler, the former Confederate cavalry commander, and now in command of the cavalry division in the Fifth Corps, determined to set things in motion right away. He had received information from some Cuban troops that a force of some 1,500 Spaniards was entrenching near a little crossroads, known as Las Guasimas, about three miles northwest of Siboney. It was not General Shafter's intention to tangle with any Spanish forces until he had been able to land all of his troops, as well as all supplies necessary to carry out active campaigning. In fact, he made it very clear from his headquarters offshore when he ordered General Lawton to seize and hold the village of Siboney, some seven miles up the road from Daquirí toward Santiago. "I wish you to make a strong position there," wrote the commanding general, "because we may have to hold it a week. I won't move until I can make provision to move rations and ammunition, so make yourself solid."[36]

Wheeler, however, took advantage of a slight ambiguity in Shafter's order and jumped the gun. Shafter had addressed his seize-and-hold order to General Lawton "or the senior officer at the front." It was this last phrase that gave "Fighting Joe" the chance he sought to cover his beloved cavalry with the glory of opening hostilities in Cuba before the more numerous infantry could get into position. He ordered all his available cavalry to move up the path toward Siboney on the afternoon of June 23. It was hot, and the men were nearly exhausted from helping to unload supplies onto the beach at Daiquirí, but they plodded forward. It was dark when the tired troopers of the First and Tenth U.S. Cavalry and the First U.S. Volunteer Cavalry (the Rough Riders) reached their destination. They passed Lawton's already entrenched infantrymen and went into bivouac at what Colonel Roosevelt called the extreme front of the American lines. This meant, then, that Wheeler, who outranked Lawton by one star, was the "senior officer at the front," and he determined to undertake a reconnaissance in force at first light on the 24th.

The footsore cavalrymen sank to the ground grateful for the chance to do so. During the afternoon's march they had suffered from the heat and the burdens they carried. They were not in the habit of carrying such loads. They were cavalrymen, after all, and were accustomed to having their horses transport them and their accoutrements. As the sun continued its merciless beating and the men seemed no nearer their destination than ever, they began, in time honored tradition, to discard things they now felt they could do without. It was June, after all, so they could certainly get by without their heavy wool blankets. Next to go might have been the shelter half, or the poncho. Some men even discarded food along the trail because it was just that much added weight. By the time they reached Siboney, most of them were carrying their weapons, ammunition, and water, and very little of anything else.

If they hoped for a quiet night's slumber, however, they were to be disappointed. Some, of course, were probably too keyed up with excitement at what the morrow would bring to sleep. But even those who wanted to sleep found it very difficult. To speed up the movement ashore of men and equipment, Shafter had named Siboney as a secondary landing site, and troops and supplies continued to come across the beach throughout the night. And to make their landings easier, the ships offshore lit up the beach with their massive searchlights. Reporter Davis, now accompanying the Rough Riders, marveled at all that was going on around him that night. "It was," he wrote, "one of the most weird and remarkable scenes of the war, probably any war. An Army was being landed on an enemy's coast at the dead of night, but with somewhat more of cheers and shrieks and laughter than rise from bathers in the surf at Coney Island on a hot Sunday." It had also rained during the night, making things particularly uncomfortable for those prodigals who had tossed their ponchos and shelter halves into the jungle on the way from Daiquirí.[37]

Dawn finally arrived, and when it did it found the American assault force, four troops each from the First and Tenth U.S. and all eight troops of Rough Riders, on the move. General Wheeler accompanied the regulars, led by their brigade commander Brigadier General Samuel B. M. Young, on the main road to Santiago. This road ran northwest from Siboney along the side of a small valley before it climbed up some three hundred feet to a gap in the surrounding hills. From there it turned more to the west. Colonel Wood led his Rough Riders along a much less traveled trail farther to the left of, and roughly parallel to, this road. Both routes merged just beyond the Spanish position at Las Guasimas, about three or four miles from Siboney. One regular cavalry officer somewhat disdainfully described the road as "an ordinary Cuban highway, eroded and narrow," while characterizing the trail that the Rough Riders followed as "a mere bridle path." There was little communication between the two wings of the American advance due to extremely thick vegetation in the valley that separated them, but since their paths converged near the enemy position perhaps constant contact was not considered essential.[38]

Colonel Wood employed the services of a couple of Cuban scouts and sent them on ahead. When they had covered about a hundred yards a five-man team of Rough Riders moved forward carefully scouting for signs of the enemy's presence. Captain Allyn Capron, Jr., followed with the bulk of L Troop as a ready reaction force. And, finally, Wood and Roosevelt led the remainder of the regiment. Davis, nattily attired in a blue jacket and wearing a white puggaree around his felt hat, tagged along, as did reporter Edward Marshall, who wore a white, tropical weight jacket in keeping with the climate. A few other reporters, including Stephen Crane of *Red Badge of Courage* fame, hurried along at the rear of the column. After all, this regiment of volunteer soldiers, many of whom, like their lieutenant colonel, came from society's upper crust, made particularly good copy for the reading public back home.

The Rough Riders assumed a holiday mood as they moved along the jungle trail. They chattered among themselves amiably, or at least as amiably as the oppressive heat and upward sloping path would allow, and some even began singing one of the most popular songs of the day, "There'll Be a Hot Time in the Old Town Tonight." They stopped occasionally to rest, and when they did the conversations among the men covered a wide range of topics. Some of the New Mexicans discussed a mutual acquaintance's decision to give up the rough, outdoor life of a cowboy to open up a saloon. Others talked about the relative merits of different breeds of dogs while some complained of the pain inflicted upon their feet by their government-issued shoes. One trooper whiled away his rest times by shooting spitballs at his comrades. Another put into words what most of his fellows undoubtedly felt when he exclaimed, "[Damn]! Wouldn't a glass of cold beer taste good?"[39]

Their gaiety abated somewhat when the head of the column came upon a dead body. It was not an American. They assumed it was a Spaniard, although it could just as well have been a Cuban. Whatever the corpse's nationality had been it lay on its back with its lifeless eyes open but seeing nothing. Whoever he had been he had needed a shave when he died, and he could have used a new pair of shoes. But what drew most attention from the Rough Riders as they strode past was the bullet hole in his head and what appeared to be machete slashes across his neck. This scene had a sobering effect on the marchers. Their light, joking banter and singing of songs ceased.[40]

The dismounted regulars were a little more restrained in their conversations as they trudged through the jungle heat and early morning humidity. They also engaged in light conversation, but they were not as loud and raucous as the volunteers to their left. Many of these men had seen Indian combat in the West and knew only too well how serious an undertaking warfare could be. A few minutes after eight they came within sight, and range, of the enemy earthworks and all idle chatter stopped.

General Young sent one officer and two enlisted men forward to scout out the enemy situation, and while he awaited their return he ordered his Hotchkiss rapid-fire guns into position about nine hundred yards from the enemy. The Spaniards were using a tumble down ranch house and distillery for protection, and their position seemed quite strong so Young waited to allow time for the Rough Riders to arrive within range of the enemy so both wings of the American force could attack simultaneously. Finally, General Wheeler gave the order for the Hotchkiss guns to open the battle. The Spaniards responded immediately with a lethal volley. All four troops of the First U.S. then answered in kind from their forward positions ahead of the Hotchkiss guns. Soon the regulars began taking fire from their right front. They could not allow the enemy to move around behind them so General Young sent two troops from the Tenth U.S. to the extreme right to prevent that, while another troop of the Tenth moved off to the left front. The Spaniards, firing methodically, sent volley after volley crashing through the heavy brush, although the thick growth and the fact that both sides were using smokeless powder cartridges made it difficult for either side to locate precise targets. Sergeant Presly Holliday, of the Tenth Cavalry, later recalled that "the bullets were passing over us in a storm and it would have been instant death for a man to stand up."[41]

The progress of the Rough Riders on the parallel trail had not been appreciably slower than that of their comrades. After about an hour and a half on the trail Colonel Wood halted his men while he rode forward to converse with Captain Capron, who was returning with information that he had come upon a Spanish outpost. The main body of the enemy could not be far ahead. Wood sent Major Alexander Brodie off to the left with all four troops of his squadron so the Spanish would not overlap his force in that direction. He then ordered Roosevelt to take the three remaining troops of his squadron through the barbed wire fence paralleling the trail and into the jungle to the right to link up across the valley with the regulars. The undergrowth was so thick that it was difficult for Colonel Roosevelt even to stay in sight of his own men, much less to locate and connect with the regulars. And the individual troopers had to maintain visual contact with the men on either side of them or risk becoming hopelessly lost.

As the Rough Riders began to move slowly ahead in skirmish formation, Thomas Isbell, one of the forward scouts, spotted a Spanish soldier through the foliage and shot him. The enemy troops responded instantaneously. The fusillade of shots that poured out of their position was deadly. Isbell soon went down with a bullet through the neck, the first of seven wounds he would suffer over the next thirty minutes. Another Spanish bullet ripped into Hamilton Fish's left side and out his right and into Ed Culver's chest. Fish was the popular sergeant of Troop I who had convinced Roosevelt not to leave him behind in Tampa.[42]

Perhaps of equal concern as the loss of these men, this initial Spanish volley spooked the mules carrying the regiment's Colt machine guns, and they stampeded back down the trail toward Siboney. On the other side of the valley the mules pulling the regulars' Hotchkiss guns had been trained so well to the sound of gunfire that one was seen to be nonchalantly rubbing his neck against the trunk of a small tree while bullets filled the air. The Rough Riders, however, would have to drive their foe with only their carbines.[43]

The Rough Riders immediately sought shelter wherever they could find it. Still the casualties mounted. Captain Capron, unable to find a tree to provide shelter, fell flat to the ground to escape the storm of Mauser bullets overhead. Unfortunately for the captain, one of these bullets came in low. It entered Capron's left shoulder and angled downward into his abdomen producing a fatal wound. It was his twenty-seventh birthday.[44]

The Americans, as the attacking force, started into the battle at a decided disadvantage. The Spaniards had had time to prepare fairly strong earthworks that gave protection from almost anything except artillery fire or very carefully aimed, or lucky, shots. Occupying prepared positions also imparted a certain psychological edge to the defenders. The Americans would have to root them out, and the tangle of jungle growth and half overgrown wire fences immediately in front of their trenches meant that dislodging them would require quite an effort.

It was virtually impossible for the attacking volunteers to locate the enemy. The Spaniards were well concealed in and around the distillery and the Americans were unable to pinpoint them until they could get through the jungle and out into the open. Colonel Roosevelt, nevertheless, had his men firing in the general direction of the enemy — a reconnaissance by fire — even though he doubted its value. It allowed his men to at least enjoy the psychological effect of striking back at the invisible enemy. Roosevelt continued to sweep the jungle with his binoculars, but it was Richard Harding Davis who was the first to spot some Spanish soldiers in an advanced position off to the right front. "There they are, Colonel," he said, "look over there; I can see their hats." Roosevelt looked in the direction Davis indicated, and when he saw them he ordered several of his best marksmen to take them under fire. The first few shots were short, but the men quickly corrected the range and soon sent the Spaniards scurrying for cover.[45]

Soon another body of men appeared in the same general location, also moving toward the main Spanish lines. Roosevelt did not want his troops to open fire on them until he could positively identify them. He was able to tell that they were not the regulars, and that led him to the only likely conclusion: that these must be the promised Cuban reinforcements finally joining the fight. Only after the battle was over did he discover that these men had also been Spanish soldiers falling back on their stronger positions.[46]

As the volunteers continued to engage the enemy they noticed still more troops off to their right rear. These were the men of the Tenth Cavalry, but in the excitement of battle they mistook Roosevelt's men for the enemy and fired into them. Sergeant Joseph Jenkins Lee alertly grabbed up a red and white regimental guidon, scaled a nearby tree, and waved the flag for all he was worth. When the troopers of the Tenth saw the banner they immediately ceased their fire.[47]

As the Mauser bullets cracked through the jungle one occasionally found a target in the form of an American soldier, and he crumbled to the ground. Newspaper correspondent Edward Marshall was somewhat taken aback by how very different from the dramatic death scenes enacted in stage plays was the real thing. These Rough Riders, he noted, "did not throw hands up and fall dramatically backward with strident cries and stiffened legs." No, "they fell like clods. Two things surprised me about these episodes," he continued. "One was the strange noise which soldiers in their trappings make as they go down. It is always the same. It is a combination of the metallic jingle of canteens and guns, and the singular, thick thud of a falling human body." He described the sound as a bullet made impact in a human body as "not unlike the noise made by a stick when it strikes a carpet which is being beaten." This was what war was about, not the parades, the fancy uniforms, or the flashy sabers, but death in a place far from home. Seeing companions fall had a sobering effect on the men, and they resolutely remained at their tasks.[48]

Marshall, too, soon became a casualty. He had been popping away at the Spaniards with his pistol when a bullet ripped into him. He fell, just as he had seen the others, in a heap. His wounding, ironically, sparked the nearest thing to a panic within the American troops that day. First Lieutenant Thomas W. Hall, the regimental adjutant, saw, from a distance, Marshall slump into the grass. Hall mistook the correspondent's light colored jacket for Colonel Wood's khaki uniform coat. With his commander thus supposedly *hors de combat* he panicked and raced down the trail back toward Siboney telling all who would listen that Colonel Wood was dead, and the Rough Riders had been wiped out.[49]

The American soldiers meanwhile, both volunteers and regulars, moved forward in individual rushes. Each man picked a bush or tree somewhere to the front of his current position and made a run for it. There he hunkered down, fired a few shots toward the enemy, and then sprang up and moved forward again. As Colonel Roosevelt discovered, the value of these natural barriers was more in obscuring the enemy's view of a target than in providing any real protection. He had taken up a temporary position behind a palm tree and cautiously peered around it toward the Spaniards when a bullet ripped through the trunk, sending dust and debris into his left eye and ear.[50]

For over an hour the battle waxed hot as the cavalrymen slowly worked their way forward and angled for clear shots at the Spaniards. The sun continued its rise in the eastern sky, and its rays added to the physical discomfort of men on both sides. General Wheeler began to be concerned as his casualties mounted with no significant compensating gain in real estate. With many of his men facing heat exhaustion he sent back to Siboney for reinforcements. General Lawton responded by immediately dispatching Brigadier General Adna Chaffee's brigade up the trail behind Wheeler and Colonel Evan Miles' brigade by way of another trail a little to the north.[51]

By about 9 A.M., the Americans on both sides of the little valley had worked themselves close enough to the enemy works to begin a direct assault. This was also about the time that the Spanish commander decided that his force had served its purpose of slowing the American advance and began a prearranged withdrawal toward Santiago. As the Americans began their final rush, the Spaniards in and around the distillery buildings fired a final volley or two and then retreated. General Wheeler, temporarily lost in the fog of war, forgot that he was no longer the gray-clad cavalryman of Civil War days and shouted enthusiastically, "We've got the Yankees on the run." After a moment of sheepish silence, those around him laughed, and he joined in.[52]

When the fighting was over, and the adrenaline had ceased to flow at such a fantastic rate, the men slumped down exhausted. They were more than willing to see the enemy go. They were too worn out to mount any kind of pursuit, only able to occupy the recently abandoned works and congratulate one another on their "victory." The Rough Riders had performed as well as could be expected of raw, unprofessional soldiers, but many among the regulars did not share this conviction. Lieutenant John Pershing, of the Tenth Cavalry, described how enfilading fire from his regiment relieved the Rough Riders from an intense Spanish fire, and another member of Pershing's regiment declared: "I don't think it an exaggeration to say that [but] for the timely aid of the Tenth Cavalry, the Rough Riders would have been exterminated."[53]

Regardless of who saved whom, the men were glad to have put the day's fighting behind them as they compared close calls and near misses that they had experienced or witnessed. In addition to Colonel Roosevelt's experience alongside the palm tree, one man who entered the fight with his pipe clenched firmly between his teeth had its bowl shot away, and several men emerged unscathed from the fight but with numerous bullet holes in their clothing. They asked after their friends trying to learn who had been killed, who wounded. Some of the Rough Riders began to question one of their number about the weird incantations he had intoned throughout the fight. Those near him had heard him repeatedly mutter at first and then fairly shout out what seemed like the sound "Slimpnthx," as he fired his carbine at the enemy. He seemed puzzled by their questions. "Never said such a thing in my life," he insisted. But as his comrades kept insisting on the veracity of their accounts the man in question slowly began to smile as he realized what had happened. "I'd heard," he said, "that it was a good thing to keep one's mind off himself in time of danger just to say over and over again some formula. I was afraid maybe I'd be rattled, so when the bullets began to sing I tried to remember some rhyme or something, and the only thing that came into my head was, 'six slim slick saplings.' ... I guess I got it pretty well mixed up, but by the time I got fairly into the fight I must have forgotten to stop saying it. I know my tongue feels kind of tangled yet."[54]

One of the Spanish soldiers captured that day expressed his amazement at the American battle tactics. Instead of retreating every time the defenders fired into them, as the Spaniards expected, the Americans kept coming forward. "That is not the way to fight," he said of the Rough Riders, "to come closer at every volley." A Spanish officer was in awe of the regular black American cavalrymen. "What terrified our men," he remembered, "was the huge American Negroes. We saw their big black faces through the underbrush and they looked like devils. They came forward under our fire as if they didn't care the least about it."[55]

American reinforcements began arriving from the rear shortly after the fighting stopped. Many of them expressed bitter disappointment that they were too late to have participated. Nevertheless, they moved through the recently captured position and stationed themselves a little closer to Santiago.

The victory did not come without a price. In the words of Confederate General Nathan Bedford Forrest, "War means fightin', and fightin' means killin'." For sixteen of the assaulting American cavalrymen (and ten Spaniards) the war — and their lives — was over. Fifty-two Americans and about half that many Spaniards were wounded. And even though some Cuban troops were camped within earshot of the battle, they were nowhere to be found until after the shooting stopped — an ominous sign.[56]

As had been the case with the Marines killed at Guantánamo a couple of weeks earlier, the dead from this battle were buried virtually where they fell. Some of the volunteer cavalrymen reverently carried Captain Capron's body back down the trail for interment at Siboney, but the other fallen Americans were buried in common graves the next day. In the case of the Rough Riders, when the common burial trench was completed a thick cushion of palm leaves and grass was put into the bottom of it before Chaplain Henry A. Brown read the Episcopal burial service and those attending sang "Rock of Ages." The blanket-wrapped bodies were then lowered into the grave one by one and covered with another layer of palm leaves before being covered with dirt.[57]

After burying their dead and regaining their strength, the cavalrymen moved a few miles farther up the road toward Santiago the day after the battle, and soon the rest of the Army went into camp nearby.

Chapter 6

Heavy Fighting in Cuba

General Shafter had assured an anxious Admiral Sampson that he would attack Santiago "as soon as the command is all ashore, with sufficient rations and ammunition." By June 26, although he remained aboard the *Seguranca*, he had virtually all of his Fifth Corps ashore, it had been augmented by the arrival of some 3,000 Cuban troops, and he was getting ready to supervise the landing of even more American troops, reinforcements who had arrived from Fortress Monroe, Virginia. Shafter then had to devise the strategy with which to make good on his promise.[1]

The soldiers themselves were dealing with the almost daily monsoon-like rains, the heat, the mosquitoes, and poor food. In spite of this, or perhaps because of it, they were anxious to strike a blow against the Spaniards. One disgruntled sergeant, perhaps after overhearing some of the newspaper correspondents discussing strategy, made it clear how he felt. "Well, now," he said, "so this is what they call strategy, and you find it in the books. Well, damn Strategy! I've never read about it, but I am getting blooming tired of the demonstration of it. There's Santiago, and the dagoes, and here we are, and the shortest distance between two points is a straight line; which is something everybody knows, and don't have to study strategy to find out. I am in favor of going up there and beating the faces off them dagoes, and then let the war correspondents make up the strategy, as they seem to be the only ones who are worrying about it."[2]

While Shafter waited for a reliable amount of supplies to be landed, General Linares was also making plans. He no longer had to wonder, of course, where the Americans would come ashore, but he still could not be sure just where they would attempt to test his defenses. Keeping a reserve force of almost 2,000 men within the city, he distributed the remaining 8,000 or so in a wide arc along hilly terrain east of the city known as San Juan Ridge. He also assigned three infantry companies from the San Luis Brigade and about fifty Cuban guerrillas to defend the tiny village of El Caney, five or six miles to the northeast. The rugged jungle terrain and the scarcity of roads in this general area would hold the invaders to some rather well defined avenues of approach.[3]

By June 28, General Shafter learned that an 8,000-man Spanish relief expedition had set out from Manzanillo and could reach Santiago within four or five days. The report overstated the size of this contingent by more than a factor of two, but Shafter decided that he could not wait much longer. He must take the city before this force could strengthen it.[4]

The almost daily rains had turned the roads and trails into quagmires. The generally debilitating effects of the tropical heat and various illnesses caused several leaders to be less than effective. General Wheeler, commanding the cavalry, was ill and confined to his tent, replaced by Brigadier General Samuel S. Sumner. General Young was also sick and had to turn over control of his cavalry brigade to Colonel Wood. This in turn elevated Lieutenant Colonel Roosevelt to regimental command of his beloved Rough Riders. Even General Shafter found the heat and humidity to be almost too much for his 300-pound body.

Shafter called all of his division commanders to his tent early on the afternoon of June 30 to inform them of his battle plans for the morrow. He would send the Cuban troops around to the northwest of the city to intercept the Manzanillo reinforcements. He assigned Brigadier General Henry M. Duffield with the recently arrived Thirty-third Michigan volunteers to make a demonstration against the Spanish defenses at the mouth of the harbor. The Navy would cooperate by providing supporting fire. Shafter did not know if he could count on the untried volunteer troops in the main effort, but their move against this enemy position would at least force General Linares to keep his forces there instead of sending them against the left flank of the primary American assault. Nor could he ignore the tiny garrison at El Caney. He did not feel justified bypassing this handful of troops on his way toward the San Juan Heights lest they fall upon the right flank of his Army. And even if they did not attack his flank, they could, if left unhindered, move south onto his supply line from Siboney and Daiquirí. With the supply situation already quite tenuous, he could not afford a disruption. Shafter decided to detach one brigade from Brigadier General Henry Lawton's division to keep an eye on the village while the rest of the corps made the assault on the heights in front of Santiago. Lawton and Brigadier General Adna Chaffee, one of his brigade commanders, both spoke up to suggest that rather than just sending a brigade to monitor every movement in and around the village, Shafter should order a full scale attack. They knew that there were only about 500 defenders, and informants had entered American lines the day before with the observation that these troops would probably evacuate the town rather than try to defend it against a determined effort by the Americans. Shafter therefore ordered an attack on El Caney to begin as soon as it was light enough to see on July 1.[5]

Lawton declared that he could neutralize the village in only two hours' time. Then, the victorious American troops would swing around to the west to become the right wing of the main assault against the heights of San Juan. The plan certainly looked workable on paper. By sunset on July 1, Shafter planned to have his troops safely situated along the crest of San Juan Ridge. Having thus captured the outermost line of Spanish defenses he would be that much closer to forcing the surrender of the rest of the garrison at Santiago. Several things intervened to keep his plan from being accomplished smoothly and rapidly.

Meanwhile Major Maxfield and his balloon company had reached Siboney, and he soon reported to Shafter's headquarters near El Pozo to learn just what the commanding general had in mind for his company. It had begun to rain so the signalmen were unable to unpack the balloon (now christened *Santiago*) to check for any more heat-induced damage. When the rain finally let up, on the morning of June 30, the fragile envelope again exhibited several places where the melting varnish had stuck the balloon to itself as well as some more serious tears in the fabric. Major Maxfield declared the damage to be such that he would not have risked an ascent in peacetime. This was war, however, and he had little choice. The damage was hastily repaired, and the men began filling the balloon with gas.

Late in the afternoon, when the bag was full, Major Maxfield and Sergeant Ivy Baldwin climbed into the observation basket and gave the signal for the men on the four guy lines to begin paying out the rope. Slowly the balloon rose over the surrounding treetops causing soldiers of both armies to gaze upward in open-mouthed wonder. Having satisfied themselves of the balloon's performance the two signalmen came down while another signal officer took

Cuban general Demetrio Castillo Duany up to survey the area between themselves and the Spanish positions. Maxfield went up a third time with Shafter's chief engineer officer, Lieutenant Colonel George M. Derby. At the end of the third ascent the sun had settled far enough into the west to make any further aerial observations pointless, but the ascents provided valuable general information about the landscape between the two armies and verified once and for all that Admiral Cervera's squadron was indeed in the harbor of Santiago. But the balloon had still been almost a mile and a half from San Juan Ridge, too far away for Colonel Derby to glean any precise information about Spanish strength there so he told Maxfield to be prepared to move closer in the morning and go up again. That night the men of the balloon company tied down their precious charge as securely as they could and hoped that the nighttime winds would not open any more holes in the frail fabric.

Meanwhile General Chaffee personally undertook to reconnoiter the ground over which the Americans would have to advance toward El Caney the next morning. After riding along some of the various bridle paths as close to the town as he thought prudent, Chaffee dismounted and proceeded on foot. British military attaché Captain Arthur Lee accompanied him on a couple of these scouting expeditions and later related that they even got close enough to overhear the meal time conversations of Spanish soldiers in the works surrounding the town. They got so close, in fact, that Captain Lee feared they would be discovered and captured or killed. "I began to speculate," he mused, "on the probable efficacy of the British passport that was my sole defensive weapon." Their luck held, however, and Chaffee returned to American lines with valuable information about the layout of the town and its defenses.[6]

El Caney was a fairly typical Cuban village. Many of the houses had thatched roofs, but a few, those of the more prosperous residents, were sheltered from the elements by red tiles. Some of the houses on the periphery of the village — along with a stone church — were loopholed so Spanish riflemen could fire from within the protection of their walls. About 500 yards southeast of the town a steep hill rose to a height of about a hundred feet. On top sat a small, but formidable, stone fort called El Viso. Between this fort and the four or five wooden blockhouses on the northern and western edges of town the Spaniards had dug deep, narrow protective trenches and had installed barbed wire entanglements.[7]

As soon as General Lawton's men learned that they would attack El Caney they broke camp and began trudging toward their objective. They wanted to get as close as they could before nightfall, in preparation for the early morning attack the next day. A handful of Cuban scouts led the way along the narrow trails, and the American force looked like a long blue snake as it wended its way in fits and starts ever nearer its goal. Lawton ordered a halt as the sun began to sink behind the mountains, although it was some time later before the last of the American troops were able to quit the trail for the night. Orders circulated among the men that there were to be no cooking fires this night because of their proximity to the enemy. There was some grumbling as the men partook of a supper of cold, uncooked bacon and hardtack that they had to wash down with nothing stronger than water. Officers even forbade the lighting of pipes, lest the flare of the match or the glow of the tobacco give away the American position. There was some concern that if the garrison at El Caney learned that it was about to be attacked that it would evacuate the village before the Americans could spring their trap. Captain Lee accompanied Chaffee's brigade and later remarked: "In the light of future events this anxiety seems somewhat ludicrous, for the enemy had no idea whatever of retreating and was apparently quite as anxious for a fight as we were."[8]

July 1 dawned just like so many days in the tropics — hot and getting hotter. General Duffield's planned diversion at Aguadores got off to an inauspicious start. His troops boarded a train at Siboney that would take them all the way to their objective. Duffield, however, cautiously had his men detrain about a mile and a half from the Spanish position and proceed the rest of the way on foot. The same problems of weather and terrain that bedeviled all of the marching American troops in Cuba slowed the Michigan volunteers down also. By the time they neared the 700-foot railroad bridge over the Aguadores River they were almost three and a half hours behind schedule. They also discovered that the Spaniards had destroyed about forty feet of the bridge on the western side. So even though this American force outnumbered the one opposed to it by a ratio of about ten to one, there was no way for it to close with the enemy. Finally, without doing any measurable damage, Duffield led his men back to Siboney early in the afternoon.[9]

Still for these volunteers this had been their baptism of fire as Spanish artillery shelled their formation and inflicted some casualties. One of the wounded men wrote a vivid description of his introduction to the horrors of war for his hometown newspaper. The Spanish artillery shell that had hit him had also killed and wounded four of his comrades. He described how the projectile went through one man before it hit him "and you could have thrown your hat clear through the hole it made." It then struck him on the left elbow, and passed completely through another soldier before it even exploded. The shrapnel from the explosion led to the amputation of one man's arm and another's leg.[10]

General Lawton, meanwhile, had a very tight, and, as it proved, unrealistically optimistic time schedule to maintain. He was to begin the assault on El Caney at 7 A.M. and attain complete victory by 9. Then, with an hour to move down the road from El Caney toward Santiago, his men would join in on the attack on San Juan Heights at 10. Lawton placed Brigadier General William Ludlow's brigade, consisting of the Eighth and Twenty-second U.S. Infantry Regiments and the Second Massachusetts Volunteer Infantry on his left, southwest of the town. From there it would be able to cut off El Caney's defenders from retreating into Santiago as well as prevent any reinforcements from reaching the village from that direction. General Chaffee's brigade, the Seventh, Twelfth, and Seventeenth U.S. Infantry Regiments, made up the right of the line, east of town. Colonel Evan Miles held two of his regiments, the Fourth and the Twenty-fifth U.S. Infantry, in position directly south of town, adjacent to the El Caney–Santiago road, while the First U.S. supported Captain Allyn Capron, Sr.'s battery. Bates' brigade—the Third and the Twentieth U.S.—served as a ready reserve force, to be committed to battle where it was most needed.

Capron's four little field guns, opened the ball at 6:30 on July 1 from a position about 2,300 yards south of the village. A sergeant, standing atop a caisson with his binoculars aimed toward the town, shouted excitedly when he spied a group of enemy horsemen moving away from El Caney toward Santiago. Captain Capron, in shirtsleeves among the guns, finally located them in his glasses and gave the order to fire. All four guns were loaded and ready, and one of them sent a shrapnel shell hurtling toward the distant column. It seemed to take forever from the time the gun fired until observers witnessed a puff of white smoke above the Spaniards. "You're a hundred yards too high," Capron called out. "I want to tear 'em all up! I want 'em cut *all to pieces*!" As soon as the range was adjusted another gun barked, and another until the enemy scattered. The elder Capron had begun to avenge the death of his son—and namesake—at Las Guasimas.[11]

A half hour later the American infantrymen, who had moved up to within six to eight hundred yards of the village before daylight, opened up with their rifles. The outnumbered Spanish garrison held out gamely. General Joaquín Vara del Rey's men faced ten-to-one manpower odds and had no artillery or machine guns with which to defend the village, but they used their rifles with deadly effect. The reduction of El Caney was not an easy task. Capron's light guns were too far away to have much effect, and the Spanish riflemen delivered their fire from within the protection of their trenches and blockhouses.

Huge clouds of smoke issue forth from Capron's battery as it fires at targets in El Caney on July 1 (Library of Congress).

The exchange of fire had already begun by the time the far right of the American line came into position. A soldier in the Seventeenth Infantry observed Spanish soldiers scampering about in the village and mistakenly assumed that they were running away. "Bah!" he thought, "the fight won before we got to it!" Spanish rifle fire soon disabused him of this misperception. He soon heard a sound that he later described as "like the pattering of heavy hail-stones coming from a great height, among the leaves of the little trees by our side." The "hail-stones," of course, were Spanish rifle bullets searching the jungle for soft flesh.[12]

Ludlow's brigade soon became hotly engaged southwest of town. The regulars responded to the Spanish fire with their modern Krag rifles, and the men from the Second Massachusetts did the same with their obsolete Springfields. Although the Springfield fired a heavier bullet, the massive clouds of smoke that issued from every muzzle furnished the defenders with precise targets. After a few smoke-laden volleys, along with the hot return fire, the men from the Bay State realized that they were drawing too much unwanted attention in the form of Spanish bullets. For the rest of the afternoon they fired as individuals rather than as companies. The smoke was still there, of course, but it was in smaller quantities at any given time.[13]

The fight for El Caney soon degenerated into a long-range sniping contest. The Americans had a difficult time locating individual targets because the Spaniards did not usually expose themselves except long enough to fire, and then it was back under cover. "We could see nothing to fire at," recalled one of the regulars of the Seventh U.S., "except buildings and blockhouses, for no Spaniards were in sight." American casualties mounted, however, and it seemed plain to the attackers that unseen Spanish snipers up in the trees in front of them were inflicting much of the damage. Knowing the enemy sharpshooters were there and finding an effective way of getting rid of them, however, were two very different things. They could

Volunteers fire their Springfield rifles across a valley, illustrating the tell-tale clouds of smoke that their rifles produced (U.S. Army Military History Institute).

fire blindly into the foliage of the trees, but unless they then saw a Spanish soldier drop to the ground they could not be sure that the trees they were shooting actually contained enemy soldiers. With no telltale puff of gun smoke to give away their locations the Spaniards could continue their deadly work all day.[14]

On the far right of the American line, Colonel J. T. Haskell led his Seventeenth Infantry into battle as if he were again on some battlefield of the Civil War. Unfortunately, times, and bullet trajectories, had changed since the 1860s. As the colonel, accompanied by Lieutenant Walter M. Dickinson, strode forward ahead of his men, saber in hand, three bullets cut him down—two in the leg and a fatal one in the chest. The same burst of fire caught Dickinson in the arm. Unable, with only one useable arm, to drag the fatally wounded colonel back to the relative safety of a small lane in which most of the men had taken cover, Dickinson ran back and asked for volunteers to help him. Four men immediately responded and followed Dickinson back to where the colonel lay. Working as fast as they could they removed him to some cover, but in doing so three of the five-man rescue party were wounded, including Lieutenant Dickinson who took another bullet to the body.[15]

The lane in which these men huddled was not as much of a haven as they had at first supposed. Spanish rifles inside the stone blockhouse enfiladed the road from the southwest while fire from another blockhouse swept the lane from the east and entrenched riflemen kept up constant volleys from in front of the American position. The lane was even within range of Spanish snipers in the tower of the town's church. Officers commanded the men to not give up this position so they responded with all the Krag fire they could muster. Casualties mounted. Even Lieutenant Dickinson, already suffering from two wounds, was hit again two more times. He died before sunset.[16]

By ten o'clock most of the American troops had pushed forward to the outskirts of the village. At that time, General Lawton sent word for the men to disengage temporarily for a brief rest. Most were able to do so where they were; others fell back to safer positions. The Spaniards obviously knew where the Americans were now so there was no longer a need to prohibit cooking fires, and the men kindled these as quickly as they could. Soon coffee was brewing and those men who still had any bacon in their haversacks were cooking it as well. For two to three hours, only the sound of occasional sniper rounds broke the stillness of this lunch break. Early in the afternoon, however, the battle resumed its fury, with Miles's brigade moving up on Ludlow's right and Bates filling in between Miles and Chaffee.[17]

By about 2 P.M., Shafter began to think that he might have overextended his forces by having them fight what amounted to two separate battles in one day. He also seems to have decided that his earlier assessment of the danger posed by the Spaniards at El Caney had been overly cautious. He sent word to Lawton to break contact and move his men toward Santiago. "I would not bother with the little blockhouses," he wrote. "They can't harm us." This message caught Lawton by surprise. It was obvious to him that the Fifth Corps commander was too far to the rear to have an accurate picture of what was happening at El Caney. Lawton knew that to stop now would be an admission of defeat. Furthermore, as he replied to Shafter, some of his units were so hotly involved with the Spaniards that they could not withdraw without considerable danger. The commanding general then withdrew his original order, although with some anxiety.[18]

Meanwhile, Lawton's men still lay in whatever cover they could find from Spanish bullets, although cover from the broiling sun was almost non-existent. Two men of the Twelfth Infantry had previously crawled all along their section of the line, within 200 yards of the enemy positions, carefully snipping the barbed wire fences so that when the order for the final assault came they would not have that obstacle to hinder them. But they tempted fate — in the form of Spanish marksmen — every time they moved. As one man in a neighboring regiment recalled: "The quickest movement from point to point, or a temporary rise to snap one's camera, was inevitably rewarded with a special visitation of bullets that cut the grass round one, raised little puffs of sand, and generally made one wish one hadn't done it!"[19]

General Lawton finally decided that, since the hours-long expenditure of rifle ammunition by his troops had not measurably weakened the Spanish resolve to hold out, it was time for an assault on particularly troublesome El Viso. He selected General Chaffee's brigade to push forward and drive the enemy from the fort. Chaffee's men were already close to their goal. In fact, when Chaffee spotted two Spaniards rise from a trench and sprint toward the stone fort, he called: "Up on your knees there, two men, and pick off that delegation!"[20]

A black hen provided a few moments of levity in the midst of the carnage when she ran out of the fort and along the trench line. She seemed particularly indignant with all the noise and commotion around her. She flapped her wings angrily and made pecking motions at the air, as if she could catch one of the thousands of bullets that were flying around her. "Poor creature!" wrote one observer, "She escaped ten thousand bullets only to have her neck wrung by a hungry soldier that night."[21]

By this time, Captain Capron had brought his guns up to within a thousand yards of El Caney. At that distance, even though they were field guns and not really intended for heavy siege work, they began hitting El Viso with regularity. One lucky shot splintered the enemy's flagpole and caused a cheer from the attackers as the red and yellow banner fell. Capron told his men that the Spaniards would undoubtedly send a man out on the exposed roof to replace the flag on its staff. "Get him with shrapnel if you can," he ordered. As predicted, a soldier soon appeared on the roof. One of Capron's guns fired, and the crew watched and waited tensely as the projectile screamed toward the fort. After a few seconds they saw the tell-tale puff of white smoke right over the blockhouse, and the man was swept away. "Got him!" the artillerists jubilantly shouted.[22]

The foot soldiers were probably glad to have a chance to attack. They were out of options. "The only thing left," wrote a soldier in the Twenty-fifth U.S., "was to go ahead or die; or else retreat like cowards. We preferred to go ahead." At least they would be moving. They would not have to continue to lie in the punishing sun and worry about being shot by the unseen enemy. They advanced under cover of a ravine until they were almost upon their objective. A news correspondent who was present declared that the men then "swarmed over the wire fences and the trenches beyond like a hive of angry bees, and amidst the cheering of the rest of the line drove the enemy helter-skelter over the crest of the hill."[23]

When the sweating attackers reached the enemy works they saw the toll that the day's fighting had exacted on the Spaniards. Dead and wounded men lay in the trenches, and those who were able seemed only too happy to throw down their rifles and throw up their hands in surrender. The first Americans into the stone fort found that rifle and shell fire had killed most of its occupants and the rest, like their comrades in the trenches outside, were quick to surrender. One man, in fact, had a piece of white cloth tied to the end of a stick with which to signal the small garrison's intention, but he found the incoming fire so intense that he did not dare approach an open window to display it for fear of being shot down before he had a chance to use his flag.

A soldier of the Twelfth U.S. clambered onto the roof of the fort and lustily waved an American flag as a symbol of the hard fought victory. But not everyone on the other side was willing to concede just yet. As the man's comrades hoarsely cheered his bit of bravado, several Spanish bullets hit the roof very near to him, and he immediately grabbed his flag and fell flat, obviously not wanting to have survived the day's fighting only to fall victim to a vengeful sniper. But up he sprang again, waving Old Glory until one of his officers ordered him down.[24]

James Creelman, a news correspondent for William Randolph Hearst's New York *Journal*, had attached himself to Chaffee's brigade and was one of the first Americans into the Spanish position. A reporter's natural inquisitiveness propelled him to be where the story was, but he also had another reason. He wanted to get possession of the Spanish flag that had only recently been shot from its staff. "It was the thing I had come to get," he later recounted. "I wanted it for the *Journal*. The *Journal* had provoked the war, and it was only fair that the *Journal* should have the first flag captured in the greatest land battle of the war." Just after he picked it up, however, a bullet struck him in the left shoulder. He described the sensation as like that of being punched in the shoulder with a closed fist, and although the force of the impact spun him around it did not knock him down. Almost immediately, however, his arm turned numb and he experienced sharp pain all the way down into his hand and in his back. His arm, he wrote, "hung loose as though it did not belong to me." A soldier of the Twelfth Infantry was hit at about the same time, also in the left shoulder. As he was attempting to dress this wound he was struck again in the left arm, and then a third time in the left leg. "I thought that sufficient punishment," he recalled, "but the spiteful devil, who was concealed in a tree, seemed determined to finish the job, and kept pegging away, and finally landed the sixth [fourth] shot. This took effect in my right leg, just below the knee, and taking a downward course passed out through my heel." El Viso and its new defenders were under fire from Spanish positions elsewhere throughout the village.[25]

The capture of El Viso, however, seemed to have broken the spirit of the few surviving Spaniards as the Americans swept slowly through the village. By 5 P.M., ten hours after they had originally attacked, the American troops finally took El Caney. It had been a costly day's fight for both sides. The attackers, as is usually the case, lost more men than the defenders, but the Spanish lost a greater percentage of their total force. About 235 Spaniards were killed or wounded and another 120 became prisoners out of a force that only began with about 520. Among the dead were General Vara and two of his sons. The Americans lost 81 killed and 335 wounded. Hardest hit among the American units was the Seventh U.S. It had begun the day with 916 officers and men and lost 132 to death or wounds.[26]

With the fighting at an end, it was time to tend to the wounded and to bury the dead. Medical personnel had set up field hospitals and they quickly saw a constant inflow of wounded Americans and Spaniards. The Americans wrapped their dead in blankets and buried them in common graves with all the honors of war. They buried the Spaniards in the very trenches they had so bravely defended. A sergeant of the Twenty-fifth Infantry, put into words what many of the Americans undoubtedly felt as he viewed the dead bodies of the Spaniards. "Oh! what a terrible sight. God grant I may never behold such a piteous spectacle again."[27]

Policing up the small town in the aftermath of the fighting meant more than just burying the dead. The Americans also gathered up the Spanish rifles and destroyed them, along with extra ammunition. The Massachusetts volunteers would probably have gladly thrown their obsolete Springfields onto the scrap heap in exchange for an equal number of Mausers, but they were not allowed to do so.[28]

The exhausted Americans filed out of the village and back to where they had left their blanket rolls and haversacks early that morning. The men of the Second Massachusetts watched from the side of the road as the black soldiers of the Twenty-fifth Infantry filed by. The volunteers had watched earlier as these men took part in the final valorous charge on El Viso, and now they showed their appreciation by a spontaneous outburst of applause and cheers. "Those men think you are soldiers," observed a man accompanying the regulars. "They *know* we are soldiers," replied the sergeant to whom the remark had been directed.[29]

The rest of the Fifth Corps had not stood idly by while Lawton's men were braving the scorching heat of both the tropical sun and Spanish rifle fire. The road to Santiago passed between two hills, both of which were occupied by enemy troops. General Shafter ordered General Kent's infantry division to make up the left wing of the attacking force. It would attack the fortified Spanish home — dubbed the blockhouse — and its supporting works atop San Juan Ridge while General Wheeler led the cavalry division against Kettle Hill, somewhat in front of and to the right of Kent's goal. Both divisions had to share a narrow jungle road to reach their respective staging areas.

As Lawton's men headed toward El Caney that morning, Kent's and Wheeler's men began moving toward El Pozo. Captain George Grimes set up his four-gun battery of 3.2-inch rifled field pieces atop El Pozo Hill, approximately a mile and a half from San Juan Ridge. Although considered rather small for siege work, these guns certainly had the range of the Spanish works and would provide as much cover fire for the advancing infantrymen as possible when the assault finally began. The artillerists were not alone as they waited for orders on the hill top. High ranking infantry and cavalry officers, newspaper reporters, military observers from various European nations, Cuban soldiers, and sketch artists for American magazines and newspapers also waited there for the battle to begin. One of these artists, Howard Chandler Christy, decided that even being on this hill did not offer him the vantage point he sought, so he climbed up into a tree somewhat behind the guns where he would have, he hoped, a truly panoramic view of the drama about to unfold. Below the hill on the east, and out of the direct line of fire from Santiago, much of the Second Cavalry Brigade was in the yard of a farm house or sugar factory, and several Cubans occupied the building itself.[30]

General Shafter had over-exerted himself in the hot sun the day before and was unable to accompany his troops to the front. He sent his adjutant, Lieutenant Colonel Edward J. McClernand, to issue attack orders in his stead. The colonel did not want to signal the beginning of this second phase of the day's battle until General Lawton had had plenty of time to reduce El Caney and be ready to participate in the assault on the San Juan Heights. Finally, well over an hour after the beginning of what McClernand believed would be the two-hour battle for El Caney, he gave Grimes the long awaited orders to fire at about 8:20 A.M. A ranging shot from one of his guns was soon on its way. Those anxiously watching from the hilltop saw that it sailed completely over the Spanish blockhouse at which it had been aimed. Grimes ordered the range reduced by 150 yards for the second shot, but it, too, was long. After another adjustment, the number three gun sent its shell plowing into the earth just in front of the target. The precise distance had now been determined through trial and error, or what artillerists call bracketing the target, and the next shot of the early morning found its mark, crashing through the red tile roof of the blockhouse and causing shouts of exhilaration all around. The American artillerists tempered their joy with the certain knowledge that the Spaniards would not be long in replying. They knew that the huge clouds of smoke that billowed forth with every one of their shots clearly marked their locations for the Spanish gunners.

Very shortly, those on El Pozo heard the first enemy shells whistling through the air. The Spanish gunners also overestimated the distance to their intended target, but these first shots were not without deadly effect. The first two or three shells burst beyond El Pozo Hill but over the heads of the Americans and Cubans assembled below it. Colonel Roosevelt was slightly wounded by a shell fragment from the second round, which also wounded half a dozen other cavalrymen nearby. Almost immediately another round landed squarely on the building housing the Cubans, killing and wounding a number of them and scattering the rest "like guinea hens," not to be seen again until the fighting was over for the day. Luck intervened to prevent even greater casualties when shrapnel penetrated a box full of 175 Hotchkiss shells but failed to set them off. It did not take the Spanish gunners long to adjust their fire and soon their shells began falling into Grimes's battery position. The various non-essential personnel and other casual lookers-on quickly sought safety. Christy had seen enough from his leafy perch and decided to finish his sketches from memory. Grimes continued to pepper away for another thirty minutes or so, but then the increasingly effective counter-battery fire caused him to order a halt. With no more smoke clouds to guide Spanish gunners they also ceased firing.[31]

Major Maxfield, anxious to demonstrate the value of aerial observation under battlefield conditions, had his men up with the sun on the morning of July 1, once again repairing new holes in the balloon and using up some more of their dwindling reserve supply of hydrogen to re-inflate it. When they had again gotten it airworthy they moved about half a mile closer to the Spanish works. Maxfield met Colonel Derby there, and the two men once again clambered into the basket and rose into the morning sky.

From their vantage point they could see, at a distance, Lawton's troops engaging the Spaniards at El Caney. They could also see the lines of soldiers beneath them trying to move along the clogged road from El Pozo toward the San Juan Heights. They saw no evidence of Spanish reinforcements coming out of Santiago toward the heights, nor could they locate the Spanish artillery that had given Grimes's Battery such fits. They were not able to get a very detailed picture of the enemy defenses. They could see the blockhouse on top of San Juan Hill and could occasionally pick out individual enemy riflemen, but that was about it.

Maxfield, having studied the use of balloons in European warfare, knew that he should be able to see everything in sufficient detail from an altitude of a thousand feet without having to get any closer to the enemy lines. Derby, on the other hand, had apparently not read those same reports and after a brief time aloft ordered the balloon lowered to just a few hundred feet and dragged forward for a closer look. Maxfield was reluctant to risk his fragile craft any closer to the enemy guns and tried to point out to the colonel that by moving so far forward it would be difficult for the Spaniards to resist making the 15,000-cubic-foot balloon a target of both rifle and artillery fire. Derby would not be swayed, however, so forward it went.

The ground crew below hauled on the tether ropes until the two officers were barely above the treetops, and then they moved forward. When they reached the point where the road continued across the Aguadores River, Colonel Derby decided they were far enough forward and asked that the ground crew begin paying out the tethers so he and Maxfield could again make their observations from a thousand feet up. Even though they were now well within the horizontal range of the Spanish Mausers, they would be relatively safe at that altitude. Unfortunately, the guy ropes became inextricably tangled in the jungle tree limbs nearby, and the balloon's occupants were forced to make their observations from a much more dangerous elevation of only about fifty feet!

From the Spanish position there was no way to determine by direct observation just where in the jungle the American troops were. Spanish officers of course knew that they would have to come by way of the few trails in the area, but they had no way of knowing when. The progress of the *Santiago* removed this doubt. As the balloon moved slowly forward, just above the treetops, the Spaniards could see the four guy lines hanging down from it and knew that whoever was on the other ends of those ropes were on one of the trails. The Spaniards wasted little time in opening fire on this big new target. Almost miraculously, the balloon and the balloonists remained unscathed for quite a long time. In fact, the Spaniards may not have actually been trying to shoot down the balloon since it gave them such a wonderful marker. All they had to do was drop their shells into the jungle in the immediate vicinity of the balloon and they were sure to hit the marching Americans.

As more and more bullets found their way into the *Santiago*'s gas bag, Maxfield noted a decided loss of buoyancy and called down to the men to pull the balloon down. Upon reaching the ground he found over a dozen bullet holes and at least one fairly substantial rip apparently caused by an exploding artillery round. The damage was probably repairable, but with no more reserves of gas there was no way that another ascent could be made. Instead, the balloon company gathered the deflated bag, stuffed it into its basket, and retreated on foot to a safer place. They would retrieve their aircraft when the shooting stopped.

A sergeant in the Tenth U.S. Cavalry described what the men on the ground thought about the use of the balloon. "So much has been said about this balloon," he recalled, "that it hardly seems necessary to say more; why was it there, no one of the line could tell, as the only information its occupants furnished, so far as we knew, was that the Spaniards were firing on us—information which at that particular time was entirely superfluous." A New York volunteer described the sounds made by the bullets and pieces of shrapnel as not, at first, sounding very threatening. "Not quite a click and not quite a whine, and now and again, a *buzz* when a Spanish bullet smacked into a tree.... We were under fire! This is what we had come for." Of course, along with the realization that people were now actively trying to take his life caused a tenseness in his "throat, a dryness that was not a thirst, and little chilly surges" in his stomach.[32]

In spite of the costs, Colonel Derby had spotted a little-used trail running off to the left of the main road. It did not appear on maps of the area, and he could not be sure where it ultimately led, but it seemed to offer a good way to relieve the congestion on the main jungle trail. Prior to its discovery both divisions of troops jostled along the single trail the infantrymen on the left and the dismounted cavalrymen on the right. The new path offered relief to this congestion. Two infantry regiments of Brigadier General Hamilton S. Hawkins' brigade had already passed the entrance to the trail when Colonel Derby reported its existence to General Kent. The general immediately turned the rest of his division into the trail.[33]

The first regiment into the trail happened to be the untested, volunteer Seventy-first New York, the only volunteer regiment in Kent's entire division. Entering the side trail with the New Yorkers were three of the earliest civilian combat cameramen. They were employees of the Vitagraph Moving Picture Company and were there to capture the upcoming action on their relatively new medium. One onlooking soldier noticed that they must not have gotten very far down the trail because in about one minute they were back again on the main road with their cumbersome equipment. The enemy fire had now become quite heavy, and that may have caused the intrepid cinematographers to reassess their strategy. In fact, Spanish fire at this point would have caused many regular soldiers to have second thoughts about continuing to expose themselves to it. When the apparently random Spanish artillery fire began bursting around them, inflicting casualties from an unseen enemy, some of the men in the lead battalion panicked and refused to go on. Because of the narrowness of the trail their action stopped the forward progress of the entire brigade. It was too much for some of the New Yorkers as they stopped along the trail looking for places of concealment from the Spanish fire. One man, even while chills rippled through his cold, clammy stomach in time with his pulse, saw that the flies and the birds seemed to take no notice of the lead bullets and iron shot ripping through the vegetation around them. "It was," he remembered, "a comfort — almost — to bury one's nose in the rank vegetation of the jungle floor; anything to shrink in size." Staff officers pleaded with the men to keep moving forward, and most of them did. Those who simply could not muster the courage to move, however, were ordered rather harshly to at least crawl off the trail and into the jungle so that those soldiers who *would* go forward *could* go forward. When General Kent learned of the situation he was in no mood to waste time. He simply told the New Yorkers that if they were not willing to go forward they should get off the trail and let the regulars through. While a few of the New Yorkers dragged themselves into the brush, most of them, along with the bulk of the division, hurried forward. They finally debouched at the edge of the jungle, crossed the meandering San Juan River, and went into line of battle facing San Juan Hill.[34]

After the final combat troops entered the trail the bandsmen of the Sixteenth U.S. followed. They carried their instruments with them but were prepared to act as stretcher-bearers for their wounded comrades if necessary. At least some of the musicians, however, had other plans. As one would come across a dead or wounded soldier he would pick up the rifle and ammunition belt and leave his instrument behind. "Pick up that goddam horn," yelled the furious drum major on such occasions. "You pick up that goddam horn! An' that's an order!" he roared at a bandsman he caught in the act. "Not by a goddam site," came the reply. "You think I'm agoin to get shot at an' not shoot back!" The drum major then went sputtering off toward another musician gathering up a rifle, but his remonstrations met with a similar response.[35]

Colonel Charles A. Wikoff's Third Brigade of Kent's Division, consisting of the Ninth, Thirteenth, and Twenty-fourth U.S. Infantry Regiments, had pushed the Seventy-first New York along the trail in front of them. As soon as they emerged from the jungle and presented themselves as visible targets to the Spaniards the volume of fire increased. One of the first to fall was Colonel Wikoff. Upon his fatal wounding, command of the brigade passed to Lieutenant Colonel William Worth of the Thirteenth Infantry, but within minutes he was hit in the right arm. Unwilling to leave the field, he picked up with his left hand the sword he had dropped and continued waving it to encourage his men onward. Loss of blood soon weakened him to the point that he turned over brigade command to Lieutenant Colonel Emerson Liscum of the Twenty-fourth Infantry. A few minutes later, Liscum too, was among the wounded and Lieutenant Colonel E. P. Ewers of the Ninth Infantry led the brigade. Only about ten minutes had elapsed since Wikoff fell. Waiting for orders to go forward, the infantrymen took what shelter they could along the bank of the San Juan River.[36]

And the Spanish fire was deadlier than ever. So many of the dismounted cavalrymen were killed and wounded as they crossed the river in the shadow of the balloon, that they later referred to this location as the "Bloody Ford." As they lay along the relative safety of the river banks, a British military observer marveled at the task awaiting them. "Was this [hill] to be taken," he asked himself, "practically without the aid of artillery? Artillery should have battered, and battered, and battered the position, and then the infantry might have swept up at the run." But the attempt to provide covering fire had long since been proven less than effective. As they waited in formation for some order to go forward the soldiers continued to suffer casualties from the accurate Spanish fire. A trooper from the Tenth Cavalry found shelter very hard to come by and, like many others near him, looked for protection wherever he could find it. Standing in the waist deep water did not seem adequate so he unapologetically ducked so low "that it was no trouble for him to sip the water from that welcome stream without bending his body."[37]

The popular Rough Rider captain of Troop A, Irish-born "Bucky" O'Neill, tried to calm and inspire his men by his own behavior. Instead of trying to protect himself from the enemy's fire, this former mayor of Prescott, Arizona, strode up and down in front of his men, and in full view of the Spaniards, puffing on a cigarette and acting unconcerned about his own welfare. His men got the message, and although they appreciated what he was trying to do they begged him to take cover. He pooh-poohed the notion that any harm could come to him on this day by declaring, "the Spanish bullet isn't made that will kill me." A few moments later a Spanish bullet entered his mouth and carried away the back of his head, killing him on the spot.[38]

Some of the wounded, particularly if their injuries did not seem to be life-threatening, probably headed for the rear with a sense of relief. They would not have to try to cross the bullet-swept terrain at the base of the hills and then up to the top. Others seemed angry that their wounds kept them from sharing what they were certain was to be the glory of capturing the enemy positions. In any case, wounded soldiers were not out of danger as they headed for medical treatment in the rear. Spanish sharpshooters—some dressed in green clothing for camouflage—fired from the treetops at stretcher-bearers and walking wounded. One of the men carrying a wounded Sixth Infantry man was shot in the head and killed just after giving the injured man some water and tobacco. In another case, two of three stretcher-bearers were shot before the third man dragged the initial casualty off the road and into some bushes to wait for help.[39]

By 1 P.M. all of the assault elements—all, that is, except General Lawton's division, which still had its hands full at El Caney—were ready to go forward against their respective targets along the San Juan Heights. General Shafter could hear the noise of battle from his headquarters, but he was about two miles from the firing lines and probably not entirely aware just how desperate things were becoming. The defense of El Caney had caused a serious disruption in the American timetable for victory, and the troops huddled in front of San Juan Heights could not long afford to remain there while they awaited the outcome at El Caney. When no orders were forthcoming from headquarters the various generals and colonels looked toward one of Shafter's representatives at the front, Lieutenant John D. Miley, for instructions. The lieutenant was just as baffled by the lack of guidance as they were. Finally, however, the young officer took the initiative and told those around him that "the heights must be taken at all hazards. A retreat now would be a disastrous defeat." Finally, they could go forward![40]

An infantryman on the left of the battle line recalled that he was almost paralyzed with fear at the thought of standing up and trying to move up the hill toward the enemy position. "All I know," he said, "is that when I looked up that ... hill, and I knew I was going to cross that open space in the face of that hell fire, I got cold all over. I could feel my hair move on my scalp, and my teeth chattered. I tried to pray, but I couldn't. I didn't think of my mother or anything like that. I only tried to think of some way to get out of going up that hill.... While I was trying to make up my mind what to do, our sergeant jumped up and hallooed: 'Come on, boys; give 'em hell!' and it felt as though he had grabbed me by the shoulders and yanked me out of my cover, for the first thing I knew I was at the bottom of the hill and beginning to go up." As he and those around him started forward they heard a wonderful sound from behind them. Some thought it sounded like woodpeckers hard at work. Others were reminded of the sound of a stick being drawn across the pickets of a fence. It was neither. Second Lieutenant John H. Parker had put into action three of his four rapid-fire Gatling guns. These guns consumed ammunition at a prodigious rate and were only in action for a few minutes. But during those minutes they poured fire onto San Juan Hill at an equally stupendous pace, forcing the Spaniards to keep their heads down and allowing the attackers time to move up the hill unimpeded.[41]

General Hawkins knew that his brigade had to attack San Juan Hill, but with no more covering fire than that provided by the Gatling guns and the light field guns again firing from El Pozo Hill he was reluctant to order his men forward. He had seen in the Civil War what well directed defensive fire could do to an attacking force even when that force had massed artillery paving the way for it. Lieutenant Jules Ord, brigade quartermaster, volunteered to lead the brigade against the hill, but Hawkins still hesitated, not wanting to even ask for volunteers for such a suicidal undertaking. Ord then told his commander that he did not expect him to ask for volunteers, but he was volunteering anyway. He only asked that the general not *forbid* him from going forward. "I will not ask for volunteers," Hawkins reiterated. "I will not give permission and I will not refuse it. God bless you and good luck."[42]

Ord immediately seized upon this tacit approval and, waving his sword to rally the men, started up the slope. Immediately to their front was an expanse of high grass with barbed wire entanglements and then the rather steep slopes of the hills. Just as with the men of the Second Division attacking El Caney, these American troops now faced barbed wire for the first time, and wire cutters were in very short supply among the troops. An *ad hoc* pioneer company formed in General Hawkins's brigade and attacked the wire with what clippers were available, and with axes.[43]

When the infantrymen neared the crest the Gatling guns and other covering fire ceased to avoid hitting them. By that time, however, the defenders had had all they could take and rapidly moved down the far side of the ridge and toward the next line of defenses, leaving their dead and wounded behind. Lieutenant Ord was among the first to reach the abandoned works and noticed a wounded Spanish soldier lying along the edge of the trench, still in the line of fire. Ord instructed a couple of nearby men to move the injured man to a safer place. The Spaniard, perhaps misunderstanding this humanitarian gesture, drew a pistol and shot the popular young officer in the head as he stepped across the trench. It was the last thing that Spaniard did in this life, as the soldiers who were about to carry him to safety now beat him to death with the butts of their rifles.[44]

Over on the right, in front of Kettle Hill, Colonel Roosevelt had almost decided not to wait any longer for orders to attack. His cavalrymen were taking more and more casualties where they were, and unless they attacked soon they might not have the numerical strength to carry their objective. One American officer was hit almost simultaneously by several bullets and left a vivid recollection of the event. "I felt as if my left leg were struck by a cannon-ball, the little finger of my left hand caught in a stone-crusher, and my right shoulder clawed by a wild-cat."[45]

General Sumner soon relayed Miley's order to Roosevelt and his other regimental commanders. The First Cavalry Brigade — the Third, Sixth, and Ninth, all under Lieutenant Colonel Henry Carroll — would lead the attack, and the Second Brigade — the First, and Tenth U.S., and the Rough Riders, under Colonel Wood — would follow up in support of the First. Roosevelt wasted no time. He mounted his remaining horse, "Little Texas," and rode to the front of his regiment. His men, lying on the ground to avoid the bullets whistling overhead, took courage from his example and rose up to begin the assault. Moving forward from the rear of the brigade formation, the Rough Riders soon came upon the still-prone forms of the regulars of the First and Ninth. Roosevelt, failing to spot an officer of higher rank, finally told a captain that he was there to support the regulars, but he could not very well support them until they got up and started moving forward. The captain hesitated to obey this order from an officer in another command, and a volunteer command at that, so Roosevelt lashed out: "Then let my men through, sir." The blustery colonel would lead the attack himself if that was what was necessary. As the rowdy volunteers began passing through the lines of the regulars, they jumped up and joined in, for they had been waiting such orders just as anxiously as had the Rough Riders only moments before.[46]

As the newly inspirited troops moved up from the base of the hill they too encountered barbed wire fences. A captain of the Tenth Cavalry vainly tried digging up one of the fence posts supporting the wire with his bare hands in order to remove the obstacle. He was equally unsuccessful in trying to rock the pole back and forth until he could pull it out of the ground. Finally, he climbed the strands of wire like they were steps on a ladder and jumped to the other side. One of his men then discovered that a bayonet made a fairly efficient wire cutter.[47]

It has often been said that even the best tactical plan seldom survives the first few minutes of combat, and that was certainly the case at Kettle Hill as men of both brigades quickly became intermingled. The experience of a sergeant in Troop B of the Tenth Cavalry was probably not atypical. "I heard the constant commands—'B Troop, forward!'" he recalled. "Thinking all the time that my troop was meant and not knowing that B of the First Cavalry as well as B of the Rough Riders were just ahead of me. I soon found that I had obeyed other officers' commands and was in the front rank with a troop of Rough Riders." In fact, most of the men in this man's regiment wound up veering off to the left and attacking San Juan Hill.[48]

The Spanish gave way in the face of the determined American assault and began to abandon their works and flee toward Santiago. Among the first Americans to the top of Kettle Hill was the intrepid Colonel Roosevelt who had ridden part way up on horseback. With no more work to be done on Kettle Hill, Roosevelt led his troops, along with men from the other cavalry regiments, down and across to San Juan Hill to help out there. By the time the Rough Riders reached the crest of San Juan Hill most of the defenders had fled, although Roosevelt shot one fleeing Spaniard with his revolver. A tired trooper from the Tenth U.S. Cavalry, scornful of the media coverage of Roosevelt's men and remembering the fight at Las Guasimas, remarked that "this was the second time we came to the rescue of the Rough Riders."[49]

As the exhausted soldiers reached the crest of San Juan Hill they saw that the Spaniards, in their haste to leave, had left their flag flying over the blockhouse. Several of the men immediately moved to take it down. A man from the Thirteenth U.S. ultimately captured this prize. While he and a friend proudly held it up for the admiring inspection of a couple of envious cavalrymen some Spaniards, mortified to see their beloved banner being treated so cavalierly by the conquerors, sent a fusillade of shots toward the small knot of men. Two of the men were hit, although not fatally, and thereupon heightened the enemy's frustration by angrily ripping the flag into fragments.[50]

The enemy kept up a long-range fire from the next row of hills, and even though most of the Americans rested on the lee side of San Juan Hill and Kettle Hill, there were still casualties. One man, taking advantage of the lull in activity, decided to have a snack. As he lifted an Army hardtack to his mouth a Spanish bullet splintered it in his hand. He was not hit, however, and nonchalantly ate the remnant. A New York volunteer had a similar experience. While munching on one of the hard crackers he bit down on what he thought was a rock. His companion, however, saw blood running down his chin and neck. When the man spit out the "rock" he saw that it was a Spanish bullet that had ricocheted into his jaw and temporarily lodged between his teeth.[51]

The worn out Americans worked through the night erecting protective breastworks of their own on San Juan Heights. The last thing these men wanted to do was to spend the next several hours in hard physical labor. "That morning," recalled an exhausted regular, "everyone would have been outraged at the thought of sitting near the enemy's lines without throwing out the strongest posts provided for in the books of regulations. Now we were without any; our columns of smoke rose up conspicuously, and all the world sat around the shrine of bacon unconcerned. A long day's fighting knocks the corners off one's sensitiveness to the military proprieties, and makes one apathetic to dull and conventional forms of risk." In spite of the men's physical condition, however, it was vitally important to be prepared for any Spanish counterattack that might develop. A difficult chore even for men who were fresh, an insufficiency of tools rendered this task more difficult. One regiment, for example, was issued a total of two picks and four shovels for the use of over 900 men. Some of the troops found abandoned Spanish tools and put them to good use. Others used knives, forks, spoons, and even their empty ration cans to dig at the stubborn earth. The complaints of some of the Rough Riders reached the sympathetic ears of their regimental adjutant, and he rode to General Wheeler's headquarters to seek some sort of modification to the orders.[52]

Wheeler had returned to his sick bed after the fighting for the day had ended, but he graciously arose to receive the junior officer. "General," the younger man reported, "I am afraid our men can't dig the trenches." Wheeler was somewhat taken aback by this information, and when he asked the adjutant which men he was talking about he learned that the entire cavalry division was balking. He then instructed the messenger to go back to the division and bring the man who could not dig trenches to his quarters. The young man must have thought that the general's hearing had failed him. It was not just one man, he emphasized, but every man in the entire division. Wheeler understood perfectly, but he wanted to interview only one man who declared that he could not dig a trench. The officer departed and shortly returned with an enlisted man from the Ninth Cavalry. By this time Wheeler was fully dressed, and he asked the soldier if he was the one who could not dig trenches. The embarrassed trooper admitted that he was one of hundreds of such men. "You can go to sleep now, my man," the general said as he exited his tent, "and I'll go up and dig your trench for you. When the sun comes up to-morrow morning the Spaniards are going to open on us, and every man who isn't protected is not only in danger of being killed, but will be unable to help us maintain our own position. The trenches have to be dug, and if you are unable to dig yours I'll just go out and do it for you. Where's your pick?" "Boss," the embarrassed soldier said to the diminutive general, "you ain't fit to dig no trenches. If they done got to be dug, I'll just naturally do it myself. I'm dog tired, but that ain't work for you." "I know it isn't work for me to do," the general replied, "but I am going to need soldiers in the morning, and I am going to save your

Volunteers along San Juan Ridge prepare for a Spanish counter-attack (U.S. Army Military History Institute).

life, if possible. Do you think now that you can dig the trench?" Without a word the chastened soldier turned and headed back to the top of the ridge.

Wheeler turned toward the officer and told him to go and find him another man who could not dig a trench. The adjutant rode off and did not return. The next morning the cavalry division was well-ensconced in strong earthworks, but the expected attack never came. General Linares had been wounded during the day's fighting and had turned command over to General José Toral. Toral chose to concentrate and strengthen his inner line of defenses closer to the city rather than harass the Americans with a counterattack.[53]

By sundown on July 1, American forces controlled El Caney and San Juan Heights, but this control had come at a considerable cost. In addition to the losses of General Lawton's command, 147 men had died storming the heights and 929 suffered wounds. General Shafter should have foreseen such losses since his troops were attacking fortified positions all along the line. A soldier advancing in the open is always an easier target to hit than one who is at least partially protected by earthworks or blockhouses. Still the magnitude of American losses came as something of a shock because of the previously held notion that the Spaniards were not worthy foes and would turn and run away at the first sign of a determined American offensive.[54]

The dead, of course, were beyond caring about anything, but many of the wounded still faced terrible ordeals. Some who had fallen in the tall grass or along jungle trails were not discovered for a day or two. And because General Shafter had only gotten three ambulances ashore by this time, others faced a long jolting ride back to the division hospital east of El Pozo in mule drawn wagons bouncing over the merest excuses for roads. This combination contributed to the further discomfort and indeed the deaths of untold numbers of wounded.

Those who survived the ride reached hospital tents that were vastly overcrowded and medical personnel overwhelmed with work.[55]

As darkness fell over eastern Cuba, the five Army doctors at this hospital had already performed over 150 surgeries, and the number of injured men still lying in the grass waiting for attention continued to increase. Regimental surgeons who had been on the firing line administering first aid began arriving back at the hospital throughout the evening, and that alleviated some of the problems. Working in the operating tents by candlelight, or outside with a combination of moonlight and candlelight, these doctors stayed at it all night long.

The number of patients greatly overtaxed the hospitals, and even after the surgeons had tended the wounded they faced difficult conditions. The first hundred wounded men filled the tents set aside for patient recovery, and even they were forced to lie on the bare ground. There were no mattresses, no cots, few blankets, and almost no clean clothing. In most cases hospital workers lifted the wounded men from the operating tables, carried them outside, and laid them down on the grass where they were subject to the hot daytime sun and the frequent tropical showers. They had neither blankets to lie on nor under, and the only articles of clothing they had on were whatever they had been wearing when wounded that the surgeons had not cut away to do their work.[56]

General Shafter now had more problems to sort out. With his losses in killed and wounded, and a growing sick list, a further offensive seemed temporarily out of the question. What seemed of much greater importance was the ability of those men remaining on the firing line being able to repulse a Spanish counterattack. The commanding general even began to consider pulling his troops back from the San Juan Heights to a position five miles farther removed from Santiago. There, his overtaxed supply system could keep the men in food, ammunition, and the other necessities more easily, and there he could wait for reinforcements from the United States. Shafter consulted with his division commanders about the advisability of a withdrawal. Generals Lawton, Bates, and Wheeler opposed such a move. General Kent, although personally opposed, had polled his brigade commanders and they favored it. A regular enlisted man, although not an attendee at the meeting, seemed to speak for the majority of soldiers when he expressed his belief that they could hold their position until hell froze over and "then we would fight it out on the ice."[57]

Back in Washington, the slightest hint of such a retrograde movement caused considerable concern. Such a move might look to all the world as if the Fifth Corps had suffered defeat at San Juan Heights instead of scoring a victory. Secretary of War Alger and President McKinley wired their concerns to Shafter and promised that he could have all the reinforcements to be had as soon as proper transportation could be arranged. They realized that they could not possibly have an accurate picture of things in Cuba from their offices in faraway Washington and did not go so far as to issue Shafter any orders with regard to the Army's movements. "Of course you can judge the situation better than we can at this end of the line," their message read. "If, however, you could hold your present position, especially San Juan Heights, the effect upon the country would be much better than falling back." They seemed to have a marvelous grasp of the obvious.[58]

There was a flurry of messages back and forth between General Shafter and Admiral Sampson on July 2. The general earnestly implored his naval counterpart to force his way into the harbor even though the batteries protecting the entrance were still just as strong as before. "I am at a loss," he stated, "to see why the Navy can not work under a destructive fire as well as the Army." He further justified his request by alluding to his heavy losses of the day before and suggesting that the Navy could enter the harbor with less loss of life than would occur if the Army had first to silence the batteries.[59]

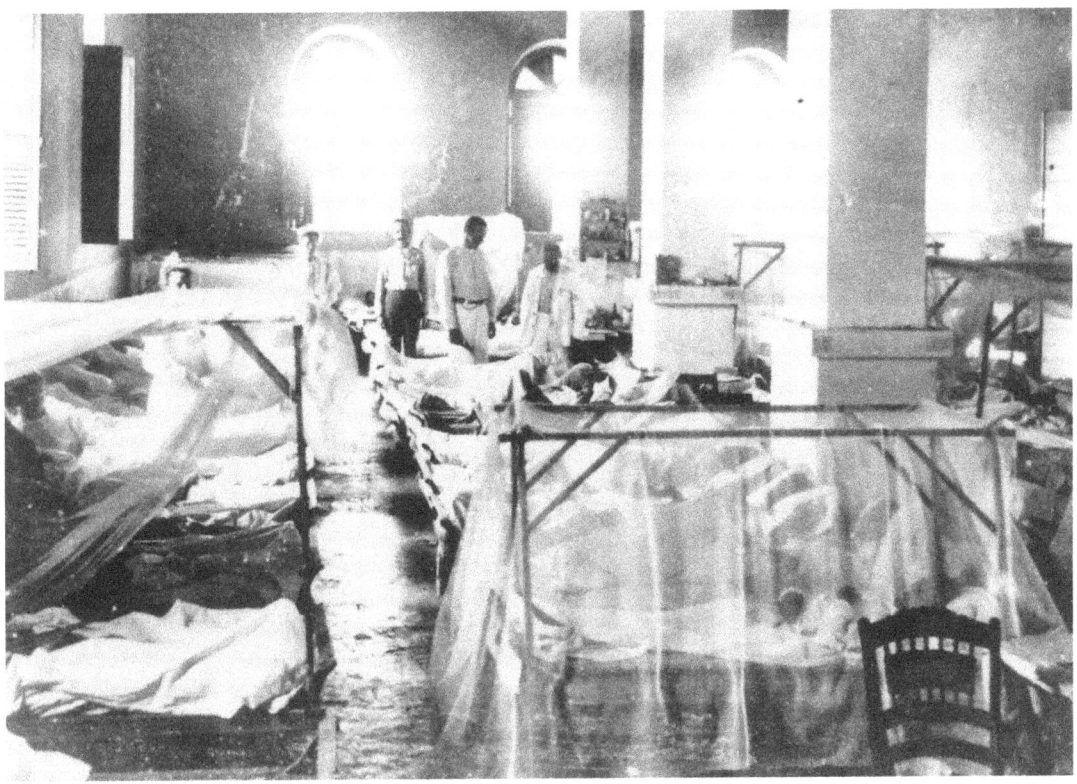

Hospital in Cuba, with some beds outfitted with mosquito netting (U.S. Army Military History Institute).

Admiral Sampson pointed out to Shafter that he was not afraid of losing Navy lives, but he was decidedly averse to losing Navy ships. After all, human casualties, whether in the Army or the Navy, could be replaced with relative speed. Lost ships could not. If the Navy forced its way past the protective batteries and into the channel there was still the danger of submarine mines to consider. Quite a few of them had been detonated trying to stop the *Merrimac*, but it would only take one strategically placed mine to sink one of Sampson's warships in mid-channel. If the Spaniards allowed a couple of ships to pass before activating the mine, they would then be effectively cut off from the rest of the blockading squadron and at the mercy of Cervera's ships. No, Sampson was not anxious to risk his ships in that way.

Telegraphic, or even telephonic, communication still left something to be desired between the communicants, so Sampson decided to come ashore and meet with Shafter face to face. Perhaps that way he could impress upon the general how sensitive his situation was. Maybe they could agree on some combined plan of action that would see the defenses at the harbor's mouth defeated, thus giving Sampson the necessary freedom to clear the mines out of the channel before going in after Cervera.

Sunday morning, July 3, dawned clear and bright, promising another hot day. At a few minutes before nine, a signalman on Sampson's *New York* ran up the flags that told the rest of the blockaders to disregard the movements of the flagship. The *New York* then lifted anchor and headed eastward toward Siboney where the admiral would go ashore for his meeting with Shafter. After about thirty minutes, and after having covered some seven miles, someone on the ship looked back and saw gun smoke. Cervera had decided to make a run for it.

CHAPTER 7

Naval Battle Forces Surrender

ADMIRAL CERVERA'S DECISION TO venture into the open seas was one that was forced upon him. As American ground forces approached Santiago, Cervera's gloom only deepened. If the American Army captured the city he and his command would face three possible fates, none of them particularly attractive. He could surrender his ships, which would certainly be an ignominious end. He could scuttle them to keep the Americans from having them, but this was only slightly less shameful than surrender. Or he could run the gauntlet of the blockaders and hope that at least some of his ships could fight their way out of the trap.

Cervera and all of his ship captains agreed that the time for escape had long since passed. The blockading squadron was too strong. In fact, Cervera confided to General Linares, "I have considered the squadron lost ever since it left Cape Verde, for to think anything else seems madness to me, in view of the enormous disparity which exists between our own forces and those of the enemy." Even if the two squadrons had been more evenly balanced the physical setting worked against a successful extrication. For Cervera's ships to reach open water they would have to steam, in single file, down the narrow, twisting channel from the harbor to the sea. They could not follow one another very closely because the pilot of each ship would have to maneuver slowly and very carefully. The sunken hulk of the *Merrimac* also impeded navigation. The escaping ships would have to pass so close to it as to risk fouling their port propellers in its sunken rigging. Thus the entire American squadron could concentrate its fire on one Spanish ship at a time as it came into view. Therefore, Cervera wrote to Linares, "There is no possibility of stratagem nor disguise, and the absolutely certain result will be the ruin of each and all of the ships and the death of the greater part of their crews."[1]

Unfortunately for the Spanish admiral, men far removed from the scene of battle were making decisions for him. On June 26, Minister of the Marine Ramón Auñón y Villalón, several thousand miles away in Spain, strongly suggested that Cervera's ships should run the blockade at night. On the same day, Governor General Ramón Blanco y Erenas in Havana chided the admiral for putting an unnecessarily pessimistic face on things and also suggested a nighttime escape. What neither of these men understood from their distant locations was that sneaking out under cover of darkness was not a viable option, because there was no cover of darkness when the blockaders played high power searchlights directly up the channel.[2]

Following the American successes at El Caney and San Juan Heights on July 1, Cervera once again tried to dissuade Blanco from issuing final orders for a sortie. He pointed out that he had dispatched quite a number of his gunners to help man the batteries on land and that they were essential to the defense of the city. What is more, if he attempted to leave now it would appear to the city's defenders that he was abandoning them in order to save himself. The governor was not to be swayed. That night he sent unequivocal orders. Cervera's ships were to leave as soon as possible. Sadly, the admiral prepared to comply.

Cervera made final preparations—it required twelve hours just for the ships to get up steam—and issued sailing orders on the morning of July 2. The ships would leave late that afternoon as soon as the sailors who had been detached to the land batteries could be reembarked. The *Infanta María Teresa*, the most powerful of the squadron, would lead the procession down the channel and would attack the first blockader that presented itself. Next would come the *Vizcaya*, the *Cristóbal Colón*, and the *Almirante Oquendo*, which were to hug the coastline and try to escape to the west while the *Maria Teresa* distracted the American ships. The speedier torpedo boat destroyers *Furor* and *Plutón* were to attempt to outrun all pursuit instead of staying around to fight. Any vessels that successfully outfought or outran the enemy were to make for Havana or Cienfuegos. Some of the sailors doing duty in the trenches had a considerable march back to the harbor and finally arrived, exhausted, about 4 P.M. Cervera then postponed his squadron's escape until early the next morning to allow time for much needed rest.³

Fog accompanied the dawn on July 3, but it burned off in a few hours. The Spanish gunboat *Alvarado* steamed down to the mouth of the channel so Captain Victor Concas y Palau, commander of the *Infanta Maria Teresa*, could make one last reconnaissance. The report he brought back to Admiral Cervera was that one of the American battleships that was usually on blockade duty appeared to be absent, but there were more than enough ships remaining to give the Spanish gunners plenty of work. Then, with guns loaded and anchors raised, the ships waited for the signal from the flagship to get underway. It soon appeared—"Viva España"—and was met by rousing cheers from the decks of all the vessels in the harbor.⁴

Aboard the blockaders, the American sailors remained watchful and anxious for a fight. A rumor then current throughout the fleet was that the Spanish captain of the *Vizcaya* had boasted that he would tow the *Iowa* all the way back to Spain if the two ships ever met in combat. The crews on some of the ships maintained a fifty percent watch. Never were fewer than half the men awake, and those who slept did so at their duty stations instead of in their hammocks. The long hours of watchful waiting gave the men time to reflect on their own mortality. A sailor on the *Texas* probably spoke for many when he remarked to Captain John Philip: "I don't know about this thing of standing up to get shot at.... The truth is, if Cervera ever comes out of his hole and begins throwing eleven-inch shells at me, I am very much afraid that I *shall* be very much afraid."⁵

As luck would have it, and July 3 was certainly a day when Admiral Cervera needed all the luck he could find, the blockading squadron was at reduced strength when the breakout began. Admiral Sampson, of course, was absent on his way to Siboney to converse with General Shafter. Along with the flagship went the armed yacht *Hist* and the torpedo boat *Ericsson*. The battleship *Massachusetts*, the cruisers *New Orleans* and *Newark*, and the converted tender *Suwannee* had all gone to Guantánamo for coal, and the rest of the blockaders were conserving fuel by not having fires under all their boilers. That left, from east to west and covering an arc of about eight miles, the converted yacht *Gloucester*, the battleships *Indiana*, *Oregon*, *Iowa*, and *Texas*, the armored cruiser *Brooklyn*, and finally another converted yacht named *Vixen*. But although the relative sizes of the two squadrons were almost the same, the firepower advantage was definitely with the Americans.⁶

Because July 3 was a Sunday, the crews of the American warships turned out in their white uniforms for a 9:30 inspection. The fog had cleared by then and it was already hot, with only a slight northwest breeze providing any relief. Few of the men were looking forward to the prescribed reading of the Articles of War to them. It would probably take an hour or more, and most had heard them enough times before to be very familiar with the ones that had any impact on their daily lives. Few, if any, of the American sailors had any inkling that this day would be any different from those that had gone before them since mid May.[7]

As the *Infanta María Teresa*, with flags flying and bright work highly polished, loomed into view in the lower part of the channel at about 9:35 A.M., there was surprise aboard the American ships. Many found it hard to fathom why Cervera had chosen such a bright, clear day to come forward when he had not done so on so many other occasions when dark of night or stormy weather might have been to his advantage. Captain Philip, of the *Texas*, declared that "Cervera's sally had been so long expected that when it actually came it was unexpected." Some figured that after being bottled up in Santiago harbor for six and a half weeks, and with the fall of the city apparently imminent, Cervera would simply blow up his ships to keep them out of the hands of the victorious Americans. Nevertheless, the American sailors quickly overcame their initial surprise and sprang to their battle stations. Signal flags throughout the American squadron fluttered with the message: "The enemy is attempting to escape." Finally, all the waiting was over.[8]

As the American naval officers realized what was happening they lost no time in issuing the necessary orders. "Sound the general alarm!" "Clear ship for action!" "Turn on the current of the electric [ammunition] hoists!" "Steam and pressure on the turrets!" "Hoist the battle flags!" (No one on the *Texas* had thought to have the battle flags ready, and they were still locked in a flag locker until the ship's navigator ordered some nearby sailors to break into the locker to get them.) "Lay aloft range-finders in the tops and give us our distance from the Morro!" "Engines ahead full speed!" "Be ready with the forced draft!" "The starboard battery will engage!" "Set your sights for four thousand yards!"[9]

One of the *Texas*' young officers sat comfortably in the ship's barbershop that morning, having his luxurious auburn beard trimmed to a more comfortable Van Dyke style. The barber had completed his work on the right side but had not yet started on the left when the alarm sounded, and the officer bolted out of the chair and ran off to his battle station.[10]

The men were well drilled, and they scrambled to their assigned places as fast as was humanly possible. Still, however, to some it seemed as if they were moving in slow motion. An officer on the *Indiana* hurried the men of the powder division below by shouting, "They [the Spanish ships] will all get away; two of them are outside the Morro already!" So eager were the men to do their duty that they recklessly threw themselves down the narrow ladders and through the hatches until the ammunition deck "was swarming with bruised and bleeding men, staggering to their feet, and limping to their stations." The ammunition passers on the *Texas* quickly handed up their first twelve-inch shell, upon which they had chalked:

> In God we trust,
> This shell will bust,
> And blow the Dagoes
> Into dust.[11]

On board the *Infanta María Teresa*, Captain Concas positioned himself outside the conning tower. If it was his fate to become a casualty this day he wanted to do it out in the open so his crew might be emboldened by his heroic death and fight even harder. Receiving permission from Admiral Cervera, Concas gave the order to commence firing at the nearest enemy ship. "It was the signal," he later wrote, "that the history of four centuries of grandeur was at an end and that Spain was becoming a nation of the fourth class." He turned to Admiral Cervera and said, simply, "Poor Spain!" The equally fatalistic admiral seemed silently to agree.[12]

With its two forward-firing guns in action as soon as it left the channel, the *María Teresa* faced the combined fire of the entire American squadron. Nevertheless, an Associated Press correspondent aboard Sampson's flagship expressed a certain admiration for the doomed squadron. "Out they came," he observed from a distance, "gallantly, these fine cruisers, the pride of Spain's navy, ... pushing their gun-smoke before them in thick, tumbling clouds like the chariot of Vulcan." As Cervera ordered his ship straight toward Commodore Schley's *Brooklyn* the water rushing by his vessel's bow gave it the appearance of a dog with a bone in its teeth. This attempt to ram the American ship caused some tense moments among its officers and crew. The helmsman put the wheel hard to starboard to avoid a collision, but this maneuver brought the *Brooklyn* directly into the path of the *Texas*, which was making for the Spanish ship with all speed. The *Infanta María Teresa* then turned away to the west and attempted to escape toward Cienfuegos.[13]

The American ships gave chase, but there was no way that all of them could catch up with the speedy Spaniard. Captain Evans, aboard the *Iowa*, hoped to be able to ram the enemy ship, or, when it appeared he would not be able to catch up with it, fire torpedoes into it. After a short chase he realized that this, too, was impossible. It had been seventeen months since his ship had been in dry dock and had the barnacles and other marine growth scraped from its hull. Its speed was further retarded by the fact that its cylinder heads had not been removed and cleaned for six months. Giving up on the *María Teresa*, the captain instead ordered his helmsman to turn the big ship hard to port so the *Iowa*'s starboard broadside could come into play briefly. Turning back to starboard allowed some of the *Iowa*'s portside guns to continue firing at the fleeing *María Teresa* while its starboard guns began playing on the *Vizcaya*, which had followed the flagship out of the harbor ten minutes later.[14]

The *Vizcaya*, too, escaped the *Iowa*'s ram and torpedoes. Perhaps Captain Evans could get close to the *Cristóbal Colón* as it steamed westward after the others. The growing palls of gun smoke made sighting targets difficult in both squadrons. Captain Philip, on the *Texas*, opined that "we might as well have had a blanket tied over our heads." When gunners aboard the *Colón* opened on the *Iowa* they either must have taken advantage of a brief break in this smoke cover or else they were very lucky. One shell blew a hole in the starboard side about four feet above the waterline and then exploded on the berth deck destroying the ship's dispensary. Quickly following this shell another struck just at the waterline. It did not explode, but it tore a hole in the hull through which seawater rushed. After these two shots the *Colón* turned its attention to other targets as it left the *Iowa* behind.[15]

Heedless of the damage, Captain Evans pushed his ship as hard as it would go, trying to intercept the *next* Spanish ship, the *Almirante Oquendo*, so he could use his torpedoes on it. When he saw that once again his ship was too slow, he turned and ran parallel to the *Oquendo* at a distance of about fifteen hundred yards. From that vantage point the *Iowa* poured everything it had into the enemy vessel. Not only did the big broadside guns wreak havoc, but the smaller caliber rapid-fire guns and the machine guns also joined in. According to Evans, the Spanish ship soon "rolled and staggered like a drunken thing."[16]

Meanwhile, the *Infanta María Teresa*, having gotten safely past the *Iowa*, now fell back as if to cover the other ships of the Spanish squadron. Actually she was already in her death throes. An American shell hit the Spaniard's main steam pipe almost as soon as it began its turn to the west. This caused a serious reduction in its speed, and the escaping steam suffocated the men manning one of the ammunition hoists. The ammunition hoists for the five-and-a-half-inch guns became unserviceable early in the battle. Each of these cumbersome devices could raise five fully loaded projectiles up to the guns, but they were so linked mechanically that when a shell hit one of them it disabled all the others at the same time. One of the hoists fell back into the magazine, where one of its shells exploded but, miraculously, did not detonate the rest of the contents of the magazine. Another American shell soon pierced one of the fire mains, and when fires began to break out, such as the one in Cervera's cabin where some 2.24-inch rounds were stored, there was no way to douse them. By 10:35, only an hour after leaving the safety of Santiago harbor, the concentrated fire of the American ships had smoke billowing up in several locations. Captain Concas lay wounded, and the admiral took over direct control of the *Maria Teresa* and ordered it toward shore. The gunnery officer on the *Oregon* made note of the fact that even though the stricken ship was evidently out of the fight, its captain had not stricken its colors. Since it was still a viable target the *Oregon*'s big guns raked it again as it steamed by. Soon the crippled Spanish ship beached itself, just west of Punta Cabrera.[17]

The hail of American fire directed toward the *Infanta María Teresa* at the beginning of the day's battle allowed the remaining Spanish ships a little breathing space as they began their runs to the west. Each of them, however, soon encountered a virtual firestorm from the American ships.

Each of the twelve- or thirteen-inch guns on ships like the *Texas* and the *Oregon* were capable of firing every two or three minutes under ideal conditions, but their actual rate of fire was reduced by the dense gun smoke that blanketed the sea and made it difficult to sight targets. The air inside the gun turrets quickly became stifling, even though big powerful fans pushed the gun smoke out through the barrels of the guns between shots. Each of the half dozen men had specific duties, but the process of loading and firing was necessarily laborious. First, a trap door behind the gun opened and an elevator lifted the projectile and powder bags up to a position in line with the open breech. A hydraulic rammer then pushed the projectile, sometimes weighing as much as 1,100 pounds, forward into the gun, followed by a couple of powder bags, each of which weighed over two hundred and fifty pounds. The ammunition hoist then disappeared into the floor, and a sailor swung the heavy breech block closed. The gun captain stepped forward to install a primer and hook up the electrical firing wires, while an officer peered through the telescopic sight and prepared to press the firing handle. When the gun fired, the noise was deafening as the half-ton projectile hurtled toward the target with enough energy to penetrate two feet of armor at 1,000 yard. And in spite of the presence of the exhaust fan the turret filled with acrid smoke. As soon as the gun recoiled from the shot two men wrestled open the breech, and a third played a stream of cooling water into it. Then the whole process began again as the second of the two guns in the turret fired.[18]

Spanish gunners were certainly not standing idly by. While the *Texas* dueled with the *Almirante Oquendo*, an enemy shell destroyed most of its pilothouse on the flying bridge. Another one exploded in the air over the forward portion of the ship and the concussion alone splintered one of the ship's cutters and shattered the eardrums of a naval cadet on board. Several officers, including Captain Philip, were thrown to the deck by the blast. "I remember pitching up in the air," the captain recalled, "with my coat-tails flying out behind me, as if I had been thrown by one of Roosevelt's broncos." The concussion of the *Texas*'s big guns was so severe that it threw a sailor down a hatchway, causing him to break his leg. On the *Iowa* the concussion that resulted every time an eight-inch gun let fly hurled the crew members working the nearby six-pounders to the deck.[19]

Damage aboard the *Oquendo* was much more significant. One of the Spanish five-and-a-half-inch guns burst at the breech as it was firing only its fourth round, blinding the gunner and killing or wounding the rest of his crew. An eight-inch shell from one of the American ships burst inside an eleven-inch gun turret and wiped out that entire gun crew. And, as on Cervera's flagship, the ammunition hoists for the five-and-a-half-inch guns were out of order

Wreckage of the *Almirante Oquendo* (Library of Congress).

almost from the beginning of the action. Other hits started so many fires that the crewmen were unable to flood all the affected compartments. Near the rear of the ship, burning wood from the officers' mess fell through an ammunition hoist hatch threatening to detonate the magazine beneath it. Two sailors alertly closed up the compartments holding the eleven-inch shells and then worked feverishly stuffing wet bedding into the hatchway to keep sparks and flames away from the five-and-a-half-inch shells below.[20]

Soon the *Oregon* pumped shells into the *Oquendo* from nearly point blank range of eight hundred yards. It was too much. With all of his guns knocked out of commission, fires spreading rapidly, and his decks littered with dead and dying sailors, the *Oquendo*'s captain finally gave the order to head for shore. He remained on board his beached and burning ship to the last. As the last handful of officers and crewmen urged him to join them in abandoning the crippled vessel he suddenly clasped his chest and collapsed to the deck. Perhaps the humiliation of defeat was too much for his heart to bear, and it just stopped beating. His comrades tenderly covered his body with a flag before they went over the side.[21]

On the *Oregon*, one of Captain Clark's officers urged him to finish off the crippled Spanish ship, but he answered, "No, that's a dead cock in the pit. The others can attend to her. We'll push on for the two [the *Vizcaya* and the *Cristóbal Colón*] ahead." White flags soon appeared on the *Oquendo*, and the sailors aboard the *Texas*, which was just then catching up with the faster Spanish vessel, burst into cheers at the sight of the flaming vessel joining Cervera's flagship on the beach. From the bridge, however, Captain Philip yelled an admonishment at his jubilant crewmen. "Don't cheer boys; those poor devils are dying."[22]

The two Spanish torpedo boat destroyers had similar luck. Although the American capital ships concentrated on chasing down their opposite numbers, they did turn their secondary batteries on the small English-built vessels. One Spanish officer later commented sorrowfully that "the Americans sprang on the *Plutón* and *Furor* like cats on two mice. We couldn't even bite, the Americans were too quick." Lieutenant Commander Richard Wainwright's armed yacht *Gloucester* headed straight for the *Plutón* which was the last Spanish ship out of the harbor and which, momentarily, turned to the east instead of following all of its sister ships. The proximity of the *Gloucester*, however, and the speed with which it was closing on his craft quickly convinced the captain of the Spanish destroyer that his only hope for escape lay to the west and he turned about.[23]

American shot and shell quickly riddled the lightly armored Spanish destroyers. Aboard the *Furor* one shell destroyed a shell room, while another hit the hatch of a boiler ventilator, causing the engine to lose pressure and slowing the vessel down just when speed was most important for the little craft's survival. A Spanish boatswain was literally cut in half by a projectile, and half of his body fell in among the tiller-ropes causing them to be useless until shipmates could lift the grisly mess out of the way. Finally, with his rudder disabled and his ship nearly shot to pieces, the *Furor*'s captain ordered his helmsman to try to reach shore. He never made it. An officer on board the *New York* watched as a shot pierced the *Furor*'s boiler. The rapidly escaping steam reminded him of an ostrich feather "that leaped five hundred feet into the air." The little vessel blew up with a roar and sank almost vertically, stern first, into the sea near Punta Cabrera. Almost fifty of its 70-man crew died.[24]

The *Plutón* was not in much better shape. It had begun to take on water when its captain realized that the only hope for the survival of many of his crewmen was to head for the beach. A projectile from one of the American ships soon changed things. It roared into the *Plutón*'s forward boilers, blowing pieces of them up through the deck and making it impossible for men in the stern to communicate with those in the bow. Almost immediately, the little ship scraped up on the beach just west of Cabañas, allowing its surviving crewmen to scamper to the relative safety ashore. It must have been sweet revenge for Commander Wainwright, who had been the executive officer of the ill-fated *Maine* when it met its end in Havana harbor.[25]

American sailors switched roles as soon as the firing stopped. Now, instead of doing their utmost to destroy their opponents, they worked just as hard to save the lives of those Spaniards who struggled to stay afloat in the water or who suffered from wounds and were still aboard the burning wreckage of their ships. Commander Wainwright ordered three boats lowered from the *Gloucester*, and volunteers immediately pulled toward the wrecked *Plutón*. The sailors pulled as many men as they could out of the water and either returned to the *Gloucester* or rowed ashore and deposited their human flotsam on the beach before going back for more.

Boarding the wrecks and rescuing those who were too badly injured to make it into the water was a more difficult task. Some, like a young lieutenant on the *Furor*, were badly mangled. This officer was not so seriously injured at first that he could not jump into the water before his ship went down, but he somehow got his foot entangled in its propeller, wrenching it off at the ankle. He was still able to work his way to the beach where he used a remnant of clothing to fashion a rude tourniquet for himself.[26]

When nothing more could be done aboard the *Plutón*, Ensign John T. Edson and a boat crew from the *Gloucester* pulled for the burning *Infanta María Theresa* about two hundred yards from the shore. The surf breaking around the flagship was too rough to attempt to load the Spanish casualties directly into the cutter. Edson decided to try to get a line from the ship to the beach where it could be secured and used as a lifeline. Unable to speak Spanish, Edson held up a piece of rope and, through pantomime, indicated to the Spaniards that they were to throw him one end of a rope. A rope soon sailed over the water to the cutter, and, although it was old and not likely to hold up to much stress, it was the only rope on board that had not already burned up. Edson then asked for a volunteer to swim the line ashore, and Otto Brown quickly jumped up, looped the rope around his neck and jumped into the surf.

Brown found the swimming to be very difficult, and he tired rapidly. Finally, he had to give up. The cutter meanwhile was also moving closer to the shore and picked up an almost exhausted Brown. "Brown," the ensign said, "you were a little too hasty. I didn't mean you to jump overboard at the present time. I was getting the boat a little nearer before I sent you off."

Finally, the boat reached a point that was about as near to the beach as it could go, and Brown, by this time somewhat recovered from his early escapade, again volunteered for the job of taking the line to the beach. Boatswain's Mate Peter Keller also volunteered. Both men reached land safely and quickly tied off the line to a tree. The rescue could now begin in earnest.

Many Spaniards had already stripped down to their undershirts and drawers and swum to the beach, including Admiral Cervera and his son, Lieutenant Angel Cervera. After the arrival of the American rescuers, many of the crewmen still aboard their ship jumped into the water near the cutter, and the Americans hauled them aboard until the small boat was full. The rescue vessel then made toward shore. Upon reaching a point about seventy-five yards out Edson put the men back into the water near the safety line where Brown and Keller waited to help them the rest of the way to the beach. After three or four trips the *Gloucester*'s gig appeared and joined in, measurably increasing the efficiency of the operation. There was some concern that the *María Theresa*'s forward powder magazine might remain unflooded and could blow up at any minute if the flames reached it. Some individual shells were already exploding in the fire and heat making the rescue work even that much more dangerous. The ship had run aground with some of its big guns still loaded, and when the fire reached them the heat worked its way through the steel breeches and cooked off the rounds in the chambers. One of these shells struck dangerously close to the *Gloucester*'s cutter.

More and more Spanish seamen made it to the beach as the rescuers worked feverishly to evacuate the ship before the fires reached the forward magazine. Armed Cubans also soon appeared along the shore headed for the sailors. Boatswain's Mate Keller quickly intervened and asked the first Cuban he saw, in rather fractured Spanish, to point out to him his commander. After being directed to "el capitan," the American remonstrated with him that these unarmed, half-naked men on the sand were prisoners of war of the United States, and he and his men were to cause them no harm. The Cuban officer accepted that, and a potential bloodbath was averted.

Finally the *Gloucester*'s gig deposited the last of the Spanish crewmen on the beach and prepared to return to its ship. Admiral Cervera was among those on the beach, and Keller and Seaman Brown, through several successive trips through the surf, escorted the admiral, his son, Captain Concas, and a few other members of the admiral's staff out to the boat.

Upon arrival back at the *Gloucester*, Commander Wainwright had his chief boatswain's mate pipe this high-ranking prisoner and his staff aboard as if they had been long time allies instead of recent enemies. The admiral had somehow secured a coat, a white sailor's cap, and a torn pair of trousers by the time he reached the American ship. There were about a hundred prisoners aboard already, including the commanding officers of the *Plutón* and the *Furor*, and the officers of the *Gloucester* did everything in their power to alleviate their dismal situation. They fed them, provided them with clothing from their own wardrobes, and looked to the medical needs of those who had suffered wounds.[27]

Meanwhile, the heavier American ships continued to pummel the last two Spanish vessels. As the *Brooklyn* closed the distance between itself and the *Vizcaya* Commodore Schley called down from the bridge to Ship's Yeoman George H. Ellis for a reading. Ellis, who had been prudently shielding himself from enemy fire by standing behind the forward gun turret, immediately stepped out onto the open deck with his stadimeter. He had no sooner called back up that the enemy ship was now but 1,400 yards away than an enemy shell decapitated him, splattering four nearby sailors with his blood.[28]

At about the same time, and in the same general part of the ship, an unusual drama was playing out. One of the starboard six-pounders jammed, and efforts to extract the shell resulted in its separation — leaving the projectile stuck in the barrel. One of the Marine gunners from the idle port-side six-pounder battery volunteered to try plunging a rammer into the muzzle of the piece to drive the round back out through the breech. This would not have been an easy task had the seas been calm and had there been no hostile fire. But the enemy shells and bullets along with the fierce concussion of the *Brooklyn*'s own turret guns directly overhead made it almost impossible. Nevertheless, the Marine got to work. The gun barrel was too hot to hold onto so he had to hang onto a Jacob's ladder with one hand and try to maneuver the rammer with the other. After several attempts he had to admit defeat. Almost immediately, a fellow Marine took his place, but he met with no more success than had his comrade. Yet a third Marine, 23-year-old Harry MacNeal, stepped forward to make another attempt. If he also proved unsuccessful, the gun would have to be abandoned until after the battle. MacNeal swung into action. Each time one of the big guns overhead fired it nearly knocked him overboard, but at last he was able to dislodge the stubborn projectile. The gun crew immediately put the gun back into action, and MacNeal, according to one of his officers, "resumed his duties as coolly as if what he had done was a matter of every day routine."[29]

The gunners on the *Iowa* skipped their 13-inch shells across the waves toward the Spanish ships like a small boy skips a stone across the surface of a millpond. One Spanish officer noted that "the skipping ... shells appeared to slide along the surface of the water and hunt for a seam in our armor.... Three of these monster projectiles penetrated the hull of the *Vizcaya* and exploded there before we started for the shore." After about an hour and a half of steady pounding, the *Vizcaya* had absorbed all the punishment it could take. Fires now roared out of control both fore and aft. Its five-and-a-half-inch guns had proved to be only slightly better than totally useless. Breeches would not close, firing pins malfunctioned, and the condition of the ammunition meant that some of the gun crews had to load seven and eight rounds before finding one that would fire. Casualties were so heavy that soon there were not even enough men to operate the few guns that remained functional. In a desperate attempt to salvage something from his awful predicament, Captain Antonio Eulate ordered his helmsman to turn sharply to port. He would try to ram the *Brooklyn*, but the American ship matched the maneuver. Worse for Eulate, however, was the fact that when his ship turned away from shore it presented its broadside to the forward turret guns of the *Oregon*, which was close behind. A thirteen-inch shell in his port bow, along with his inability to close on the *Brooklyn*, caused Eulate to turn back to starboard. Then, after a hurried consultation with some of his officers, he decided that they had defended their nation's honor to the best of their ability. Continuing to fight would only lengthen the casualty list, so he finally gave the order to head for shore just east of Asseraderos. And so that the Americans would not have the satisfaction of capturing the ship's beautiful silk battle flag, he ordered someone to hoist a fresh one and lower and destroy the one that had flown throughout the fight.[30]

The *Oregon* and the *Brooklyn* recognized the inevitable and wasted no more energy or ammunition on the *Vizcaya* as they continued to chase the *Cristóbal Colón*. As the *Texas* drew near, its officers observed the devastated condition of the *Vizcaya*, but there was still no evidence of a white surrender flag. True, her stern flag was no longer flying, but the Americans were not sure if this indicated an intention to lower all her flags or if gunfire had merely shot this one away. "But we could not fire on her," Captain Philip recalled, "even if she had not surrendered. Flames were shooting from her deck fore and aft, and as her nose touched the beach two tremendous explosions literally shook her to pieces." An officer aboard the doomed vessel later wrote that "while we were walking the deck, headed shoreward, we could hear the roar of the flames under our feet above the voice of the artillery. The *Vizcaya*'s hull bellowed like a blast furnace." Meanwhile, Spanish survivors hauled down their ship's battle flag and cut up the precious emblem of their bravery to keep it out of the hands of the soon-to-be victorious Americans. One of them, badly wounded and apparently knowing that he could not live much longer, took a piece of the flag and wrapped it around him before he died.[31]

Again the victorious American sailors metamorphosed from warriors to saviors as they got rescue operations underway to save the men of the *Vizcaya*. Captain Evans ran the *Iowa* in as close as possible before lowering his boats to begin shuttling Spaniards off of their ship and onto his. The torpedo boat *Ericsson* and the converted yacht *Hist* were close by, and Evans signaled them to assist. This rescue was as difficult, and as dangerous, as that of the *Maria Theresa* crewmen. Still-loaded cannons discharged when the heat became excessive, and one sailor informed his father that "we had a sample shot from every piece of ordnance in the ship. Every minute or so the fire would reach a box of rapid-fire ammunition and an explosion very much like a 'flower pot' would occur, thin, feathery trails of smoke shooting far heavenward in a dozen different directions."[32]

The honorable reception extended to Admiral Cervera by the officers and crew of the *Gloucester* was echoed by the men of the *Iowa* toward Captain Eulate of the *Vizcaya*. The captain, bloodied by three wounds and weakened by a loss of blood, was hauled aboard the American ship from a boat filled with wounded sailors. Since, unlike his admiral, he had not been forced to abandon his ship in his underwear, he was still fully clothed, although disheveled and with a bloody makeshift bandage around his head. When presented to Captain Evans he sadly unbuckled his sword belt and kissed the hilt of his sword before offering it as a typical token of surrender. "I never felt so sorry for a man in all my life," Evans later wrote, and after symbolically accepting the sword he returned it to the gallant Spaniard.

Eulate appreciated Evans's gesture and began accompanying him below to his cabin for treatment of his wounds. Just as the two officers were leaving the deck, the Spaniard stopped and saluted his burning ship with upraised hand. "Adios, *Vizcaya*!" His salute was returned almost immediately with a deafening roar as the once proud ship's forward magazine blew up.[33]

By this time, Admiral Sampson's *New York* had finally caught up to the chase, and he ordered the *Indiana* and the *Iowa* to break off and return to blockade duty. He did not want the two remaining Spanish ships, the *Reina Mercedes* and the *Alvarado*, to slip out of the harbor and attack the unprotected American ships at Siboney.

The American ships were having a hard time gaining on the faster *Cristóbal Colón*. Without its long range guns, however, the Spaniard would be a sitting duck if the American battleships got within range. Still, it might be able to outrun the *Oregon* and *Texas* while outfighting the faster but more lightly armored *Brooklyn*. What followed was a sea race, and the heroes were not the gunners on the respective vessels, but the overworked engine room crews in the stifling heat below decks. The guns on both sides fell silent, but the chase continued. Although the Spanish ship had the advantage of speed over most of the Americans, it was following a course approximately parallel to the coastline while the *Oregon* pursued a straight, and therefore somewhat shorter, course. Slowly the American ship gained on the Spaniard.[34]

Finally, at a little after noon, Captain Clark ordered a ranging shot. The gunnery officer estimated the range at 9,500 yards, but the shot fell short. Another hour went by before those on the *Oregon* noticed a slackening of the *Colón*'s speed. The Spanish stokers had by this time used up all of the ship's high grade fuel and were now forced to use an inferior coal taken aboard at Santiago, thereby slowing their speed. The range had now closed sufficiently that the *Oregon*'s occasional shells were falling close enough alongside the *Colón* to cause Captain José de Paredes to consider surrender rather than face the fate of the rest of the squadron. "I decided to run ashore and lose the ship," he later wrote in his official battle report, "rather than sacrifice in vain the lives of all the men who ... had fought with brilliant heroism and great discipline and coolness." At about 2 P.M., he turned his ship toward shore near the mouth of the Tarquino River, ordered the sea valves opened, and, still at full speed, ran it up onto the beach. His ship had made it about fifty miles.[35]

The crewmen of the victorious American ships hardly had time to catch their breaths after the firing ceased when Admiral Sampson sent word that he had a report of one, or maybe two, Spanish warships bearing down on the remainder of the blockading fleet off Santiago. His information was that they were the *Pelayo* and the *Emperador Carlos V*, and he immediately ordered the *Brooklyn* and the *Oregon* to meet and either capture or destroy them. Captain Francis Cook, of the *Brooklyn*, was doubtful if the *Pelayo* would have been capable of crossing the Atlantic from Spain so quickly, but stranger things had happened in the emergencies of war, and he wasted no time ordering full power from the engine rooms and steaming eastward.

Captain Evans of the *Iowa* likewise received word of the approaching threat from the commander of the *Harvard*. Evans's situation was made a little more difficult by the fact that he had taken about three hundred prisoners on board by this time. It would take too long to land them all on the beach before responding to the alarm. He could not, in good conscience, merely leave them under guard on his decks where they stood a good chance of becoming casualties to the gunfire of their own country's warship. And he could hardly quarter them below decks out of security considerations for the safety of his own ship and crew. He finally went to Captain Eulate and told him that he was putting him and his men under a parole of honor to do nothing to assist the unknown vessel in its upcoming fight with the *Iowa*. He then ordered the prisoners into protected areas and cleared for action.[36]

After a short while lookouts aboard the *Brooklyn* made out the outline of a large warship heading toward them at a fairly rapid speed. Even though the *Oregon* had stayed behind to attempt to salvage the *Cristóbal Colón* and had not accompanied the *Brooklyn*, Captain Cook sent his men to their battle stations. Alone and with ammunition at a low supply after having expended a great deal of it over the previous few hours, the American ship nevertheless pushed forward. The men were confident — maybe even a little cocky — and eager to do battle with this latest arrival from Spain.

As the ships drew nearer to one another, a gunner's mate brought Captain Cook the ship's recognition book of naval vessels. From the looks of the approaching stranger, it could be neither the *Pelayo* nor the *Carlos V*. The Spanish ship that most nearly matched the silhouette in the book was the new cruiser *Cardinal Cisneros*. This puzzled Cook, as the latest naval intelligence he had indicated that this ship was still in Spain and not yet completed. Commodore Schley continued to study the stranger, perplexed by its peacetime white color. "I don't believe she is Spanish," he concluded. But then he, too, consulted the recognition book and exclaimed, "By Jove! It is the *Pelayo*, after all!"[37]

Captain Cook called up to the signal bridge to see if the lookout could identify the other ship's flag. "Not yet, sir," he called back. But then, a few moments later, "We have raised her colors, sir, and she is Spanish." Schley turned to Cook and told him to send his men to their battle stations "and start an eight-inch shell for her when I give the word." There was still a tiny amount of doubt in Schley's mind, however, and he called up to the signal bridge to reconfirm the nationality of the other ship. The original opinion was confirmed, but something just did not look right to the commodore. "Cook," the commodore spoke again, "that fellow is not at quarters. His guns are turned away from us. He is not up to snuff. Watch him closely, and the moment he sends his men to quarters or moves a turret, let drive. Give him everything you have. We will sink him in twenty minutes, unless he gets a shot under our [armor] belt." Likewise, aboard the *Iowa*, Captain Evans ordered his gunners to open fire as soon as they had closed the distance to within 5,000 yards.[38]

By this time the sun had set, and the captain of the mystery ship began to worry about the intentions of these American warships bearing down on him. It was obvious that the *Brooklyn* was not just out for a Sunday cruise as it rushed through the water toward his ship. Perhaps the Americans mistook his ship for something it was not. He therefore ordered a spotlight on his ship to play full upon his flag so that there could be no misidentification. It was the flag of Austria, not Spain![39]

A short time later the commander of the Austrian battleship *Maria Theresa* was rowed over to the *Brooklyn* to pay a call on Commodore Schley. Schley told him that the only thing that kept the Americans from opening fire was the peaceful demeanor of the other warship. "If you had sent your men to quarters or moved a turret I should have raked you," he told his opposite number. "Your flag is so like Spain's, saving that you have a white stripe where she has yellow, that it is hard to tell them apart at any considerable distance, and I came very near letting drive at you." The Austrian acknowledged his good fortune and then, since it was now full dark, asked how far from shore his ship should spend the night to avoid any other accidental confrontations. "Twenty miles off the coast, at least," Schley advised. "This is a bad coast tonight for strangers." The Austrian thanked him for his courtesy and took his ship forty miles off just to be safe.[40]

This second great American naval victory of the war was almost as lopsided as that of Commodore Dewey at Manila. The *Iowa*'s captain rejoiced that "God and the gunners had had their day." Yeoman Ellis was the only American killed by hostile fire and Fireman J. Burns of the *Brooklyn* was the only one wounded. Losses among the Spanish were staggering. Over 14 percent, or 323 men, were killed and another 151 suffered wounds. Commodore Schley later remarked that "there is no fun in being under fire. When you hear a man say that he likes to fight you can tell him with truth that the liars are not all dead."[41]

The decisive factor in the battle appears to have been the relative accuracy of the gunnery displayed by the respective sides. Captain Evans's remark about the excellent work of the American gunners notwithstanding, the crews of the 8-inch guns hit their targets only about three times for every one hundred rounds fired — and they were the most accurate of all. The six-pounder guns had to fire a hundred times to effect a single hit on the target. As abominable as these firing statistics appear to be, however, the Americans seem to have been better shots than their opponents. The Spanish sailors had had virtually no target practice, and only the *Brooklyn*, the *Texas*, and the *Iowa* were hit at all, and none of them suffered any irreparable damage.[42]

Farther west Admiral Sampson signaled Captain Clark to send a prize crew from the *Oregon* to try to re-float the *Colón*. These men had a very difficult task before them. By the time the Americans got on board there was fifteen feet of water in the engine rooms making any salvage attempt extremely difficult. Despite these difficulties the men worked energetically. At one point it was necessary to deploy the *Colón*'s anchor. As the *Oregon*'s chief boatswain's mate made the necessary preparations he heard a flurry of Spanish commands. He looked around to find the *Colón*'s apparently inebriated boatswain's mate issuing orders as if he were still in charge. The American sailor brooked no insubordination from American crewmen under his control, and he certainly was not going to allow this interference in his assigned task. He drew his revolver, pointed it at the Spaniard, and announced, "I'll have you understand that *I* am chief boatswain's mate of this ship now!"[43]

Working tirelessly through the night the salvage crew made little progress. They finally decided, at about 11 o'clock, that they could not save the *Colón* and headed back to the *Oregon*. They had barely got away from the damaged ship when it began to list dangerously to starboard, and within minutes the once-proud ship lay on its side in the shallow water near the beach.[44]

Although unable to save the Spanish ship, the Americans had been able to remove all the wounded enemy sailors. They also found a veritable menagerie on board. On the forecastle they found five cows, which they cut loose and urged over the side and toward shore. There were also chickens, two cats, a dog, and a coal-black pig, which they named "Dennis Blanco" and adopted as the *Oregon*'s mascot.[45]

André Proctor, the assistant engineer of the *Gloucester*, wrote how grateful the Spaniards were to their recent enemies. "They wound their arms around our men's necks, and covered them with kisses." Of course this shower of affection was rather alien to the Americans. "One man tried it on me," Proctor continued, "but I couldn't stand it, and had to repulse him."[46]

Admiral Sampson, the Johnny-come-lately of the battle, had no problem taking the lion's share of the credit for the outcome. "The fleet under my command," he wrote in his first official notification to Washington of the battle, "offers the nation as a Fourth of July present the whole of Cervera's fleet." He made no mention of the very major part that Commodore Schley played, and thereby engendered that man's undying antipathy.[47]

On shore that morning Colonel McClernand entered General Shafter's tent and found him once again on his sick bed. Both men may have wondered how much longer the commander could hold up, even in this limited manner, to the rigors of active campaigning in the tropics. McClernand suggested that, with the Americans and Cubans in fairly good positions from which to begin a siege of Santiago, it might be a good time to demand the garrison's surrender. Shafter agreed and prepared a message to be sent in to General Toral under a flag of truce. It was short and to the point. Toral had until 10 A.M. on July 4 to surrender. "Unless you surrender," read the note, "I shall be obliged to shell Santiago de Cuba." Such a bombardment of the city would almost surely create unwelcome collateral casualties among the civilians, so Shafter asked Toral to inform the civilians of this latest turn of events so they could evacuate before the deadline. Toral's reply was equally succinct. He would not capitulate. Perhaps Colonel Federico Escario's arrival from Manzanillo the day before with 3,000 troops buoyed his hopes for the future.[48]

By the time Toral's answer reached Shafter, early that evening, preliminary reports of Commodore Schley's victory over Cervera had arrived. With no more Spanish ships to worry about, the American fleet could use its long-range cannons to pummel Santiago from the sea while Shafter's artillery applied pressure from inland. If necessary, Shafter reasoned, his Army could starve the defenders into submission.

Toral remained adamant. He would not surrender.

On the morning of July 4, meanwhile, streams of civilians moved out of the city headed for the relative safety of El Caney. They were in desperate straits. Many were sick; all were hungry. As future General John J. Pershing, then a lieutenant in the Tenth Cavalry, observed them he was moved to state that "the suffering of the innocent is not the least of the horrors of war."[49]

In light of the continuing evacuation, by which perhaps 80 percent of the civilian population left the city, Shafter postponed his bombardment and temporarily turned his attention to more humane matters. He wanted to obtain the release of Navy Lieutenant Hobson and the seven *Merrimac* crewmen who had been captured with him. On July 5, therefore, he unilaterally released twenty-eight Spanish prisoners of war. The next day, Lieutenant Miley, of Shafter's staff, met with a Spanish major under the shade of a large ceiba tree between the opposing lines. He took with him three blindfolded Spanish officers who had been captured. He would allow his counterpart to select one of them to be exchanged for Hobson. The major recognized a wounded acquaintance among the trio and chose him. Since none of the seven men captured with Hobson were officers, the arrangements for their exchange were much less formal. Seven captured enlisted men were traded for them. The American soldiers welcomed Hobson into their lines as if he had single-handedly won the war.[50]

With surrender negotiations apparently at an impasse, Shafter notified Toral that unless he surrendered unconditionally by 3 P.M., July 10, a previously threatened naval barrage would begin one hour later. In the meantime, the first reinforcements from the United States—volunteer regiments from Massachusetts, Illinois, Michigan, Ohio, and the District of Columbia—had arrived and were taking up positions in the firing line. "If they [the Spaniards] don't [surrender]," wrote a bloodthirsty Michigan volunteer in a letter home, "we will blow them off the face of the earth. We want to leave one Spaniard alive to tell the queen how it was done."[51]

At 4 P.M. on July 10, the *Brooklyn* and the *Indiana* lobbed a few eight-inch shells into the city without causing any measurable damage to the Spanish military position. The next morning, the *New York* joined in a three-and-a-half-hour bombardment, but General Shafter had been so concerned about the Navy's big shells landing by accident among his own troops that he had specified targets only in the western part of the city. The fire was fairly accurate, but there were no significant military targets in that part of town. Shafter's artillery, out on the hills surrounding the city, also joined in for about two hours. Spanish artillery could not, of course, reach the American ships, but it put up a spirited reply to the Army's guns. And the infantry on both sides also traded volleys vigorously. A trooper from the Tenth U.S. Cavalry accorded more value to this exchange of fire than was warranted when he wrote to a friend that "the cannons and Gatling guns roared. While the cannons tore away their defenses, the Gatling guns mowed their men. Our dynamite gun, nearly every shot, blew a company of them a hundred feet in the air." One must wonder whether this man was even anywhere near the firing line that day or not. Before the Navy could add the fire of the twelve- and thirteen-inch guns of the *Oregon* and the *Massachusetts*, Shafter postponed further firing in the face of renewed negotiations.[52]

Besides the occasional flurries of small arms and cannon fire, life in the trenches overlooking Santiago was marked by other problems for the soldiers. The daytime heat was almost unendurable, the only respite coming from the rains. And what rains they were! An Ohio officer was convinced that the only difference between the wet season in Cuba and the dry season was that "in the dry season it rains all the time, and in the rainy season it rains a good deal more." During the night of July 11, the rain was especially heavy. "The rain came down like it was poured from buckets," recalled a New York sergeant, while a Massachusetts officer thought that it could be described more accurately as "coming down in tubfulls." A New York officer, deciding to make the most of a dismal situation, wrapped his rain poncho around him and sat on a wooden box letting the rain run off his hat and wash over his bare feet. In the midst of this deluge an enlisted man poked his head out of his small two-man tent and saw the lieutenant sitting in the rain. "Sir," he yelled above the roar of the storm, "I wish to report that my tent has sprung a leak and is sinking fast."[53]

The weather, along with the rigors normally associated with active campaigning, had also reduced the Army's clothing to rags. An inspection of the Twenty-first U.S. Infantry Regiment late in July revealed the destitute state of the soldiers. "The men are filthy," the report disclosed. "Campaign hats are worn out, full of holes, shapeless, and sweat through. Blue flannel shirts are rent, ... sleeves tattered to the elbows. Trousers are mud-bedaubed below the knee, and shine from grease and dirt accumulations above the knee. The damp soil and humid climate causes feet to swell; then the shoes become too tight; enlarged joints, corns, etc., follow and the men cut or slit their shoes for ease. In many cases toes project." On the very day this report was written workers at Siboney began unloading a ship that had been there for a week. It contained, among other supplies, 5,000 blue Army shirts and trousers, 25,000 sets of underwear and hats, almost 25,000 shoes, and 14,000 complete canvas uniforms. This illustrated the sad fact that throughout the Cuban campaign much of the men's suffering came about not because the means to alleviate it were not available, but that they were still on ships or in warehouses somewhere.[54]

Major General Nelson Miles and a contingent of volunteers had arrived off Santiago, and the Commanding General of the Army seemed anxious to put his troops to work against the fortifications guarding the harbor entrance. Before committing them to action, however, Miles, Shafter, and Toral sat down together on July 13 under the large shade tree between the lines to discuss the situation further. It was obvious that Toral knew he was finished, but he was too proud a man to go down without a fight. And, as he pointed out to the Americans, his government expected him and all its military commanders to continue to fight as long as his Army had food to eat and ammunition to expend. Even so he agreed to consult his government one more time. Secretary of War Alger, meanwhile, authorized Shafter to let Toral know that once he and his men had given up, the United States would transport them on American ships back to Spain. Miles thought Toral was simply stalling and urged Shafter to discontinue negotiations and attack the city. Shafter counseled moderation. He was sure that a Spanish surrender was imminent.[55]

By this time it was obvious to all that the Santiago garrison was doomed either to surrender or to starve. It seemed wiser now to risk losing part of the empire in a peace settlement than to fight on and risk losing all of it. Toral informed Shafter on the morning of July 14 that he was ready to appoint commissioners to work out details of capitulation. The commissioners from both sides met that afternoon. The Americans further conceded that Spanish officers could retain their sidearms, but the Spanish negotiators wanted to keep all their small arms as well as their military records. They also wanted the United States to allow the Cuban volunteers in their Army to stay in Cuba rather than be transported to Spain. The talks were inconclusive, the Spanish claiming that they could not sign formal surrender documents without express permission from Spain. Officials in Washington would in no way allow the defeated Army to retain its arms. "The way to surrender," wired Adjutant General Henry Corbin privately to Shafter, "is to surrender, and this should be fully impressed on General Toral."[56]

Commissioners signed the formal document at 6 P.M. on July 16. Not only did its terms apply to the beleaguered garrison of Santiago but to all of the other 12,000 Spanish troops in eastern Cuba. Under the terms of the agreement, of course, all hostilities between Spanish and American forces in eastern Cuba ceased immediately. And since the United States had nothing to gain by being vindictive, it allowed the defeated soldiers to keep their personal property, and for the officers this meant even their sidearms. Spanish forces agreed to help clear the underwater mines from the entrance to the harbor so American ships bringing food and other supplies could sail right up to the city. The Americans agreed to transport all the Spanish troops back to Spain, but they allowed any of the Cuban auxiliaries who had fought for Spain to remain on the island after signing a parole promising not to take up arms against the Americans for as long as the war with Spain continued. Spanish officers had also asked that their men be allowed to take their individual weapons back with them to Spain, but American officials said no.[57]

The next morning, General Shafter sent word to all general officers and their staffs to report to corps headquarters to witness the formal surrender ceremony. Admiral Sampson declined to send a representative ashore to participate, and General Garcia refused Shafter's invitation upon learning that the American commander intended to retain Spanish civil officials in power in Santiago. Nevertheless, when all of his officers had assembled, Shafter, with General Wheeler by his side, led them on horseback out through the lines and toward Santiago, accompanied by two troops of the Second U.S. Cavalry and a delegation from the Ninth U.S. Infantry. The entourage passed the huge tree, under whose branches so much of the preliminary agreement had been worked out, and rode into a large field to meet its Spanish counterpart.[58]

As Shafter and Toral shook hands in friendly greeting they presented quite a contrast. The American commander wore the same uniform, somewhat rumpled now, that he had worn for the last three weeks while Toral was resplendent in his blue linen uniform trimmed in gold lace and with medals on his chest. Some of those present — some of the Americans at least — might have thought back to another surrender scene thirty-three years before when another victorious American general, wearing a mud bespattered campaign uniform accepted the surrender of a general whose clothing was immaculate. Their names, respectively, were Ulysses S. Grant and Robert E. Lee. Shafter showed himself to be just as magnanimous as Grant had been when he presented to Toral the sword and spurs worn by General Vara del Rey when he was killed at El Caney. He told the surprised Spanish leader that it was the wish of the American officer who had captured these items that they return with Toral's men to Spain and be given to the dead general's family.

After this exchange of pleasantries the ceremony began. A Spanish naval officer stepped toward Shafter to formally surrender the only remaining Spanish gunboat in the harbor. Shafter apologized for not dismounting, as protocol dictated, but explained that his size made remounting very difficult. Toral then took up a position in front of his one-hundred-man delegation, drew his sword, and said simply: "I surrender the Spanish troops under my command, and this place." Shafter, facing him about twenty feet away, accepted the surrender on behalf of the government of the United States. Finally, a small representative body of Spanish troops filed past the Americans and ceremoniously stacked their weapons.[59]

The group then rode through the Spanish lines and into the city of Santiago. Hundreds of Spanish soldiers lined the road to get a look at the Americans. These troops still had their rifles, but they were true to the surrender document and posed no threat. In addition to the soldiers, the Americans passed by numerous dead and decaying horses whose foul smell did little to make the ride enjoyable. Human graves were also visible along the road, and vultures and other predators had partially uncovered the contents of some of them. "The odor," according to a news correspondent who accompanied the delegation, "was horrible in the extreme."[60]

The officers from both sides conferred again inside the governor's palace until just before noon, when they came out into the plaza. At precisely 12 o'clock, the cavalry band struck up "The Star Spangled Banner" while Captain William H. McKittrick and First Lieutenant John D. Miley, of Shafter's staff, and Lieutenant Joseph Wheeler of his father's staff, raised the Stars and Stripes to the top of the flagstaff on the roof of the palace. Out along the hills outside of town, American artillery boomed in salute, and the soldiers yelled until they were hoarse. Throughout the process of negotiation that ultimately brought hostilities to an end there had

Soldiers celebrate news of the Spanish surrender in Cuba (U.S. Army Military History Institute).

been an undercurrent of dissatisfaction in the American camps. Many, notably Theodore Roosevelt, thought General Shafter was wasting time trying to talk the Spaniards into surrendering and favored an attack on the enemy works and capture of the city by force of arms. By the time the opposing commanders signed the surrender documents, however, much of this sentiment had disappeared. In its place was relief that a direct assault had *not* become necessary. As the colonel of the Thirty-fourth Michigan observed, "If we had been ordered to charge their works they would have piled us up 10 deep, and then we could never have reached them."[61]

The signing of the armistice did not mean the end to the fighting for the Americans. They now fought sickness instead of enemy soldiers. Yellow fever, the most dreaded of the tropical diseases, made its appearance in the Fifth Corps on July 6, and Army medical officers immediately took what steps they could to control its spread. Compounding the problem, of course, was the fact that no one was sure just how the disease spread from one person to another. Medical science had not yet isolated the *Aedes aegypti* mosquito as the guilty party, but doctors believed that better personal hygiene would probably help keep a man healthy. It was another mosquito-borne disease, however, that was far more common than Yellow Jack. It is estimated that malaria probably affected 75 percent of Shafter's men while they were in Cuba. Victims usually suffered several days—perhaps a week—of fever at the outset. But then, even after the fever broke, they were too weak to return to their normal military duties for some time.[62]

The treatment of fevers of all kinds had not, at least in some military hospitals, advanced much beyond the Middle Ages. One way in which medical personnel sought to reduce the patient's fever used both external and internal methods. First, they placed the ailing patient on a rubber sheet. Then, after dipping a bed sheet in ice-cold water, they wrung out the excess and placed it over the suffering soldier, making sure that it made contact with as much feverish skin as possible. An attendant then took a small block of ice and repeatedly rubbed it all over the wet sheet. When the man's teeth began to chatter uncontrollably the attendant removed the icy sheet and carefully patted him with dry towels until his skin was dry — but not warm — before returning him to his bed. (It was such treatment that, when applied to the wounded Confederate General "Stonewall" Jackson in 1863, led to a fatal onset of pneumonia.) And since this treatment only dealt with the patient's exterior symptoms he might also receive ice-water enemas to purge the fever from his interior.[63]

Colonel Charles R. Greenleaf, the Army's chief surgeon, handed down a list of recommendations within a week of the first malaria case's identification. Troops should pay special attention to keeping themselves clean and cooking their food in a sanitary manner. They should also have as little to do with Spaniards and Cubans as possible, since the prevalence of disease in these populations seemed to indicate a causative link. Although it was relatively easy to implement these suggestions once the importance was grasped, it was sometimes difficult to impress upon the volunteers how important these suggestions were to their continued well-being. Another of Colonel Greenleaf's prescriptions was for the soldiers to relocate their campsites every couple of days. He did not mean simply moving from one side of a road to the other. These relocations should be a minimum of two miles from previous sites, perhaps even up into the mountains where the air was cooler and incidence of disease was demonstrably less. Upon hearing of this, one young officer labeled the idea "absurd," confiding to his diary that "not one-third of our army could march five miles, so weakened are we by disease." The almost daily rains turned the roads and jungle trails into soupy mires, and the majority of the men were soon so weakened from sickness that they would not have been able to move from one camp to another even on hard, paved turnpikes.[64]

Efforts were also under way to recruit ten regiments of men immune to yellow fever for service in Cuba. Common belief was that once a man had survived a bout with the disease he built up immunity to recurrences. Four of these regiments of "immunes" were to be composed of African-Americans because of a presumed immunity to yellow fever within that race. These troops would arrive in Cuba as soon as possible and take over occupation duty from the Fifth Corps. Shafter's men could then return to the United States or some other duty station, perhaps Puerto Rico.

While waiting for the arrival of these replacement troops, the number of men struck down by fever continued to increase. On July 11, General Miles ordered the destruction of every building in Siboney that might have housed fever victims. Virtually the entire village soon lay in ashes, and still the fever cases crowded into the available facilities. Colonel Greenleaf petitioned General Shafter to send a company of men to assist his meager medical staff in caring for the sick, but Shafter was unwilling to weaken his combat force by even this small amount. The doctor remonstrated that battling yellow fever was just as important as battling the Spaniards, but Shafter was unmoved. Greenleaf, however, remained convinced of the importance of additional personnel at the hospital so he went over Shafter's head and appealed to General Miles. Miles did not want to order men to such duty, but he told the colonel of the Twenty-fourth Infantry to see if he could get even as few as a dozen volunteers to suit the doctor's needs. It was not to be a short-lived assignment. The men who volunteered had to be ready to spend as much time at this chore as conditions dictated. Knowing this, every man in the regiment stepped forward. They served valiantly, and in spite of the belief that, because they were black they would be safe from the fever, 95 percent of these supposedly immune men got sick.[65]

While the incidence of yellow fever among the troops seemed to draw the most attention from the press, dysentery was probably more widespread and caused more deaths. A Rough Rider wrote that "nearly everyone in camp is fairly putrid with dysentery. Chills come around each day to shake the majority of us to see if we are still alive. When the chills get tired, along comes a most diabolical kind of fever which is warranted to burn a man up entirely in just three hours; it usually stops a trifle short of that spontaneous combustion point, much to the disappointment of the poor victim."[66]

The longer the Army stayed around Santiago the longer grew the sick lists. By July 28, almost 4,300 men lay sick. This represented about one quarter of Shafter's force and did not take into account those men who had left the hospitals but were still too weak to do duty nor those in the early stages of disease who had yet to report themselves to the hospitals.[67]

On August 2, Shafter informed his superiors that he was becoming more and more concerned with the likelihood of a serious epidemic of yellow fever. He wanted to move his entire corps back to the United States. Surgeon General George Sternberg insisted that yellow fever did not, indeed could not, exist in higher altitudes, even in the tropics, so Secretary of War Alger repeated his earlier advice to Shafter. Stay in Cuba, but simply move the Army into the higher elevations north of Santiago. The poor transportation network in eastern Cuba and the high percentage of sick soldiers made any such move impossible.

Officials in Washington obviously did not appreciate the logistical difficulties facing Shafter. The single railroad into the interior was in disrepair, and even after it was put into running condition it was of such a small capacity that it would take weeks to remove the entire Army from the coastal fever zone. Theodore Roosevelt, never one to shy away from a confrontation or a headline, very matter-of-factly addressed his commander: "To keep us here ... will simply involve the destruction of thousands. There is no possible reason for not shipping the entire command North at once." He was convinced that half of the Army would die of disease if it had to remain where it was until the fever season ended in the fall. Most of the officers shared his opinion and directed a joint — "round robin" — letter to Shafter. Their note was perhaps a little more diplomatic in tone but no less forceful in content. "This army," they opined, "must be moved at once or it will perish." And Shafter received yet a third missive on the subject from the Army doctors on site. He then transmitted copies of this correspondence to Washington along with yet another personal plea to rescue his Army by transporting it back to the States. Then, as if to put even more emphasis on the abysmal conditions in Cuba, he ordered 500 caskets to be sent to him.[68]

CHAPTER 8

Eighth Corps to Manila

COMMODORE DEWEY'S DECISIVE VICTORY over Admiral Montojo raised a question. Now that Dewey had defeated the Spanish squadron, what was to become of the city of Manila? Although his ships could probably compel the city's surrender, Dewey did not have enough bluejackets or Marines on board to occupy it. The only solution was to raise another Army expeditionary corps as quickly as possible and dispatch it to the Philippines. Dewey estimated that a force of 5,000 men would be necessary.

The War Department chose Major General Wesley Merritt, the second most senior officer in the Army, to lead this command, designated the Eighth Army Corps, and on May 13, he wrote to the president asking that his force be increased to 14,000 men. He doubted that the level of training of the volunteers from the western states was adequate for the task ahead, so he also requested that regular troops make up the majority of his force. The Army's commanding general, Major General Nelson Miles, readily assented to a larger expedition, but balked at the notion of it having a predominance of regulars.[1]

Whatever the ultimate size of the force was to be, Army officials needed a campsite that was large enough to house it and that was near enough to the docks at San Francisco to make embarkation easy. They first set up Camp Merriam, near the Lombard Street entrance to the Presidio, but soon relocated the troops to a location about four miles west of the city, and a mile from the ocean, just south of the Presidio. The area had been the site of a racetrack, complete with infield pond. With the pond filled in the available camping and drilling space, christened Camp Merritt, was sufficient for several thousand men.

The location of this camp and the physical conditions surrounding it had little to recommend themselves to the soldiers. Several inches of sand covered the old racetrack, which made merely walking, much less drilling, very difficult. The sandy soil, combined with the windy, drizzly weather that seemed to predominate, meant that the men's tent pegs never really got a firm grip, and it was not uncommon for a soldier to have to claw his way out from under a pile of wet canvas after his tent had collapsed on him. "It is horrible," one man complained, and another was certain that the weather there was "as bad as could be imagined."[2]

The camp was close enough to the gaslights and entertainment of San Francisco to draw men into the city whenever they had time and money to spare. There were the usual restaurants, beer halls, and theaters. One establishment featured a belly dancer calling herself Little Egypt, who had supposedly scandalized fair-goers at Chicago's Columbian Exposition of 1892–1893. Among the other popular bawdy attractions were, according to an Oregon volunteer, "institutions that told the story of the bees and flowers in practical fashion."[3]

Camp Merritt was, first and foremost, a training facility to prepare raw recruits for active military service. The level of expertise that the incoming recruits exhibited was as widely varied as it had been at Camp Alger, Camp Thomas, or any of the other camps in the East. Sometimes the officers were as unfamiliar with military life as were their eager students and contented themselves with not much more than teaching their men how to march in formation. "If marching up a hill and marching down again," noted one rather callous observer, "is all that is necessary to constitute a soldier then most of the volunteer troops at the Presidio have nothing more to learn. By the same token," he went on, "if giving the orders that dispatch the soldiers aimlessly up and down the aforesaid elevation, and when that is done with mounting a pedestal for the adoration of the throngs of mothers, sisters, wives, and sweethearts who daily and hourly swarm through the camp, is essential to wearing shoulder straps successfully, the officers can throw away their blue books [Army Regulations] in the knowledge that they are letter perfect, in the art of war."[4]

On May 23, five companies of the Fourteenth U.S. Infantry Regiment — some of General Merritt's beloved regulars — as well as two volunteer regiments made up the first contingent of the Eighth Corps to depart for the seat of war. Brigadier General Thomas M. Anderson commanded them as they marched down the streets of San Francisco from the Presidio to the docks. The people of the city gave them a glorious sendoff, fueled in part by the fact that California's own volunteer regiment was among them. Virtually the entire police department marched ahead of the soldiers as the citizens cheered and waved. The crowds of well-wishers pushed into the street and made it difficult for the marching troops to retain any semblance of military precision. The citizens came well armed with flowers — long stemmed red roses, carnations, geraniums, pansies, violets, and sweet peas. They left the sidewalks to place their scented offerings over the men's shoulders, around their necks, and into their hands. Many just tossed their floral offerings into the path of the procession. American flags, likewise, were everywhere. It was hard to find a window anywhere along the parade route that was not decorated with the Stars and Stripes. San Franciscans offered small flags to the soldiers with as much enthusiasm as they had the flowers. These miniature symbols of patriotism soon showed up pinned to the soldiers' hats, protruding from rifle barrels, knapsacks, blanket rolls, and, in fact, every conceivable place on or about their persons.[5]

The triumphant march ended at the docks, where the men, some of them physically spent from their five-mile hike, boarded the waiting transports *Australia*, *City of Sydney*, and *City of Peking*. Actual departure was not immediate, and well-wishers crowded the decks for one last farewell to a son, husband, or friend. There simply was not room for all who wanted to come aboard, so others thronged the docks calling out their good-byes to the soldiers who lined the rails above them. Women threw bouquets of flowers or small, rolled up flags to the men as mementos of home. The soldiers responded with brass buttons from their uniforms. It took a couple of more days to get everything in order, and this first expedition steamed past Fort Point and out through the Golden Gate on the afternoon of May 25. Dozens of sightseeing craft accompanied the three liners out to sea, almost reluctant for them to leave.[6]

The U.S. Army had never before undertaken to move so many troops over such vast distances of water, and it was totally unprepared to do so. The government owned no troop ships so had to lease as many commercial vessels as possible. Army quartermasters eventually chartered fourteen ships and purchased two more with which to move the men, animals, and equipment of the Eighth Corps the 7,000 miles from San Francisco to the Philippines. The officers traveling on these ships, due to their rank, had staterooms, but the quarters provided for the men were not as comfortable. Carpenters had hurriedly built wooden bunks stacked three high in the enlisted men's quarters. Typically, each man had plenty of sleeping room as long as he was no taller than 5'9", nor wider than twenty-three inches. He also had a twenty-three-inch clearance between his straw-filled mattress and the woven wire springs of the next bunk above him. A two-foot wide aisle ran between each two rows. Most of the ships were also rigged with electric lights and ventilating equipment for the comfort of the troops, as well as galleys for turning out hot meals.[7]

Almost all of the troops making this trip were seeing the ocean for the first time. And as soon as the ships passed out of San Francisco's protected harbor, through the Golden Gate, and into the Pacific Ocean, the men encountered their first lesson in ocean travel—seasickness. A news correspondent traveling on a later ship that encountered an ocean storm commented on the amount of seasickness that followed. "Perhaps it is well to leave to the imagination the scenes on the *Newport* during the raging of the storm, certainly it would be unwise to chronicle the expletives which this record surprise of the Pacific wrenched from the pallid lips of those whose pleasant anticipations of a trip across summer seas had thus been rudely shattered." Seasickness affected large numbers of soldiers. "I thought," noted a North Dakota volunteer, "that I had cast up my entire internal organism." A regular cavalryman who left San Francisco on the fourth expedition discovered that most of his comrades refused to bear the "stigma" of having submitted to seasickness. By the second day at sea he found that he and one other man were the only ones who would admit to having been so afflicted. "And so I am forced to conclude," he wrote, "that the long, sad line along the ship's side last evening, and the unhappy sounds that punctuated the night watches below, were all a bad dream." On the ship carrying Nebraska volunteers the concept of seasickness had just begun to suggest itself, but of course none of the men wanted to risk the ridicule of their comrades by being the first one to the side of the ship. Frank Johnson, in a letter to his parents, told what happened next. "Just then one of the officers came running down along the deck saying all right boys you can get sick if you want to. Your Captain has began [*sic*] to feed the fish and you have the same privilege, and in a half hour there was about 100 along the railing throwing up." Another Cornhusker, describing the same event, recorded that "words fail to express in even slight degree the utter and abject horror of those two or three days of sickness when 1,000 men paid tribute to Neptune with wrenchings and travail which spoke of untold wretchedness." After a few days at sea most of the soldiers recovered and tried to enjoy the rest of the trip.[8]

After the initial excitement and seasickness wore off the voyage became monotonous. The men felt crowded, and there was little chance for exercise. Some officers tried to relieve the situation by allowing one company at a time up on deck to take the fresh sea air, walk around, and stretch their muscles, but after an hour or two it was back down to their quarters so another company could have its turn.[9]

Because of the great distance to Manila an intermediate stop was necessary in Honolulu to replenish the ships' coal and fresh water supplies. There, too, the ships would link up with the protected cruiser U.S.S. *Charleston* to escort them on the final leg of the journey. It usually took a week or so to reach Honolulu, and the islands were always a welcome sight. In early July, the captain of a transport of the third expedition offered a bottle of wine to the first man aboard who spied land. Perhaps such a contest would help to alleviate the boredom on board. A North Dakota volunteer, claimed the prize when he sighted what he assumed was the island of Oahu. It turned out that he had spotted another island in the Hawaiian group, Molokai—site of the leper colony. Oahu, and the capital city of Honolulu, was still eighty miles away but the proximity to Honolulu caused no small amount of excitement among the men. That night, after dark, two other men from the same regiment sneaked past the guard and shinnied up one of the ship's masts to look for the lights they knew would represent land.

When they spied the lights a little before midnight, they let out such shrieks as to awaken their sleeping comrades and cause them to crowd the rails in expectation.[10]

The soldiers were anxious to get their feet on dry land again and to see the marvelous sights of this tropical paradise. Few, if any, were disappointed by their reception as crowds of people thronged the docks to welcome them. When the *Charleston* reached the islands on May 29, it was the first American ship to arrive on its way to the Philippines. Not even waiting for the cruiser to reach the dock, a welcoming committee on another ship steamed out to escort the visitor to its mooring place. The welcoming craft, as well as every other vessel in the harbor, had red, white, and blue bunting streaming from every available location as cheers rocked the harbor. The scene was even more chaotic three days later as the first three transports neared the island. Tipped off by coast watchers far from Honolulu, ships and boats of every size and description cast off to welcome the new arrivals and usher them into the harbor. The *City of Peking* was the first of the three to enter the harbor where the *James McKee* was waiting with the official welcoming committee and a Hawaiian band. As the soldiers on the *Peking* stood at rigid attention the band blared out the "Star Spangled Banner." The band of the California volunteers answered from the *Peking* with Hawaii's national anthem, and cheers resounded across the harbor. "It looked as if the entire city was down by the water front to welcome the strangers," recalled a Honolulu resident, "for from the stringers of the wharves to the crosstrees of every vessel in the harbor, there was not a single point where a human being could cling which was not occupied by some welcome-giving resident."[11]

Some of the details of the welcomes differed from one expedition to another, but all remarked upon the carnival atmosphere surrounding the arrival of American troops in the young Hawaiian republic. As the S. S. *Peru* arrived and approached the Pacific Mail dock, the soldiers aboard crowded the rails and climbed into the ship's rigging to get good close up views of Honolulu. Tired of military food they quickly set up chants of "Where's the pie wagon?" and "Give us some fruit!" The happy civilians eagerly obliged, at least so far as the requests for fresh fruit were concerned, as they tossed bananas and pineapples up to the outstretched hands of the troops. "The men," recorded one who was among them, "were more than hungry for the fruit, and showed more greed than manners in their wish for the 'free lunch.'"[12]

An Oregon enlisted man on the first expedition arrived on June 1, and immediately wrote his mother of his initial impressions. "If you could sit in my chair this moment, you would not have missed the trip for the world," he gushed. "This is my first day in paradise." A lieutenant in the same regiment was equally impressed when he wrote home that "this is as near paradise as any place I expect to see on this earth." To most of the soldiers Oahu was simply, in the words of a Nebraska volunteer, "the finest Island in the world."[13]

Local women prepared sumptuous dinners for them. The welcoming committees, many of whose members sported badges with an eagle-and-crossed-flags motif and the motto "Aloha nui to our Boys in Blue," laid out these feasts on long tables amid the gardens of former Queen Liliuokalani's royal palace in the center of the city. (Although, as one soldier informed his correspondent, with the overthrow of the monarchy and its replacement by an American-supported republic four years earlier, one was not to use the term "Royal Palace," but was to refer to that edifice as the "Executive Building.") And what feasts they were! Enough rows of tables were set up on the shady grounds to seat 3,000 to 4,000 hungry troops at once. The tables fairly groaned with the load of food placed upon them. After the men had all seated themselves, dozens of young ladies began serving them an almost endless supply of all types of edibles. There was chicken, roast beef, breads, and cakes. The tropical locale also yielded immense quantities of figs, coconuts, pineapples, oranges, bananas, mangroves, dates, and grapes. The hostesses were ever ready to fill and refill empty cups with "coffee made with real milk." And for desert there were pies and cakes, unlimited quantities of soda water, and cigars. "I'll tell you," wrote one happy diner, "we did it Justice after being on Salt meat and rations served by the army." And when they had finished eating, many of the men strolled the grounds or shook hands with Hawaiian President Sanford Dole and his wife, who were usually on hand for these open-air banquets.[14]

Members of the expedition who were Masons, or who belonged to such other fraternal organizations as the Knights of Pythias, found that local lodge brothers had also set up banquets for them and their friends. And when the feasting was over there seemed to be no shortage of local residents eager to conduct the visitors on tours of the city and surrounding points of interest. And if time permitted there were leisurely horseback rides up through Nuuanu Valley to the crest of the mountains for a spectacular view of the Pacific Ocean on both sides of the island. Bicycle and carriage rides were also popular. There was a wonderful museum of Hawaiian culture that offered hours of enjoyment to those who visited it. And for those who wanted a different bathing experience than that offered by Waikiki there was a tile-bottomed, fresh water swimming pool in the shape of a Maltese cross. The sugar mill at Ewa, which was capable of producing 18,000 tons of sugar per year, was another curiosity worth seeing.[15]

The idyllic stopover, whether it lasted for a few hours or a few weeks, ended too soon for most, as the ships prepared to get underway for their final destination. A correspondent ruefully commented that there was probably more American "patriotism to the square inch" in Honolulu than anywhere in the United States.[16]

When it came time to leave not all of the men reported back to their ships. Some undoubtedly balanced the prospect of two or three more weeks on a hot, crowded troopship against the beautiful Hawaiian climate and opted for the latter. The difference between the two situations was even more marked for some of the ships' civilian crewmen. The heat generated in the boiler rooms of ships in the tropics could be brutal. When the third expedition prepared to leave Oahu it was found that the S.S. *Morgan City*'s entire gang of stokers and coal handlers had melted into Honolulu's population. The ship's captain scraped together a motley assortment of men to fill the vacancies, but they were not as experienced or as efficient as those who had deserted. Most soldiers, however reluctant they might have been to leave the islands, knew that their duty called them to proceed to the Philippines.[17]

There was some excitement of a military nature for those traveling in the very first convoy. Before leaving Honolulu, Captain Henry Glass of the escort cruiser *Charleston* received sealed orders, not to be opened for twenty-four hours. When he did open and read them he learned that there had been reports of one, and possibly two, Spanish gunboats at the Spanish island of Guam and he was to capture or destroy them on his way to Manila. When he had his signalman wigwag this information to the transports it was met with keen enthusiasm. Perhaps the soldiers would not have to wait until they got all the way to the Philippines to see action.[18]

The transports buzzed with rumors about Guam and other islands in the group known as the Ladrones, or Mariannas. There was also considerable interest in this latest turn of events on board the *Charleston*, and the members of the gun crews quickly began sharpening up their aims. Whereas there had been some target practice earlier in the voyage it seemed more to relieve boredom than anything else. Someone on board a troopship tossed wooden boxes overboard, and the *Charleston*'s gunners took pot shots at them with their small guns. Now, however, with the prospect of real actions looming, Captain Glass had a regular pyramidal cloth target deposited on the waves. Then, from a range of about two miles, the 6-inch guns on both sides of the *Charleston* took turns, and the 8-inchers on the bow and stern also joined in. The reported accuracy was surprisingly good. Each gun fired two rounds at the target, and every shot except the very first one hit it.[19]

The convoy arrived off Guam early on the morning of June 20, and the *Charleston* cleared for action as it approached the harbor at Agaña. Rain squalls dimmed visibility, but it quickly became apparent that the rumored enemy gunboats were nowhere to be seen. If shore batteries were present, as Captain Glass assumed, they remained silent. Continuing westward, the *Charleston* reached the harbor at San Juan d'Apra. It was here that the men on board first caught sight of the masts of a brig just inside the reef protecting the inner harbor. As was customary, the *Charleston* ran up the Stars and Stripes as if to challenge the unknown ship to respond in some fashion. Those aboard the anchored craft quickly perceived the military nature of this newly arriving ship and broke out their own national ensign — the rising sun of Imperial Japan — before the stranger mistook their ship for a Spanish gunboat and opened fire.

As the *Charleston* swung through the opening in the reef and eastward into the harbor itself it passed under Point Orote. This dominating headland was an ideal place for defensive works, and it was so high above the water that no ship's guns would be able to elevate high enough to return fire from there. Luckily for the Americans, the Spanish had long since abandoned any fortifications there. There was still one obstacle before the *Charleston* reached the village of Piti, which served as the port for the capital city of Agaña, and that was Fort Santa Cruz directly ahead.

A Captain Hallett, described as "an old whaler," had entered this bay many times in more peaceful pursuits, and he now came aboard the *Charleston* from the *Australia* to act as a pilot. He was surprised that the defenses he had seen on Point Orote on previous trips were inactive and wondered if the same could be said for Fort Santa Cruz. Captain Glass ordered his gunners to fire a few ranging shots at the fort to discover whether they would provoke any return fire. The transports remained safely out of harm's way, and as each shot from the cruiser kicked up dust on shore the soldiers lining the rails cheered lustily. After firing about a dozen shots and receiving no reply, the *Charleston* pushed on toward Piti.

On shore, meanwhile, the sudden appearance of these American ships caused several local officials to get together to prepare for their visitors' ultimate arrival at Piti. Guam was apparently such a backwater of the decaying Spanish empire that no one in Seville had notified those on the island that a state of war existed with the United States. When the *Charleston* opened fire on Fort Santa Cruz, one of the party at the dock, Captain Pedro Duarte Anducar, seemed mortified that there was no Spanish artillery close at hand with which to return the ritual salute! He quickly dispatched a note to his troops at Agaña to hasten to Piti with whatever small artillery pieces they could round up so they could fulfill their obligation of welcoming this visitor from the United States.[20]

Anducar then, along with the captain of the port, a naval surgeon and quarantine officer, a paymaster, and a civilian interpreter, pushed off in a small boat flying the Spanish flag to greet the *Charleston*. Frank Portusach, the interpreter's brother and, by virtue of naturalization ten years before the only American citizen on Guam, followed in his own boat, with the U.S. flag flying. When the port officials went on board, Navy officers broke the news to them that their country was at war with the United States, and demanded the surrender of Guam. They, of course, did not have the authority for such an act but promised to bring the governor, Juan Marina, back to the ship later that afternoon. Instead, the governor sent word that his government's regulations would not permit him to visit another nation's warship in such circumstances, but he offered to meet with Captain Glass the next morning in the village of Piti.[21]

Glass was suspicious of Marina's intentions so he instructed Lieutenant William Braunersreuther to take a boat's crew ashore the next morning to demand that the governor capitulate. To lend a little urgency to this demand, Glass also ordered Marines from the *Charleston* and the *Peking*, as well as a battalion of the Second Oregon Volunteers, to form a landing party. The soldiers and Marines were slow to organize. It was the first time the volunteers had been issued ammunition, and, as one of them later wrote, "none but a few old-time guardsmen had ever fired a shot with our antiquated long tom." Braunersreuther was anxious to accomplish his task so he and his immediate group went ahead without their reinforcements. On the way to the shore he impressed upon the Spanish pilot that he would not brook any trickery on his part. "You have come," he said, "to pilot us to the landing where you say we shall find your Governor. In taking us there remember that we are prepared for any emergency, and at the slightest sign of treachery you die first."[22]

Braunersreuther reached shore without any incidents, and upon being presented to the governor the American officer spoke to him in Spanish. "I have the honor," he said, "to present a communication from my commandant. I am authorized to wait one half hour for your reply. In presenting this communication I call your attention to the fact that we have, as you see, three large ships in the harbor, and a fourth [the *City of Sydney* had not yet crossed the reef] outside and ready to come in. One of these ships is a modern war vessel of high power, with large guns. The others are transports full of soldiers. We have a large force here. I call your attention to these facts in order that you may not make any hasty or ill considered reply to the note of my commandant." The note, of course, demanded that the governor immediately surrender all within his domain.[23]

While all this was going on a steam launch towed several boatloads of Marines and soldiers — about half of the total landing party — toward shore. The rest of the landing force waited expectantly on board the *Australia* for the launch to come back for them. Finally, after forcing Lieutenant Braunersreuther to cool his heels for twenty-nine of the allotted thirty minutes, Governor Marina gave him his answer to take to Captain Glass. Braunersreuther informed the governor that he acted with Glass's permission and that he would receive the communication. "Sir," the message began, "in the absence of any notification from my government concerning the relations of war between the United States and Spain, and without any means of defence, or the possibility of defence in the face of such a large opposing force, I feel compelled, in the interests of humanity and to save life, to make a complete surrender of all under my jurisdiction." The Americans then took the governor and his party out to meet with Captain Glass aboard the *Charleston*.[24]

After Captain Glass greeted his guests, he and one of his officers got into the captain's barge and headed for silent Fort Santa Cruz. There the captain ran a large U.S. flag up the abandoned fort's flagpole to the thunderous cheers of all the American sailors and soldiers lining the rails of the ships off shore. The crews of the *Charleston*'s six-inch guns began firing a twenty-one-gun salute, and the bands on the transports struck up "The Star Spangled Banner."[25]

The final act of conquest remained to be played out, and that was the physical surrender of the Spanish troops on the island. Governor Marina sent orders for all of the troops to assemble, with their weapons, in the boathouse at Piti. The garrison, which Captain Glass had been led to believe might amount to as many as a thousand troops, numbered only slightly more than a hundred, and only half of these were Spaniards. The rest were natives.

Lieutenant Braunersreuther, along with a couple of other officers, got back into one of the *Charleston*'s boats and headed back to shore to accept the surrender. His ship's Marine detachment accompanied him to provide security. Inside the boathouse, the Spanish regulars lined up along one side and the Chamorros faced them along the opposite side. Once by one the Spanish soldiers stepped forward and turned over their late model German-made rifles and accoutrements to the Americans, who stowed them in the boat for return to the *Charleston*. The native troops then followed suit, turning in their American-made Remington rifles and related equipment. Next, Braunersreuther ordered the Spaniards onto a barge for transport, as prisoners of war, out to the *Charleston*. The Chamorros, on the other hand, he paroled and allowed them to remain on their home island. Their reaction at this good news was one of near ecstasy as they ripped Spanish buttons and insignias off their clothing and jubilantly raced back home.[26]

The American ships remained in the harbor over the next couple of days while the *Charleston* took on coal from the *Peking*. They steamed away from the new American possession of Guam on June 22, and arrived without further incident in Manila Bay on the 30th.

By that time two more convoys of ships had left San Francisco for the Philippines. Brigadier General Francis V. Greene commanded the men of the Eighteenth and Twenty-third Infantry, the First Colorado, the First Nebraska, the Tenth Pennsylvania, and two batteries of the Utah Volunteer Artillery that set sail on June 15 aboard the transports *China*, *Colon*, and *Zealandia*. With no perceptible Spanish naval threat to contend with, these three vessels proceeded without an armed escort.

This was the only other expedition to interrupt its voyage after leaving Hawaii. On July 4, the men on these vessels celebrated their nation's birthday by laying claim to tiny, uninhabited Wake Island, some 2,300 miles west of Honolulu. Wake Island is actually an atoll of three islands, all that breaks the ocean's surface of a long ago volcano. A correspondent for *Harper's Weekly* described it as "a dreary sun-beaten spot ... glistening with white coral and shells, and covered with a sickly growth of low shrubs." Upon arrival the *China* lowered two open boats, and General Greene led a party ashore to raise the Stars and Stripes and officially lay claim to this Spanish-discovered island.

The stopover was brief because, as the *Harper's* correspondent noted, there was nothing there of any interest. Underway again, the men enjoyed a Fourth of July celebration, and the accompanying banquet was much more than canned beef and hardtack. It consisted of prime rib of beef au jus, stewed corn, boiled potatoes, rice pudding, cream sauce, freshly baked bread, peach cobbler, and lemon sauce, all to be washed down by the individual diner's choice of mocha or java coffee or lemonade. After dinner pipes, cigars, and cigarettes were lighted as the general program of commemoration began with the singing of "America." The chaplain of the Colorado regiment led the men in a brief prayer and then read to them the Declaration of Independence. General Greene then addressed the troops:

> Fellow soldiers and comrades—When Thomas Jefferson wrote the immortal words which you have just heard read, he little dreamed that one hundred and twenty-two years later they would be read in the middle of the Pacific Ocean to an expedition of American soldiers bound to the conquest of a group of islands off the coast of China that, were he alive to-day, he would be the first to seize the opportunities which Admiral Dewey's glorious victory in Manila Bay has placed within our grasp; In Jefferson's mind there would be no hesitation as to our duty to hold the Philippines and accept the destiny which has been suddenly thrust upon us....
>
> War is a serious business. Only those who have seen it can realize what it will be like when we get really into the midst of it. But it brings forth the noblest qualities with which man is endowed—courage, devotion, self-sacrifice. To those who survive, the memory of its hardships and dangers will ever bring a feeling of pride which no other acts of a man's life can produce. And those who fall will have the eternal satisfaction of knowing that by their death they have contributed to the accomplishment of a great result.
>
> Let us go onward, then, to our duty, come what may, in a just cause, confidently relying on the gratitude of our fellow-men, the approval of our own consciences, and the blessing of Almighty God.

Following these sobering thoughts was more music — "Battle Hymn of the Republic," "Hail Columbia," "The Star Spangled Banner" — along with more patriotic oratory. Similar celebrations took place on the other ships.[27]

By the time of General Greene's patriotic oration, Brigadier General Arthur MacArthur's command was already at sea. His seven ships left San Francisco over a period of five days near the end of June. This third contingent of troops consisted of the Third U.S. Artillery, the First Idaho, the Thirteenth Minnesota, the First North Dakota, a battalion of the First Wyoming, a company of regular Army engineer troops, and those members of the Eighteenth and Twenty-third Infantry Regiments who had not sailed with General Greene. General Merritt, Eighth Corps commander, sailed with this group. His command totaled nearly 11,000 men with a modest assortment of field artillery and Gatling guns.[28]

For all of the expeditions the part of the trip between Honolulu and the Philippines was when boredom, heat, poor food, and a shortage of fresh water began to be apparent. With the initial novelty of an ocean voyage worn off, there was little for the men to do with themselves. For some, the high point of each day may well have been the noontime ritual of setting their watches back fifteen minutes to account for their westward travel. One of the Minnesota volunteers, aboard the *City of Para*, gave a typical day's happenings: "To get up at 5 A.M., take a bath, eat breakfast, drill an hour, loaf till dinner, eat dinner, loaf again till supper, eat supper, loaf a couple of hours, take another bath and then turn in, constitutes the day's excitement."[29]

On some of the ships, officers required their men to participate in regular drill. Because of the lack of deck space in which to maneuver, however, these sessions were usually limited to some basic calisthenics and practicing the manual of arms. In spite of the lack of room on deck, the North Dakota officers aboard the *Valencia* decided that some form of regularly scheduled physical activity would be useful in combating the men's boredom. They assembled the troops in a column of twos and proceeded to march them around the deck of the ship. Few besides the officers saw the value of this. Most seemed to share the sentiment of the soldier who wrote that "several of us only went around once and then we dodged down the first stairway."[30]

Some of the officers began to realize that, since many of the volunteers were less than proficient with their rifles — indeed some had never fired them at all — perhaps some desperately needed target practice would help dispel the boredom of the men. The ships stopped while the men of the *China* hoisted a large makeshift target into the water and watched it drift slowly away. In the meantime, the Utah volunteers had tied the wheels of their field pieces down to the deck to prevent uncontrollable recoil. When the ship and the target were about 1,500 yards apart the gunners opened fire. Enough water in the vicinity of the target was stirred up to convince a reporter on board that the shooting was excellent, and they continued to shoot until the target was some three miles away. Nor were the volunteer infantrymen left out of these noisy festivities. Another target — a box with a piece of white cloth floating from a jury-rigged flagpole — was set over the side. When it had drifted to a point representative of the assumed combat distance, firing began. Each man received a grand total of five rounds of ammunition and blazed away. Their accuracy was also rated very high.[31]

After leaving Honolulu the men exhibited less and less of a military appearance. "Beards have sprouted from chins," observed one soldier, "and moustaches have made their appearance on lips which up to this time have never known the fruits of the razor." Even though most of the officers remained clean-shaven, this soldier continued, "so far as the enlisted men are concerned, they don't know that a razor is on board." Dress, too, had become much more casual as most of the men spent their days wearing nothing more than shirts and trousers, foregoing footwear altogether, with perhaps a wet towel draped over their heads and necks to keep cool. "Now, no person cares what he looks like," wrote a Minnesota volunteer, "and we slop about the decks in old shoes, red with age and salt water, worn-out trousers, frayed to a fringe at the bottoms and a much-abused army shirt. Some of the boys still wear hats, but the majority have discarded all headgear except that supplied by nature in the shape of hair, which now is ragged and unkempt. Our chief ambition in life is to keep cool, and the fewer clothes a man wears the easier is the problem for solution."[32]

A growing lack of personal cleanliness accented the slovenly appearance of some of the men. This failure to bathe regularly was almost certainly due to mere laziness, as there was plenty of opportunity for seawater showers. The *Peru*, for example, had two seawater shower baths on the forward section of the main deck and two more aft. Therefore there was, as one soldier aboard put it, "surely no excuse for the unwashed." He assured his mother that he was showering twice a day and changing his clothes every three days. A soldier from another ship in the convoy undoubtedly learned from the misfortune of two of his fellow warriors who chose to ignore the two-baths-per-day requirement of their company officers. Each of them was taken to a lower deck, where "under the direction of a non-commissioned officer and assisted by a detail of men, large bars of soap and a scrub brush, he is soon placed in a thoroughly sanitary condition, and reaches that degree of popularity supposed to be akin to godliness."[33]

The enforcement of sanitation rules extended, on some ships at least, to a regular, daily sweeping out of the sleeping quarters. Those men found guilty of such heinous crimes as spitting on the floor soon found they had four days of kitchen duty assigned to them. Peeling potatoes, washing pots, and generally assisting in the preparation of meals for all aboard was not, in itself, particularly onerous. But when that duty is performed for twelve hours at a time, and in a confined space whose temperature reaches well over a hundred degrees, it is anything but pleasant. Rare indeed was the man who suffered this penalty more than once.[34]

Laundry was another problem for the men cooped up on the ships, but they quickly found a way to solve it. They discovered that if they bundled their dirty clothes up and tied the bundle all to a rope, tied the other end of the rope to the ship's rail, and threw the bundle into the sea, that in about twenty minutes they could reel in their clothing, and it would be "as clean as new driven snow." A few men discovered, however, that with regard to this method of cleansing their clothes, more is not necessarily better. A Minnesota officer calculated that if twenty minutes in the salt water would get his two shirts clean, then several hours would make them absolutely spotless. Unfortunately, the turbulent seawater in the wake of the ship, as well, perhaps, as the actions of sharks, meant that when he sought to retrieve his laundry nothing remained of his shirts on the other end of the rope but their collars.[35]

As each expedition neared the equator the heat became a major factor in the men's daily attempt to remain comfortable. At least one of the ships was fitted out with a pair of square canvas water tanks where the men could splash around to their hearts' content. Six feet on a side, they were large enough for several men to use at one time. The decks of the ships were now too hot to go barefoot, and every bit of shade was at a premium during the day. Some men spread their shelter tents in such a way as to gain some shady respite from the tropical heat. Others rigged makeshift awnings from the auxiliary sails on board. At night, the sleeping quarters below decks were almost completely empty as the men sought escape from the stifling heat. The cool evening breezes topside converted the decks into vast sleeping platforms. Some men, with the help of sympathetic crewmen, emptied the straw out of their mattresses and converted them into hammocks that they slung from every available space on deck at night. One soldier observed that sleeping soldiers took up so much space that "the main deck resembles a huge morgue."[36]

The heat sapped the strength of the idle soldiers, even though they had little more to do with their time than play cards or chess, or read. Spanish grammars were popular among some officers and men. Some even found it almost beyond their abilities even to go down to get their dinners. Of course, the heat was not the only reason for this indifference toward food. The soldiers' diet on this trip was boring at best and downright inedible at worst. One soldier claimed that he ate "pork, beans, spudds [sic] and sea coffee about eight days in the week." Army regulations called for a daily "travelling ration" of approximately one pound of bread, one twelve-ounce can of beef, five ounces of canned baked beans, coffee, and sugar. Even this unimaginative menu might have been acceptable had it not been for the fact that much of the canned meat ration was spoiled. A Minnesota soldier on the *City of Para* observed that when this canned meat was opened, "it was found that much of it was tainted and several pieces had engendered in itself minute animal life; in other words and to use plain language it was simply rotten and filled with maggots." Another described it as "stringy and soupy." Much of this meat, including 400 pounds on the *Valencia*, was dumped overboard.[37]

The men might even have overlooked the spoiled meat somewhat if everyone in the expedition was eating the same food. Officers, however, paid for their own food and generally ate much better than the men. One soldier reported that the officers enjoyed such breakfast fare as fruit, boiled pike, sirloin steak, ham, sausages, hot rolls, toast, corn muffins, tea, coffee, and cocoa. "The officers' meal," he continued sarcastically, "is just an ordinary one — nothing extra — while at the same time the enlisted men breakfasted on the following delicacies: 'Coffee, bread and corned beef.'"[38]

The hungry volunteers soon resorted to devious means to augment their meager fare. Singly or in small groups they raided the officers' kitchens and made off with pies and other creature comforts not on their own menus. Three members of the First North Dakota managed to steal a case of canned salmon from the supplies aboard ship, and this made a delicious supplement to their boring diet. While they shared their bounty with some friends the next morning, however, the officer of the day caught them. The regimental commander recognized the extenuating circumstances surrounding this bit of larceny and realized that it probably would never have happened if the government rations had been adequate. He therefore released the men with no more serious consequences than a reprimand. Over the length of a long voyage, however, with perhaps a thousand hungry men on board each ship, the total results of such forays could be significant. A Minnesota soldier informed his parents that in spite of the presence of guards in the hold of the ship, and in spite of officers making the rounds every fifteen minutes, the men of his regiment had "taken, stolen, over a *ton* of canned fruit and nearly a hundred bottles of Burbon [sic] whiskey besides lots of other stuff." On this same ship hungry soldiers stole carrots that were intended to feed the few cattle that were aboard to provide fresh beef.[39]

Soldiers with money in their pockets were able sometimes to buy such edibles as canned fruit, jelly, condensed milk, lime juice, cranberry sauce, and even cigars from the commissary. The ships' cooks and stewards were also frequently willing to surreptitiously "hand out a bowl full of scraps or a piece of plum pudding or a hunk of bread and butter in return for a piece of silver." Minnesotan Fred Gregory probably came up with the best scheme of all. He learned that the chief cook on his ship had been born in Trinidad. Gregory had visited the island for a few days some years before and still had some tourist literature in his personal baggage. He studied diligently until he felt he could easily pass himself off as a native and then sought out the cook. With tears of mock joy in his eyes he pumped the hand of the galley boss as he introduced himself as a fellow native of Trinidad. For the next three hours the two men exchanged information on "their" home island and talked over old times. For the rest of his voyage, Fred Gregory ate the best food the ship had to offer.[40]

Men who were short of disposable income were not above victimizing the sailors for extra food either. The ships' working crews quite naturally got more nutritious food than their sedentary passengers, and it did not take long for the troops on board to figure out ways to share in this better fare. Often there was very little sophistication involved in these foraging expeditions. They simply stood around while the sailors were eating and waited for one of them to look away from his food for an instant. Then, as one volunteer confided to his diary, "some one will steal his meat and another will grab his tea. The ships people don't dare to leave any thing in the shape of food down for even a moment as they are sure to find it missing."[41]

The colonel of the Minnesota regiment soon tired of all the complaining he heard from his men about the food. He finally addressed them:

> Warriors and heroes, when we started out on this little picnic we did not altogether anticipate that it was going to assume the proportions it has, and I can assure you I regret exceedingly that the supply of strawberries and ice cream has played out and we are compelled to subsist on hard tack, pork and other delicacies of a like nature. I am certain the constitutions of the majority have suffered to a very considerable extent and propose when we reach Manila to give the entire regiment a week's holiday in which to recuperate its health. I am sure that you will make as many friends in Manila as the regiment has made in the other places where it has been quartered, and I am satisfied that you will spend a most enjoyable holiday. I should like to have enough men in camp to keep a guard on Post 1, but if it is considered best that all should be absent I shall certainly not insist upon this.

General complaining lessened noticeably after this sarcastic address.[42]

At least as bad as, and perhaps worse than, the unimaginative diet aboard the transports was the short supply of fresh drinking water available during the latter stages of the voyage. On some of the ships, the manner of distribution of the water that was available caused a lot of grumbling. When a man wanted a drink he took his tin cup to the ship's sole fresh water hydrant. There, under a guard's watchful eye, he poured some water into his cup and drank it. He was not allowed, for some reason, to take the water away with him to drink later. The problem with this regulation was that this desalinated seawater was heated in the process of its distillation and was often still very warm when it came out of the spigot. (Some Minnesota soldiers claimed to have tested some and found its temperature to be 122°.) After a few days of this the rules changed and, although a guard remained posted near the water tank, the men were allowed to fill their canteens once a day and take them to some cooler, shadier part of the ship where the water could cool down before they drank it. Many still grumbled about the water rationing, but it could have been worse. The frequent rain showers that they encountered at this time of year allowed them to catch rainwater to add to their canteens.[43]

While the travelers had much to grumble about with regard to their food, their water, and the heat, they also found time to note the natural wonders they saw. A couple of weeks after leaving Honolulu, while one convoy stopped for repairs to one of its ships, the soldiers on board noticed several small sharks near their vessel. Attempting to practice their marksmanship, they loosed a fusillade of pistol shots at these creatures, but without effect. Perhaps they were encouraged by the experience of a Minnesota volunteer several days earlier. The ships were again stopped when someone spotted a large shark. This particular soldier borrowed a shark hook and a stout line from one of the sailors, cajoled one of the galley crew into parting with a large chunk of meat, and dropped the bait over the side. Very shortly the shark hit the bait. The struggling soldier managed to wrestle his catch clear of the water and one of his companions then administered the coup de grace with a revolver. The happy fisherman soon had a pocketful of sharp, menacing shark teeth for souvenirs. An enterprising shark fisherman on another ship was not as lucky. He, too, baited his hook with a piece of meat, and with the typical irreverence of a soldier remarked that "the bait'll kill him with indigestion if I don't catch him with the hook." The big fish that hit the bait, however, did not share the man's low opinion of the morsel. The soldier was soon hauling his prize up toward the deck when his rope broke, and the shark splashed back into the sea. Undeterred, the man fashioned another hook, attached another piece of meat, and lowered it into the water. He soon had another shark on the line, but the result was the same. Before he and his eager helpers could haul it aboard the rope broke again, and the fish escaped. After yet a third unsuccessful try, the weary would-be fisherman gave up.[44]

Although the travelers periodically sighted such other aquatic creatures as flying fish, porpoises, and whales, the most dramatic natural phenomenon they saw on their voyage was inanimate. As the ships passed through the northern reaches of the Mariannas Islands, known then as the Ladrones, they came in sight of the actively volcanic island of Farallon de Pajaros. The first evidence of this island was the column of smoke that was visible from several miles away. If the convoy should pass within just a few miles of the island after nightfall the view was magnificent. One observer described it as "vomiting billows of smoke and sheets of flame to heaven's high vault." Even from the distance of three miles, he wrote, "every crack and crevice in the rugged sides could be seen distinctly. Vast sheets of flame would rise and light up everything for a moment, only to be replaced by billows of smoke pouring out of the crater's mouth in great rolling masses." Another soldier thought "the eruptions of lava and fire from its crater seemed to set the very heavens afire." Still not everyone was as impressed by the volcanic fireworks. One man dryly commented that the "pyrotechnic display would not do credit to an ordinary Fourth of July celebration in Minnesota."[45]

Before the men of the Eighth Corps reached the Philippines sickness, accidents, and suicides had thinned their ranks. Measles, malaria, and typhoid were the major culprits. More than one ship's captain sought to avoid the spread of these maladies by having all of the bedding, thought to be the breeding ground of disease, thrown overboard.

Several ships reported men overboard sometime during their ocean crossing. One soldier was up in the rigging of the *Ohio* and somehow lost his grip and fell. He bounced off a tightly stretched awning over the deck and fell into the sea. By the time the *Ohio*'s boats were in the water and the rescue effort begun there was no sign of him, and he was listed as lost at sea. The man, meanwhile, realized as soon as he hit the water that his chances of rescue were slim, but when he saw the *Morgan City* coming toward him he swam toward it. An alert man aboard this ship spotted him, and he was hauled aboard, wet but otherwise not harmed. Unfortunately, a man falling into the ocean was usually lost before the ship could be brought to a halt and search boats lowered. Nor were all the men who went over the rail the victims of accidents. Several reports mention civilian crewmen who committed suicide in this manner. They were coal passers or stokers who, apparently driven mad by the heat in their workspaces, sought relief in the cool ocean waters.[46]

CHAPTER 9

The Philippines Campaign

AFTER COMMODORE DEWEY'S VICTORY in Manila his squadron remained relatively inactive for the next couple of months. With not enough Marines on board his ships to capture and hold the city of Manila, Dewey had to content himself with merely setting up a blockade and waiting for troops from the United States. He did not want to tangle with the heavy Spanish guns along the Manila waterfront so he anchored his squadron close to Cavite, where he set guards up over the captured arsenal stores.

There seemed to be no real threat of any Spanish ships arriving to challenge Dewey, although there were still a couple of small torpedo boats lurking in the Pasig River. There was also a little apprehension with regard to possible underwater mines, new ones, being floated out from shore to destroy the American vessels. Nor was all the danger man made. The summer months brought typhoons to this part of the world, and one of these tremendous storms, even within the confines of Manila Bay, could do a considerable amount of damage to Dewey's ships.

Nevertheless, life aboard the warships soon settled down to a regular routine. At 5 A.M. the harsh notes of reveille shattered the stillness of dawn and turned each ship into a churning mass of humanity as the crewmen arose, rolled and stowed their hammocks, took care of morning ablutions, had their first cups of coffee, and began scrubbing down the decks. By 7:20, breakfast was ready, and for the next forty minutes the men ate and relaxed. Precisely at eight o'clock every ship in the squadron ran up the Stars and Stripes, and on ships large enough to have their own bands the musicians played the "Star Spangled Banner" while everyone aboard stood rigidly at attention. Occasionally a steam launch towed a small boat several hundred feet behind it, and the gun crews on some of the ships engaged in sub-caliber target practice, firing at a red flag on the target boat. There was not much else to do for the rest of the day.[1]

At about noon on June 30, the pace of life quickened with the arrival of the U.S.S. *Charleston* and its three-ship convoy. The men on these ships were glad to leave the rolling China Sea, which had caused many of them to experience seasickness for a second time. Dewey's crews welcomed these newcomers with hearty cheers, and the soldiers yelled themselves hoarse in response. General Anderson met with Dewey and finalized arrangements for his men to go ashore at Cavite where they would occupy abandoned Spanish Army barracks until the rest of the reinforcements arrived from the United States.

The landing began the next day with small boats ferrying groups of soldiers from their ships to the docks of Cavite. The sea ran fairly high, and the men had to exhibit a certain amount of acrobatic prowess to time their step from the boat to the dock so that it coincided with the boat's position on the crest of a wave. Failure to do so meant that a man would have to wait while the boat descended some five or six feet into the trough of the next wave and then rose back up again until it was even with the surface of the dock. It took the better part of two days to get all the men and supplies ashore.

Life for the Americans at Cavite soon settled down to a routine reminiscent of stateside training camps. On days when the weather permitted, they drilled from 7 to 8 in the morning and then again in the late afternoon from 5 to 6. Sometimes individual companies of men, straining under the burden of rifles and packs, made practice road marches in the general direction of Manila, twenty-seven miles away. At other times they practiced their marksmanship by firing at half a dozen man-shaped targets specially erected on the wreckage of one of the Spanish ships out in the bay.[2]

By the middle of July the steady arrival of soldiers from the United States began to overtax the facilities at Cavite. Army commanders also wanted to establish a staging area for the attack on Manila much closer to that city. Cavite was only a few miles from Manila by water, but troops traveling on foot would have had to endure a long, tiring march before reaching the enemy capital. Consequently, one battalion of California troops moved across the bay on July 15 to a position just south of the Manila suburb of Malate. The remainder of the regiment followed two days later. The new camp, on the site of a former peanut field near the small hamlet of Tambo, was named in honor of the hero of Manila Bay, and the second expedition began arriving the next day. Camp Dewey was relatively flat and extended from the beach on the west almost to the main road connecting Manila to Cavite on the east. Officers' tents occupied the section nearest the beach, and the company streets stretched inland from there.[3]

Landing troops and supplies at Camp Dewey was rather a makeshift proposition, just as it had been in landing the men of the Fifth Corps in Cuba. There were no specialized landing craft available to deposit men and cargo safely on the beach. Instead, ships' boats and native *cascos* were used. These latter vessels, with their woven mat awnings and bamboo decks, were well suited to their originally intended purpose, but their rather fragile construction sometimes proved to be insufficient for their current role. Adding to the difficulties was the fact that it was the middle of monsoon season in the Philippines, and near gale force winds frequently lashed the waters of the bay.

It was during one such stormy day in late July that the third expedition began landing at Camp Dewey. Their ships anchored at a safe distance offshore while soldiers scrambled into the native *cascos* for the ride to the beach. When five such craft were filled, a steam launch took them in tow and headed in. In spite of the stormy weather, most of the boats made it without difficulty, getting close enough so that the men only had to wade the last several feet to the beach. The *casco* carrying the men and supplies of the Astor Battery, however, was not as fortunate. As it neared the beach its towrope broke, and the waves pushed the fragile craft sideways allowing waves to break over it from stem to stern. The boat was soon swamped and broken up. It was close enough to shore so that none of the men drowned, but they were thoroughly drenched by the time they reached dry land. Of more important potential consequence was the fact that all of the ammunition for their field guns was rendered inoperable due to the wetting of the powder. They would have to laboriously remove the propellant from each cartridge and replace it with dry powder before they could use their guns. Compounding their difficulty was the fact that it was almost impossible to find a source of dry powder with which to fill their shells. Only through the good offices of the Navy were they able to reload their spoiled ammunition. They had to offload the guns themselves into four or five feet of water and then haul them ashore by hand.[4]

During one landing, when another of the *cascos* had broken loose and was about to be wrecked by the waves, the soldiers on board stripped off their clothes before the inevitable ducking. Then, with bundles of clothes in one hand and their rifles and ammunition in the other, they worked their way through the waves to the beach. A member of the band struggled to keep his tuba out of the salt water, but at times the waves broke over him leaving only his extended arms and huge instrument visible. "He looked," noted an observer, "like some strange sea-god of classical fable."[5]

Sometimes, albeit in milder seas, enterprising Filipinos earned some money by offering to carry Americans on their shoulders from the *cascos* to the shore. Unfortunately for these human packhorses, they sometimes attempted too much. When the Utah artillerists were landing, one of the natives eagerly accepted the task of thus conveying one of them to shore. In this instance, however, the American tipped the scales at something over two hundred pounds while his porter barely weighed half as much. The smaller man did his best, but his burden was just too much for him, and he disappeared beneath the waves along with his rider. Both men were teased unmercifully, and it has not been recorded whether the Filipino got to keep his fee.[6]

In spite of such occasional difficulties all of the Americans got ashore without loss of life or irreplaceable equipment. The men at Camp Dewey would not, of course, be able to enjoy the shelter of stout stone buildings as those had at Cavite but had to rely on tentage. A part of each man's issued equipment was a shelter half. This rectangular piece of canvas had buttons and buttonholes along the edges, and when two men buttoned theirs together and rigged up the necessary poles they had a two-man tent. These provided shade from the tropical sun but, as one man recalled, "were but little better than nothing in the severe tropical downpours which visited this region almost every day and flooded the camp inches deep in very few minutes." The soldiers also quickly realized that if they did not want to sleep in the mud, which of course was a natural result of the heavy rains, they had to improvise. They quickly found out what a remarkable building material bamboo is. Almost all of the men built bamboo platforms for their tents that were from one to two feet above the ground and kept them out of the mud. Occasionally, four soldiers went together and built two-story structures.[7]

Camp life in the tropics brought entirely new experiences to the soldiers at Camp Dewey — many of whom had come from the decidedly non-tropical climates of Oregon, Minnesota, and North Dakota. One of the newspaper correspondents with the Eighth Corps marveled at the lack of mosquitoes and the insignificant number of flies. His reading had led him to expect great numbers of these pests. A North Dakota volunteer, however, found all the mosquitoes he could have wanted at Cavite. One of his sergeants had been stung during the night on his eyelid, and he was unable to open that eye for several hours the next morning due to the swelling. The number of red ants also more than made up for any perceived scarcity of flying insects. One reporter described "active armies" of them appearing suddenly as if out of thin air. Their sting was quite vicious, and if they climbed the bamboo legs of the men's sleeping platforms the only solution was to evacuate the tents. To prevent such an infestation the soldiers quickly learned to put discarded tomato cans to use by filling them half full with water or petroleum and then setting each of the platform's legs into one of these cans.[8]

Another irritating aspect of life at Camp Dewey was the lack of clean drinking water. The men found that they could reach water by only digging down about a foot or two. This water looked pure and was not unpalatable, but it was full of invisible impurities that made the men sick. Camp officials issued orders to boil all water before using it for drinking purposes, but this order was probably more honored in the breach. Some of the men went through the motions, bringing a cup of water *to* a boil before drinking it, but that was not long enough to destroy the impurities. Even when the men wanted to leave the water on the fire longer the relative scarcity of firewood made this problematic. The company cooks did not want to use their precious supply of wood to boil water for the men when they could more profitably be using it to cook with. After enough bouts of water-related illnesses had afflicted the camp the men began to find ways to trap rainwater — of which there was an overabundance. A method that was popular with some soldiers was to split a few pieces of bamboo lengthwise and rig up a system of rain gutters that fed into some empty tin hardtack boxes.[9]

As more and more soldiers arrived on the outskirts of Manila the political situation grew more tense. Emilio Aguinaldo had proclaimed himself the head of a new, independent Filipino government. Government leaders in the United States had not yet decided what they thought the political fate of the Philippines should be, and until they did Aguinaldo's strident maneuvering was a potential source of embarrassment. His forces had thrown a loose cordon around the city of Manila and had every intention of forcing a Spanish surrender. Although not yet strong enough to accomplish this, Aguinaldo's Army put more and more pressure upon the Spanish, and the arrival of the U.S. Eighth Corps beginning in July put a successful Spanish defense out of reach. Governor-General Don Basilio Augustín realized that unless he negotiated some kind of settlement, the combined forces besieging the city would launch an attack that he could not hope to repel. There was now, with the defeat of Cervera's squadron and the recall of Cámara's, absolutely no hope of receiving reinforcements or supplies from Spain.

There were also difficulties on the other side of the equation. As Aquinaldo's force grew stronger and stronger Admiral Dewey and General Merritt became more concerned. They, of course, wanted to effect the surrender of Manila, but they did not want Aguinaldo to be involved. There was some fear that the Filipino soldiers might prove to be vengeful victors and carry out a bloodbath against their former colonial rulers — a fear that General Augustín also embraced.

Spanish troops in Manila were in greater strength than Aguinaldo's force and also outnumbered the U.S. Eighth Corps, but the combined weight of Filipino and American troops tipped the balance against the Spaniards. The Spanish anchored their defenses south of the city on the western end by the stone Fort San Antonio de Abad and its cannons. Trench works then extended eastward toward Blockhouse #14. This blockhouse, and others, was of similar construction to those encountered by Shafter's men in Cuba. It was about twenty-five feet square and two stories tall. It was sheathed in two-inch planks that were stout enough to slow down rifle bullets but of no protection against artillery. Concrete reinforced the walls of the upper section to provide an increase in protection against American small arms fire, and a sandbag breastwork surrounded the structure. The hipped roof had an observation cupola at its apex, and a square piece of tin with "14" painted on it identified the building. Field batteries also dotted the Spanish works.

The Filipino positions left little room for any American military maneuvering. In order to get an American presence in the siege lines, General Greene summoned Filipino General Mariano Noriel and solicitously informed him that he had noticed that the only cannon the native troops had opposite Fort San Antonio de Abad was an old ship's cannon that had thus far proved of dubious value. Greene then magnanimously offered the use of some fine new American field pieces in that part of the line. Of course, they would require their own American crewmen and infantry protection. Noriel saw that this arrangement made perfect sense, and, after receiving the approval of Aguinaldo, ordered his troops out of the trenches there. On the morning of July 29, therefore, the men of the Eighteenth U.S. Infantry and one battalion of the First Colorado Volunteers moved into the trenches to support two guns from each of the Utah Light Artillery Batteries.[10]

Although this Spanish blockhouse is in Cuba, it is typical of those in the Philippines (Library of Congress).

Minnesota volunteers pose in the trenches outside of Manila (U.S. Army Military History Institute).

The new American position was about a quarter of a mile southeast of Fort San Antonio de Abad. Work began immediately to improve the position, which stretched inland from the beach for about 270 yards. About 125 yards in front of this primitive trench line was a large abandoned two-story brick and stucco building, described variously as a private residence and as a Capuchin convent. Regardless of what its original use had been, this structure's location made it an excellent site for observing the Spanish because its upstairs windows offered a view of Fort San Antonio and the adjacent works almost as far east as Blockhouse #14. General Greene moved his men forward to incorporate this building into a new line of entrenchments, and men of the First Colorado, serving their twenty-four-hour stint in the trenches, moved forward and began working. The Spanish works, now only a couple of hundred yards away, were strangely silent while this work went on, but the busy volunteers must have cast quick looks toward them every now and again as they shoveled dirt.[11]

Digging in this soil was not easy. The location of the water table, in some places only slightly more than a foot below the surface, meant that any trench would necessarily be full of water most of the time. Still the men worked to stack shovelfuls of wet dirt into an embankment that would shield them from the enemy bullets. Spanish riflemen finally realized what was happening and begun to snipe at the Americans, but by that time the works had reached such a stage as to provide good protection against such fire. The Coloradoans worked on through the night, and by morning had erected a breastwork almost 200 yards long and offering protection up to a height of five to seven feet.[12]

The First Nebraska replaced the Colorado volunteers the next morning, and as the tired laborers marched back to Camp Dewey an errant shot from a Spanish sharpshooter finally inflicted a casualty. William Sterling was hit in the left arm from a distance of some 400 yards. He thus became, apparently, the first American soldier wounded by Spanish fire in the Philippines.[13]

Duty in these forward trenches was relatively uneventful for the first couple of days, although the level of sniping increased, but the Americans did not have long to wait for their baptism of fire. On the morning of July 31, Colonel Alexander Hawkins sent two battalions of his Tenth Pennsylvania Volunteers into the trenches, along with Battery H of the Third U.S. Heavy Artillery, in support of four rapid-fire 3-inch guns of the Utah volunteers. There was, of course, nothing to indicate that this day would be any different from the day before, and the soldiers spent most of their time working on their defensive works.

After supper that evening residents of Camp Dewey spotted several newly arrived ships offshore. They proved to be the *Indiana*, the *Ohio*, the *Morgan City*, the *City of Para*, and the *Valencia* with more troops. The arrival of these reinforcements sparked an outburst of loud cheering from shore. "Now we shall get some action!" was a common refrain. "It won't take us long to get into Manila now."[14]

Spanish officers in Fort San Antonio also saw the ships and knew the nature of their human cargo as well as did the cheering soldiers in Camp Dewey. Their reaction, however, was one of foreboding rather than elation. This latest increment of American troops, combined with those already on shore and the men of Aguinaldo's Army, now outnumbered the defenders of Manila by a significant margin. Perhaps if the Spaniards attacked the Americans immediately, before the reinforcements out in the bay could land, they might win some time for diplomatic negotiations to salvage at least some of Spain's fast dwindling empire.

After dark that night the rains began again, but Major H. C. Cuthbertson sent five squads of men from the Tenth Pennsylvania out into the no-man's-land between the American and Spanish positions to act as listening posts through the night. If the Spanish chose to attack, perhaps counting on the noise of the storm to mask the sounds of their advance, these men would be able to hear them coming and raise the alarm to prevent total surprise. And the Spanish did have plans for that night. About 11 o'clock, their line exploded in artillery and rifle fire. The Pennsylvanians occupying the forward trenches had standing orders not to fire toward the enemy positions unless the Spaniards fired first. That restriction was now moot, and the volunteers from the Keystone State returned fire, and the gunners of Utah's Battery B pumped round after round into the darkness from their two guns. A news correspondent nearby waxed poetic in describing the opening moments. "Volley after volley," he wrote, "cut the murky air; part of them possessing the twang of the Mauser, the rest carrying the unmistakable ring of our Springfields, the full sentences of conflict bearing plenty of punctuation in the shape of the roar of artillery, first that of the heavier guns at Fort San Antonio Abad, and then the wicked bark of Utah's guns at the left of our line. It was a battle sure enough."[15]

At Camp Dewey the noise of battle had soldiers stumbling into their clothes and rubbing sleep from their eyes even before the various buglers began signaling for assembly. General Greene immediately dispatched a battalion of the First California to the Pennsylvanians' assistance, while that regiment's other two battalions stood by in close support. He also sent Battery K of the Third U.S. Artillery (serving as infantry) forward and ordered the First Colorado Volunteers to stand by as a ready reserve force behind the left of the American line. The Spaniards targeted the roads leading from Camp Dewey toward the American trenches and swept them with shot and shell. American reinforcements thus had to move forward in the dark through the muddy fields. Even there, however, they were in great danger from bullets and shells that passed over the forward trenches. Captain Reinhold Richter, the popular commander of Company I of the First California, was one of the first to fall while crossing this danger zone. Captain Charles W. Hobbs of the 3rd Artillery was another early casualty, shot through the left leg. Being shot was nothing new for Hobbs. He had twice been wounded in the Civil War, and when he felt the bullet strike his thigh this time he urged his men to continue forward without him. A cursory self-examination indicated that his injury was not serious, and in less than a minute he rejoined his men. "It must have been a spent ball," he announced. It was only the next morning that he realized that the bullet had passed completely through his upper leg without hitting any bones. In addition to the two officers wounded, Spanish fire at this point also killed one enlisted man and wounded eight others.[16]

After a half hour of furious shelling, Major Cuthbertson heard the unmistakable sounds of a Spanish infantry assault to the right of his Pennsylvanians. Fearful of having that flank turned, he pulled in his pickets from that area and ordered three companies forward from their reserve positions to extend his line to the east. The roar of battle from this sector soon reached enormous proportions as the two forces, unable to see each other except by the light of the occasional lightning flashes, traded volleys. The two guns of Utah's Battery A fired shrapnel rounds with the fuses set to burst almost as soon as the rounds left the muzzles. An American officer later left a vivid description of the fighting:

> The bullets were flying over their [the Americans] heads in swarms. They whizzed, they whistled, they sang as a telegraph wire does in a wind. They zipped, they buzzed, they droned like a bagpipe far away, like a June bug seeking a light on a hot night, like a blue bottle [fly] buzzing against a window pane. They beat against the outside of our embankment with a sound like hailstones striking soft mud, like the faint hoof beat of the horses going up the backstretch in the Suburban as it comes to you on the patrol judge's stand at the middle distance. They rattled against the old Capuchin chapel and ripped through its iron roof with a noise such as children make with a stick on a picket fence running along and drawing the stick across the pickets, or like a man drumming on a window blind.
>
> Did you ever hear the cook beating up eggs on a platter with a big spoon? If that noise were magnified a thousand times it would give a suggestion of the tattoo the bullets beat on that old chapel. And all this time there were the shells. Men who were in the civil war [sic] say the shells came through the air saying "Where is you?" "Where is you?" all run together. They sound like the ripping of silk, and they give you the same feeling down the back that it does to pull a string through your teeth.[17]

A near tragedy occurred when the reinforcing California regiment reached what it thought was the main trench line and opened fire. Instead it had reached the original works erected by Aguinaldo's men, and, apparently unaware of the advanced breastworks, opened fire into the backs of the Pennsylvanians. Fortunately, the error was discovered and corrected before this "friendly" fire killed anyone.[18]

After discovering their error the Californians hurried forward into the correct trench line, where they discovered that the troops already there were dangerously low on ammunition. Lieutenant Colonel Maurice G. Krayenbuhl attributed some of this to what he considered reckless, unaimed fire and immediately took steps to stop it. He drew his revolver and jumped up onto the works with his back to the Spaniards. He then threatened to shoot any man who fired toward the enemy without orders. One of his sergeants further sought to calm the volunteers by showing that in spite of all the noise of battle the Spanish fire was almost all going well over their heads. To illustrate his point and to show them that they had relatively little to fear in their present location he clambered up on the works exposing himself to the full force of Spanish fire. The well meaning, but unlucky, sergeant soon tumbled from the works with a bullet in his head.[19]

As the firing reached a level of great intensity it became obvious that the men in the forward trenches must soon run out of ammunition altogether. Major Sam Jones, a quartermaster officer, sent Pvt. Francis Finley, of the First California, with six carts full of ammunition forward. This small relief caravan soon entered the danger zone behind the forward works where Spanish fire was fierce. A horse drawing one of the carts went down; then one of the Filipino drivers was wounded. The rest of the hired drivers quickly determined that whatever they were being paid to deliver these supplies to the front was not enough to compensate for the risk involved, and they abandoned the carts and scurried back out of harm's way. Finley was unable to convince them to stay so he got some soldiers to take their places and completed the mission.[20]

Finally, sometime around two or three on the morning of August 1, the firing ceased. American losses were ten men killed or mortally wounded and forty-three with lesser wounds. With regard to Spanish losses, a sergeant in one of the Utah Batteries euphemistically stated merely that "when morning dawned it was ascertained that several Castillian voices had been added to the Choral Society in that land beyond the river."[21]

Over the next several nights the enemy subjected the men in the forward trenches to bouts of artillery and infantry fire of various degrees of severity. On the night of August 1, the Spaniards opened fire at about 9:15 P.M., but the American response was limited to the guns of Battery B of the Utah Artillery with only a token amount of rifle fire from the infantry. The exchange, such as it was, stopped after less than an hour, but the Spaniards played reveille with their cannons at 5 o'clock the next morning. This half-hour bombardment elicited no reply. There was another forty-five minute bombardment that night.

The losses suffered on the right of the American position on July 31 emphasized the need for stronger works there. Over the course of the next twelve days whichever troops happened to be in the line, usually three battalions with a fourth in reserve, spent as much time as they could extending and improving the breastworks. It was not easy work. The men were in almost constant danger from sniper fire, and Mother Nature also seemed to be conspiring against them. It rained almost continually, often filling the trenches with as much as two feet of water. Nor was the incessantly saturated soil a very stable material with which to work, and the sides of the trenches sometimes caved in as fast as the men could repair them. Piles of sandbags helped to stabilize things, although the content of the bags was not sand at all but the same sticky black mud that was everywhere. In spite of these difficulties, the Americans succeeded in erecting fairly solid works that stretched 1,200 yards, all the way to the Pasay Road where the Filipino trenches began.

The arrival of General MacArthur's force on the very day of the battle brought American troop strength up to about 8,500, and the American trench works soon extended another thousand yards eastward. General Merritt anxiously consulted with Admiral Dewey, urging an immediate joint attack on the city. Dewey counseled patience. He wanted to wait for the arrival of the *Monterey*, a sea-going monitor with two ten-inch and two twelve-inch guns. He also wanted to continue exploring the possibility of convincing Spanish authorities to capitulate without a battle.

On August 1, General Merritt placed General Anderson in charge of his Second Division for this campaign. General MacArthur led the division's First Brigade, numbering slightly over 5,000 men, and his job was to neutralize Blockhouse #14 and any other positions between him and the walled city of Manila. The enemy was well entrenched and too far inland to allow the First Brigade the benefit of the Navy's big guns to help dislodge them. MacArthur also had to deal with the potential crossfire from Spanish trenches that overlapped his line to the east. The Filipino position, a prolongation of MacArthur's right flank, faced the Spaniards, but the Americans were determined to effect a victory without the overt assistance of Aguinaldo's forces. The Filipinos, understandably miffed at the Americans' actions, refused to give way and allow them to usurp more of their trenches. MacArthur did what he could. He positioned three small field pieces from Battery B of the Utah Light Artillery on the extreme right of his position, and he stationed the Astor Battery in reserve close by.

General Greene commanded the Second Brigade of Anderson's Division and positioned it on the left of the line, running inland from the beach. Greene's 4,000 men were to drive the Spanish defenders out of Fort San Antonio (any, that is, who survived the expected supporting naval bombardment).

By August 6, a discouraged General Augustín had turned over control of the local government to General Fermín Jáudenes y Alvarez, who had to deal immediately with an American demand that he surrender. If he failed to do so by noon on August 9, Dewey would feel free to begin a naval bombardment of the city. When Jáudenes failed to accede, the Americans sent in another note on August 9. Before responding to this demand, Jáudenes polled his senior subordinates. Seven favored entertaining the possibility of a negotiated surrender. Seven others obstinately refused to consider such a thing and voted for continued resistance. Jáudenes himself cast the tie-breaking vote by deciding to try to postpone the inevitable. He notified Dewey and Merritt that he would have to consult with his superiors in Madrid before giving them a definite answer. This response was unsatisfactory to the Americans.

What evolved very quickly over the next few days was a partially choreographed battle. Jáudenes' personal and national pride would not allow him to give up his command without a fight, so he made arrangements with Dewey to surrender the city without losing face. The American ships were to open fire on Fort San Antonio de Abad, a considerable distance away from the center of the city and where no civilian casualties were likely. After a time, the ships would cease firing and one of them would hoist the international signal asking if the Spaniards were ready to surrender. In reply, the Spaniards were to raise a white flag indicating their acceptance — finally — of Dewey's demand, now that their honor had been satisfied by gunfire. General Jáudenes would then surrender to the Americans with the understanding that the Filipino troops were not to be allowed into the city.

Of course, a mere naval cannonade would not fool anyone in Manila into thinking that surrender was inevitable, so American ground troops also had a part to play. They would advance against the Spanish positions to their front, but only after enemy fire had slackened considerably. General Merritt was very specific about this. "It is intended," he ordered, "that these results shall be accomplished without loss of life." To avoid the costly results of a Spanish double-cross, however, he did not inform his subordinate commanders that the enemy was poised to surrender after only a token resistance. He did not want his troops to become overconfident in case Jáudenes reneged on the arrangement.[22]

On the morning of August 10, the date designated for the attack to take place, all was excitement aboard the American warships. Some of the sailors grumbled about having to do all the real work of capturing the city, but having to share the glory with the Army, and they were understandably optimistic about their chances. After all, they had destroyed Spain's entire Asiatic squadron without losing a man to enemy guns. In fact, many sailors on the sick list found themselves remarkably recovered with the prospect of action looming.[23]

General Merritt came out to the *Olympia* a little before 10 A.M. to tell Admiral Dewey that the Army was not quite ready for the proposed joint action. Dewey, disappointed at the delay, signaled his ships to stand down for the time being. Delays such as this were particularly frustrating because peace talks had begun already back in Washington, and there was a certain apprehension that the talks would produce a peace treaty before Manila could be taken. If that occurred, of course, the United States would have no justification for taking over the Philippines. From a purely military standpoint, however, all agreed that it was best not to rush into any operation until they had completed all necessary preparations.

One of these preparations was to make sure that the soldiers understood not only their duties in the coming battle but also their responsibilities as representatives of the United States. Therefore, much as Winfield Scott had done over a half century earlier, during America's first foreign war, General Merritt issued a general order to his Army. They had come to these islands, the order reminded the men, with the lofty goal of helping to free an oppressed people from the tyrannical rule of Spain. "It is believed," the order read, "that any acts of pillage, rapine or violence ... committed by soldiers or others in the employ of the United States ... will be considered not only as crimes against the sufferers, but as direct insult to the United States flag, and they will be punished on the spot with the maximum penalties known to military law."[24]

The Army was ready by the 12th, and Dewey ordered his ship captains to be ready to commence operations by 9 A.M. the next day. That evening, meanwhile, shortly after dark, the alarm sounded on board the *Olympia*, sending officers and men scrambling to their battle stations. A lookout had spotted a ship approaching suddenly and without warning. In a matter of minutes four 8-inch guns, five 5-inch guns, and numerous 6-pounders were leveled at the interloper ready to send it to the bottom of the bay. Seeing this, the terrified captain of the intruder frantically signaled his friendly intentions. He was a member of Aguinaldo's force who had come requesting permission to leave the bay. He must have played the event over in his mind more than once, reflecting on how close he had come to being forever entombed in the depths of the bay.[25]

The next morning Dewey's ships got up steam and prepared to get underway. As it left its anchorage at Cavite the *Olympia* passed near the visiting British warship *Immortalite*, whose band immediately broke into "See the Conquering Hero Comes," followed by the "Star Spangled Banner" and "El Capitan." Once again, as when the American seamen left Hong Kong back in April, their British counterparts expressed their support. Heartened by this display the American sailors eagerly awaited the beginning of hostilities. The *Olympia* led the little procession through the drizzling rain toward Malate and Fort San Antonio. Behind the flagship came the *Raleigh* and the *Petrel* as well as the two captured Spanish vessels *Callao* and *Barcelo*. The *Monterey* followed for a time but kept on going until it lay off Manila and the big Krupp guns along the waterfront. It almost seemed as if the monitor's commander was trying to goad the Spanish gunners into action by his near presence so he could respond in kind. Supporting the *Monterey*, but out of immediate range of the shore batteries, were the *Charleston*, the *Baltimore*, and the *Boston*. If the Spanish gunners violated the plan and opened fire from Manila's waterfront the *Monterey* and her consorts would move in to destroy them and the town. Finally, the *Concord* lay off the mouth of the Pasig River.

Reveille sounded early in Camp Dewey that morning, and the men eagerly prepared for battle. One officer, seeking perhaps to inspire his men, told them, "Boys, you look as if you could eat those Spaniards up." "Give us a chance," was their immediate shouted reply. The rain that fell in torrents definitely did not dampen the enthusiasm of the soldiers. As a Minnesota volunteer observed, "they had put ten thousand miles between themselves and home for the purpose of paying their little tribute to the memory of the *Maine*, and now was the time and here the place."[26]

General Greene's headquarters ordered every man in his brigade to equip himself to handle a wide range of circumstances, and now they checked and re-checked their gear. In light of the season of the year it almost went without saying that the men would carry their rain ponchos with them. Because there was no guarantee against Spanish treachery in not adhering to the "script," each man also carried 200 rounds of ammunition, most of which he stored in his haversack. That canvas pouch was also where he carried his mess kit and two days' rations of meat and hardtack. Half of the men were to fill their canteens with coffee and half of them with water so they could share both beverages with one another. And at least one of every four infantrymen carried a shovel, axe, pick or some such tool in case it became necessary to dig in and build protective works. Many of the Colorado soldiers received wire cutters with which to open passageways through any Spanish barbed wire entanglements they might encounter. A company of engineer troops was also on hand to do what it could to ease the passage of the infantrymen through any physical obstacles they might meet. These hard working men had previously cut enough bamboo to be able to bridge any stream or gully that might require crossing, and they had prepositioned this material just behind the forward trenches.[27]

The gunners of the Astor Battery jumped the gun on the morning of August 13 by opening fire on Blockhouse #14 at 6 A.M. The Spaniards wasted little time in replying with both rifle fire and artillery. The infantry supporting the Astors was from the First North Dakota, and even though the jungle in front of them was too thick for them to see the enemy they fired several volleys in their general direction. The rifle fire soon dwindled away, and after about an hour the bigger guns also fell silent.[28]

Shortly after 9:30, and at a range of about 4,200 yards from Fort San Antonio, Admiral Dewey ordered the *Olympia*'s 5-inch guns to commence firing. The *Raleigh* and the *Petrel* joined in, and although the first couple of salvoes fell short, the naval gunners soon found the range and began pounding the enemy positions. The *Callao* and the *Barcelo* meanwhile steamed close into shore and enfiladed the Spanish trench lines with fire from their rapid fire Nordenfeldt and Hotchkiss guns and machine guns. There was no response from Spanish artillery and only scattered volleys of musketry directed at the two small boats near the shore. On shore the field artillery opened up on both sides.

Finally, after about an hour of softening up the Spanish positions, the American infantry assault began. General Greene sent the First Colorado Volunteers forward, half of them along the beach and half directly toward Fort San Antonio, while the Eighteenth U.S. Infantry and the Third U.S. Heavy Artillery advanced straight ahead. Before the Coloradoans on the left could reach their objective, they had to wade across a stream that entered Manila Bay a couple of hundred yards in front of the fort. Holding their rifles and flags over their heads they plunged into the water. Behind them, the regimental band trailed along playing with, as one man later reported "wonderful persistence and questionable harmony." Still the band's rendition of such favorites as "The Star-Spangled Banner" and "There'll Be a Hot Time in the Old Town Tonight" were appreciated by most of their infantry comrades. When they reached the fort they discovered it virtually deserted. A handful of dead and badly wounded defenders still lay about, but all the able-bodied Spaniards had retreated toward the walls of Manila. The exuberant Americans immediately tore down the red and yellow Spanish flag and replaced it with the Stars and Stripes.

Over on the American right, the First Brigade began receiving enfilade fire from its right front, just as MacArthur had feared. General Anderson then authorized him to unmask the Astor Battery, disregard the feelings of his Filipino neighbors, and press the attack forward. The volunteer artillerists once again unleashed a firestorm against Blockhouse #14 and its neighbor to the northeast, Blockhouse #13. And the Spanish gunners once again wasted little time in focusing their attention on their opposite numbers. One enemy cannoneer sent a shot screaming into the American lines with either superb precision of aim or a tremendous amount of luck. It hit one of the Utah guns and wounded three of its crew. Whether or not luck was involved with the placement of the shot there is no doubt that luck was involved with the amount of damage it did. Even though one of the wounded Americans later died of his wound, the carnage would likely have been much greater if the Spanish projectile had actually exploded. There were additional casualties. At one point a sergeant knelt down to help a battery mate wounded in the leg. The wounded man was sitting up watching his friend apply a dressing when he suddenly fainted away and fell back. A bullet had entered the mouth of the sergeant and blown the back of his head away. The wounded man later recovered.[29]

In spite of these losses the American field guns hammered away, rapidly blasting holes in Blockhouse #14 and making it untenable to the enemy. As the surviving Spaniards fell back, the men of the Thirteenth Minnesota and the Twenty-third U.S. Infantry charged forward. Thick brush and swampy ground impeded their progress, but they soon reached and occupied the most forward of the enemy's trenches. The American field pieces also advanced, although with no horses to pull the guns this was extremely difficult. A dozen Utah gunners had to do the job of six horses to haul their gun and limber over very difficult terrain. The Astor Battery faced the same problem, but infantrymen helped pull its guns forward.

Most of the soldiers on both sides did their duty bravely this day, but it was at this phase of the fighting that a rare instance of cowardice occurred. As the Thirteenth Minnesota pushed past the blockhouse they came under a rather intense fire from Spanish soldiers nearby. One company had advanced farther than the rest and now found itself fairly pinned down. Orders came down for the captain of another company to lead his men to its assistance, but the captain suddenly declared that he felt ill and unable to follow this order. One of his lieutenants immediately jumped up and led the men forward while the captain took a shovel and began furiously to pile up earth in front of his position.[30]

The next obstacle for MacArthur's brigade was Blockhouse #13, a few hundred yards northeast of #14. Built primarily of stone, it was not as easily harmed by the field guns of the Astor and Utah Batteries. Soon, however, wooden portions of this structure were on fire, causing much of the stored small arms ammunition therein to cook off. The noise of this exploding ordnance caused many in the area to suppose that it was the sound of fierce Spanish resistance.[31]

On the American left the Colorado volunteers, having found Fort San Antonio unmanned, continued onward. General Greene sent the Nebraska volunteers in the wake—literally—of the Coloradoans through the surf along the beach while the other regiments of his command advanced along parallel roads. As they sloshed along the shore past the Spanish fort they observed the effect of naval gunfire on Fort San Antonio. "What guns were not dismounted," one man wrote, "were covered up with debris. His [Dewey's] shells and solid shot had tore their works all to pieces. The body of one Spaniard could be seen hanging over the wall, tore all to pieces by one of Dewey's shells."[32]

As American soldiers from both brigades moved through the suburbs toward Manila's old city walls they met scattered resistance, but the heavy fighting seemed to be over by early afternoon. Out in the bay Admiral Dewey flew the internationally recognized signal "Do you surrender?" from the forward signal halyard of his ship, and, leaving the *Callao* and the *Barcelo* in place, began moving the rest of his ships closer to the city. As the minutes dragged by with no response from the city there was some speculation about whether Jáudenes intended to honor his earlier promise. Finally, at noon, a full hour after the American surrender request, the Spaniards raised the appropriate flags indicating their wish to hold a conference. Then it was Dewey's turn to make his opposite number wait. Shortly after 2 P.M. he sent Flag Lieutenant Thomas M. Brumby and Lieutenant Colonel Charles A. Whittier, of Merritt's staff, ashore in the Belgian consul's launch to confer with Spanish officials. Within twenty minutes Brumby

Colorado volunteers atop the ruins of Fort San Antonio de Abad after the surrender of Manila (Library of Congress).

was back with the news that the Spaniards had indeed capitulated. Why, then, Dewey inquired, was the Spanish flag still flying prominently from the battlements of the city? Brumby informed him that the Spanish troops feared that the local inhabitants might do them harm when they saw the symbol of four centuries of imperial rule come down the pole. They wanted American protection, and Dewey quickly ordered the Second Oregon Volunteers, who had been kept afloat on the *Kwonghoi*, to land at the city to replace the flag and begin occupation duty.[33]

Lieutenant Brumby then went back ashore with the biggest American flag that the *Olympia*'s flag locker contained. A lieutenant of the recently landed Second Oregon, along with a couple of sailors and some reporters, made up the small flag raising party. Curious knots of Spaniards, soldiers and their wives, watched the group approach the flagstaff. When it became obvious what the Americans' intentions were, most of the men sadly turned away, not wanting to actually witness the last symbol of their country's grandeur being removed. Some of the women broke into sobbing entreaties to their men to not allow their flag to be desecrated by the touch of these invaders. The Americans apprehensively fingered the butts of their revolvers and began to mentally make note of possible escape routes in case there should be resistance. There was no interference, however, and just as the Stars and Stripes reached the top of the pole the sun broke through the clouds for perhaps the first time all day and bathed the scene in golden light. At this point, wrote one of the reporters who had been part of the flag crew, "we all breathed a bit more freely and proceeded with our work of transforming Luzon into an American colony."[34]

The capture of Manila had cost the Americans 122 casualties during these first two weeks of August — nineteen killed and 103 wounded. It had also led to the capture of 13,000 prisoners of war, 22,000 small arms, 10,000,000 rounds of small arms ammunition, 70 pieces of

One of the gates into the walled city of Manila (U.S. Army Military History Institute).

fairly modern artillery, and hundreds of old muzzle-loading cannons. Most of the city's 300,000 civilians were glad to have the yoke of Spanish colonialism finally lifted.[35]

Aguinaldo's forces did not sit idly by while the battle took place. They were, of course, unaware of the arrangement between the Spanish and the Americans but attacked the Spanish right along with their "allies." Some of the attacking Americans found themselves in as much danger from Filipino bullets as from Spanish. The California regiment, for example, had just reached the walls of the old city at Calle de Nozaleda and was hurriedly escorting some Spanish troops within when gunfire erupted behind them. A Filipino force, seeing Spanish troops ahead and on the city walls, had opened up. The Spanish, along with the Californians, returned the fire and, for a few almost incomprehensible moments, Americans and Spaniards stood virtually side-by-side fighting a common foe. The Filipinos soon stopped shooting and marched away. Spanish and Filipino casualties as a result of this clash are unknown, but two Californians died and another was wounded.[36]

As soon as the Spanish surrendered, the American commanders began shifting their men into positions from which to prevent armed Filipinos from entering Manila. They wanted no more incidents such as that which had befallen the California volunteers, and they did not want the recently surrendered and disarmed Spanish soldiers to be victimized by the local troops.

The Filipino leaders were understandably unhappy in not being privy to American battle plans to capture Manila, and the situation was further exacerbated by their now being forbidden, by armed American soldiers, from entering the city unless they went in without their weapons. The potential existed for more violence.

On August 14, an officer and eight men of the Colorado regiment took over a just-abandoned Spanish work about a mile east of the suburban village of Rotonda. They had barely settled in when they came under rifle fire. Advancing up the road toward them were about 250 Filipinos, firing as they came. The American captain sent for reinforcements and ordered his men to retreat in an orderly fashion. The timely arrival of a company of Americans from Rotonda ended the fracas. The Americans disarmed the native troops and demanded explanations from their leaders. These officers claimed that they never would have ordered the attack if they had realized that American soldiers now faced them. They claimed that they thought the Spanish still occupied the position. This excuse seemed plausible so the insurgents were freed, although their weapons were retained "as a lesson not to trifle with American troops."[37]

Timing, the saying goes, is everything, and it was certainly true with regard to this battle. Locally, the white flag appeared while General MacArthur's troops were still involved in heavy fighting to the southeast. Had MacArthur been aware of this he could have saved himself several casualties. Internationally, the effects were much greater since only hours before the battle began, diplomats in Washington had agreed to end the war. However, with the telegraph cable that connected the Philippines to the rest of the world still severed, word of the truce did not reach Manila for several days. Had General Jáudenes been aware of the agreement to end hostilities he might have chosen not to surrender the city when he did, trusting instead to diplomats to determine its ultimate fate.

CHAPTER 10

The Puerto Rico Campaign

THE REDUCTION OF SANTIAGO de Cuba and the concurrent destruction of Admiral Cervera's squadron were the primary goals of American military men, but this did not mean that they neglected other operations. Spain's other major Caribbean colony, Puerto Rico, also drew considerable attention. Army and Navy leaders deemed the capture of Puerto Rico a military necessity in order to deny Spain any kind of a foothold in the Western Hemisphere from which to launch attacks on Cuban targets or send reinforcements to Spanish garrisons there.

General Miles desperately wanted to lead an expedition to Puerto Rico. It would probably be the last chance for him to add more martial honors to his already illustrious military career. Even while he was at Tampa helping General Shafter's Fifth Corps get ready for the voyage to Cuba he urged that a Puerto Rican campaign begin as soon as Santiago was secure. Even though Miles' campaign took a back seat to Shafter's expedition, the War Department had to begin planning right away. On June 7, with Shafter's transports barely loaded and even then waiting to leave Tampa's docks, Miles received orders to prepare 30,000 more men for departure within ten days.

On June 26, Secretary Alger authorized General Miles to draw the troops he needed from the stateside camps of the First, Third, and Fourth Army Corps. Should General Shafter be able to release some of his force, those men would also be added to the Puerto Rican venture. And in spite of the woeful record of the Fifth Corps's experiences at the overcrowded facilities at Tampa, that port was also designated as Miles's embarkation point. As it turned out, however, several ports were used.[1]

The Army's success on the ground in Cuba and the Navy's victory over Cervera at sea lent increased urgency to the Puerto Rican campaign. Miles's troops began leaving the states for Santiago where they could either assist Shafter in cleanup operations or steam directly for Puerto Rico. This force began arriving off Santiago on July 9, and Miles arrived two days later. Shafter's negotiations with General Toral were ongoing, and it did not look as if the reinforcements accompanying Miles would be necessary in effecting a Spanish surrender. Moreover, the increasing sickness within the Fifth Corps already was causing Miles to decide against embarking any of them to join his force. He also decided to leave the Puerto Rico-bound troops aboard the transports where they would not have contact with Shafter's sick men. He then ordered them eastward to Guantánamo Bay to await developments.

After wrangling with the Navy about available shipping, Miles' 3400-man force steamed away from Guantánamo on the afternoon of July 21. Brigadier General Theodore Schwan and another 2,900 men left Tampa on the 24th, and Major General John R. Brooke left from

Newport News, Virginia with a 5,400-man brigade on the 28th. Although the expeditions from the mainland proceeded without armed naval escorts, steps had been taken to give the transports a measure of self-defense capability. The *St. Louis*, for example, sailing from Newport News with the Third Illinois Volunteers aboard, was replete with five six-inch guns, fourteen four-inch guns, and a score of smaller rapid-fire weapons.[2]

With the Fifth Corps successful in Cuba and the Eighth Corps already arriving in the Philippines, it was obvious that the Puerto Rican expedition would be the last major campaign of the war. This meant that the thousands of soldiers still at stateside training camps would likely not take an active part in the war. This realization led to a flurry of telegrams and letters to the War Department in Washington from newspaper editors, influential private citizens, governors, U.S. senators, and congressmen around the country begging that regiments from their respective states be included in Miles's force.

The justifications put forth for including particular units were varied. Some were based on some real or perceived historic precedent, such as the claim that the First Troop Philadelphia City Cavalry had been George Washington's bodyguard during the American Revolution and had participated in every armed conflict since then. Others claimed heroic Civil War service, such as one supplicant who cited the valorous performance of Minnesotans in the Iron Brigade at Gettysburg. "If there be more fighting," he pleaded, "their sons seek the field of honor and danger." Others employed lightly veiled hints at the political consequences of leaving a particular regiment at home. Some were much more direct. "If you want to make some good votes this fall, have the Twenty-second [New York] regiment sent to Porto Rico."[3]

In most cases the response from Washington was almost formulaic. The petitioner's pet regiment would be given every consideration if the campaign needed more troops than had already been scheduled. There was one notable, and immediate, exception in the case of Indiana volunteers. Senator Charles W. Fairbanks pointed out to the secretary of war that every state surrounding his had sent troops either to Cuba, the Philippines, or Puerto Rico, yet none of Indiana's five volunteer infantry regiments had left the United States. The senator was certain that the secretary had not intentionally overlooked Indiana, but he felt that some remedy was appropriate. Upon receipt of this wire, and verification of its assertions, the secretary immediately issued orders that an Indiana regiment be substituted for an Illinois regiment slated for deployment to Puerto Rico. While this salved sore feelings in Indianapolis, it created a furor in neighboring Illinois. The Fifth Illinois had already prepared to board trains at Chickamauga for movement to the coast when orders arrived that it would not be going after all. The men of the regiment, "the flower of Illinois," were heartbroken at their fate. Adjutant General Corbin explained to Illinois Governor John W. Tanner that his state had already sent three regiments to the front and that it was only in fairness to Indiana that the Fifth's orders had been countermanded. Illinois citizens, nevertheless, held protest rallies over what they considered unfair discrimination. The War Department ultimately felt so much pressure on this issue that it relented and reinstated orders for the Fifth Illinois to go to Puerto Rico. Governor Tanner thanked General Corbin, but then, in the same message, made a case for also sending the *Eighth* Illinois![4]

The soldiers en route to Puerto Rico had to deal with many of the same problems that had faced the men on those earlier voyages to Cuba and Manila—cramped, often unventilated sleeping quarters and poor food and drinking water. An Ohio volunteer was full of sarcastic praise for the accommodations on the *St. Paul*. He described spacious quarters with lots of room on deck for taking exercise. He tempered his description, however, by stating that the ship was perfectly adapted to carry a regiment of 600 men, but unfortunately his regiment contained more than twice that number. An artilleryman complained that the enlisted men's quarters on his ship had two decks of horses and mules above them and two more below, and "the ammonia makes the place almost unbearable." A Pennsylvania volunteer was sure that life on board the *City of Chester* was "a perfect hell. We had on board two hundred mules, and they traveled second class; we had twelve hundred men, and we traveled steerage."⁵

Some of the ships were fitted with brand new hammocks, which should have been considerably more comfortable than hard wooden bunks. But in an effort to get as many men as possible aboard, workmen had placed the hooks from which the hammocks were slung so close together that each man had a space only eighteen inches wide for his berth. This tight spacing made sleeping unpleasant in the best of conditions, but it was especially uncomfortable when, as a news correspondent on the *St. Louis* reported, "you are trying to sleep in terrific heat, and the ship is rolling in the bargain." After the first night of such conditions, the decks of the ships became littered with the sleeping forms of officers and men. The steel decks were not as soft as the hammocks, but the ocean breezes more than made up for that, at least on nights when there were no tropical showers.⁶

The soldiers grumbled not only about their sleeping facilities but about the quality and quantity of food and water available to them. Travel rations consisted of canned roast beef, canned baked beans, canned tomatoes, hard tack, and coffee (sometimes with sugar). In the best of circumstances the soldiers would readily eat these items, that is, if served only once or twice a week. But some of the troops had been subsisting entirely on the travel ration for some weeks before sailing. The quality of this food made quite an impression on an Ohio soldier aboard the *St. Paul*, who went to great lengths to describe it in his published account of the war. He found the label on the canned beef, which touted it as "Prime Roast Beef," to be very deceiving. In fact, he said, "The English language absolutely does not contain an expression more deceptive than that combination." It was of the lowest quality to begin with, he decided, and packed in its cans only after having lain in storage for an indeterminate length of time. "In many cases the stuff was spoiled," he declared, "if indeed it ever had been fit for the use of human beings." The rest of the menu was not much better. The aforementioned Ohio volunteer discovered that the canned beans "were often spoiled and disgusting even to think of." Served to the men straight from the cans, uncooked and unseasoned, they were anything but "a tempting viand." This man also found the canned tomatoes to be "stale, sometimes spoiled, [and] sickening at best." Nor was this a case of a coddled citizen-soldier facing a situation routinely accepted by the regulars. A regular artilleryman on another ship was no less condemning of the canned meat. Even though it was slimy and smelled terrible he forced himself to eat it, but became violently sick after only three mouthfuls. He decided to save an unopened can as a souvenir, but when he accidentally dropped it on the deck of the ship it exploded and showered him with its filthy contents. A bucket of warm water served as the basis for each mess's coffee. The men of the mess threw crushed coffee beans and a little sugar, if they had it, into the water and waited. A few minutes later, when the solution had darkened in color, someone pronounced it to be coffee. A Massachusetts volunteer noted that food conditions aboard the *Yale* had so deteriorated that "men who live on Beacon Street grabbed food from the refuse of the officers' table which was being thrown overboard, while Harvard men chased small potatoes down the scuppers with an eagerness which could be explained only by the pangs of hunger." When the officers caught their men throwing the tainted food overboard they chastised them for this waste. The men on the *Yale* did not see it as wasting good food. In fact, one of them composed a limerick about this rejected food:

> Near Cuba there lived a young shark,
> Who fed always about some new barque.
> He ate meat from the "Yale,"

Then turned up his tail—
The end of the tale of the shark.[7]

The men did not have much to do during the day but sit around and complain about their plight. A few men engaged in target practice by firing at empty wooden boxes that were thrown into the water. "This was," recorded one of these men, "the only rifle practice we had in the service."[8]

Some of the troops received new canvas uniforms before departing the United States, and still others traded in their heavy blue wool for the tan uniforms while on the transports. This lighter weight clothing helped make things a little more bearable. Some got a little more respite from both the heat and the dirt and grime by having salt water hoses played upon them as a form of early morning baths.[9]

General Miles had set Fajardo, on the northeastern coast of Puerto Rico and about forty miles east of San Juan, as his proposed landing site, but announced en route that the expedition would land instead at Guánica on the south coast.

The invasion force steamed along the northern coast of the island until after dark on the night of July 24. Then, with darkness hiding the fleet's movement from any Spanish eyes on shore, the ships reversed direction—except for the cruiser *Columbia* left behind to alert Major General James Wilson's expedition to the change of plans—and headed around the western side of the island and toward Guánica. Arriving there the next morning, the shallow draft *Gloucester* nosed into the harbor to investigate the situation. The gunners aboard the small craft let fly with one of their three-pounders at a blockhouse displaying a Spanish flag, and then a naval landing party went ashore to reconnoiter further. The sailors hastily erected a barricade of stones and barbed wire across Guanica's one and only street and employed their Colt machinegun against a few inquisitive Spanish soldiers. When it began to look as if the resistance might be more than this small group could deal with they signaled back to the waiting ships for reinforcements. While the *Gloucester* shelled suspected enemy positions in the hills surrounding the town, some regular artillerymen landed to assist the sailors. The exchange was short-lived, the handful of Spanish defenders opting to run away, perhaps to fight another day. The transports then began disgorging Miles's troops, and soon the Sixth Illinois and the Sixth Massachusetts Volunteers came ashore, as well as the rest of the artilleryman accompanying them from Guantánamo.

The natives seemed happy to see the Americans, and, with few exceptions, welcomed them to Puerto Rico. Late that afternoon, however, Brigadier General George Garretson received word that the Spaniards who had so hastily departed that morning had not gone far. In fact, reports were that a large enemy force was nearby and had fired on an outpost of men from the Sixth Illinois on the road to Yauco. He immediately dispatched two companies from the Sixth Massachusetts to reinforce the position. After dark they received more random fire, but it did no damage. Thus under fire for the first time most of the Americans performed coolly with no outward display of fear. "At the first [enemy] volley I was simply surprised," remembered a Massachusetts volunteer. "I did not have the slightest tremor." One man even took the time to calmly light his pipe, while for another the most urgent task was to recover his hat, which a gust of wind had sent skittering down the road.[10]

A little after midnight the men sent word back to Garretson that they expected the Spaniards to attack in force at any moment. The general responded with five more companies of Massachusetts volunteers that he personally led out of Guanica at 3 A.M., arriving at the outpost a little before dawn.

He found the Illinois troops dug in on the side of a hill and the enemy apparently posted in a field somewhat to the left. Garretson deployed two of his companies to seek out the

Spaniards and left three more in reserve. The American attackers had only covered a couple of hundred yards when the Spanish opened up on them from a hillside to the left. Enemy fire also found the American reserves, who were standing in a relatively compact formation on a roadway they thought was secure. Almost immediately two men dropped, wounded, while the others, taken by surprise and never having been under fire before, continued to mill around on the road. Major Frank Anthony, the surgeon for the Illinois regiment, recognized what a tempting target such a crowded mass represented for the Spanish and ordered them to disperse to more effective cover before more of them were injured.

Although General Garretson later estimated the strength of the enemy force at between 600 and 700, the fighting did not last long. However many Spanish soldiers there were, they soon broke contact and retreated back toward Yauco. Two more American volunteers had been slightly wounded, bringing the total to four, while two Spaniards died and fifty more suffered wounds of varying severity.[11]

After the day's excitement, the Americans were particularly alert for any suggestion that the enemy was returning. They were so alert, in fact, that several times that night they saw or heard things that convinced them that the entire Spanish Army was about to descend upon them. About nine o'clock, some of the Massachusetts men heard the unmistakable sound of horses' hooves upon the road, but it was too dark, even with the occasional sweep of a searchlight's beam from one of the ships in the harbor, to make out anything definite. One of the men, therefore, called "Halt" to the invisible rider. Receiving no response he repeated his challenge. When silence again answered him he fired in the direction of the hoof beats, whereupon the intruder galloped away. About an hour later more horses approached but stopped some distance away on the road. Seven or eight Americans moved quietly toward them, rifles at the ready. When the horses began running toward the American outpost the little squad quickly moved to the side of the road and prepared to ambush their unknown, and unwelcome, visitors. The horses were almost on top of them when the volunteers unleashed a fusillade. One of the horses was down, badly wounded, but all of the others escaped. As the men approached the crippled horse to investigate the condition of its rider they were surprised to see that not only was there no rider, but no saddle or other trappings. The "attackers" had simply been riderless horses. It is surprising that not more damage was done by the wild firing in the night. Some of the errant shots even hit ships in the harbor, including the one upon which General Miles was sleeping. He was not amused, but the sentinels congratulated themselves on handling the matter as they had been taught.[12]

The results of such firing in the night were not always so harmless. One man, standing guard near a bridge, heard a noise in the dark and immediately called out a challenge. Receiving no response, he called out again, and this time he was sure that he saw the figure of a man. Finally, after a third challenge went unanswered the soldier fired with deadly effect. And this time the target was not a riderless horse, but a sleepwalking private from the Fourth Ohio.[13]

On July 27, General Miles welcomed the first expedition sailing from the United States directly to Puerto Rico. General Wilson's force — the Second and Third Wisconsin Volunteer Infantry Regiments, two more companies of the Sixth Illinois, and a company of signal corpsmen — had sailed for Fajardo, according to the original plans, and had then come on to Guánica. With the arrival of Wilson, Miles's available force doubled, and he wasted no time in expanding his beachhead. He sent Brigadier General Guy V. Henry with Garretson's brigade on toward Yauco, only about five miles northeast of Guánica. From there his men could use a railroad and a good highway to descend upon Ponce, Puerto Rico's largest city, about twelve miles to the east. At the same time the commanding general ordered Wilson to move by ship to Ponce, effectively putting it in a land-sea vise.

When the water-borne force reached the port that served Ponce there was no immediate show of resistance, and Ensign Roland I. Curtin, from the *Wasp*, went ashore in a small boat with a letter for the Spanish commander demanding that he surrender. It was difficult for the Spanish Captain of the Port to take this 24-year-old officer seriously. He was, as an American correspondent described him, "about the youngest-looking boy in the navy." The local official informed Curtin that he was not authorized to take such a step as surrendering, but that if the young American wanted to travel to Ponce, a scant two miles inland, he might then take it up with the military commander. Curtin told him to telephone the commander at Ponce and inform him that he had thirty minutes in which to come down to the port and surrender. Otherwise, said the diminutive Curtin, "I shall bombard Ponce!"[14]

As Curtin was being rowed back out to the *Wasp* after delivering his ultimatum he met Commander Charles H. Davis on his way into shore from the *Dixie*. He told the senior officer what had transpired. Davis approved of what he had done but decided to lengthen the grace period by an additional half hour, by which time the surrender was duly carried out. This was probably the first time in history that the telephone had been used to demand the surrender of an enemy garrison.[15]

While all this was going on, the Spanish defenders experienced even more pressure as General Henry's force easily captured Yauco and then made its way to Ponce. Spanish soldiers were undoubtedly dispirited by this turn of events, but the citizens seemed relieved to have the Americans in their midst. Loyalist militia units dissolved amid mass desertions, and General Miles issued a proclamation assuring the people of Puerto Rico that the American forces had not been sent among them out of any but the purest of motives. "The chief object of the American military forces," it read, "will be to overthrow the armed authority of Spain, and to give the people of your beautiful island the largest measure of liberty consistent with this occupation. We have not come to make war upon the people of a country that for centuries has been oppressed, but, on the contrary, to bring you protection, not only to yourselves, but to your property; to promote your prosperity, and bestow upon you the immunities and blessings of the liberal institutions of our government."[16]

That afternoon, Generals Miles and Wilson both appeared in full dress uniforms on the balcony of the *alcalde*'s palace to review a parade in their honor. The march did not exactly go off without a hitch. As the local fire companies paraded by, their members apparently were so eager to get a glimpse of their deliverers that they did not watch where they were going. Three of their number were run down by their own equipment. And although the men were not seriously injured, the local Red Cross personnel were adamant to demonstrate their prowess in front of the foreign dignitaries. They insisted on bearing the injured men off on stretchers even though none were very seriously injured, and, as an American correspondent noted, "the firemen preferred to walk."[17]

On the last day of July, General Schwan arrived from Tampa at Ponce with 2,900 men: two regiments of infantry, two batteries of artillery, and one company of cavalry, all regulars. The next day, in anticipation of the impending arrival of General Brooke and 5,000 more troops, the *Wasp* and the *Gloucester* left their anchorage at Ponce and headed east looking for another landing site behind the suspected position of the Spanish troops along the southern coast. As the two ships neared Port Jobos the inaccuracy of their navigational charts only seemed reinforced. The depths shown on the charts seldom matched those measured on the scene. The Puerto Rican pilots kept assuring the American naval officers that they were in no danger, but in spite of slow speed and careful handling the *Wasp* soon hung up on the reef. The engines quickly reversed and increased power, easily pulling the ship off, but by this time it was obvious that Port Jobos could not serve as a place of debarkation for the heavy troop ships on the way.[18]

The *Gloucester* signaled that it was going farther east, to the port of Arroyo, and the *Wasp* followed. The charts for the bay at Arroyo were no more accurate than for Port Jobos, but visual observation showed that the waters were much less treacherous. The *Gloucester* stopped and dropped anchor at eleven o'clock, the *Wasp* a few minutes later, and officers on both ships scanned the shoreline for any evidence of a Spanish military presence. They spotted the Union Jack of Great Britain and three French tricolors but no Spanish flags. A couple of miles inland to the northwest lay the city of Guayama, but it appeared equally peaceful.

By the time a small boat from the *Gloucester* reached the beach under a white flag there was quite a gathering waiting to meet it. The *alcalde* and the local priest welcomed the Americans, and within minutes the Stars and Stripes was fluttering in the breeze over the customs house. American authorities immediately enlisted the aid of a messenger to go to Guayama with a demand for the surrender of that city and its small force of Spanish defenders. The soldiers at the latter place, many of them Puerto Rican volunteers, did not relish the idea of surrender, and late that night they entered Arroyo. There were as yet no American troops ashore, and only the presence in the harbor of the *Wasp* and the *Gloucester* gave any indication of anything out of the ordinary. The enemy volunteers furtively made their way down to the beach and opened a rifle fire on the *Gloucester*. The Americans could not very well reply without the risk of heavy civilian casualties. However, when the ship's big spotlight swept the beach, the brightly illuminated riflemen lost their nerve and beat a hasty retreat.[19]

With the enemy threat at least temporarily dissipated at Arroyo it was now safe for the transports to land. The *Cincinnati*, the *St. Louis*, and the *St. Paul* arrived on the afternoon of August 2, with part of General Brooke's force. There were no dock facilities so Brooke's men went ashore in lighters towed by the navy's launches. It was slow, but with only token Spanish resistance, it proceeded throughout the afternoon. Army engineers eventually succeeded in constructing a usable dock by sinking two lighters in the shallow water and covering them over with boards.

By August 5, General Miles had about 15,000 troops ashore along the southern coast of Puerto Rico, and began formulating his strategy to seize San Juan, the capital. Speed was essential because negotiations to end the war had already begun in Washington. The United States would have a much better chance of wresting Puerto Rico from Spanish control if Miles's troops could conquer Spanish forces there before a cease-fire was announced. General Schwan would lead one contingent northwest from Ponce to Mayagüez on the west coast. From there he was to work his way toward Arecibo on the northern coast. The second prong of Miles's offensive, under General Garretson, would also originate at Ponce, but it would move almost straight north over the mountains to Utuado and then on to Arecibo. When these two forces linked up, General Henry would lead them eastward toward San Juan. General Wilson was to lead a third force from Ponce northeast along a major highway to a strong Spanish position at Aibonito. From Arroyo, General Brooke's 5,000 troops would march northwest toward a linkup with Wilson near Aibonito. From there, this combined force would move against San Juan from the south. Against a strong enemy this strategy might well have proven disastrous for the Americans, as it seemed to invite defeat by detail. But the Spanish forces on the island were by this time neither strong in numbers nor strongly inclined to offer great resistance.

Nevertheless, final orders for the American offensive began emanating from Miles's headquarters on August 6. On that date, General Schwan received instructions to "drive out or capture all Spanish troops in the western portion of Porto Rico. You will take all the necessary precautions and exercise great care against being surprised or ambushed by the enemy, and make the movement as rapidly as possible, and at the same time exercising your best judgment in the care of your command to accomplish the object of your expedition."[20]

General Schwan's small independent brigade was made up entirely of regulars—although many of them were fresh recruits—and somewhat resembled a twenty-first-century combined arms unit. It consisted of Troop A, Fifth U.S. Cavalry, the Eleventh U.S. Infantry and two companies from the Nineteenth U.S., and Light Battery C, Third U.S. Artillery and Light Battery D, Fifth U.S. Artillery. As it left Yauco on the morning of August 9, the cavalry pushed ahead as a screening force. These troopers would spot any trouble spots early and relay the information back to the main body by way of mounted couriers. Behind the cavalry about two miles marched an advanced guard of two companies of the Eleventh Infantry, one platoon of artillery, and two Gatling guns. Next came the main body: the remaining infantry companies, one battery and two platoons of artillery, and the brigade's other two Gatling guns. The supply trains plodded along in the wake of this force, protected by another company of infantry.[21]

The tropical sun was punishing, and the march quickly became uncomfortable. A regular artilleryman, writing about the campaign later, was hard pressed to describe the ordeal as he and his comrades went "tramping along in a blinding dust, parched of throat, empty of belly, and loaded down with a pack that would make a quartermaster's mule to fake the glanders." The friendliness of the Puerto Rican people that the column occasionally encountered made up for some of the discomfort. The natives willingly supplied the foreign soldiers with cool fresh water, cigars, and various fruits. Although Army medical authorities had previously cautioned the men not to eat local fruits, they were hard to resist. An artilleryman expressed a typically adverse—or maybe perverse—reaction to such regulations when he recalled: "Because we were forbidden to eat of the fruit, we stuffed ourselves with it, and looked for more." An Illinois soldier wrote that "half ripe bananas fried in grease was considered a treat although lacking in nourishment."[22]

By the afternoon of August 10, Schwan's brigade had reached within about a half dozen miles of Mayagüez without yet having met the enemy, but things were about to change. The men noticed civilians hurrying across the fields and away from the road. Spanish troops must have been near enough for the people to want to escape the effects of a pitched battle. At about 3:30, after having passed through a brief but furious summer shower, the brigade turned right off the main road toward the village of Hormigueros, less than a mile away. As the cavalrymen crossed an iron bridge over the Rio Rosario, Spanish troops hidden in the thick brush some 500 yards ahead opened fire on them.[23]

The main body of the American brigade rushed forward and deployed on either side of the road. Unable to ford the Rio Rosario, however, they were obliged to take to the road again and cross on the bridge. In spite of the danger of presenting such a mass target to the unseen enemy there was no other way to get the men across the stream and at the Spaniards. "Bullets whistled by our heads, or kicked up the dirt at our feet," recalled one soldier, "but, though the pop of rifles made up a continuous sound like the opening of a hundred thousand beer-bottles, not a vestige of smoke rose in the clear air, not a patch of hostile uniform was to be seen." Luckily, in spite of enjoying the advantages of surprise, smokeless powder, and concealment, the Spaniards did not do much execution on the Americans as they hurried across the bridge and deployed to either side of the road.[24]

The American Gatling guns soon added their chatter to the "beer-bottle" popping of the Mausers and Krags, and American field pieces soon roared as well. After about two and a half hours, the Spaniards had had enough and withdrew. Only one American was killed in this skirmish, while an officer and fifteen enlisted men suffered wounds.[25]

A young cavalryman tried to explain to his parents back home what it had been like to be under fire. "It is," he wrote, "a mighty queer sensation—not fear exactly.... But take it all in all, I would rather be at home, lounging in that large armchair in my room, smoking some Old Gold tobacco." Another soldier expressed a certain disappointment in what he saw taking place around him. It was not at all like the popular representations of battles that appeared in picture books, with thousands of soldiers on a vast open field shooting at one another from point blank range. "There were no clouds of dust," he moaned, "no heaps of slain, no cheers, no desperate charges, and not even a glimpse of the stars and stripes." For the handful of casualties, however, it was certainly real enough.[26]

It was one of the wounded who furnished a macabre bit of humor after the fighting was over. This man, painfully wounded through both cheeks, was sitting propped up against a fence waiting for medical attention. One of his comrades, fortunate enough to have come through the action unscathed, went to his side to see if there was anything he could do to make him more comfortable until the stretcher bearers arrived. He half expected the injured man to inquire about the outcome of the battle or to beg for a sip of water, as wounded men always did in the novels. This man, however, wanted neither information about the fight nor water. Instead, he had been lying there trying to remember the words to a popular song, and when the healthy soldier asked if he could do anything to ease his pain he said: "If you'll tell me how the beginning of 'Sweet Marie' goes," he said, spitting out a couple of teeth, "I'll give you a piece of my face for a souvenir. I've been trying to get that blame tune straight for the last fifteen minutes, but keep getting off my trolley."[27]

Schwan's column camped near the battlefield for the night, but it was on the march again early the next morning. His scouts reached Mayagüez at 8:30 and found that the Spanish garrison, after learning of the American victory the afternoon before at Hormigueros, had abandoned the city and set out toward Lares. By 11 A.M. the rest of Schwan's command had entered this third largest city on the island. The general allowed his men to rest while he sent detachments of cavalry to learn how far the enemy troops had gone. They reported back that the Spanish rear guard was still within five miles and retiring slowly.

On the morning of August 12, Schwan dispatched a reconnaissance in force. It contained six companies of the Eleventh Infantry along with a platoon of cavalry and a platoon from the Third Artillery. The men had no idea how long they would be on the march, so they carried enough food to last them for three days. The road was difficult, the heat was oppressive, and the rain rendered them even more uncomfortable. By the end of the day they had covered only about nine miles.

The next morning the Americans caught up with the retreating Spaniards a few miles north of the village of Las Marías and opened fire on them. As the firing continued an American courier galloped back to Mayagüez to let General Schwan know what was developing. The messenger was unable to give the general a precise estimate as to the strength of the enemy force, but it seemed certain that it far outnumbered the 700 Americans it then faced. When Schwan arrived on the scene, however, he found that the Spaniards were rapidly retreating, and that the firing had subsided to long-range rifle fire with an occasional round from one of his field pieces thrown in for good measure.

General Schwan was proud of the performance of these men. They were regulars, and they were also very proud of themselves. One of the men, in a post-war reminiscence, compared the performance of regulars and volunteers. He had little to write about the latter that was positive. "Because we had no Volunteers with us," he began, "we were not granted even one little word-spattering newspaper scribe, and so relinquished at the outset any fugitive hopes of glory that otherwise might have been entertained. We were out for the business,—hard marching, hard living, hard fighting,—and the opening vista was fringed with gore. We were none of us the darlings of any particular State, nor the precious offspring of a peripatetic statesman with a practiced pull. We were at no time decimated by disease through ignorant or insubordinate disregard of the primary principles of hygiene. We didn't write long wailing letters home because we were obliged to sleep on the damp ground, and had neither hot rolls, chocolate, nor marmalade for breakfast. We were ragged, hungry, tough, and faithful. In other words, we were regular army men, and, distinctly *not* Volunteers."[28]

The only thing that Schwan's regulars had not accomplished, which the general would have liked, was the taking of some prisoners. He sent the cavalry off to try to bring in some prisoners so he could learn of the enemy's intentions. They returned to camp toward evening empty handed. Schwan then asked for infantrymen to follow up the retreat of the Spaniards and try to make some captures. Virtually the entire company volunteered, in spite of the exhaustion of the day's work, and returned with forty Spaniards and their weapons.[29]

Only one of the American supply wagons had been able to traverse the difficult road and reach the camp that night so supper was scanty. By the next morning no more wagons had come in so breakfast was also scarce. Nevertheless, the troops had a wonderful chance to follow up their victory of the day before and destroy the Spanish force they had faced.

The force with which General Schwan was to link up at Arecibo meanwhile had begun its movement from Ponce northward under General Garretson on August 8. Each man of the Sixth Illinois and the Sixth Massachusetts began the march well prepared. A Massachusetts volunteer reported that in addition to his rifle and bayonet and the forty or fifty rifle cartridges he carried in his cartridge belt, there were fifty or sixty more in his haversack. He carried a canvas shelter half, a rubber rain poncho that was essential during that time of year, and a canteen of water to help combat the effects of the summer heat. In addition, many men carried a change of socks and underwear, an extra shirt or two, and a mess kit. Some of the men may have been even more burdened than that. A Massachusetts soldier, while still in the United States, had described his marching load: "I have everything I need and not a thing else. I am carrying a woolen blanket, a rubber blanket, a canvas shelter [half], a change of fine underclothing, three or four pairs of stockings, one towel, a comb, a tooth-brush, my dishes, a little paper and a pencil, my camera, 48 films, and my brown trousers. It may weigh, altogether, 45 pounds, not a bit heavy to carry, and not a bit lacking of what I want." This, of course was in addition to his rifle, bayonet, canteen, and ammunition. This same soldier, when faced with the march from Guánica to Ponce, found a local youth willing to carry his pack for him in exchange for 25 cents.[30]

After a few hot hours on the march, the men began to reduce the amount of baggage they carried by unceremoniously tossing unwanted articles into the bushes alongside the road. Extra clothing went, along with the blankets and shelter halves. Some even went so far as to discard their bayonets and much of their extra ammunition. The New Englander who had earlier found that his forty-five-pound pack contained only those items essential to his health and comfort no longer had a porter and soon changed his tune. "We are fast learning how to live on the march," he wrote home. "Much that was superfluous has been thrown away. For instance, I am carrying a towel, a toothbrush, and one pair of stockings.... My brown coat has long been a thing of the past."[31]

It took a while, however, for the men to lighten their loads and become hardened to the trail. The first day's march from Ponce only took them nine miles, to Hacienda Florida. Stragglers continued to reach camp after dark, and some of the ox carts carrying food and extra ammunition did not make it until the next day. It took the brigade two more days to reach Adjuntas, just a few miles farther, and on the 12th it finally reached Utuado.

General Wilson, meanwhile, had the consolation that at least his assigned route was over a fairly well maintained macadamized road that led all the way to San Juan. Because it was such a good road, some said the best in all the West Indies, the Spaniards would certainly attempt to deny its use to the invading Americans. Careful reconnaissance revealed such to be the case. Wilson received reports that about 2,000 Spanish soldiers occupied the town of Aibonito, about thirty-five miles northeast of Ponce, and were daily strengthening its defenses. In addition, at least 250 enemy troops were at the little town of Coamo, eight miles nearer Ponce on the same road. The enemy positions were too strong to risk attacking them in a frontal assault without heavy losses. Wilson decided, therefore, on a flanking movement.[32]

On the evening of August 8, Wilson pondered the situation before him. He found that he and two of his officers were the only members in his entire command who had ever seen a gun fired at another human being, the only ones ever to have seen men killed in war. He must have wondered how well his men, who had only traded in their obsolete Springfield rifles for the more efficient Krags five days earlier, would stand up to Spanish gun fire.[33]

He ordered Brigadier General Oswald H. Ernst to send the Sixteenth Pennsylvania Volunteers of his brigade on a cross-country march around the enemy's right flank. He estimated that this regiment, under Lieutenant Colonel John Biddle, should arrive on the main road between Coamo and Aibonito by 7 A.M. the next morning. Ernst was then to push the Second and Third Wisconsin Volunteers, assisted by a regular artillery battalion and a troop of New York volunteer cavalry, forward up the main road toward Coamo. If the timing was right Wilson would smash the Spaniards with the hammer of this latter force against the anvil of the Sixteenth Pennsylvania.

The Pennsylvanians had rough going. They set out at about 4:30 in the afternoon and marched until it got dark when they stopped for a temporary camp. There was little in the way of a trail, and the thick growth meant that much of the time the men had to march in single file, which slowed their progress considerably. A little after midnight, Colonel Biddle and a staff officer, accompanied by a twelve-man pioneer squad, moved forward to clear any obstructions from the trail. After traveling about a mile, the colonel sent a couple of men back to bring the rest of the regiment up to that point while he continued forward with the pioneers. In the dark and difficult terrain these men got lost and did not bring the regiment forward until well after the time planned for. Consequently, by 7 A.M. the tired infantrymen were still two or three miles from where they had hoped to be by then.[34]

Wilson had gone ahead and ordered the rest of Ernst's brigade forward, as scheduled, at 6 A.M. The firing in this sector began about forty minutes later when four guns of Light Battery B of the Fourth U.S. Artillery, parked in an open field to the right of the highway, opened fire on a Spanish blockhouse on the Los Baños road, just south of Coamo. The riflemen in the blockhouse returned fire, but it was less than effective. The battery commander stated that it was "so wild that I hardly realized that we were under the fire of an enemy." Nor did the Spaniards have time to improve their aim. After the fifth shot from the American guns the gunners had the exact range and began firing shrapnel rounds into the target. That was enough for the defenders, and they rapidly abandoned what had become a death trap. Even though the target had been rendered impotent the guns kept firing shell and shrapnel for another forty minutes "for practice." By the time the American guns quit firing the blockhouse was in flames.[35]

The Second Wisconsin attacked Coamo eastward along the main road, while its sister regiment moved across country to and across the Coamo River to be able to assault the town from the south. Finally, one company of New York cavalry followed the Third Wisconsin across the river to gain control of the road from Coamo to the coastal village of Santa Isabel. The horsemen were to ferret out any resistance in Los Baños that might make itself felt on the right and rear of the Third Wisconsin.

Among the news correspondents watching the battle that day from the relative safety of the American artillery positions was Richard Harding Davis, fresh from covering the fighting in Cuba for the readers of *Scribner's* magazine. Having determined that the one-sided contest at hand would soon end, and hoping to "scoop" his competition in covering the inevitable surrender, he slipped away with a couple of commissary officers anxious for some excitement and headed forward in the wake of the Second Wisconsin. The trio had barely started, however, when three other correspondents and a British military observer hurried to join them.

Their path took them closer to a shallow place in the river than to the bridge, and they eagerly splashed across. When they intersected the road toward town they saw empty Spanish rifle pits and the detritus of war. Pots still boiled over small campfires and unfired cartridges lay on the ground. The Wisconsin boys must have pushed through here in an awful hurry. Davis feared the worst and urged his small horse to greater speed. He shouted to his companions that the American infantry must have crossed the bridge a half hour earlier and that they would really have to hurry if they were going to arrive in time to witness the town's surrender. One of the other reporters then informed Davis that the Spaniards had destroyed the bridge, and the troops would have to have crossed the stream at the same ford that they had so recently used. It dawned on Davis that his small group was ahead of friendly troops! By now it was too late to stop and turn back so the handful of unarmed men sped on into the town of Coamo.

The Spanish forces on the west side of the town had not waited for the American infantry to attack but had abandoned their positions and tried to escape toward the east. They soon made contact with the Sixteenth Pennsylvania. The Pennsylvanians had not quite reached their assigned position when the firing began on the west side of town, and they were afraid that they would miss out on the fighting. In spite of being somewhat preoccupied with the attack of the Wisconsin troops, the Spaniards learned the location of the Pennsylvanians and laid an ambush for them from behind a low stone wall. Half a dozen unsuspecting Americans went down under the first withering enemy volley, but their comrades quickly recovered and began returning fire with great effect. Caught in a situation from which there seemed no chance for escape, and with mounting casualties, the Spaniards soon began waving their hats, handkerchiefs, and anything else they could think of to signal the Americans their intention of surrendering. The fight for Coamo was over.

Davis's party, meanwhile, thundered into the empty streets of the village wondering whether a Spanish ambush would end their adventure. This anxiety was soon allayed when the *alcalde* and dozens of other civilians approached with white flags. While the citizens plied their deliverers with wine, rum, and cigars, Davis formally accepted the surrender of the town and (even though he had no military standing) named himself military governor, mayor, and chief of police. His administration was short-lived. Within about twenty minutes, General Wilson arrived at the head of about a thousand soldiers and bemusedly relieved Davis of his authority.[36]

In terms of relative numbers of casualties, this battle resembled the naval contests in Manila Bay and off the coast of Santiago more than it did the fighting at El Caney or along San Juan Ridge. American losses were very light. None were killed. In fact, the six enlisted men wounded were all in the Sixteenth Pennsylvania. None of the attacking Wisconsin volunteers suffered a scratch. The Spanish commandant and four of his soldiers paid the ultimate price, and between thirty and forty were wounded. On top of that the Americans captured five enemy officers and 162 men. The battle for Coamo was quite a success.[37]

That night General Ernst's brigade made camp in the valley just beyond Coamo, with outposts pushed forward almost to Aibonito to keep a sharp eye on enemy movements. For the next couple of days the principle objective was to reconnoiter further before planning any more movements. The Spaniards were at Aibonito, and after receiving information from various scouts General Wilson again decided that the tactical plan that offered the greatest hope for success was to attack and turn their right.

The preliminaries for this movement began early on the afternoon of August 12, when five guns from Battery F of the Third U.S. Artillery opened up on suspected enemy positions at a range of 2,150 yards. The Spaniards wasted little time in replying with rifle and artillery fire. The plumes of smoke issuing forth from the American guns every time they fired gave the enemy a tremendous edge in target location, and counter-battery fire soon began to find its mark. After almost an hour, return fire slackened and the Spanish appeared to vacate their trenches and gun positions.

The American guns went silent for about a half hour, and then the gunners began to see Spaniards returning, and soon the air again was filled with enemy fire. Major J. M. Lancaster, commanding the American artillery, ordered his gunners to keep up a slow harassing fire until their ammunition was all gone.

While all this was going on, Lieutenant Edward P. O'Hern positioned Battery F's remaining field piece directly on the road to add to the volume of fire coming from the hillside to his left. During the lull in the firing Major Lancaster directed Lieutenant J. P. Haims to take his gun out of battery and join Lieutenant O'Hern on the road. Spanish infantrymen were only about 800 or 900 yards away from these two guns and began firing heavy volleys in their direction. Haims soon went down with a bullet through the body. Then the American guns on the hillside ran out of ammunition and retired, leaving the two pieces on the road as the Spaniards' sole target. The firing soon became so hot that Lieutenant O'Hern decided not to wait until his ammunition was gone before he pulled back.[38]

Casualties among the Americans were fairly light. Lieutenant Haims' painful wound was the only one inflicted on American artillerists. A Spanish shell had exploded amidst the men of the Third Wisconsin, however, killing one man and wounding three of his comrades, one mortally. rifle fire also felled an infantry officer and an enlisted man.

The purpose of this exercise had been to develop more precisely the strength of the enemy before committing to the planned flanking movement, which was to begin at dawn the next morning. The enemy show of resistance was a cause of some concern for General Wilson. He would have a difficult time driving them out of their positions. In order to forestall the possibility of heavy American losses he decided on a rather audacious gamble. That afternoon he sent one of his staff officers, Lieutenant Colonel Tasker Bliss, under a flag of truce to see the Spanish commander at Aibonito. The purpose of the visit was for Bliss to hand over a demand that the Spaniards surrender! "While I had but little, if any, expectation that the Spanish commander would yield to my cheeky demand," General Wilson remembered in his memoirs, "I had long years before learned that it was no mistake in war to ask for what you would like to have, even if you should be forced to accept only what you could get away with."[39]

Wilson's "cheeky demand" probably caught his opposite number a little off guard, as he told Colonel Bliss that he would have to communicate by telegraph with his superiors in San Juan. Bliss could return the next morning for the Spanish reply. General Ernst, meanwhile, had already received his attack orders. He was to move against the Spanish left at daylight of the 13th, unless the enemy acceded to Bliss's demand. The next morning, at first light, Bliss returned to the Spanish lines for the answer. Not only did the Spaniards refuse to surrender, but their message was especially blunt about any future attempts to negotiate. The Spanish commander announced that he would accept no more messengers under white flags, and that the Americans would be well advised not to attempt to assault his works.[40]

General Brooke was also busy, sending two regiments toward Guayama on August 5. A little after 10 A.M., and about a mile east of Guayama, as Company A of the Fourth Ohio wended its way up a small slope in advance of the rest of the column, Spanish forces opened fire. The Ohioans immediately moved off the road seeking shelter behind trees, rocks, or anything at all that might stop a bullet. Unable to spot the location of the ambushers the men began firing toward the assumed position of their assailants along the top of the rise. "They are just [as] afraid of us," encouraged an officer of the Fourth Ohio, "as we are of them so just be careful and pump it to them." Apparently taking heart from this exhortation, his men, after having been pinned down for a half hour, began moving forward up the hill. Singly and in small groups they dodged from one source of protection to another. When they reached the top they found the enemy gone.[41]

From this elevation the Americans could easily see the city of Guayama. They also learned very quickly that the Spanish troops they had driven from the heights had not gone far. From the underbrush, cacti, and fields between the Americans and their goal the Spaniards kept up a lively fire. The Ohioans spread out on both sides of the road in heavy skirmish order and began working their way toward the city. Progress was slow, the enemy elusive. Upon reaching the outskirts of the town, the American advance halted. It would be foolish to go any farther without some sort of reconnaissance to determine the strength and location of the enemy force. While the men rested and their officers pondered their next step civilians began making it known to the soldiers that the town was in their hands. The Spaniards had chosen not to engage in urban warfare, and had completely evacuated Guayama.

The formal occupation ceremony, complete with flag-raising, went off without all of the customary flourishes. The band of the Fourth Ohio ordinarily would have played the "Star Spangled Banner" and other patriotic airs to commemorate this momentous occasion, but it was not able to perform. Cross-trained as stretcher bearers, the bandsmen had left their instruments in Arroyo and had come forward as ad hoc members of the hospital corps. Nevertheless, the local *alcalde* made a welcoming speech to the Americans, and the colonel of the Fourth Ohio congratulated his men for their actions that day.

Rifle fire marred the ceremony when a handful of Spaniards crept back near the city determined to cause mischief and fired into the town. A battalion of Ohioans immediately responded. Captain J. D. Potter's Company F had charge of the two Sims-Dudley dynamite guns, which they now trundled by hand to the edge of town and began to shell the hillside where the snipers were apparently concealed. Potter estimated the range to the Spanish position to be about 1,200 yards when he gave the order to fire. While the dynamite projectiles gouged the countryside, the infantrymen added the fire of their rifles to the action. The combination was enough, after only the second dynamite round, to discourage any further disruptions by the Spanish, but the guns fired three more rounds just for, as Captain Potter put it, "moral effect." The conquest of Guayama had come at relatively low cost to the Americans. They came through the hot day's work without any fatalities and only four men suffered wounds, none of which proved life threatening. Still, however, rumors of an enemy counterattack prompted American authorities to have suspected Spanish sympathizers lodged in the jail overnight.[42]

Two days later, General Brooke received orders to begin his next movement by attacking and capturing the village of Cayey, on the way to Aibonito. A scouting patrol brought word back to General Brooke that the Spaniards had indeed occupied a fortified position along the road to Cayey. General Miles exhibited his well-known penchant for husbanding the lives of his men when he directed Brooke to "envelop or outflank the enemy rather than attack in front, and under no circumstances assault entrenched lines." Miles obviously did not want his men to suffer the kind of casualties that had befallen the Fifth Corps on the heights of San Juan.[43]

Brooke ordered General Haines to scout the road toward Cayey. Haines in turn ordered Colonel A. B. Coit to send a company from his Fourth Ohio Volunteers to undertake the assignment. There had been a report of an explosion somewhere along the road, and Brooke wanted to find out the details before attempting to lead his entire brigade forward. He expressly cautioned the colonel not to bring on an engagement with the enemy. Coit responded immediately. He decided that if one company was sufficient for the task at hand, then certainly two companies would make the job that much easier, so he named Companies A and C to carry out the general's order.

The reconnaissance patrol was on the road by 8 A.M. on August 8, but progress was slow. The column matched the speed of the flankers, but those on the left had to work their ways along the side of a hill while those on the right were in a valley. By noon Coit's command had only progressed a few miles, and he had called in the flankers due to the rugged terrain. The patrol soon found what it had been sent to find. At a rather abrupt turn in the road they saw the place in the road that had been blown up. And a short distance behind it were the trenches and gun positions of the enemy. The column proceeded only a short distance farther when bullets rent the air about it like so many angry hornets.

The first few volleys whistled harmlessly overhead, but the Spaniards' aim was bound to improve. To advance would have been to disobey General Brooke's instructions. To stand fast was both pointless and dangerous. The only option left open to Colonel Coit was to fall back. This, too, had an element of danger since to do so meant that the men would be exposing themselves to Spanish fire as they sought the safety of a bend in the road farther back. Colonel Coit ordered the men to fall back in twos and threes. Small squads of men then waited for a Spanish volley to rip over their heads and, while the enemy soldiers were working the bolt actions of their rifles for another fusillade, the Americans broke for the rear.

As progressively more and more soldiers reached safety one of them, for some inexplicable reason, was seized by panic. "The [Spanish] cavalry is coming!" he cried. "Run for your lives!" His fear communicated itself to a handful of his comrades, and they began heading back to Guayama as fast as they could go. A Sergeant McConnel planted his feet in the middle of the road and vowed to shoot the next man who tried to run past him for the rear, and the junior officers were able to restore order in the ranks.[44]

By the time Sergeant McConnel had taken his stand some men already had rushed past and on toward Guayama with their tales of gloom and doom. Officers there quickly gathered up those companies of the Fourth Ohio that could be spared from other necessary duties and headed for the scene of the fighting. By the time the reinforcements arrived the Americans had taken what cover they could find, and the lack of suitable targets had caused the Spanish fire to slacken considerably. The large body of additional America troops moving forward along the road, however, gave the enemy something to shoot at again, and they reopened their fire.

The purpose of the reinforcing troops was only to escort their comrades to safety, but the commander of the relief party decided to give his men a chance to return fire before returning to Guayama, and he ordered them to the top of a ridge from which they had clear shots at the Spanish trenches. After a rugged climb, during which the men had to move in single file, they reached the top of the ridge and commenced firing.

Although both sides blazed away at one another little damage was apparently inflicted. This began to change when the sweating members of Company F, Fourth Ohio manhandled two dynamite guns into position. The first shot at the enemy fell short, but the effect of the explosion was enough to convince many of the Spaniards that they did not want to be around when the American gunners' aim improved. Unable to counter this weapon successfully, the Spaniards rapidly began abandoning their works. Another round from one of the dynamite guns exploded amidst the enemy soldiers and killed twenty-seven of them. After a few such shots, the Americans packed up and returned to Guayama with no further molestation by the enemy.[45]

On August 12, General Brooke prepared to take the field again. He directed General Haines to take a regiment of infantry and try to get around behind the enemy, who were reported to be near a village known as Pablo Vasquez on the road toward Cayey. Brooke would then personally lead the rest of the brigade up the road and drive the enemy into Haines's blocking force. General Haines selected the Fourth Ohio Volunteers for this task, and at 7:15 A.M. on the 13th, the Ohioans, weighed down with two days' rations and 100 rounds of ammunition, left Guayama. Brooke controlled the Third Illinois and the Fourth Pennsylvania Volunteer Infantry regiments, along with two troops of cavalry, and four batteries of field artillery. A successful fight here would clear the way for the Americans to march into Cayey, where they would be in a position to block the retreat of any Spaniards from Aibonito toward San Juan.[46]

Meanwhile, shortly before three o'clock on the afternoon of August 12 in Washington, a French diplomat called on U.S. Secretary of State William Day to inform him officially of Spain's acceptance of peace terms. It was a gloomy day in Washington, with rain falling in sheets, but inside the cabinet room of the White House the feeling was anything but gloomy. It was 4:23 P.M. when the treaty was signed.[47]

General Miles sent telegrams to all of his field commanders in Puerto Rico announcing that the United States and Spain had agreed to a truce and that all military action was to cease immediately. American soldiers reacted in different ways to news of the cease fire agreement. General Shafter's troops viewed the news with some relief. Some were already at sea, on their way to Long Island to recuperate from their campaign, and the truce meant that, more than likely, a formal peace treaty would soon follow. When that happened they would no longer be needed for an attack on Havana or indeed any other targets. In Puerto Rico, where the men were generally healthier than their brethren in the Fifth Corps, there was some disappointment upon hearing the news. All across the island American troops were poised for a final push on San Juan. Many believed that if hostilities had continued for another couple of days they would have completely occupied the island. In the Philippines, news of the cease-fire came as something of an anticlimax since the Spanish forces at Manila had already surrendered the city. In the stateside training camps there was a mixed reaction. Many of the men were disappointed. After all, they had volunteered in the hope that they would see combat. Now those hopes were dashed. Others, however, having already despaired of seeing any action, welcomed the armistice as the first step in their separating themselves from the drudgery of Army camp life and getting on with their lives at home.

CHAPTER 11

Coming Home

THE INK WAS HARDLY dry on the armistice before citizens from all over the country began bombarding officials in Washington with complaints about the treatment of the sick soldiers in Cuba. The fighting was over, but the soldiers still remained in that sickly climate. Of course, it was not a simple matter of sending the sick men home to recuperate because of the fear that they would bring the fevers home with them. The solution seemed to be to bring the troops to some point in the United States where they would be both out of the fever zone and yet not in close contact with civilians until they fully recuperated. The August 4 newspaper publication of Roosevelt's letter and the round robin note further stirred up the public and finally moved Secretary Alger to issue the long-awaited movement orders to General Shafter. He was to begin preparations for the immediate evacuation of the Fifth Corps from Cuba.

Only a couple of days before, the War Department had leased a 5,000-acre parcel of land located 125 miles from New York City at Montauk Point, at the far eastern tip of Long Island. It had dock facilities and a few buildings, and the landowner agreed to install extra rail sidings and erect warehouse and terminal buildings at no additional cost to the government. The site was far enough away from any concentrations of civilians as to pose little danger of exposing them to the diseases carried home by sick soldiers. At the same time it was far enough north of the fever zone as to drastically reduce the danger of new fever cases breaking out among the troops and allowing those already sick to convalesce.[1]

The original purpose of the camp, dubbed Camp Wikoff, was as a training base for the proposed attack on Havana tentatively scheduled for December 1898 and secondarily as a recuperation site for those who had contracted various illnesses in Cuba. By the time the first veterans of the Cuban fighting arrived, however, the United States and Spain had agreed to a truce, so there would be little training at Montauk.

All arriving troops spent a period of quarantine in one section of the camp. Those not exhibiting symptoms of communicable diseases, after a period of several days, moved into the general camp area. The men lived in floored tents, but there was also a need for mess halls, bathing facilities, offices, and other fairly substantial structures. Civilian workers were hurriedly hired, often at rather extortionate wages, and work began on August 5.

According to original instructions only those soldiers who were free of disease were to be allowed on board the transports. Those exhibiting any symptoms of fever were to be left behind to recover in hospitals in Cuba or would come north later on hospital ships that had the facilities to care for them. The reality was that any man who was strong enough to walk on board a ship did so. To be left behind, most believed, was to ensure death.

The first contingent of soldiers left Santiago headed north aboard the transport-cum-hospital ship *Seneca*. It had carried the Seventy-first New York Volunteers part of the way to Tampa as that regiment went off to war. One of its members even then described the ship — with its hard wooden bunks — as far from luxurious. The accommodations had not been revised for the comfort of the ninety sick and wounded men going north. Two civilian contract surgeons accompanied the wounded on the *Seneca*, but both were young and relatively inexperienced. To make matters worse, there were apparently no medical supplies or instruments to spare for this shipload of patients. The total supply of medical instruments amounted to a couple of pairs of forceps and scissors. Lacking were such basic items as thermometers and even the simplest of medicines. Janet Jennings, a news correspondent who had attached herself to the Red Cross as a way to get to Cuba, stepped forward and volunteered to accompany the patients on the *Seneca* back to the United States.[2]

Clean water for drinking and bathing was in such short supply that wounded men had to have their injuries bathed in seawater or not at all. The fresh water tanks had not been flushed in several weeks, rendering the "potable" water almost undrinkable. Ice would have alleviated that condition somewhat, but the supply of ice on board ran out after two days at sea.[3]

Jennings was everywhere on the ship trying to make the patients more comfortable. She talked all but two of the forty civilian passengers on board (they had been on board before it was thought to have the *Seneca* transport sick and wounded) into giving up their staterooms so that some of the patients might be made more comfortable. With virtually nothing to ease the pain of wounds or the flush of fever, she distributed liberal doses of whiskey to all who seemed to need it. In fact, so tirelessly did she work that one soldier on board said "she almost worked herself to death.... She was an angel!" The *Seneca* finally reached its destination, delayed three days at sea by weather, without having lost a single patient. Four days later the hospital ship *Relief* arrived from Santiago — but only half full.[4]

Conditions on the *Mobile*, formerly used to carry livestock to England, were also bad. It had undergone a thorough cleaning and whitewashing before taking on its human cargo at Santiago, but that seemed to make little difference to the 1,600 to 1,700 men crammed aboard. Available toilet facilities could only serve about fifteen men at one time, and the men's hammocks were hung so close together that every time the ship rocked on the waves at night the sleeping men bumped into one another. Those who became sick were placed on the upper deck for the benefits of fresh air, but the temporary wooden roof built to shelter them from the rain did a poor job. Still they fared better in that respect than their healthier comrades below. They were quartered below the deck upon which horses were being transported, and, as one passenger later related sarcastically, "it was the privilege of the men ... to receive the drainage from the leaky floor above, as they lay in their hammocks."[5]

Not all of the soldiers returned from Cuba amid such horrid conditions. The Army doctor aboard the *Hudson*, for instance, insisted that the ship be completely fumigated and well stocked with necessary supplies before it took on passengers in Santiago. As a result, it made the trip with no outbreaks of sickness at all. Likewise, the *Miami*, which provided passage for the Rough Riders, was well maintained and had minimal health problems. Colonel Roosevelt even characterized his men as living "high, with milk, eggs, oranges, and any amount of tobacco, the lack of which during portions of the Cuban campaign had been felt as seriously as any lack of food."[6]

The celebratory spirit exhibited by the Rough Riders caused their progress northward to be delayed somewhat. According to a Troop E lieutenant, several of the men decided to protect their already fragile health by buying bottles of liquor into which they would mix quantities of quinine to dispel the effects of fevers. Had the inebriating effects of the mixture been confined only to the Rough Riders there would have been no problem. But the more they drank the more generous they became with their miracle cure, sharing it liberally with members of the ship's engine room crew. The captain of the ship appealed to Colonel Roosevelt when he found, upon preparing to leave Santiago, that "he had no steam, no engines, and no one to operate the ship." Roosevelt told his men that they must turn in to him all alcohol. When they reached the United States he would return it to them. If he discovered liquor that had not been voluntarily surrendered he would throw it overboard. About seventy men turned in bottles and flasks to him, but others decided to risk the penalty by keeping theirs. Some twenty of these unfortunates saw their bottles confiscated whereupon Roosevelt, true to his word, consigned them to the ocean waves.[7]

Reporters were quick to cover the arrivals of the victorious soldiers from Cuba, but in many cases they were shocked by what they saw. A newspaperman from the Boston *Herald*, reporting on the arrival of the Second Massachusetts Volunteers at Montauk, characterized the ship on which they had come as "a floating charnel house." He described the experience of some three dozen Boston women who had traveled to Montauk to welcome home the Massachusetts volunteers. "They were prepared to wave handkerchiefs and clap their hands," he wrote, "but the sight that met their eyes struck horror to their souls." "They simply could not bear to look upon the suffering that was passing in review — a kaleidoscope of misery."[8]

When the first of Shafter's men arrived at Montauk on August 14, they found a scene of confusion. Some 3,500 cavalrymen, along with 5,000 horses, had already arrived by train from their camps in Florida. And more sick men were on the way from Cuba. Workmen were still striving to get the camp into a habitable condition, but the relative remoteness of the site meant that the labor force from which to draw was necessarily scant. The Second Regiment of United States Volunteer Engineers soon arrived to add their labors. A lot had to be done. They had to construct pumps and pipelines to supply the camp with fresh water. They had to dig drainage ditches to carry off wastewater and excess rain. They had to keep roads in good repair. They had to erect numerous hospital and other structures, as well as tents for the soldiers to inhabit.

The size and location of sanitary facilities contributed to the ill health of the camp before the arrival of the engineers. Latrines, or sinks, were located rather haphazardly, many of them dangerously close to the hospital or on wet swampy ground. Hospital attendants, in most cases completely ignorant of basic sanitation procedures, routinely dumped the contents of bedpans at the most convenient locations for themselves. This usually meant that this waste wound up on the ground surface or in drainage ditches adjacent to the hospitals. They discarded dirty and infected bedding in similar fashion. Wet, and often moldy, blankets, mattresses, and pillows piled up close enough to the hospitals to be dangerous to the patients therein.

The engineers had to prepare sanitary latrines for the use of thousands of men, many of whom suffered from dysentery. They immediately set to work and dug two trenches eight feet deep, four feet wide, and a hundred feet long. They then added shed roofs and walls to furnish privacy. When complete, each of these structures could handle forty men at one time, and every effort was made to keep them as sanitary and odor-free as possible. A six-man team had a full-time job of keeping the floors and the seats clean. And once every hour they covered the contents of the latrines with lime, dry earth, and copperas in an effort to disinfect them.[9]

Government officials worked tirelessly to make the constantly arriving soldiers as comfortable as possible. Individual civilians and private charities contributed food and clothing to make up for any slack of the War Department. Helen M. Gould, for example, hired women who needed work to make pajamas, nightshirts, and bandages for the convalescent soldiers at Camp Wikoff. The daughter of railroad tycoon Jay Gould, she was thus able to add to her previous $10,000 gift to the government for the war effort. Helen Long, whose father was the secretary of the navy, volunteered, along with some of her classmates at Johns Hopkins University, to help out at a naval hospital in New York City. Many other women also did what they could to make life at the camp a little more comfortable for the returned soldiers.[10]

Secretary Alger and President McKinley made personal inspection trips to the camp to assure the men that they truly cared about their welfare. During the president's visit he, like many other less official visitors, gravitated toward the camp of the colorful Rough Riders. He and his party came upon a group of men busily engaged in a crap game on a blanket spread upon the ground. One of the gamblers casually asked the commander-in-chief if he cared to place a fifty-cent wager on the roll of the dice. McKinley good-naturedly accepted the challenge, laid his coin upon the blanket, and rolled the dice. "The president craps," announced the soldier as he nonchalantly collected the bet, "who is the next lucky guy?"[11]

As soon as sick men were well enough to travel they received furloughs to go home. By the end of September the camp was empty. It had seen over 20,000 men pass through and had been the place where 257 of them had breathed their last.[12]

Soldiers who never left the United States during the war became more and more restive after the truce went into effect. Most were disappointed that they had not had the opportunity to face the Spaniards, but now that there was no longer a need for them to remain in uniform they wanted to go home as soon as possible. The War Department transferred some volunteer units back to their home states for eventual mustering out, but others prepared for deployment as occupation troops to the recent Spanish colonies to prevent, as much as possible, any friction between the natives and the defeated Spanish forces as they awaited transportation back to Spain. There was a very real concern that the indigenous people might boil over into revenge against their former colonial rulers.

In Cuba, even as Shafter's command prepared to leave, healthy men of the so-called immune regiments began to arrive. There were ten of these regiments, raised mainly in the South from among men who had built up immunities to tropical diseases like yellow fever. Five of them eventually served in Cuba, and one in Puerto Rico. The first occupation troops arrived in Cuba in August and were parceled out all over the eastern end of the island. Some stayed in Santiago while others occupied Guantánamo, Holguin, Siboney, Manzanillo, and numerous other towns and villages. Later, volunteer regiments from Georgia, Illinois, Texas, Ohio, and several other states sailed directly to Havana and other Cuban and Puerto Rican ports to continue the pacification of the islands. The Philippines were so far away that the troops already there remained rather than being replaced.[13]

The Americans had plenty of time to acquaint themselves with Cuban and Puerto Rican culture. One of the first things that many of them noticed and commented upon was the architecture. In large cities like Havana or Matanzas the public buildings were not unlike structures they had seen in the United States. It was the private dwellings that seemed so different. City dwellings, with their whitewashed or pastel tinted walls, were so solidly built that they appeared to be small fortresses. This image was furthered by the fact that, although window glass was a rarity, iron bars and wooden shutters protected window openings. An Indiana volunteer's first impression of Havana was that it resembled some "huge penitentiary (and makes one curious to know what is going on within)." When the shutters were open pedestrians passing along the narrow sidewalks abutting the houses had no difficulty looking right into the front rooms.[14]

In the small towns and rural villages there was a greater mix of architectural styles. Some villagers of Puerto Rico used corrugated iron sheeting to build their homes while others built clapboarded structures or used whitewashed brick. The poorer residents lived in thatch-roofed huts made of poles and scrap boards. Some could not even afford these materials and kept the elements at bay with woven grasses and huge leaves. The apparent beauty of the tropical seacoast villages they saw from the decks of their ships often favorably impressed newly arriving troops. An Ohio colonel arriving at Siboney thought "the white or light blue huts of the natives under the glaring rays of a noonday sun looked clean and inviting.... That was the way the picture looked from a steamship a mile out to sea. But when we got ashore.... it was different! Those white huts were filthy comfortless hovels such as civilized men would hardly house their dumb animals in. They were evidently designed to keep out the rain and sun and to keep in the filth and poisonous air of the occupants."[15]

Soldiers arriving in the Philippines thought the town of Cavite looked rather charming and quaint from the decks of their transports. There seemed to be lots of open park-like areas with plenty of trees, under whose branches an abundance of cool shade was sure to exist. Upon landing, however, and actually walking the streets of the crowded village this initial impression faded. The newcomers saw that what they had perceived to be solid stone columns and arches was instead mere stucco, and not very well executed stucco at that. An impressive statue rising above a square turned out to be carved from wood and badly in need of having its numerous coats of paint freshened. A civilian correspondent left a graphic description of the effects of the damp climate on the structures of the village. "In bright sunshine," he wrote, "the green mould which stained everything, creeping up the walls, accenting all the joints and spreading over all perpendicular surfaces in great patches, varying from intense purplish black to vivid metallic greens and yellows, was picturesque enough to look upon from afar, but close at hand, and particularly in the rain, it seemed repulsively noxious."[16]

A Massachusetts volunteer — posted to Matanzas — found "everything ... including streets, people, buildings and language, ... at first matters of great curiosity to the soldiers.... The streets were narrow and ill kept.... and most of the roadways were so rough that it would be impossible to drive a light American wagon over them without great discomfort." Another Bay Stater found similar conditions in Santiago where sewage flowed along the streets. "I have seen a pool of green, slimy water in the middle of a thoroughfare," he related, "and dead dogs, cats and decaying matter floating on its surface." A New Yorker described the "nauseating stench from the green slime which covered the unpaved streets [as] unbearable." An Illinois volunteer reported that "if cleanliness is next to godliness, then" the Puerto Rican civilians he had encountered "were certainly an ungodly lot, as the condition of the streets and interior of nearly all of the store buildings was indisputable evidence against them."[17]

The native populations reacted to the occupation troops in a generally positive manner. Troops from the First Texas Infantry, for example, landed at Havana on the day after Christmas and paraded through the liberated city to their campground in the suburbs. From the reception accorded them by the local populace one would have thought that it was these very men who had stormed San Juan Ridge some months before. They were hailed as liberators with shouts of "¡Viva los Americanos!" and "¡Viva los Americanos soldados!" One Texan declared: "With viva this and bravo that, I never heard so much cheering in all of my by no means prosaic life." In addition to the vocal welcomes, the residents of Cuba's capital city showered the Americans with oranges, bananas, cigarettes, candy, and silk handkerchiefs. "The mere pleasure of having participated in that march," wrote one of the men, "has amply repaid me for all the past nine long months of toil and privation and hardship which has been my lot as a soldier to endure."[18]

Many of the American occupying troops had probably never left the county of their birth, and their letters home were filled with observations of the people and things they encountered in these alien climes. The common soldiers seldom came into contact with the upper class civilians, but they had plenty of comments about the people they did observe and, with few exceptions, it was negative. Unfortunately, most Americans first encountered the insurrectionists, most of whom came from near the bottom of the economic ladder. The fact that so many of the native soldiers were impoverished and underfed led many of them to appropriate for their own use any unguarded American food or other property. After all, compared to them the American soldiers in their midst seemed to have so much. The petty thievery certainly did not engender kind feelings among the occupation troops. "Barefooted and with little to cover their nakedness," remembered one volunteer officer, "your sympathies are at first aroused, but don't turn your back upon them to express this sympathy to your companions, else in the meantime they steal all your belongings." Even the chaplain of the Rough Riders expressed an opinion hardly in keeping with his calling as a man of the cloth. "I haven't found a man in the entire army," he said, "who has any use for the Cubans.... Those I have seen, which number several thousand, are lazy, ignorant, cowardly, and worthless creatures."[19]

A North Dakota officer in Manila found the Filipinos to be good natured and friendly to the Americans, but he also thought they were lazy and immoral. A Minnesota man wrote that he was "disgusted with the place" and that the "poor people here have absolutely nothing to live for." One volunteer characterized the Puerto Ricans he had seen as "a servile, lazy-looking lot" while another man was even less charitable when he described a "typical" Puerto Rican man as "black, dirty, lazy, ignorant, immoral, naked and diseased. He would steal the clothing from a corpse and while the [Fourth Ohio] regiment was in the field before Guayama, some of these fellows robbed the knapsacks of the soldiers who were fighting for their liberty." A Massachusetts volunteer wrote home that "the majority of the natives are pretty destitute, and if it wasn't for the sugar-cane would starve." Another man from the same regiment was repulsed by one instance of poverty and made no pretenses when it came to passing judgment. This family lived in a bark-covered hut "with no furniture, the children naked, and their parents in rags squatting like apes in the front of the shack. An indescribable loathing of the inanity and inactivity of such a life made one long for rocky New England and an honest day's work. Men or women followed by children creep out in the morning and hunt their breakfast of bananas or fruit just as a pig will hunt its breakfast of acorns."[20]

But the Americans found that, regardless of skin complexion or station in life, most natives of all ages were infatuated with tobacco. While pipe smoking was almost unheard of, cigars and cigarettes were everywhere. An Illinois volunteer expressed surprise to see men, women, and even children going about "puffing at a big black cigar or inhaling the fumes of a cigarette." The locals quickly learned that the newcomers among them represented a profitable market because the use of tobacco among the American troops was also quite widespread. Puerto Rican vendors loaded cigars into baskets or cloth bags and sold them to the soldiers throughout the camps. Some of the Americans found the Puerto Rican cigars distasteful. They attributed the poor taste of the finished product to the method of manufacture rather than the quality of the leaf. Ohio volunteers went so far as to refer to the island as the "land of the vile cigars." In spite of an initial lack of enthusiasm for the local product, many men found it difficult to pass up the low prices prevalent. "For anyone who cared to smoke," wrote one of the Ohioans, "could get a fine cigar, at first for part of a hard tack, then for a whole one and finally the price was raised to two hard tacks, the quality of the goods decreasing as rapidly as the price increased." The demand for tobacco, even that of diminished quality, soon outpaced the available supply and prices shot skyward. One man offered to pay $42.50, all the cash he had and representing almost three months' pay, for a one-pound bag. Even at this he could find none. One of his companions was able to find enough of the weed to fill the bowl of his pipe a couple of times, but it cost him 184 pieces of hard tack.[21]

The exotic location of the Philippines in the South Seas gave rise to much expectation among the American soldiers as to the availability and comeliness of the native women. Extant letters indicate that this anticipation went largely unfulfilled. More than a few of the men were anxious to make the acquaintance of the dark-eyed senoritas in Manila. "The boys haven't caught a good look at a skirt since leaving San Francisco," complained a North Dakotan, "except, of course, those seen during the short stay at Honolulu." A curly-haired sergeant was this regiment's champion "lady killer," and he anticipated "doing great execution among the susceptible Philippino [sic] lassies" as soon as he got the chance. One man commented upon the grace with which native women carried baskets on their heads, comparing their litheness with Venus herself. "But in almost no case," he continued, "does one see a pleasing face.... They mostly all have nice white teeth except those who chew the [betel] nut, and their skins are a yellowish brown color, their features rather suggestive of a low grade Chinese." A volunteer sergeant categorically declared: "The women are ugly looking and repulsive, almost all of them go along the streets puffing away either at a big cigar or a cigarette." In spite of these men's low opinions the venereal disease rate — as high as 40 percent of the sick according to one account — indicates that many of them overcame their initial repulsion.[22]

The same condescending attitude toward the native populations did not make itself evident with regard to the un-repatriated Spanish prisoners of war. The Americans seemed to recognize that their recent enemies had fought valiantly and therefore deserved a certain measure of respect. That this feeling was reciprocated was evidenced by an open letter from a Spanish prisoner to the American troops. "You fought and acted in compliance with the same call of duty as we," he wrote. "You fought us as men, face to face, with great courage."[23]

Of course, being a prisoner of war at any time has never been a welcome experience. There have always been minor — and often not so minor — annoyances engendered by prison life. At Siboney, two Spanish officers were imprisoned in one of their former blockhouses, and they complained to a visiting journalist that they had not been allowed out of their enclosure even to bathe themselves. The reporter relayed their complaint to an American officer for some kind of resolution. It was probably not the first complaint that these officers had registered, and the American decided that lack of bathing opportunities would be one thing that henceforth they could not complain about. He sent another officer and a squad of armed men to the blockhouse. "We have come to take you to your bath," announced the American. The Spaniards apparently had had a change of heart in the intervening few minutes, but their protestations were of no avail. They had complained of a lack of opportunity for bathing, and now that opportunity was to be furnished whether they were ready for it or not. The squad of troops escorted them to the beach from whence the officer pointed toward the ocean and said, "There is your bath ready for you." The crestfallen officers finally waded into the surf for their bath. Upon returning them to their quarters the American officer told them: "I am permitted to promise you that you shall have a bath once a day hereafter. Should you desire two per day, I think it can be easily arranged."[24]

Because the anticipated violence of the Cuban and Filipino populations toward the departing Spaniards failed to occur as feared, occupation duty for many seems to have consisted for the most part of sight-seeing, occasional drill or guard duty, letter writing, and lounging in hammocks in the shade. The Army even hired local laborers to do much of the hard physical work associated with setting up and maintaining a camp. The price of indigenous labor was so low, by American standards, that many local women found employment in doing the laundry of the occupation forces. The laundresses took the clothing to nearby creeks where, by dint of some cocoa soap, the naturally cold water, and liberal amounts of elbow grease, they soon had the garments spotless. Lacking washboards, the women rubbed the clothes vigorously over rocks in the river, pushing and prodding with corncobs and wooden paddles. Then, after squeezing the soapy water out of the clothes, rinsing them, and beating them on more rocks, they spread them in the hot sun to dry. By most accounts, the results were the equal of any laundry in the United States.[25]

Occupation troops usually did not have much to keep them busy. The strains of early reveille roused the sleeping soldiers from their tents. Roll call followed, and then breakfast, which a volunteer on duty in Puerto Rico described as nothing more than a half cup of watery bean soup and five hard tack. "The boys have offered a reward," he confided to a friend, "to the one finding a bean in his soup." After breakfast, and before the sun had made much progress in its path toward mid-day, the men might drill for an hour or so, but they spent the greater part of the day trying to avoid the heat. They might drill again late in the afternoon or, in some areas, they might engage in rifle target practice before eating a sparse supper. They filled their considerable free time in a variety of ways. Many found the weather too hot to want to do much more than stay in their tents and read newspapers or magazines that had arrived from the United States. Those camped near the beach at Manila enjoyed surf bathing although the occasional painful jellyfish sting made this activity less than inviting to some. Officials further enjoined them from bathing during the heat of the day.[26]

After the temperature abated somewhat later in the year many of the men turned their attention toward athletics. Some took up football, which was only then emerging as a sport distinct from rugby. The tropical climate, however, was not conducive to this sport. As a Utah volunteer described it: "The requirements for a good football game are a temperature of 6 degrees below zero, and a field covered with a four-inch layer of snow, and a corresponding thickness of soft mud underneath. As the Philippines are sadly deficient in the first two articles, it was decided to drop 'Rugby' in favor of baseball." Individual companies formed baseball teams and competed against one another for regimental championships. Sometimes there were regimental teams, and the American Commercial Company presented a silver championship cup to the team representing the Utah Light Batteries in the Philippines when they defeated all challengers. Dr. James Naismith's newly devised game of basketball also found favor with the troops.[27]

A Massachusetts volunteer on guard duty at Matanzas managed to inject a measure of excitement into his duty. This particular man was patrolling near his colonel's tent in the midst of a very stormy night, when he noticed movement in the dark shadows. It was two men sneaking furtively toward the tents from the direction of a nearby hill. They could have been nothing more threatening than a couple of soldiers trying to sneak back into camp after curfew, or they could have been a couple of bandits up to no good. Remembering proper policy he challenged them to halt and be recognized. When they made no effort to obey him, but instead kept coming toward the camp, he had no choice but to fire. The nearest thing to him that he could use to steady his aim was the colonel's tent. He rested the fore end of his rifle across the corner of the tent and fired. The shot brought a strong oath from one of the men — perhaps he had been hit — and they both beat a hasty retreat. The sentry undoubtedly felt proud of himself for having protected his post from possible attack. A quick investigation showed that the two intruders were probably a pair of goats, while the swearing that the man heard had come from his colonel. After all, his rifle muzzle was directly over the head of the sleeping officer inside his tent when he fired.[28]

Occasional holidays relieved the tedium of occupation duty. As Thanksgiving approached, plans were afoot to celebrate it in as fine a style as if the men had never left home. In Manila, for example, each company of the Thirteenth Minnesota invited the corresponding company of the First California to a grand holiday feast. One of the hosts assured his mother in a letter that "we have made a stand and will have Turkey and Mince pies no matter what they cost. Turkeys are $6.^{50} and $7.^{00} Mex[ican] apiece and pies 50¢ Mex but it makes no difference. We have $240.^{00} Mex in our Co fund and each boy puts in $1.^{00} while guaranteeing another so we are going to spend between $400.^{00} and $500.^{00} Mex for the blow out."[29]

Some holidays were less festive but just as important. On February 15, 1899, for instance, all non-essential duty in Havana was suspended in memory of the men who had lost their lives on the *Maine* just one year earlier. To further mark this sad anniversary, Marines and sailors from the *Brooklyn*, the *Resolute*, and the *Lebanon* helped escort a large procession of carriages to the cemetery where many of the *Maine* victims still lay buried. As the Navy band from the *Brooklyn* played patriotic airs, the crowds of people filed past the graves, leaving so many flowers that they nearly covered the ground. A twenty-one-gun salute to the fallen sailors and Marines completed the ceremony. A week later all unnecessary chores were dispensed with to honor the birthday of the first President.[30]

Like soldiers everywhere, the American occupation troops eagerly sought out souvenirs to take back home with them. These men may not have had the chance to face the Spaniards in battle, but they were determined to bring home some evidence of the war nonetheless. Among the most sought after items were Spanish rifles and Cuban machetes. Prices that the Americans were willing to pay for such items quickly eclipsed their utilitarian worth many times over. Canny Cubans soon realized that with an appropriately blood-curdling provenance even the most innocent of knives used to chop sugar cane became an almost priceless relic of the recent war. An Indiana chaplain noted that after the excitement of the war had passed such items "sold for a few dollars without a history, but during those early days one could almost see the blood dripping from the famous machete and hear the dying yell of an innumerable host of Spaniards shot down by this or that rifle as they were brought near the camp by some illustrious patriot 'del ejercito Cubano.'" The Americans even sought such mundane items as brass buttons and insignias from Spanish military uniforms. Many Spanish soldiers waiting for repatriation were eager to oblige when they learned that the Americans would trade food for such trinkets. And not all of the souvenirs were of an inanimate nature. Some Pennsylvania troops, returning from Puerto Rico, offered a fourteen-year old local boy a ride in one of the Navy's ships. He seemed eager for the experience, but his happiness soon faded when he found that the ship was headed for the United States. Other volunteers brought another young boy home with them, but he seemed happy to come.[31]

Another pastime that found favor with those who still retained any of their pay was to visit the local markets to augment their Army rations with fresh fruits, vegetables, eggs, or milk. Fruit was abundant and cheap, but the men sometimes became quite ill if they ate great quantities and washed it all down with local liquor. (Of course it is open to speculation whether it was the fruit or the liquor that caused the distress, but some believed it was the combination of the two. They believed that the liquor caused the fruit to ferment in their stomachs, leading to considerable discomfort.) A New England volunteer relished a dish that a local woman prepared for him. It was "rice boiled with cocoanut and filled with raisins." It was not unusual to see an American soldier waiting patiently at the marketplace with his tin cup in his hand for the arrival of a milk cow. He would then get his pint of milk straight from the source. A prudent shopper could often buy a couple of eggs, a small loaf of bread, a quart of milk, and three or four bananas for a total outlay of about twelve or thirteen cents.

A Bostonian described what was for him, apparently, a typical day's diet: "Today I had for breakfast a big dipper of milk, two boiled eggs, and a loaf of bread, For dinner I had eggs—scrambled this time—bread, and coffee; and for supper bread, rice, and wine—the best wine I ever tasted, and the cheapest. It all cost me a little over fifty centavos—perhaps 30 cents in our money." As the calendar receded farther and farther from a payday, however, the amount of disposable income among the soldiers grew scant and these expeditions into the local economy became less frequent. With no more access to the local food they had to look for imaginative ways to make their issue rations more palatable. One such delicacy was prepared by saving the grease that cooked out of their pork when they fried it. Then, after soaking their hard tack in water until it assumed the consistency of mashed potatoes, they poured the grease over it and fried it up.[32]

With so much free time it is not surprising that some of the troops sampled the available alcoholic beverages. One observer believed that there must have been something magical in the local distilling processes "to judge from the effects [their products] have had on some of the boys who possessed the temerity to tackle them. A small jag from them generally means three or four days riotous inebriety on the part of the victim, followed by about a week of hopeless stupidity and two or three days in the guard house. The experience with an aquadiente [sic] jag shall last one a lifetime."[33]

There did occur at least a smattering of cross-fertilization of cultures. Some Americans attempted to master the Spanish tongue, and many natives eagerly sought to learn English. Sometimes these attempts met with interesting results. One soldier went into a local shop on a quest to buy some fresh oranges. A weakness in his newly acquired Spanish vocabulary, however, resulted in the proprietor proudly displaying his inventory of dried fish. Some Illinois volunteers in Puerto Rico spent time teaching some local youths the proper pronunciation of certain English terms—swear words for the most part. The eager students repeated the terms over and over again until they had mastered the pronunciation and inflections. The soldiers had not, however, spent as much time explaining the meanings of these terms. "If a soldier spoke to one of them with the air of one expecting a reply," one of the Illinoisans later recalled, "the native would pay strict attention to every word and appear to be weighing it in his mind and looking up innocently, would reply by repeating a string of oaths that would put a drunken sailor to shame."[34]

The tedium of seemingly endless occupation duty led some volunteers in the Philippines to pray for relief, although the prayer was certainly one that would have been unfamiliar to stateside churchgoers.

> Our father who art in Washington
> McKinley is thy name;
> I wish you'd come with a fleet of ships
> And take us home again.
> We've done all we bargained for,
> And are sure 'twould be a treat
> To be taken back to old Nebraska,
> Our loved ones there to greet.
> The weather here is kind of hot,
> And a trying on the brain,
> And then, the way they've fed us
> Would give any man a pain.
> Hard-tack, rice and mule meat,
> With salmon on the side,
> Would drive most anyone to drink,
> Or get a hobo's hide.

> I guess I'll bring this to a close;
> The thought drives me insane,
> But I'll know enough to stay there
> If I get home again.
> We've done what we enlisted for—
> Remembered well the Maine:
> We freed the Filipinos
> And whipped hell out of Spain.
> Humanity I'll fight for still,
> But keep it in your pate,
> The fighting I do when I get home
> Will be in my dear old State.[35]

In Havana the official transfer of power from Spain to the United States occurred at noon on January 1, 1899. By early February the last of the Spanish troops in the West Indies were on their way home, and it was no longer necessary to keep large contingents of American troops in the islands. Most were eager to leave. At San Juan, Puerto Rico, the departing soldiers gaily sang such familiar songs as "The Girl I Left Behind Me." Then, possibly to show that the wounds of their fathers' war had healed, they sang both "Dixie" and "Marching Through Georgia." Shiploads of soldiers leaving the Caribbean during the fever season faced quarantine periods when they reached the United States. Local health officials wanted to ensure that no sick men were landing to spread disease. According to one account, "the men were to be stripped and steamed until all the Cuban brown would leave their skin and they were to go home as fair faced as a new-born child." After this personal cleansing, recalled another, "all our clothes and the ship's bedding were passed through a great cylinder heated with dry heat to 220 degrees." And lest there be any doubt as to the efficacy of the process, an Indiana man wrote that "the most skeptical had but to lay the tip of his little finger on them [clothes and bedding] as they emerged to be most thoroughly convinced that every flea, United States grayback [louse] and every vermin of every kind, carrying concealed about his person any contagious microbes of smallpox or yellow fever, had suffered a most horrible death; but they deserved it all for what they did to us in Cuba." After the men had subjected themselves and their personal gear to this fumigation the sailors used carbolic acid on the decks and burning sulfur in the holds to disinfect them.[36]

Returning Alabama volunteers found no organized welcome at Montgomery, but the citizens of Birmingham made up for the apparent lack of interest in the state's capital. Thousands of them lined the streets yelling and waving flags as their veterans marched. Citizens of Columbus, Ohio welcomed Ohio volunteers with a huge feast in the civic auditorium. But the welcome extended to the men of the Sixth Illinois mirrored the celebration that most units enjoyed upon *leaving* their home states. People living all along the route from New York City to Springfield seemed to vie with one another to welcome these returning warriors. "It seemed to us," recalled one man, "that they must have been preparing for our coming for weeks as the number of pies, cakes and cans of jelly given us was little short of astonishing. Great cans of pure, sweet milk were brought into the cars and carried from one end to the other and an open invitation was extended to each man to fill his cup as often as he liked. Large baskets of various kinds of fruits were brought to the train and bushels of sandwiches were found at almost every stopping place." At a welcome home banquet at one of Springfield's premiere hotels, however, the soldiers pointedly avoided the pork-and-beans entrée.[37]

Soldiers returning from the Philippines had to endure another long sea voyage before reaching the States. And once again the soldiers complained about the voyage. Food came in for severe criticism. A returning Utah artilleryman commented that the "epicurean tastes" of

Citizens of San Francisco welcome the Minnesota Volunteers home from Manila (U.S. Army Military History Institute).

his fellow veterans "could not totally harmonize with the bogus coffee and cows that had a flavor strangely akin to that of horse flesh." Some ships encountered storms, with all of the resultant seasickness that one might expect. San Franciscans welcomed all of the returning soldiers, but, of course, went all out to welcome their own First California volunteers. A special committee appropriated $70,000 for a lavish three-day celebration.[38]

CHAPTER 12

Epilogue

AMERICAN AND SPANISH DIPLOMATS met in neutral Paris on September 29 to iron out the terms of a formal peace treaty. The results of the war—America's second foreign war—were geographically vast and far-reaching. Spain agreed to give up Cuba (and also conceded the loss of Puerto Rico). Cuban independence, after all, had been what had propelled the American Congress to authorize war in the first place. Peace commissioners finally signed the treaty on December 10, 1898. Under its final terms Spain lost Cuba and Puerto Rico, and accepted $20 million to transfer the Philippines to the United States. The United States also insisted on possession of the island of Guam.

But at what cost had the United States become an imperial power? Spanish shells and bullets killed fewer than 400 American soldiers on the battlefields of Cuba, Puerto Rico, and the Philippines. Much deadlier by far were diseases like typhoid, malaria, yellow fever, and dysentery. These and other illnesses caused the deaths of approximately 2,500 men, many of whom never even left the training camps of the United States.[1]

More than a century after the Spanish-American War, there are few tangible reminders of it. War correspondent Richard Harding Davis returned to eastern Cuba in 1912 but was disappointed to see what changes nature had wrought on the once-bloody battlefield. The course of the San Juan River had shifted somewhat, obliterating the site of the makeshift first aid station at what the soldiers dubbed "Bloody Bend." San Juan Ridge itself has been preserved, like many other battlefields, with statues, cannons, and a modern interpretation of a Spanish blockhouse. Visitors can try to recapture the sights and sounds of those long ago July days while enjoying the park-like setting of today.

The ships that made Manila Bay echo with gunfire and those that fought each other in the running battle that stretched out along the Cuban coastline west of Santiago are almost all gone now. Most of the Spanish ships, were, of course too badly battered to be salvageable, although the captain of the *Cristóbal Colón* beached his ship before it suffered much battle damage. American salvage crews neglected to make it water tight before they pulled it off the rocks and into open water again, and it immediately sank. They had slightly better luck with the *Infanta Maria Teresa*, Admiral Cervera's flagship. It had suffered significant battle damage but was still deemed worthy of restoration. It was refloated and taken to Guantánamo for preliminary repairs before being taken in tow by the Navy repair ship *Vulcan* for the voyage to the shipyard at Norfolk, Virginia. The two ships encountered a severe tropical storm in the Bahamas that threatened to sink them both, and in order to save the *Vulcan* it became necessary to sacrifice the *Maria Teresa*. The salvage crew evacuated the Spanish ship and cut the towline. The *Maria Teresa* now rests between two reefs off Cat Island where scuba divers can reach it easily.[2]

The Navy had much better luck with the *Reina Mercedes*, which it raised from the Santiago channel in early 1899, and put it back into service without an inordinate amount of effort or cost. It subsequently served as a receiving ship at various east coast ports, and in the 1950s served at the United States Naval Academy as the commandant's residence. Ultimately, however, it became too costly to maintain, and in 1957 it went to the scrap yard.[3]

Relics from some of these ships may still be seen today without having to invest in scuba lessons and chartering a boat to the Caribbean. A battle-damaged 6-inch gun from the *Vizcaya* has been preserved at a library in Lowell, Massachusetts, a gun from the cruiser *Castilla* is in Rochester, New York, a 5.5-inch gun from the doomed *Almirante Oquendo* survives in a city park in Ottumwa, Iowa, and another overlooks the Mississippi River at Jefferson Barracks, near St. Louis.[4]

The American ships, with the exception of the *Maine* and the *Merrimac*, came through the war virtually unscathed but soon faced obsolescence in the age of the mighty *Dreadnoughts*. Most of them did at least limited duty during World War I, and a few were still on the Navy's rolls by the beginning of World War II.

Perhaps the most famous ship of the war was the U.S.S. *Maine*. Its destruction in Havana harbor was, of course, one of the proximate causes of the war, but the ultimate disposition of the wreck and its crewmembers is also quite interesting. The battleship began to interfere with navigation as more and more ships called at Havana, so in 1910 the U.S. Congress appropriated almost a million dollars to raise the sunken ship and recover the remains of the approximately one hundred crewmen still entombed aboard her. The Army Corps of Engineers was in charge of the project. After more than seven months of work, the engineers had stabilized the wreckage of the once-great ship enough to allow it to float once more, and on March 16, 1912, tug boats towed the *Maine* out of the harbor past the Morro Castle and into the open sea. About four miles out, workers went back aboard the ship and opened up valves that once again let the seawater rush in. Less than an hour later, with an American flag flying, the *Maine* slipped under the waves for the final time and sank in almost 4,000 feet of water.[5]

The *Maine* had been such an inspiration to all Americans during the war with Spain that the Navy made efforts to distribute relics from the ship to civic groups and museums all across the country. The ship's main mast now watches over the graves, at Arlington National Cemetery, of the sailors and Marines who died that night in Havana. The foremast is at the United States Naval Academy at Annapolis, Maryland, along with a life preserver, a couple of porthole covers, a heavily encrusted bugle, and Captain Sigsbee's binoculars and inkwell. The Navy Historical Center at the Washington Navy Yard is now home to one of the *Maine*'s 6-inch deck guns, a spare propeller, and a pivot gun. The state of Maine has the ship's ornate bow scroll mounted in a public park in Bangor, and part of the ship's formal silver service, originally donated to the ship by the citizens of Maine, is in the Blaine House Museum in Augusta. Other souvenirs of the famous ship reside in parts of the country with little connection to the *Maine* other than a patriotic interest in its fate. There is an anchor in Reading, Pennsylvania, the mangled base of the conning tower in Canton, Ohio, one of the capstans in Butte, Montana, a 6-inch gun in Alpena, Michigan, and Captain Sigsbee's salvaged bathtub in the Hancock Historical Museum in Ohio.[6]

In 1925, the Cuban government erected along Havana's waterfront what was perhaps the most architecturally impressive monument to the victims of the *Maine*. The centerpiece of this imposing memorial consists of two of the battleship's ten-inch guns, flanking two Corinthian columns. A lintel connected the two columns at the top, with a huge spread-winged American eagle perched thereon. Dedicated "to the victims of the *Maine*," the base of the monument was inscribed with the names of the crewmembers who died as a result of the ship's sinking. Alas, the monument, like the ship itself, had a relatively short life before tragedy struck. A Caribbean hurricane raged across the island in 1926 and toppled the columns. Sixteen months later, Cuban and American dignitaries rededicated the repaired memorial — this time with a more aerodynamic eagle at the top. The major portion of the memorial still exists, but the eagle, the universal symbol of the United States, is gone now, a victim of the communist regime of Fidel Castro. Castro's government has also altered the inscription to read "To the Victims of the *Maine*, Sacrificed for Voracious American Imperialism in its Efforts to Take Control of Cuba," but the columns and the cannons remain.[7]

After the *Maine*, the most well-known ship of the Spanish-American War is the U.S.S. *Olympia*, and it is the only surviving ship from that conflict. After its service in Asiatic waters it returned to the United States for overhaul. After a few years as a training ship for Naval Academy midshipmen, the *Olympia* underwent routine modernization that included replacement of its 8-inch guns and turrets with single 5-inch guns in 1910. Two of the salvaged guns went back to Union Iron Works for display, and two of them went to the defenses of Corregidor in the Philippines. After World War I the *Olympia* sailed to France to retrieve the remains of an unknown American soldier for enshrinement at Arlington National Cemetery, and this was its last major mission. It was decommissioned in Philadelphia late in 1922, and it now rests, replete with replicas of its original eight-inch guns and turrets, at that city's Independence Seaport Museum.

Most of the other ships of Dewey's squadron were recalled from limited service to participate in patrol, training, or escort duties during World War I and then scrapped a few years later. The *McCulloch* collided with another ship off the California coast in the summer of 1917 and sank. The *Baltimore* helped lay the vast minefields in the North Sea in 1918 and was decommissioned at Pearl Harbor, Hawaii four years later and used as a storage hulk. It was still there on December 7, 1941, when the Japanese attacked. It was sold for scrap a few months later and ultimately towed out to sea and scuttled in September 1944.

The ships of Sampson and Schley suffered similar fates. The *Texas* was renamed *San Marcos* in 1911 so that a battleship then under construction could bear the name of the Lone Star State. (The "new" *Texas* went on to serve in both world wars and is now, as floating museum near Houston, the only survivor of the *Dreadnought* era.) The *Texas/San Marcos*, the *Iowa*, the *Massachusetts*, and the *Indiana* all became target ships when there were no longer any other viable uses for them. The *Massachusetts* sits today in about twenty-six feet of water only a mile and a half from Pensacola Pass. Its two main gun turrets are usually awash, and the battleship-*cum*-reef has become a popular spot for sport divers.

The mighty *Oregon* returned to the Pacific after the war with Spain and during World War I served as an escort ship for the American expedition to Siberia. It left active service the following year and in 1925 the state of Oregon "borrowed" it from the Navy for a museum. A year after the attack on Pearl Harbor the Navy decided to scrap the *Oregon*, but then decided to use it — minus its guns and other armament — as an ammunition barge to support the landings on Guam in 1944. It remained there after the war, silently rusting away until the Navy ultimately sold it to a Japanese scrap firm in 1956.

The heroism of America's combatants was recognized not only by the welcome home parades and parties, but by a grateful government as well. At that time the United States only had one medal for bravery — the Medal of Honor — and a total of 112 medals were awarded. The Army and the Navy applied slightly different criteria to acts of outstanding courage to determine who should receive the medal. For example, prior to 1915, the Navy granted the medal only to enlisted men while the Army also included officers. The Navy awarded the medal for non-combat bravery, such as heroism in the face of exploding ships' boilers or in clearing a harbor of enemy mines, and thirteen of the Navy's Medal of Honor recipients received their medals in recognition of such valor. The Army reserved the medal for actions in the face of an armed and hostile enemy.

The war's first major battle, ironically, resulted in only one man receiving the Medal of Honor. He was Chief Carpenter's Mate Franz Itrich, who had been in command of his ship's whaleboat as it moved among the burning wreckage of Spanish ships in Manila Bay, making sure that they would never pose a threat again. His brief citation gives no details of his action, but merely reads: "On board the U.S.S. *Petrel*, Manila, Philippine Islands, 1 May 1898. Serving in the presence of the enemy, Itrich displayed heroism during the action."

The Navy awarded fifty-one Medals of Honor — almost half of the total — to men who participated in the cable-cutting expedition at Cienfuegos on May 11, 1898. Virtually every man who was in any of the four boats received the medal. The only exceptions were the naval officers, who were ineligible, and, inexplicably, the Marine private who was killed and the sailor who was fatally wounded there.

The sinking of the U.S.S. *Merrimac* to block the entrance to Santiago harbor also generated a number of Medals of Honor. They went to all seven of the enlisted men who took part. Thirty-five years later, a special act of Congress also awarded the medal to the expedition's leader, Richmond Hobson.

The land fighting of July 1 and 2, 1898, resulted in the Army's awarding two-dozen medals. Nine of them went to members of the Seventeenth U.S. Infantry for actions at El Caney. The other fifteen went to men attacking the heights of San Juan.[8]

The Spanish-American War had been over for more than a century when the last Medal of Honor was awarded to a participant in that conflict — Theodore Roosevelt. On January 16, 2001, in one of his last official acts in the White House, President William Clinton presented Roosevelt's Medal of Honor to his great grandson, Tweed Roosevelt. But the story of this medal is full of twists and turns. During his lifetime, the former commander of the Rough Riders made no secret of the fact that he coveted the Medal of Honor. "I am entitled to the Medal of Honor," he wrote, "and I want it." He believed that he had a right to the medal and told his friend Senator Henry Cabot Lodge: "If I didn't earn it, then no commissioned officer can ever earn it." Nevertheless, when the official list of recipients was published in early 1899, Roosevelt's name was not on it, and there the matter died until 1996.[9]

In an effort to rectify the fact that no black American servicemen were awarded the Medal of Honor for World War II or Korean War heroism, the 1996 National Defense Authorization Act did away with the requirement that military decorations had to be recommended within a relatively short time after the deeds they were meant to recognize. This opened the door for Roosevelt's family and friends to reopen his quest for this award. A bill with over 160 co-sponsors was introduced into the House in July 1997 to bestow the Medal of Honor posthumously on Theodore Roosevelt for his actions on July 1, 1898, at San Juan Ridge. The bill ultimately passed both houses of congress without dissent fifteen months later.[10]

This political decision rankled many in the U.S. Army and elsewhere. Critics pointed out that Roosevelt's actions that day, while certainly heroic, were no more so than those of countless other officers as they led their men up the ridge, and none of them had been honored by the receipt of the nation's highest military honor. They also pointed out that even though Generals Wheeler, Wood, and Sumner recommended Colonel Roosevelt for the Medal of Honor, none of these men, contrary to requirements for the Medal, had actually witnessed Roosevelt's valor on July 1. The officers on a specially-appointed review board ultimately chose not to buck the entire Congress and approved of its recommendation. Thus, President Clinton, a Democrat, presided over the ceremony by which former president Roosevelt, a Republican, received the Medal of Honor.[11]

For most of the thousands of soldiers who survived, their war service was the most memorable event in their lives. Some went on to make important contributions in a wide variety of fields—the military, politics, business, or entertainment. Most of the senior American military leaders had begun their careers during the Civil War and left active service within a few years of the end of the war with Spain. By 1903, generals Miles, Shafter, Merritt, and Wheeler and admirals Sampson and Schley had all retired. Admiral Dewey announced his candidacy for the presidency in April 1900, but withdrew it six weeks later and remained on active duty until his death in 1917 at the age of seventy-nine. Brigadier General Leonard Wood, after a stint as governor-general of Cuba, served as Army chief of staff from 1910 until 1914, and trained a division for combat in France during World War I, although he remained stateside. After the war, he unsuccessfully sought the Republican Party's nomination for president.

Dewey's opposite number at Manila Bay, Admiral Patricio Montojo y Pasarón, returned to Spain under the cloud of defeat and shame. He was relieved of command and jailed as the result of a court martial in March 1899, although another court absolved him and released him from confinement. Admiral Cervera fared much better. Not only did he not face a court martial, but he won promotion to vice admiral in 1901 and became chief of the Navy Central Staff the following year. King Alfonso XIII named him life Senator of the Kingdom in 1903, and he retired to his home in southern Spain four years later. Valeriano Weyler, the architect of the much-reviled reconcentration policy, served about two years, in three separate short terms, as Minister of War, and outlived all the important military leaders of this war. On November 30, 1929, he celebrated his seventy-fifth anniversary of military service to Spain and died the following year at the age of 92.

Some of the younger American soldiers and sailors went on to win laurels in other military capacities. Benjamin O. Davis, who had served as a young enlisted man in one of the "immune" regiments, transferred into the regular Army after the war and rose through the ranks to become the Army's first black general officer. John Pershing as a captain of the Tenth U.S. Cavalry in Cuba rose rapidly through the ranks to lead the American Expeditionary Force in Europe during World War I. Both Tasker Bliss, who served as a staff officer during the war with Spain, and Major General Adna Chaffee rose to become the Army Chief of Staff during and before World War I, respectively.

Army and Navy veterans of the War with Spain also played major roles in the twentieth century's second great conflict. Rough Rider William F. "Frank" Knox became President Franklin Roosevelt's secretary of the navy during most of World War II while former Tennessee volunteer Cordell Hull served as secretary of state. Ensign William Leahy served aboard the *Oregon* during the momentous fight off Santiago and later rose to become chairman of the joint chiefs of staff during World War II, as well as President Franklin Roosevelt's chief of staff. Ernest J. King spent part of his first summer vacation from the Naval Academy on duty in the Caribbean with Admiral Sampson's squadron in 1898. He then went back to the academy to finish his formal naval education and rose to become chief of naval operations during World War II.

Two other veterans earned military reputations in the early twentieth century in an area that did not even exist until long after the smoke had cleared in the Caribbean—military aviation. Ensign William Moffett served aboard the *Charleston* as it escorted troops to the Philippines in 1898, and was later awarded the Medal of Honor for action during the Mexican intervention at Vera Cruz in 1914. An early advocate of naval aviation, Moffett became the first head of the Navy's Bureau of Aeronautics in 1921. His enthusiastic work there until his death in 1933 has earned for him the sobriquet of Father of Naval Aviation. Similarly the Father of the Air Force, Billy Mitchell, also served in the Spanish-American War. Enlisting in the First Wisconsin Volunteers as an eighteen-year old private, he transferred to the regular Army after the war. He learned to fly in 1916, put this new-found technology to good use during World War I, and became perhaps the early twentieth century's most outspoken advocate for military aviation.

A fair number of veterans turned to politics after returning home. The most well-known, of course, was Colonel Roosevelt. He parlayed his performance along San Juan Ridge into political success at the polls in the fall of 1898 when New York voters sent him to the governor's mansion in Albany. Two years later he was President McKinley's running mate and found himself thrust into the Oval Office upon McKinley's assassination in 1901. Many others were successful at lower levels of politics. In fact, Roosevelt used the "bully pulpit" of the White House to appoint one of his former Rough Riders to be the territorial governor of New Mexico. Richmond P. Hobson, the hero of the *Merrimac*, resigned from the Navy and served four terms in Congress, where he advocated women's suffrage and prohibition.

Among the Spanish-American War veterans who prospered in business in later years were former Rough Riders David Goodrich and John McIhenny. Goodrich rose to become chief executive officer of his family business, B. F. Goodrich Company, and his fellow trooper led the Tabasco Sauce Company.

Two icons of American Midwestern literature served in the Army. Sherwood Anderson served in an Ohio regiment, and Carl Sandburg went to Puerto Rico with the Sixth Illinois Volunteers. Edgar Rice Burroughs served briefly with the Seventh U.S. Cavalry before the war and tried unsuccessfully to enlist in the Rough Riders. He later created the popular Tarzan series of books. Tom Mix served in the Fourth U.S. Artillery and later went on to be a box office smash in early western movies. Ben Lear stayed in the Army but won a bronze medal at the 1912 Olympic Games in the Three-Day Equestrian Event. (He also later rose to the rank of lieutenant general during World War II.)

As with any group of men the size of the U.S. Army in 1898, not all led exemplary lives, either then or later. President Roosevelt offered the job of U.S. marshall for New Mexico Territory to another man from his old regiment, but this man, a lifelong Democrat, felt constrained to turn down this offer from the Republican president. Roosevelt's second choice for this position had a more concrete reason for not accepting. He was in jail on a murder charge. Tom Horn, likewise, returned to the West after service with the Army and gained notoriety by being convicted of murdering a young boy, for which he was hanged in 1903.[12]

There were, sadly, some men who felt the need to embellish their experiences. There was, for example, the trooper of the Ninth Cavalry, who, in a letter written a week after the fight for San Juan Ridge, earnestly confided to a friend that he was "sixty hours under heavy fire." Then, as if this had not stretched the truth far enough, he wrote: "Sorry to tell you that I have killed more than a hundred Spaniards." And several men claimed service in the ill-fated hot-air balloon. A Sergeant Bonanzinga left a fairly detailed account of "his" balloon ascension on July 1. According to his account, he and a telegraph operator accompanied Major Maxfield to a height of about 2,000 feet just before daylight. The Spaniards must have been sleeping late that morning for, according to the sergeant, it was a couple of hours before they spotted this large balloon overlooking their position. For the rest of the day, the enemy rifleman and artillerists tried their best to bring down these budding aeronauts. Finally, at about 5:30 in the afternoon, the Spaniards found the range and sent the balloon crashing down. "I crashed into a treetop and lost consciousness," Bonanzinga recalled. "When I came to I was on a stretcher being borne to the hospital. Here it was found that two of my ribs had been broken and I was bruised from head to foot." Sergeant Thomas Boone, of the Second U.S. Infantry, also claimed to have made an ascent that day. His account, however, has the balloon going up about 7 A.M. and being shot down at 1 P.M., at which time it was only about eighty yards away from the Spanish line. "At least two hundred bullets and four shrapnel shots went through the inflating bag," he claimed, "and we came down with a rush." He did not claim injuries as severe as his fellow non-com, but did admit to "being badly bruised and shaken up."[13]

The vast majority of men who served in the Army in 1898 did not see combat, but the fact remains that they were ready to so. A Texas volunteer probably summed up the experience for all of his fellows when he wrote: "The experience, the sights, the hardships, and happiness which we have passed through were all new to us. We left home blindly, knowing absolutely nothing [about] what was before us, and although we were never in any battle, it was not our fault. We volunteered at the call, we were ready, willing to go where ever we were sent, and although we never reached the battle field, yet we fought disease and death in other forms, hunger, hardships, the heat, and extreme cold, mosquitoes and flees [sic], and in fact most every thing that there is to make life miserable. We have passed through it all, and now it is over with the experience I have passed through is worth many a dollar to me."[14]

All of the Americans who fought the Spaniards in 1898 are gone now, regulars and volunteers, with various claimants to the title of final survivor. But whoever the last veteran was and no matter when or where he died, the men who fought in their country's second foreign war were, as a group, as brave and daring as the soldiers of any other war at any other time.

Chapter Notes

1. From Cuban Revolution to American War with Spain

1. John L. Offner, *An Unwanted War: The Diplomacy of the United States and Spain Over Cuba, 1895–1898* (Chapel Hill and London: University of North Carolina Press, 1992), 11.
2. David F. Trask, *The War with Spain in 1898,* The Macmillan Wars of the United State Series (New York: Macmillan, 1981), 9; Offner, *Unwanted War,* 80.
3. Trask, *War with Spain,* 9; Offner, *Unwanted War,* 80.
4. Charles Dwight Sigsbee, "Personal Narrative of the 'Maine,'" *The Century Magazine* 57, no. 1 (November 1898), 77.
5. Sigsbee, "Narrative of the 'Maine,'" 241–242.
6. Richard Wainwright's testimony and George Holman's testimony (first quotation) in *Message of the President of the United States transmitting the Report of the Naval Court of Inquiry Upon the Destruction of the United States Battle Ship Maine in Havana Harbor, February 15, 1898, Together With the Testimony Taken Before the Court* (Washington, D.C.: Government Printing Office, 1898), 26–27, 23; Lt. John Hood's testimony (second quotation), *Court of Inquiry,* 119; Sergeant Michael Mehan's testimony and Landsman William H. Thompson's testimony, *Court of Inquiry,* 167–169.
7. Charles Bergman's testimony (quotation), *Court of Inquiry,* 167–169; Willis John Abbott, *Blue Jackets of '98* (New York: Dodd, Mead and Company, 1899), 56–57; the final death toll was 268 — 230 sailors, 28 Marines, and two naval officers; 8 of the injured later died. G. J. A. O'Toole, *The Spanish War: An American Epic, 1898* (New York: W. W. Norton, 1984), 126; Sixteen uninjured crewmen is from Walter Millis, *The Martial Spirit* (Houghton Mifflin, 1931; reprint, Chicago: Ivan R. Dee, 1989), 105.
8. Sigmund Rothschild's (first quotation) and Louis Wertheimer's testimony in *Court of Inquiry,* 58–63; Joseph M. Rogers, "Our Action on the Maine Disaster," in *The Great Republic: By the Master Historians,* edited by Charles Morris and Oliver H. G. Leigh (New York, Pittsburgh and Chicago: R. S. Belcher Company, 1901), IV, 15 (second quotation); Frederick G. Teasdale's testimony in *Court of Inquiry,* 53–55.
9. Rogers, "Action on Maine Disaster," IV, 15.
10. Sigsbee, "Narrative of the Maine," 245–247, 253.
11. Millis, *Martial Spirit,* 110.
12. Millis, *Martial Spirit,* 110 (quotation), 108.
13. Offner, *Unwanted War,* 189–190.

2. Dewey's Battle for Manila Bay

1. John M. Ellicott, "The Naval Battle of Manila," *United States Naval Institute Proceedings* 26 (September 1900), 489–490; Thomas J. Vivian, editor, *With Dewey at Manila: Being the Plain Story of the Glorious Victory of the United States Squadron Over the Spanish Fleet Sunday Morning, May First, 1898, as related in the Notes and Correspondence of an Officer on Board the Flagship Olympia* (New York: R. F. Fenno and Company, 1898), 36–38.
2. Nathan Sargent, *Admiral Dewey and the Manila Campaign* (Washington, D.C.: National Historical Foundation, 1947), 4; Ellicott, "Battle of Manila," 489–490; Sargent, *Manila Campaign,* 5, 9.
3. George A. Loud, "The Battle of Manila Bay: I: Narrative of Colonel George A. Loud," *The Century Magazine* 56, no. 4 (August 1898), 612; Sargent, *Manila Campaign,* 18.
4. Dewey's official report of the battle of May 1, 1898, in George Dewey, *Autobiography of George Dewey: Admiral of the Navy* (New York: Scribner's Sons, 1913), 299.
5. G.J.A. O'Toole, *The Spanish War: An American Epic 1898* (New York: W. W. Norton, 1986), 176.
6. Bradley A. Fiske, *From Midshipman to Rear-Admiral* (New York: The Century Company, 1919), 240.
7. Ellicott, "Battle of Manila," 490; O'Toole, *Spanish War,* 174 (quotation); David F. Trask, *The War with Spain in 1898,* The Macmillan Wars of the United State Series (New York: Macmillan, 1981), 96.
8. Ellicott, "Battle of Manila," 493.
9. O'Toole, *Spanish War,* 177; Walter Millis, *The Martial Spirit* (Houghton Mifflin, 1931; reprint, Chicago: Ivan R. Dee, 1989), 184; O'Toole, *Spanish War,* 176–177.
10. John T. McCutcheon, "With Dewey at Manila," *The Spanish-American War: The Events of the War Described by Eye Witnesses* (Chicago and New York: Herbert S. Stone and Company, 1899), 40, 42.
11. Charles P. Kindleberger, "The Battle of Manila Bay: III. Narrative of Dr. Charles P. Kindleberger, Junior Surgeon of the Flag Ship 'Olympia,'" *Century Magazine* 56, no. 4 (August 1898), 621.
12. Joseph L. Stickney, "With Dewey at Manila," *Harper's New Monthly Magazine* 98, no. 585, 478.

13. O'Toole, *Spanish War*, 178.
14. O'Toole, *Spanish War*, 179 (first quotation); Dewey, *Autobiography*, 229–230 (second quotation); Ellicott, "Battle of Manila," 495 (third quotation).
15. John M. Ellicott, "The Defenses of Manila Bay." *United States Naval Institute Proceedings* 26 (1900), 279–280; Millis, *The Martial Spirit*, 184.
16. Ellicott, "Defenses of Manila Bay," 280.
17. Dewey, *Autobiography*, 205–206.
18. Dewey, *Autobiography*, 199.
19. O'Toole, *Spanish War*, 181.
20. Vivian, *With Dewey at Manila*, 50–51 (first quotation), 64 (second quotation); Joel C. Evans, "The Battle of Manila Bay: IV. Narrative of Joel C. Evans, Gunner of the 'Boston,'" *Century Magazine* 56, no. 4 (August 1898), 624 (third quotation).
21. Millis, *The Martial Spirit*, 188.
22. Fiske, *Midshipman to Rear-Admiral*, 245.
23. Evans, "Battle of Manila Bay," 625.
24. Vivian, *With Dewey at Manila*, 34, 48.
25. Stickney, "With Dewey at Manila," 479.
26. Vivian, *With Dewey at Manila*, 52.
27. Fiske, *Midshipman to Rear-Admiral*, 249; "Official Report of Admiral Montojo," Appendix C in Dewey, *Autobiography*, 304.
28. Loud, "Battle of Manila Bay," 613 (first quotation); Fiske, *Midshipman to Rear-Admiral*, 247 (second quotation); Kindleberger, "Battle of Manila Bay," 622.
29. "Official Report of Admiral Montojo," Appendix C in Dewey, *Autobiography*, 305.
30. Stickney, "With Dewey at Manila," 480.
31. "Official Report of Admiral Montojo," Appendix C in Dewey, *Autobiography*, 305.
32. Kindleberger, "Battle of Manila Bay," 622; Ellicott, "Battle of Manila," 507–508.
33. Loud, "Battle of Manila Bay," 614.
34. Stickney, "With Dewey at Manila," 477.
35. Kindleberger, "Battle of Manila Bay," 623; Young and Moore, *Reminiscences and Thrilling Stories*, 66.
36. Ellicott, "Battle of Manila," 511.
37. Sargent, *Manila Campaign*, 41.
38. Trask, *War with Spain*, 104.
39. Evans, "Battle of Manila Bay," 627 (quotation); Trask says that the fleet fired 5,859 shots and only 142 hit the targets, *War with Spain*, 104.
40. Sargent, *Manila Campaign*, 41n (first quotation); Robert H. Ferrell, *American Diplomacy: A History* (New York and London: W. W. Norton, 1975), 363 (second quotation).
41. Charles Musser, "The American Vitagraph, 1897–1901: Survival and Success in a Competitive Industry," *Film Before Griffith*, edited by John L. Fell (Berkeley, Los Angeles, and London: University of California Press, 1983), 33–34.
42. Dewey, *Autobiography*, 238.
43. Trask, *War with Spain*, 598.

3. Mobilizing for War

1. Actual strength on April 1, 1898, was 2,143 officers and 26,040 men for a total of 28,183. "Report of the Adjutant General," *Annual Reports of the War Department for the Fiscal Year Ended June 30, 1898*, vol. 1, part 1, 253, as cited by Marvin A. Kreidberg and Merton G. Henry, *History of Military Mobilization in the United States Army, 1775–1945* (Washington: Department of the Army, 1955), 141; Octavio A. Delgado, "The Spanish Army in Cuba, 1868–1898: An Institutional Study," Ph.D. diss. Columbia University, 1980, 131; *Annual Report of the Major General Commanding the Army to the Secretary of War, 1898*, 5, in Kreidberg and Henry, *Military Mobilization*, 152.
2. Graham A. Cosmas, *An Army for Empire: The United States Army in the Spanish-American War* (Columbia: University of Missouri Press, 1971), 13.
3. Kreidberg and Henry, *Military Mobilization*, 154–155, 159.
4. H.C. Thompson, "Oregon Volunteer Reminiscences of the War with Spain," *Oregon Historical Quarterly* 49 (September 1948), 195 (first quotation); Charles Johnson Post, *The Little War of Private Post* (Boston: Little Brown, 1960; New York: New American Library, 1961), 16 (second quotation); H. E. Webber, *Twelve Months with the Eighth Massachusetts Infantry* (Salem, Mass.: 1908), 80 (third quotation).
5. *Houston Daily Post*, April 25, 1898, 3 (first quotation); Ruby Weedell Waldeck, "Missouri in the Spanish American War," *Missouri Historical Review* 30 (1935–1936), 381 (second quotation); Charles H. Brown, *The Correspondents' War: Journalists in the Spanish-American War* (New York: Charles Scribner's Sons, 1967), 159.
6. John H. Parker, *History of the Gatling Gun Detachment, Fifth Army Corps, at Santiago, With a Few Unvarnished Truths Concerning that Expedition* (Kansas City, Missouri: Hudson-Kimberly Publishing Company, 1898), 173–174.
7. Gregory Dean Chapman, "Army Life at Camp Thomas, Georgia, During the Spanish-American War," *Georgia Historical Quarterly* 70 (Winter 1986), 635.
8. "Camps and Their Sanitation," *Report of the Commission Appointed by the President to Investigate the Conduct of the War Department in the War with Spain*, 8 vols. (Washington: 1900), I: 209–210.
9. U.S. Constitution, art. 1, sec. 8; "An Act effectually to provide for the national defence [sic], by establishing an uniform militia throughout the United States." Approved May 8, 1792, in John F. Callan, *The Military Laws of the United States, relating to the Army, Volunteers, Militia, and to Bounty Lands and Pensions, from the foundation of the Government to the Year 1863* (Philadelphia: George W. Childs, 1863), 95–100.
10. Robert Lee Mattson, "Politics is Up!—Grigsby's Cowboys and Roosevelt's Rough Riders, 1898," *South Dakota History* 9 (Fall 1979), 307 (first quotation); Richard Melzer and Phyllis Ann Mingus, "Wild to Fight: The New Mexico Rough Riders in the Spanish-American War," *New Mexico Historical Review* 59 (April 1984), 109 (second quotation).
11. Post, *Little War of Private Post*, 137; Joseph Choate King, Fiftieth Iowa Volunteers, Spanish-American War Survey, U.S. Army Military History Institute, Carlisle, Pennsylvania (quotation).
12. J. S. Crawford, Cherokee (Iowa) *Herald*, date not given, as quoted in W. Ardell Stelck, "Sgt. Guy Gillette and Cherokee's 'Gallant Co. M' in the Spanish American War," *Annals of Iowa* 3rd Series, 40, no. 8 (Spring 1971), 569 (first quotation); Joseph F. Steelman, *North Carolina's Role in the Spanish-American War* (Raleigh: North Carolina Department of Cultural Resources, Division of Archives and History, 1975), 4 (second quotation).
13. William J. Schellings, "Florida Volunteers in the War with Spain, 1898," *Florida Historical Quarterly* 41 (July 1962), 50; Donald Brooks Kelley, "Mississippi and 'The Splendid Little War' of 1898," *Journal of Mississippi History* 26, no. 2 (May 1964), 124 (quotation); "100,000 Pythian Knights," *Houston Daily Post*, April 21, 1898, 5; Peter Mickelson, "Nationalism in Minnesota During the Spanish-American War," *Minnesota History* 41 (Spring 1968), 8.

14. Kelley, "Mississippi and the 'Splendid Little War,'" 131; *Biennial Report of the Adjutant General of Illinois to the Governor and Commander-in-Chief 1897 and 1898* (Springfield, Illinois: 1898), 41; John J. Leffler, "The Paradox of Patriotism: Texans in the Spanish-American War," *Hayes Historical Journal* 8 (Spring 1989), 35 (quotation).

15. Thomas D. Thiessen, "The Fighting First Nebraska: Nebraska's Imperial Adventure in the Philippines, 1898-1899," *Nebraska History* 70, no. 3 (Fall 1989), 216.

16. Leffler, "Paradox of Patriotism," 35 (first quotation); David F. Trask, *The War with Spain in 1898,* The Macmillan Wars of the United States Series, Louis Morton, gen. ed. (New York: Macmillan, 1981), 155 (second quotation); Leffler, "Paradox of Patriotism," 35 (third quotation).

17. Christian G. Nelson, "Texas Militia in the Spanish-American War," *Texas Military History* 2, no. 3 (August 1962), 196 (first quotation); Joseph F. Steedman, *North Carolina's Role in the Spanish-American War* (Raleigh: North Carolina Department of Cultural Resources, Division of Archives and History, 1975), 5 (second quotation).

18. John Stronach, "The 34th Michigan Volunteer Infantry," *Michigan History* 30 (April-June 1946), 292 (first quotation); *Regulations for the Army of the United States, 1895* (Washington: Government Printing Office, 1900), 116-117 (second quotation).

19. "The Texas Troops," *Houston Daily Post*, May 8, 1898, 7; Sim Goddard, Third U.S. Cavalry Volunteers, Spanish-American War Surveys, U.S. Army Military History Institute, Carlisle, Pennsylvania.

20. Nicholas Senn, *War Correspondence (Hispano American War): Letters From Dr. Nicholas Senn* (Chicago: American Medical Association Press, 1899), 14-16; "Committee of Vigilance" of the Eighth Illinois Volunteers to the editor of the Springfield *Illinois Record*, January 4, 1899, in Willard B. Gatewood, Jr., "'*Smoked Yankees' and the Struggle for Empire: Letters from Negro Soldiers, 1898-1902*" (Urbana: University of Illinois Press, 1971), 216 (first quotation); "Texas Brigade," *Houston Daily Post*, May 14, 1898, 7; Elmer Ellsworth Wood, "Louisiana in the Spanish-American War, 1898-1899, As Recorded by Colonel Elmer Ellsworth Wood, Commander of the Second Regiment of Louisiana Volunteer Infantry," edited by Walter Prichard, *Louisiana Historical Quarterly* 26 (July 1943), 802 (second quotation); Post, *The Little War of Private Post*, 12-13 (third and fourth quotations); W. E. Biederwolf, *History of the One Hundred and Sixty-first Regiment Indiana Volunteer Infantry* (Logansport, Indiana: Wilson, Humphreys and Company, 1899), 25 (fifth quotation).

21. Kreidberg and Henry, *Military Mobilization*, 163; M. Koenigsberg. *Southern Martyrs: A History of Alabama's White Regiments During the Spanish-American War, Touching Incidentally on the Experiences of the Entire First Division of the Seventh Army Corps* (Montgomery, Alabama: Brown Printing Company, 1898), 119; Webber, *Twelve Months With the Eighth Massachusetts*, 50; Koenigsberg, *Southern Martyrs*, 25.

22. Wood, "Louisiana in the Spanish-American War," 796, 794.

23. Waldeck, "Missouri in the Spanish-American War," 384, 390; Kelley, "Mississippi and the 'Splendid Little War,'" 127; "An Offer From College Boys," *Galveston Daily News*, April 27, 1898, 4; "University Students," *Galveston Daily News*, April 28, 1898, 4; Willard B. Gatewood, Jr., "Virginia's Negro Regiment in the Spanish-American War: The Sixth Virginia Volunteers," *Virginia Magazine of History and Biography* 80 (April 1972), 197.

24. Thompson, "Oregon Volunteer Reminiscences," 196; Stelck, "Sgt. Guy Gillette," 567; Leffler, "Paradox of Patriotism," 24; Waldeck, "Missouri and the Spanish-American War," 381; Joshua C. Wright, "I'll Stand and Shoot From Taw," *Houston Daily Post*, April 23, 1898, 4 (first quotation); R. S. Bunzey, *History of Companies I and E, Sixth Regt. Illinois Volunteer Infantry from Whiteside County* (Morrison, Illinois: Rufus S. Bunzey, 1901), 196 (second quotation).

25. Peyton C. March, "Mr. Astor Outfits the Army," *Saturday Evening Post*, July 19, 1958, 53, 55.

26. Willard B. Gatewood, Jr., "Kansas Negroes and the Spanish-American War," *Kansas Historical Quarterly* 37 (Autumn 1971), 301 (first quotation); William B. Gatewood, Jr., "Indiana Negroes and the Spanish-American War," *Indiana Magazine of History*, 69 (June 1973), 135-136 (second quotation).

27. George W. Prioleau to the editor of the Cleveland Gazette, published May 13, 1898, in Gatewood, "'*Smoked Yankees,*'" 28 (quotation); Gatewood, "Kansas Negroes," 301.

28. Willard B. Gatewood, Jr. "An Experiment in Color: The Eighth Illinois Volunteers, 1898-1899," *Journal of the Illinois State Historical Society* 65 (Autumn 1972), 299-302.

29. Stelck, "Sgt. Guy Gillette," 570; Jeff L. Patrick, "Nothing But Slaves: The Second Kentucky Volunteer Infantry and the Spanish-American War," *Register of the Kentucky Historical Society* 89 (1991), 287-299; Wood, "Louisiana in the Spanish-American War," 798; Mickelson, "Nationalism in Minnesota," 7; John Bowe, *With the 13th Minnesota in the Philippines* (Minneapolis: A. B. Farnham, 1905), 8; Edmund P. Neill to his mother, April 30, 1898, Edmund P. Neill Papers, Minnesota Historical Society, St. Paul, Minnesota (quotation); Wood, "Louisiana in the Spanish-American War," 798, 800.

30. Arthur E. Gentzen diary entry for May 5, 1898, The Center for American History, University of Texas at Austin.

31. J[ohn] R. Johnson, "The Saga of the First Nebraska in the Philippines," *Nebraska History* 30 (June 1949), 141-142.

32. Gerald F. Linderman, *The Mirror of War: American Society and the Spanish-American War* (Ann Arbor: University of Michigan Press, 1974), 100; Sherwood Anderson, *Sherwood Anderson's Memoirs* (New York: Harcourt, Brace and Company, 1942), 124.

33. Goddard, Spanish-American War Surveys (first quotation); Edward Marshall, *The Story of the Rough Riders, 1st U.S. Volunteer Cavalry: The Regiment in Camp and on the Battle Field* (New York: G. W. Dillingham, 1899), 36-38 (second quotation).

34. Webber, *Twelve Months with the Eighth Massachusetts*, 51.

35. Koenigsberg, *Southern Martyrs*, 148, 111 (first quotation); "Texas Brigade," *Houston Daily Post*, May 14, 1898, 7 (second quotation).

36. Koenigsberg, *Southern Martyrs*, 155 (first quotation); H. C. Thompson, "War Without Medals," *Oregon Historical Quarterly* 49 (December 1948), 295-296 (second quotation); Post, *Little War of Private Post*, 28 (third quotation); Webber, *Twelve Months with the Eighth Massachusetts*, 59 (fourth quotation); Thiessen, "The Fighting First Nebraska," 216.

37. Stelck, "Sgt. Guy Gillette," 567.

38. Gentzen diary, May 23, 1898.

39. Frank E. Edwards, *The '98 Campaign of the 6th Massachusetts, U.S.V.* (Boston: Little, Brown and Company, 1899), 15-22.

40. Charles Herner, *The Arizona Rough Riders* (Tucson: University of Arizona Press, 1970), 48; James E. Payne, *History of the Fifth Missouri Volunteer Infantry*

(James E. Payne, 1899), 46; Webber, *Twelve Months with the Eighth Massachusetts*, 122 (first quotation); Payne, *Fifth Missouri*, 51 (second quotation); Webber, *Twelve Months with the Eighth Massachusetts*, 103 (third quotation); Melzer, "Wild to Fight," 118; Herner, *Arizona Rough Riders*, 38; A. D. Webb, "Arizonans in the Spanish-American War," *Arizona Historical Review* 1 (January 1929), 51; Herner, *Arizona Rough Riders*, 40; Curtis V. Hard, *Banners in the Air: The Eighth Ohio Volunteers and the Spanish-American War*, edited by Robert H. Ferrell (Kent, Ohio, and London: Kent State University Press, 1988), 9; Alexander L. Hawkins, "Official History of the Operations of the Tenth Pennsylvania Infantry, U.S.V. in the Campaign in the Philippine Islands," as an appendix in Karl Irving Faust, *Campaigning in the Philippines* (San Francisco: The Hicks-Judd Company, 1899; reprint, New York: Arno, 1970), 11–12.

41. Margaret Inglehart Reilly, "Andrew Wadsworth, A Nebraska Soldier in the Philippines, 1898–1899," *Nebraska History* 68 (Winter 1987), 186.

42. "Camps and Their Sanitation," *Report of the Commission Appointed by the President to Investigate the Conduct of the War Department in the War with Spain*, 8 vols. (Washington: 1900); I: 205–206.

43. Charles Creager, *The 14th Ohio National Guard: The 4th Ohio Volunteer Infantry* (Columbus, Ohio, 1899), 102, as cited in Chapman, "Army Life at Camp Thomas," 643 (first quotation); Chapman, "Camp Thomas," 644.

44. Roy W. Aldrich to Marcia, June 6, 1898, Roy Wilkinson Collection, University of Texas Archives, Austin, Texas; F. A. Bonebright to his mother, August 1, 1898, in "Letters Written Home by F. A. Bonebright, during service in the Spanish American War, 1898," Kendall Young Library, Webster City, Iowa; Payne, *Fifth Missouri*, 15; Hard, *Banners in the Air*, 22 (first quotation); Bunzey, *Sixth Illinois*, 170 (second quotation); Post, *The Little War of Private Post*, 21 (third quotation).

45. George P. Bowers, *History of the 160th Ind. Vol. Infantry in the Spanish-American War* (Fort Wayne, Indiana: Archer Printing, ca. 1900), 30–31.

46. John C. Rayburn, "The Rough Riders in San Antonio, 1898," *Arizona and the West* 3, no. 2 (Summer 1961), 125.

47. Melzer and Mingus, "Wild to Fight," 115.

48. F. A. Bonebright to Sister and Brother and all, June 3, 1898, in "Letters Written Home" (first quotation); Edmund P. Neill to his parents, May 25, 1898 (second quotation).

49. Frank Harper, "Fighting Far From Home: The First Colorado Regiment in the Spanish-American War," *Colorado Heritage* 1 (1988), 2; Diary of Sterling Johnston, Chicago Historical Society; *Regulations for the Army of the United States, 1895* (Washington, D.C.: Government Printing Office, 1900), 51; Ethelbert P. Moore to his sister Fannie, June 15, 1898, in Patrick, "Nothing But Slaves," 294 (quotation).

50. Post, *Little War of Private Post*, 47 (first quotation), 20 (second quotation); Gentzen diary, October 12, 1898 (third quotation); Pat to his nephew, Alex, June 30, 1898, Galt Family Papers, Filson Club, Louisville, Kentucky (fourth quotation); Post, *Little War of Private Post*, 20 (fifth quotation); *Regulations for the Army of the United States, 1895*, 176; F. A. Bonebright to ?, August 18, 1898, "Letters Written Home"; J. R. Johnson, "Nebraska's 'Rough Riders' in the Spanish-American War," *Nebraska History* 29 (June 1948), 107.

51. Hard, *Banners in the Air*, 14 (quotation); Harper, "First Colorado Regiment," 2.

52. Herner, *The Arizona Rough Riders*, 73.

53. Wood, "Louisiana in the Spanish-American War," 805.

54. Schellings, "Florida Volunteers," 53 (first quotation); Will R. Johnson to his father, July 5, 1898, David Demaree Banta Indiana Collection, Franklin College of Indiana Library (second quotation); John W. Metzger to his sister, June 13, 1898, John W. Metzger Collection, Chicago Historical Society (third quotation); Roy W. Aldrich to Marcia, August 21, 1898 (fourth quotation).

55. James A. Dineen to his mother, June 14, 1898, Mrs. Charles W. Bullard Collection, Indiana State Library, Indianapolis (quotation); James W. Russell to the editor of the *Tipton Times*, September 1, 1898, Tipton County Collection, Indiana State Library, Indianapolis.

56. Steelman, *North Carolina's Role*, 20; Webber, *Twelve Months with the Eighth Massachusetts*, 19–20; F. A. Bonebright to Lafe, July 25, 1898, "Letters Written Home"; Webber, *Twelve Months with the Eighth Massachusetts*, 20; F. A. Bonebright to his mother, August 1, 1898, "Letters Written Home" (quotation).

57. Edwards, *The '98 Campaign*, 35–36; Hard, *Banners in the Air*, 21.

58. Fred C. Hurt to Folks at Home, published in an unknown newspaper, June 26, 1898, Fred C. Hurt Collection, Indiana State Library, Indianapolis; F. A. Bonebright to Folks at Home, undated, in "Letters Written Home" (first quotation); Koenigsberg, *Southern Martyrs*, 112–113 (second quotation).

59. Payne, *Fifth Missouri*, 12 (quotation); Schellings, "Florida Volunteers," 54.

60. Schellings, "Florida Volunteers," 55; Johnson, "Nebraska's 'Rough Riders,'" 197 (first quotation); F. A. Bonebright to his sisters, June 29, 1898, in "Letters Written Home" (second quotation).

61. *Report of the Committee of the Massachusetts Reform Club Appointed to Collect Testimony in Relation to the Spanish-American War, 1898–1899* (Boston: George H. Ellis, 1899), 36.

62. F. A. Bonebright to The Girls, June 1898, in "Letters Written Home"; Webber, *Twelve Months with the Eighth Massachusetts*, 65.

63. Herner, *The Arizona Rough Riders*, 68; Koenigsberg, *Southern Martyrs*, 105.

64. F. A. Bonebright to his sister, June 1, 1898, and to his sisters and mother, June 14, 1898, in "Letters Written Home."

65. F. A. Bonebright to his sisters and mother, June 13, 1898, in "Letters Written Home."

66. E. Harry Phares to Fred Oglebay, September 6, 1898, Tipton County Collection, Indiana State Library, Indianapolis, Indiana.

67. 64,719. Trask, *War with Spain*, 152–153.

68. Gatewood, "Eighth Illinois," 301–302.

69. Donna Thomas, "'Camp Hell': Miami During the Spanish-American War," *Florida Historical Quarterly* 57 (October 1978), 149; Chapman, "Army Life at Camp Thomas," 651; Asst. Surgeon-General Charles R. Greenleaf to Adjutant General Henry C. Corbin, July 7, 1898, U.S. Senate, *Report of the Committee Appointed by the President to Investigate the Conduct of the War with Spain* 8 vols. (56th Cong., 1st Sess., Sen. Doc. No. 221), I, 612–613.

70. Greenleaf to Corbin, July 7, 1898, *Report of the Committee ... to Investigate the Conduct of the War*, I, 612–613; Dallas Bache, "The Place of the Female Nurse in the Army," *Journal of the Military Service Institute of the United States* 25, no. 102 (November 1899), 313.

71. R. Stansbury Sutton, "A Story of Chickamauga," *Report of the Commission ... to Investigate the Conduct of the War*, VIII, 265; James Parker to Adjutant General of

Camp Thomas, August 20, 1898, *Report of the Commission ... to Investigate the Conduct of the War*, I, 422 ; "Report of Gen. H. V. Boynton," October 2, 1898 (quotation); *Report of the Commission ... to Investigate the Conduct of the War*, VIII, 597.

72. "Report of Gen. H. V. Boynton," October 2, 1898, *Report of the Commission ... to Investigate the Conduct of the War*, VIII, 602.

73. "Report of Gen. H. V. Boynton," October 2, 1898, *Report of the Commission ... to Investigate the Conduct of the War*, VIII, 604.

74. General Field Order No. 6, April 26, 1898, as cited in "Report of Gen. H. V. Boynton," October 2, 1898, *Report of the Commission ... to Investigate the Conduct of the War*, VIII, 597; Surgeon General's Office, Circular No. 1, April 25, 1898, as cited in "Report of Gen. H. V. Boynton," October 2, 1898, *Report of the Commission ... to Investigate the Conduct of the War*, VIII, 600.

75. J. C. Minor, "Report on Conditions at Camp Thomas," September 30, 1898, *Report of the Commission ... to Investigate the Conduct of the War*, VIII, 259; "Report of Gen. H. V. Boynton," October 2, 1898, *Report of the Commission ... to Investigate the Conduct of the War*, VIII, 612; "Camps and Their Sanitation," *Report of the Commission ... to Investigate the Conduct of the War*, I, 207, 210; Stelck, "Sgt. Guy Gillette," 572 (quotation).

76. Lt. Col. Curtis Guild, Jr., to Adjutant-General VII Corps, August 21, 1898, U.S. Senate, *Report of the Commission ... to Investigate the Conduct of the War*, I, 415; "Report of Gen. H. V. Boynton," October 2, 1898, *Report of the Commission ... to Investigate the Conduct of the War*, VIII, 606 (first quotation); Francis Rawle to John W. Griggs, August 1, 1898, *Report of the Commission ... to Investigate the Conduct of the War*, VIII, 55 (second quotation).

77. Stelck, "Sgt. Guy Gillette," 573; James A. Dineen to his mother, May 27, 1898, Letters of John O'Connor and James A. Dineen, Mrs. Charles W. Ballard Collection, Indiana State Library, Indianapolis, Indiana (first quotation); Taliafero Miles Dewey to the editor of the *Cleveland Gazette*, printed October 22, 1898, in Gatewood, "'Smoked Yankees,'" 120 (second and third quotations); *Regulations for the Army of the United States 1895* (Washington, D.C.: Government Printing Office, 1900), 198; Bache, "The Female Nurse in the Army," 309–310, 318 (fourth quotation).

78. Surgeon-General George M. Sternberg, "Medical Department," U.S. Senate *Report of the Commission ... to Investigate the Conduct of the War*, I, 170 (first quotation); Mercedes H. Graf, "Women Nurses in the Spanish-American War," *MINERVA: Quarterly Report on Women and the Military* 19, no. 1 (Spring 2001), 10 (second quotation); Bache, "The Female Nurse in the Army," 318.

79. "Selection of Female Nurses," *Report of the Commission ... to Investigate the Conduct of the War*, I, 725–726.

80. Sister Jean Patrice Regan, C.S.J., "Of Women and War" (Archives of the St. Joseph Provincialate, St. Paul, Minnesota), 22; Sister Maria Assunta Werner, C.S.C., "The Sisters of the Holy Cross during the Spanish-American War, 1898–1899" (Conference on the History of the Congregations of Holy Cross, June 1986, Austin, Texas), 1.

81. Graf, "Band of Angels," 201.

4. Naval Blockade of Cuba

1. Pascual Cervera to Segismundo Bermejo, April 22, 1898, in Pascual Cervera y Topete, *The Spanish American War: A Collection of Documents Relative to the Squadron Operations in the West Indies* (Washington, D.C.: Government Printing Office, 1899) (Translation of *Guerra hispano-americana. Coleccion de documentos referentes a la escuadra de operaciones de las Antillas*, El Ferrol, 1899), 57; Cervera to Bermejo, April 24, 1898, in Cervera, *The Spanish American War*, 65 (first quotation), Cervera to Bermejo, April 2, 1898, in Cervera, *The Spanish American War*, 57 (second quotation); French Ensor Chadwick, *Spanish American War* I, 46, as cited by David F. Trask, *The War with Spain in 1898*, The Macmillan Wars of the United States Series, Louis Morton, gen. ed. (New York: Macmillan, 1981), 111 (third quotation).

2. Cervera to Bermejo, March 7, 1898, in Cervera, *Spanish-American War*, 34–35.

3. Cervera to Bermejo, April 8, 1898, in Cervera, *Spanish-American War*, 44.

4. Sanford Sternlicht, *McKinley's Bulldog: The Battleship Oregon* (Chicago: Nelson-Hall, 1977), 70.

5. Sternlicht, *McKinley's Bulldog*, 70–71.

6. Sam Magill to his father, unknown date, published in an unknown newspaper, Spanish-American War Scrapbook in the Collections of the North Dakota Institute for Regional Studies, North Dakota State University Library (Hereafter *North Dakota Scrapbook*); Richard H. Bradford, "And *Oregon* Raced Home," *American Neptune* 36 (October 1976), 259.

7. "The Diary of George W. Robinson, Fireman 2nd Division, No. 1 Fire Room, USS Oregon," March 31, 1898, http://www.spanamwar.com/Oregondiary1.htm, accessed October 29, 2002.

8. R. Cross, "A Sailor's Log," in Charles E. Clark, *My Fifty Years in the Navy* (Boston: Little, Brown and Co., 1917), 308.

9. Sternlicht, *McKinley's Bulldog*, 72.

10. Magill letter, *North Dakota Scrapbook*; Cross, "A Sailor's Log," 310.

11. Robinson diary, April 8, 1898 (first quotation); Magill letter, *North Dakota Scrapbook* (second quotation).

12. Clark, *Fifty Years in the Navy*, 263–264; Edward W. Eberle, "The 'Oregon's' Great Voyage," *The Century Magazine*, 58, no. 6 (October 1898), 914 (quotation).

13. Robinson diary, April 16, 1898.

14. Clark, *Fifty Years in the Navy*, 266; Sternlicht, *McKinley's Bulldog*, 74 (quotation).

15. Magill letter, *North Dakota Scrapbook*.

16. Eberle, "The 'Oregon's' Great Voyage," 920; Cross, "A Sailor's Log," 322 (quotation).

17. Clark, *Fifty Years in the Navy*, 267–269.

18. Trask, *The War with Spain*, 108.

19. Willis John Abbott, *Blue Jackets of '98* (New York: Dodd, Mead and Company, 1899), 96–97; John R. Spears, *Our Navy in the War with Spain* (New York: Charles Scribner's Sons, 1898), 128.

20. F. E. Chadwick, "The Navy in the War," *Scribner's Magazine* 24, no. 5 (November 1898), 530; W. A. M. Goode, *With Sampson Through the War: Being An Account of the Naval Operations of the North Atlantic Squadron During the Spanish American War of 1898* (New York: Doubleday and McClure, 1899), 44–47; Abbott, *Blue Jackets*, 105–106.

21. Walter Millis, *The Martial Spirit* (Houghton Mifflin, 1931; reprint, Chicago: Ivan R. Dee, 1989), 210–211; G. J. A. O'Toole, *The Spanish War: An American Epic, 1898* (New York: W. W. Norton, 1986), 203–204.

22. Trask, *War with Spain*, 163.

23. W. F. Beyer and O. F. Keydel, eds., *Deeds of Valor: How America's Heroes Won the Medal of Honor* (Detroit: The Perrien-Keydel Company, 1905), 360.

24. Cameron McR. Winslow, "Cable-Cutting at Cienfuegos," *Century Magazine* 57, no. 5 (March 1899), 711.
25. Louis Merriman to H. C. Merriman, "On Board the U.S.S. Texas," *Galveston Daily News*, June 19, 1898, 14; This account of the cable-cutting at Cienfuegos is based, for the most part, on Winslow's "Cable-Cutting at Cienfuegos," 708–717; O'Toole, *The Spanish War*, 205–207; Goode, *With Sampson*, 84–85.
26. The account of the *St. Louis'* attempt to cut the cables comes from Caspar F. Goodrich, "The St. Louis' Cable-Cutting," *United States Naval Institute Proceedings* 26, no. 1 (March 1900), 157–166.
27. Worth Bagley to his mother, May 4, 1898, in James Rankin Young and J. Hampton Moore, *Reminiscences and Thrilling Stories of the War by Returned Heroes...* (Philadelphia: Elliott Publishing Company, 1899), 75.
28. Those killed with Ensign Bagley were Firemen John Deneefe and George B. Meek, Oiler John Varreres, and Cabin Cook Elijah B. Tunnell. Goode, *With Sampson*, 83; John R. Spears, "The Affair of the Winslow," *Scribner's Magazine* 24, no. 2 (August 1898), 182–184; Millis lists the casualties as one officer and five enlisted men. Millis *Martial Spirit*, 200; Trask lists the casualties as five killed and three wounded, *War with Spain*, 110; O'Toole lists the losses at five killed, *Spanish War*, 205.
29. James A. Frye, *The First Regiment Massachusetts Heavy Artillery United States Volunteers in the Spanish-American War of 1898* (Boston: The Colonial Company, 1899), 4, 13–14.
30. W. A. Glassford, "Our Army and Aerial Warfare," *American Magazine of Aeronautics* (1908), 19; J. E. Maxfield, "War Ballooning in Cuba," *The Aeronautical Journal* (October 1899), 83; "A Balloon Plan," *Houston Post*, April 24, 1898.
31. Goode, *With Sampson*, 61.
32. William T. Sampson, "The Atlantic Fleet in the Spanish War," *Century Magazine* (April 1899), 889; Goode, *With Sampson*, 63–64; John R. Spears, "The Chase of Cervera," *Scribner's Magazine* 24, no. 2 (August 1898), 145.
33. Spears, "Chase of Cervera," 146.
34. Sampson, "Atlantic Fleet," 890; Spears, "Chase of Cervera," 148.
35. Sampson, "Atlantic Fleet," 891.
36. Abbott, *Blue Jackets*, 148.
37. Goode, *With Sampson*, 70–75.
38. Trask, *War with Spain*, 119.
39. Sampson, "Atlantic Fleet," 894.
40. Trask, *War with Spain*, 122.
41. Trask, *War with Spain*, 126.
42. Sampson, "Atlantic Fleet," 897–898.
43. Robley D. Evans, *A Sailor's Log: Recollections of Forty Years of Naval Life* (New York and London: D. Appleton-Century Company, 1938), 430.
44. Jose Müller y Tejeiro, *Battles and Capitulation of Santiago de Cuba* (Washington, D.C.: Government Printing Office, 1899) (Translation of *Combates y capitulacion de Santiago de Cuba*, Madrid, 1898), 18–19, 25; Commander J., *Sketches From the Spanish-American War* (Washington, D.C.: Government Printing Office, 1899), 21.
45. Trask, *War with Spain*, 175–176.
46. Evans, *Sailor's Log*, 431.
47. Evans, *Sailor's Log*, 431–432.
48. Trask, *War with Spain*, 132–133.
49. Sampson, "Atlantic Fleet," 899.
50. Harry W. Jones, *A Chaplain's Experience Ashore and Afloat: The "Texas" Under Fire* (New York: A. G. Sherwood and Company, 1901), 180.
51. Coxswain Osborn Deignan would therefore man the helm, while Machinist George F. Phillips tended the engine, and Water Tender Francis Kelly maintained the boiler. The *New York* furnished First Class Gunner's Mate George Charette, who had previously served with Hobson aboard the protected cruiser *Chicago*, and Chief Master-at-Arms Daniel Montague. Richmond Pearson Hobson, *A Personal Narrative of the Adventure in the Harbor of Santiago de Cuba, June 3, 1898, and of the Subsequent Imprisonment of the Survivors* (New York: The Century Company, 1899), 54–56; Osborn W. Deignan, "The Sinking of the 'Merrimac' and the Capture and Imprisonment of Hobson and His Men at Santiago," *Leslie's Monthly* (January 1899), 253–254.
52. Hobson, *Personal Narrative*, 8–10.
53. Hobson, *Personal Narrative*, 12.
54. Hobson, *Personal Narrative*, 12–13.
55. Hobson, *Personal Narrative*, 20, 15–16; Deignan, "Sinking of the 'Merrimac,'" 249.
56. Hobson, *Personal Narrative*, 36, 51; Deignan remembered that the *Merrimac* began its run in on the morning of June 2 with the *New York* prepared to chase it in as if it were a blockade runner when the torpedo boat *Porter* caught up with the *Merrimac* and ordered a postponement, "Sinking of the 'Merrimac,'" 255.
57. Hobson, *Personal Narrative*, 61–62; Sampson, "Atlantic Fleet," 899.
58. Hobson, *Personal Narrative*, 40.
59. Hobson, *Personal Narrative*, 27; Deignan, "Sinking of the 'Merrimac,'" 258.
60. Deignan, "Sinking of the 'Merrimac,'" 258; L. C. Merriman, "On Board the U.S.S. Texas," *The Galveston Daily News*, June 19, 1898, 14 (quotation).
61. Deignan, "Sinking of the 'Merrimac,'" 259 (first quotation); Hobson, *Personal Narrative*, 108 (second quotation).
62. O'Toole, *Spanish War*, 235–237; Deignan, "Sinking of the 'Merrimac,'" 264.
63. Evans, *Sailor's Log*, 439–440; John R. Spears, "Torpedo-Boats in the War with Spain," *Scribner's Magazine* 24, no. 5 (November 1898), 617; Sampson, "Atlantic Fleet," 901.
64. Robert Debs Heinl, Jr., "How We Got Guantanamo," *American Heritage* 13, no. 2 (February 1962), 19; Trevor K. Plante, "'New Glory to Its Already Gallant Record': The First Marine Battalion in the Spanish-American War," *Prologue* 30 (Spring 1998), 22.
65. David E. Kelley, "Marines in the Spanish-American War: A Brief History," *Marines in the Spanish-American War, 1895–1898: Anthology and Annotated Bibliography*, edited by Jack Shulimson, Wanda J. Renfrow, David E. Kelley, and Evelyn A. Englander (Washington, D.C.: History and Museums Division, Headquarters, U.S. Marine Corps, 1998), 6–7.
66. Robert Debs Heinl, Jr., *Soldiers of the Sea: The United States Marine Corps, 1775–1962* (Annapolis: United States Naval Institute Press, 1962; reprint, Baltimore: Nautical and Aviation Publishing Company, 1991), 116.
67. J. Robert Moskin, *The U.S. Marine Corps Story* (New York: McGraw-Hill, 1977), 304.
68. Jerry Harlowe, "Dr. Gibbs, Stephen Crane and J.E. Hill," *Military Images* 5, no. 2 (September-October 1983), 21; Stephen Crane, "War Memories," *The Anglo-Saxon Review* 3 (December 1899), 11 (quotation).
69. Jones, *A Chaplain's Experience*, 198–199.
70. Jones, *A Chaplain's Experience*, 202–205.
71. Young and Moore, *Reminiscences and Thrilling Stories*, 88, 97.
72. These Marines were Privates J. McColgan and William Dumphy, respectively. Plante, "New Glory," 24.
73. John Holden-Rhodes, "Crucible of the Corps," *Marines in the Spanish-American War*, 71.

74. Moskin, *Marine Corps Story*, 304–305; Young and Moore, *Reminiscences and Thrilling Stories*, 93.
75. Moskin, *Marine Corps Story*, 306; Heinl, "Guantanamo," 95.
76. Goode, *With Sampson*, 167–168.
77. Goode, *With Sampson*, 169; Abbott, *Blue Jackets of '98*, 258; Kennan says the three ships were the *Marblehead*, the *St. Louis*, and the *Texas*. George Kennan, *Campaigning in Cuba*. (1899; reprint, Port Washington, New York, and London: Kennikat Press, 1971), 74.
78. Goode, *With Sampson*, 169.
79. Müller, *Battles and Capitulation*, 58–60 (quotation); D. J. Scanlon to a friend, "Good Work of the Texas," *Galveston Daily News*, July 7, 1898, 7; "Diary of a Naval Officer on Board the Texas," *Galveston Daily News*, July 12, 1898, 5.
80. Cámara to Auñón, June 15, 1898, in Cervera, *Spanish-American War*, 150.
81. Auñón to Cámara, June 15, 1898, in Cervera, *Spanish-American War*, 151–153.

5. Fifth Corps' Baptism of Fire

1. Graham A. Cosmas, *An Army for Empire: The United States Army in the Spanish-American War* (Columbia: University of Missouri Press, 1971; reprint, College Station: Texas A & M University Press, 1998), 103–104; John D. Miley, *In Cuba With Shafter* (New York: Scribner's Sons, 1899), 2–4.
2. John Black Atkins, *The War in Cuba: The Experiences of an Englishman With the United States Army* (London: Smith, Elder and Company, 1899), 20 (first quotation); Richard Harding Davis, "The Rocking-Chair Period of the War," *Scribner's Magazine* 24 (August 1898), 132 (second quotation); George Kennan, *Campaigning in Cuba* (1899; reprint, Port Washington, New York and London: Kennikat Press, 1971), 2–3 (third quotation).
3. Gary R. Mormino, "Tampa's Splendid Little War: A Photo Essay," *Tampa Bay History* 4, no. 2 (Fall/Winter 1982), 45; Paul Eugen Camp, "Army Life in Tampa During the Spanish-American War: A Photographic Essay," *Tampa Bay History* 9 (Fall/Winter 1987), 17; Miley, *In Cuba With Shafter*, 11.
4. George Von Kromer, quoted by A. B. Feuer in *The Santiago Campaign of 1898: A Soldier's View of the Spanish-American War* Westport, Conn. and London: Praeger, 1993), 16.
5. Atkins, *The War in Cuba*, 48–50.
6. Kennan, *Campaigning in Cuba*, 4; M. B. Stewart, *The N'th Foot in War* (Kansas City: Hudson Press, 1906), 36 (quotation); Mormino, "Tampa's Splendid Little War," 39–40; Herbert O. Kohr, *Around the World With Uncle Sam; or Six Years in the United States Army* (Akron, Ohio: The Commercial Printing Company, 1907), 51
7. Charles Herner, *The Arizona Rough Riders* (Tucson: University of Arizona Press, 1970), 187–190.
8. William B. Gatewood, Jr., *Black Americans and the White Man's Burden 1898–1903* (Urbana, Chicago, and London: University of Illinois Press, 1975), 52–53.
9. Nelson Miles to Russell Alger, June 4, 1898, in U.S. Government *Correspondence Relating to the War with Spain and Conditions Growing Out of the Same, including the Insurrection in the Philippine Islands and the China Relief Expedition, between the Adjutant-General of the Army and Military Commanders in the United States, Cuba, Porto Rico, China, and the Philippine Islands, from April 15, 1898 to July 30, 1902* 2 vols. (Washington, D.C.: Government Printing Office, 1902), 24; Cosmas, *An Army for Empire*, 223.

10. David F. Trask breaks it down to 834 officers and 16,154 men for a total of 16,988 in *The War with Spain in 1898*, Macmillan Wars of the United States Series, gen. ed. Louis Morton (New York: Macmillan, 1981), 180.
11. Edward Marshall, *The Story of the Rough Riders, 1st U.S. Volunteer Cavalry: The Regiment in Camp and on the Battle Field* (New York: G. W. Dillingham, 1899), 56.
12. Herner, *The Arizona Rough Riders*, 82–83.
13. Frederic Remington, "With the Fifth Corps," *Harper's* (November 1898), 963.
14. Trask, *War with Spain*, 187; Ivan Musicant, *Empire by Default: The Spanish-American War and the Dawn of the American Century* (New York: Henry Holt and Company, 1998), 349–350.
15. Richard Meltzer and Phyllis Ann Mingus, "Wild to Fight: The New Mexico Rough Riders in the Spanish-American War," *New Mexico Historical Review* 59, no. 2 (April 1984), 120.
16. Trask, *War with Spain*, 190, 196.
17. Trask, *War with Spain*, 188; Atkins, *The War in Cuba*, 57; *Report of the Committee of the Massachusetts Reform Club Appointed to Collect Testimony in Relation to the Spanish-American War, 1898–1899* (Boston: George H. Ellis, 1899), 16; Marshall, *The Story of the Rough Riders*, 56–57 (quotation).
18. *Report of the Committee of the Massachusetts Reform Club*, 16.
19. Howard A. Giddings, *Exploits of the Signal Corps in the War with Spain* (Kansas City, Mo.: Hudson-Kimberly Pub. Co., 1900), 56–57.
20. *Report of the Committee of the Massachusetts Reform Club*, 8, 24 (first quotation); Charles Johnson Post, *The Little War of Private Post* (Boston: Little Brown, 1960; New York: New American Library, 1961), 67 (second quotation).
21. Virgil Carrington Jones, *Roosevelt's Rough Riders* (Garden City, New York: Doubleday, 1971), 80.
22. *Report of the Committee of the Massachusetts Reform Club*, 8, 17 (quotation).
23. Joseph Wheeler, *The Santiago Campaign, 1898* (Philadelphia: 1899), 13, in G. J. A. O'Toole, *The Spanish War: An American Epic 1898* (New York and London: W. W. Norton, 1984), 265; Caspar Whitney, "The Santiago Campaign," *Harper's Monthly* (October 1898), 795; Richard Harding Davis, "The Landing of the Army," *Scribner's Magazine* 24, no. 2 (August 1898), 185; Trask, *War with Spain*, 198, 212.
24. Walter Millis, *The Martial Spirit: A Study of Our War with Spain* (Boston and New York: 1931), 264.
25. Davis, "The Landing of the Army," 185; Herbert H. Sargent, *The Campaign of Santiago de Cuba*. 3 vols. (Chicago: A. C. McClurg & Co., 1907) II, 19.
26. H. Irving Hancock, *What One Man Saw: Being the Personal Impressions of a War Correspondent in Cuba* (New York: Street and Smith, 1900), 40.
27. Hancock, *What One Man Saw*, 40.
28. This had been General Winfield Scott's landing at Veracruz, Mexico in 1847; Jean Legrand, "The Landing at Baiquiri [sic]," *United States Naval Institute Proceedings* 26, no. 1 (March 1900), 122.
29. Legrand, "Landing at Baiquiri," 123.
30. General Order #18, June 20, 1898, Fifth Army Corps, in Miley, *In Cuba With Shafter*, 60–61; Sargent, *Campaign of Santiago de Cuba*, II, 16.
31. Whitney, "Santiago Campaign," 796.
32. General Order #18, in Miley, *In Cuba With Shafter*, 61.
33. E. J. McClernand, "The Santiago Campaign," published by the Society of Santiago de Cuba, *The Santiago Campaign* (Richmond: Williams Printing Company,

1927), 10–11 (first quotation); Charles H. Brown, *The Correspondents' War: Journalists in the Spanish-American War* (New York: Charles Scribner's Sons, 1967), 305–306 (second quotation).

34. Hancock, *What One Man Saw*, 33; Stephen Bonsal, *The Fight for Santiago: The Story of the Soldier in the Cuban Campaign from Tampa to the Surrender* (New York: Doubleday and McClure, 1899), 80; Post, *The Little War of Private Post*, 80; Trask, *War with Spain*, 214; Legrand, "Landing at Baiquiri," 125; Theodore Roosevelt, *The Rough Riders* (1899; Reprint: New York: Signet, 1961), 45, 52.

35. Hancock, *What One Man Saw*, 30–31.

36. Bonsal, *The Fight for Santiago*, 88.

37. Richard Harding Davis, "The Rough Riders' Fight at Guasimas," *Scribner's Magazine* 24, no. 3 (September 1898), 261–262.

38. Trask, *The War with Spain*, 220; G. J. A. O'Toole puts the starting time at 5:40 to 5:45 in *The Spanish War: An American Epic, 1898* (New York and London: W. W. Norton, 1984), 272. Just exactly how many Cuban troops were available is open to question. Estimates run from General Wheeler's 200 to General Young's 800. Wheeler, *The Santiago Campaign*, 16, 26; Sargent, *The Campaign of Santiago de Cuba*, II, 58 (quotations).

39. Herner, *The Arizona Rough Riders*, 104; Roosevelt, *The Rough Riders*, 61; Edmund Marshall, "A Wounded Correspondent's Recollections of Guasimas," *Scribner's Magazine* 24, no. 3 (September 1898), 273 (quotation).

40. Jones, *Roosevelt's Rough Riders*, 123.

41. The exact number of Hotchkiss guns varies according to who furnished the account. Whitney said two, Wheeler said three, and Young said four. Whitney, "Santiago Campaign," 798; Wheeler, *Santiago Campaign*, 16, 19; Young's report in Wheeler, 25; Herschel V. Cashin and others *Under Fire with the Tenth U.S. Cavalry* (London, New York, and Chicago: F. Tennyson Neely, 1899), 234 (quotation).

42. Roosevelt, *Rough Riders*, 72; Jones, *Roosevelt's Rough Riders*, 127–128.

43. Whitney, "Santiago Campaign," 798; Herner, *Arizona Rough Riders*, 105.

44. Jones, *Roosevelt's Rough Riders*, 132; Michael Blow, "'One Learns Fast in a Fight,'" *MHQ: The Quarterly Journal of Military History* 7, no. 4 (Summer 1995), 23.

45. Roosevelt, *Rough Riders*, 63.

46. Roosevelt, *Rough Riders*, 64.

47. Roosevelt, *Rough Riders*, 65.

48. Marshall, *The Story of the Rough Riders*, 118–119.

49. Jones, *Roosevelt's Rough Riders*, 135.

50. Roosevelt, *Rough Riders*, 64.

51. Bonsal, *The Santiago Campaign*, 94.

52. William D. Beach, "Some Recollections of Santiago," Society of Santiago de Cuba, *The Santiago Campaign* (Richmond, Virginia: Williams Printing Company, 1927), 411.

53. John J. Pershing in a speech at the Hyde Park M. E. Church in Chicago on November 27, 1898, in Cashin and others, *Under Fire With the Tenth*, 164; Anonymous account in Cashin et al., *Under Fire With the Tenth*, 163 (quotation).

54. Marshall, *Rough Riders*, 125; Davis, "Fight at Guasimas," 271; Marshall, *Rough Riders*, 243–244 (quotation).

55. Davis, "Fight at Guasimas," 272 (first quotation); Willard B. Gatewood, Jr., "Indiana Negroes and the Spanish-American War," *Indiana Magazine of History* 69 (June 1973), 106 (second quotation).

56. Trask, *War with Spain*, 222; Whitney, "Santiago Campaign," 797.

57. Jones, *Roosevelt's Rough Riders*, 144.

6. Heavy Fighting in Cuba

1. David F. Trask, *The War with Spain in 1898*, The Macmillan Wars of the United States Series, gen. ed. Louis Morton (New York: Macmillan, 1981), 225.

2. Trask, *War with Spain*, 227–228.

3. Trask says 1,869 and 8,429, *War with Spain*, 230; George Kennan, *Campaigning in Cuba* (1899; reprint Port Washington, New York and London: Kennikat Press, 1971), 120.

4. Trask, *War with Spain*, 231.

5. Joseph Wheeler, *The Santiago Campaign, 1898* (Philadelphia: 1899), 264.

6. Arthur H. Lee, "The Regulars at El Caney," *Scribner's Magazine* 24, no. 4 (October 1898), 404.

7. Kennan, *Campaigning in Cuba*, 120; Herbert H. Sargent, *The Campaign of Santiago de Cuba*, 3 vols. (Chicago: A. C. McClurg & Co., 1907) II, 101–102; Wheeler, *Santiago Campaign*, 264; Joseph Edgar Chamberlin, "How the Spaniards Fought at Caney," *Scribner's* 24 (September 1898), 228.

8. Lee, "Regulars at El Caney," 404.

9. Trask, *War with Spain*, 235.

10. Newspaper clipping dated July 21, 1898, in the file of John Geopfert, Spanish-American War questionnaire, U.S. Army Military History Institute, Carlisle, Pennsylvania.

11. Frank Norris, "With Lawton at El Caney," *The Century Magazine* (June 1899), 306.

12. Chamberlin, "Spaniards at Caney," 278.

13. Some accounts relate that the Massachusetts men were completely forbidden from firing after the first few volleys, but the captain of Company L wrote that only volley firing was discontinued. Frederick E. Pierce, *Reminiscences of the Experiences of Company L, Second Regiment Massachusetts Infantry, U.S.V., in the Spanish-American War* (Greenfield, Massachusetts: E. A. Hall and Company, 1900), 46.

14. Herbert O. Kohr, *Around the World With Uncle Sam; or Six Years in the United States Army* (Akron, Ohio: The Commercial Printing Co., 1907), 72.

15. Chamberlin, "Spaniards at Caney," 279, 281.

16. Chamberlin, "Spaniards at Caney," 281.

17. Norris, "With Lawton at El Caney," 307; Howbert Billman, "El Caney's Bloody Field," in *The Chicago Record's War Stories* (Chicago: The Chicago Record, 1898), 74.

18. Shafter, "Capture of Santiago," 622 (quotation); Sargent, *Campaign of Santiago*, II, 106.

19. Lee, "Regulars at El Caney," 406–407.

20. Guy Cramer, "Dogged Pluck of American Soldiers," in *The Chicago Record's War Stories* (Chicago: The Chicago Record, 1898), 194–195.

21. James Creelman, *On the Great Highway: The Wanderings of a Special Correspondent* (Boston: Lothrop Publishing Company, 1901), 201–202.

22. Norris, "With Lawton at El Caney," 307.

23. Theophilus Gould Steward, *The Colored Regulars in the United States Army* (1904; reprint; New York: Arno, 1969), 104 (first quotation); Lee, "Regulars at El Caney," 410 (second quotation).

24. Lee, "Regulars at El Caney," 403.

25. Charles H. Brown, *The Correspondents' War: Journalists in the Spanish-American War* (New York: Charles Scribner's Sons, 1967), 347 (first quotation); Creelman, *Great Highway*, 209–210 (second quotation); James Rankin Young and J. Hampton Moore, *Reminiscences and Thrilling Stories of the War by Returned Heroes...* (Philadelphia: Elliott Publishing Company, 1899), 222 (third quotation).

26. Sargent, *Campaign of Santiago*, II, 107.
27. Herschel V. Cashin and others, *Under Fire with the Tenth U.S. Cavalry* (London, New York, and Chicago: F. Tennyson Neely, 1899), 139.
28. Kohr, *Around the World*, 75.
29. Steward, *The Colored Regulars*, 220; emphasis added.
30. Charles Johnson Post, *The Little War of Private Post* (Boston: Little Brown, 1960; New York: New American Library, 1961), 115.
31. Theodore Roosevelt, *The Rough Riders* (New York: 1899; reprint; New York: New American Library, 1961), 79–80; Cashin, et al., *Under Fire with the Tenth*, 92; Post, *Little War of Private Post*, 115.
32. Cashin, et al., *Under Fire With the Tenth*, 206 (first quotation); Post, *Little War of Private Post*, 115 (second quotation).
33. General Kent's report in Wheeler, *The Santiago Campaign*, 59–71.
34. Post, *Little War of Private Post*, 119, 122 (quotation); Wheeler, *Santiago Campaign*, 62.
35. Post, *Little War of Private Post*, 120.
36. Young and Moore, *Reminiscences and Thrilling Stories*, 208, 514.
37. Most authors place "Bloody Ford" at the San Juan River, but contemporary maps suggest that it was at the Aguadores; Trask, *War with Spain*, 241 (first quotation); Corporal Walter W. Board in Cashin et al., *Under Fire with the Tenth*, 254–255 (second quotation).
38. Roosevelt, *Rough Riders*, 83.
39. Young and Moore, *Reminiscences and Thrilling Stories*, 209; Cashin et al., *Under Fire with the Tenth*, 99.
40. G. J. A. O'Toole, *The Spanish War: An American Epic 1898* (New York and London: W. W. Norton, 1984), 315.
41. Malcolm McDowell, "Another Account," *The Spanish-American War: The Events of the War Described by Eye Witnesses* (Chicago and New York: Herbert S. Stone and Company, 1899), 122–123 (quotation); John H. Parker, *History of the Gatling Gun Detachment, Fifth Army Corps, at Santiago, With a Few Unvarnished Truths Concerning that Expedition* (Kansas City, Mo.: Hudson-Kimberly Publishing Company, 1898), 127; Cpl. Walter W. Board, in Cashin et al., *Under Fire with the Tenth*, 254.
42. Post, *Little War of Private Post*, 127.
43. Young and Moore, *Reminiscences and Thrilling Stories*, 237–238.
44. Stephen Bonsal, *The Fight for Santiago: The Story of the Soldier in the Cuban Campaign from Tampa to the Surrender* (New York: Doubleday and McClure, 1899), 198.
45. John Bigelow, Jr., *Reminiscences of the Santiago Campaign* (New York and London: Harper and Brothers, 1899), 128.
46. Roosevelt, *Rough Riders*, 87.
47. Captain John Bigelow, Jr., in Cashin et al., *Under Fire with the Tenth*, 170.
48. Sergeant Pressly Holliday in Cashin et al., *Under Fire with the Tenth*, 237 (quotation); Sargent, *The Campaign of Santiago*, II, 118.
49. Cashin et al., *Under Fire with the Tenth*, 222.
50. J. Ford Kent, "The Heroic Charge on San Juan," *Hero Tales of the American Soldier and Sailor as told by…* (Philadelphia: Century Manufacturing, 1899), 81; A soldier from the 24th U.S. Infantry also claimed this singular honor, Cashin et al., *Under Fire with the Tenth*, 164; Paul B. Maime, "The Thirteenth Infantry in the Santiago Campaign," Society of Santiago de Cuba *The Santiago Campaign* (Richmond: Williams Printing Company, 1927), 101.

51. Parker, *Gatling Gun Detachment*, 130; A. B. Feuer, *The Santiago Campaign of 1898: A Soldier's View of the Spanish-American War* (Westport, Conn., and London: Praeger, 1993), 64.
52. Feuer, *Santiago Campaign*, 94; John Black Atkins, *The War in Cuba: The Experience of an Englishman With the United States Army* (London: Smith, Elder and Company, 1899), 143 (quotation).
53. Young and Moore, *Reminiscences and Thrilling Stories*, 375–376.
54. Wheeler, *Santiago Campaign*, 55–56.
55. Report of Brigadier General George M. Sternberg in U.S. Senate, *Report of the Commission Appointed by the President to Investigate the Conduct of the War Department in the War with Spain*, 8 vols. 56th Cong., 1st Sess., Sen. Doc. No. 221 (Washington, D. C.: Government Printing Office, 1900), I, 175.
56. Kennan, *Campaigning in Cuba*, 130–141.
57. Bonsal, *The Fight for Santiago*, 256–257, 298.
58. Trask, *War with Spain*, 251.
59. Trask, *War with Spain*, 253.

7. Naval Battle Forces Surrender

1. Pascual Cervera y Topete to Arsenio Linares, June 25, 1898, in Pascual Cervera y Topete, *The Spanish-American War: A Collection of Documents Relative to the Squadron Operations in the West Indies* (Office of Naval Intelligence, War Notes No. VII, Information from Abroad, Washington, D.C.: Government Printing Office, 1899), 111–112.
2. Ramón Auñón y Villalón to Pascual Cervera y Topete, June 26, 1898, in Cervera, 114; Ramón Blanco to Pascual Cervera y Topete, June 26, 1898, in Cervera, *The Spanish-American War*, 113.
3. Victor M. Concas y Palau, *The Squadron of Admiral Cervera* (Office of Naval Intelligence, War Notes No. VIII, Information from Abroad, Washington, D.C.: Government Printing Office, 1900), 68–70.
4. Concas, *The Squadron of Admiral Cervera*, 73.
5. "He Was On the Texas," *Galveston Daily News*, August 31, 1898, 4; John W. Philip, "The 'Texas' at Santiago," *The Century Magazine* 58, no. 1 (May 1898 [1899]), 87 (quotation).
6. David F. Trask, *The War with Spain in 1898*, The Macmillan Wars of the United States Series, gen. ed. Louis Morton (New York: Macmillan, 1981), 262.
7. W.A.M. Goode, *With Sampson Through the War: Being an Account of Naval Operations of the North Atlantic Squadron During the Spanish American War of 1898* (New York: Doubleday and McClure, 1899), 193.
8. Philip, "The 'Texas' at Santiago," 88 (first quotation); Goode, *With Sampson Through the War*, 193 (second quotation).
9. Henry C. Taylor, "The 'Indiana' at Santiago," *The Century Magazine* (June 1899), 65.
10. Jones, *A Chaplain's Experience*, 232–233.
11. Taylor, "The 'Indiana' at Santiago," 65 (first and second quotations); Jones, *A Chaplain's Experience*, 233 (third quotation).
12. Concas, *The Squadron of Admiral Cervera*, 74.
13. Goode, *With Sampson Through the War*, 198.
14. Robley D. Evans, *A Sailor's Log: Recollections of Forty Years of Naval Life* (New York and London: D. Appleton-Century Company, 1938), 450; Concas, *The Squadron of Admiral Cervera*, 74.
15. Philip, "The 'Texas' at Santiago," 91.
16. Evans, *A Sailor's Log*, 447.

17. Concas, *The Squadron of Admiral Cervera*, 76, 90; Cervera, *The Spanish American War*, 123; Trask, *The War with Spain*, 263; Charles E. Clark, *My Fifty Years in the Navy* (Boston: Little, Brown and Co., 1917), 295.
18. James Rankin Young and J. Hampton Moore, *Reminiscences and Thrilling Stories of the War by Returned Heroes...* (Philadelphia: Elliott Publishing Company, 1899), 441–442; George Edward Graham, "Working the Thirteen-Inch Gun," *Leslie's Weekly* (May 12, 1898), 299. Young and Moore give a firing rate of once every ninety seconds for the twelve-inch guns, and Graham specifies a rate of once every three minutes for the thirteen-inch gun.
19. Philip, "The 'Texas' at Santiago," 92 (quotation); Young and Moore, *Reminiscences and Thrilling Stories*, 126, 29.
20. Calandria to Cervera, July 6, 1898, in Cervera, *The Spanish American War*, 129; French E. Chadwick, "The Navy in the War," *Scribner's Magazine* 24, no. 5 (November 1898), 535; Cervera, *The Spanish American War*, 124–125; Report of the *Almirante Oquendo*'s Lieutenant Adolfo Calandria, in Cervera, *The Spanish American War*, 129.
21. Adolfo Calandria to Pascual Cervera y Topete, July 6, 1898, in Cervera, *The Spanish American War*, 128.
22. Clark, *My Fifty Years in the Navy*, 295 (first quotation); Philip, "The 'Texas' at Santiago," 93; Jones, *A Chaplain's Experience*, 240 (second quotation).
23. "Cervera's Flag Lieutenant," *Galveston Daily News*, July 24, 1898, 9.
24. F. E. Chadwick, "The 'New York' at Santiago," *Century Magazine* 58, no. 1 (May 1899), 113 (quotation); Jose Müller y Tejeiro. *Battles and Capitulation of Santiago de Cuba* (Office of Naval Intelligence, War Notes No. I, Information From Abroad, Washington, D.C.: Government Printing Office, 1899), 107; "Cervera's Flag Lieutenant," *Galveston Daily News*, July 24, 1898, 9.
25. Müller, *Battles and Capitulation of Santiago de Cuba*, 107.
26. William G. Cassard, "Rescuing the Enemy," *Century Magazine* 58, no. 1 (May 1899), 117.
27. Peter Keller, "The Rescue of Admiral Cervera." *Harper's* (April 1899), 786 (quotation); Harry Huse, the executive officer of the *Gloucester* says that there were no boatswain's mates on the ship and therefore there was no piping. Harry P. Huse, "On the 'Gloucester' After the Battle," *Century Magazine* 58, no. 1 (May 1899), 115.
28. Willis John Abbott, *Blue Jackets of '98* (New York: Dodd, Mead and Company, 1899), 282–283; John R. Spear, "The Great Naval Battle Before Santiago," *Hero Tales of the American Soldier and Sailor as told by...* (Philadelphia: Century Manufacturing, 1899), 165; Captain Schley remembered that the reported distance was 1,700 yards and that Ellis was killed when he, upon Schley's request, stepped from behind cover to re-estimate the range, Young and Moore, *Reminiscences and Thrilling Stories*, 20.
29. Paul St. C. Murphy, "Removal of a Jammed Shell While Under Fire of the Enemy," *Hero Tales*, 178–179.
30. "Cervera's Flag Lieutenant," *Galveston Daily News*, July 24, 1898, 9 (quotation); Eulate's report in Cervera, *The Spanish American War*, 131; Edward R. Eberle, "The 'Oregon' at Santiago," *Century Magazine*, 58, no. 1 (May 1899), 108; Report of the *Vizcaya*'s Captain Antonio Eulate, in Cervera, *The Spanish American War*, 130–131.
31. Philip, "The 'Texas' at Santiago," 94 (first quotation); "Cervera's Flag Lieutenant," *Galveston Daily News*, July 24, 1898, 9 (second quotation); Concas, *The Squadron of Admiral Cervera*, 83.
32. Young and Moore, *Reminiscences and Thrilling Stories*, 56.
33. Evans, *A Sailor's Log*, 451–452.
34. Fred T. Jane, *All the World's Fighting Ships* (London: Sampson Low, Marston and Company, 1898), 89, 197, 199, 206.
35. José de Paredes to Pascual Cervera y Topete, July 6, 1898, in Cervera, *The Spanish American War*, 127 (quotation); Clark, *My Fifty Years in the Navy*, 296–297.
36. Evans, *A Sailor's Log*, 453–454.
37. Francis A. Cook, "The 'Brooklyn' at Santiago." *Century Magazine* 58, no.1 (May 1899), 99; Henry Barrett Chamberlin. "Schley's Unfought Battle," in *The Chicago Record's War Stories by Staff Correspondents in the Field* (Chicago: The Chicago Record, 1898), 116 (quotation).
38. Chamberlin, "Schley's Unfought Battle," 116 (first and second quotations); Evans, *A Sailor's Log*, 454 (third quotation).
39. Cook, "The 'Brooklyn' at Santiago," 100.
40. Chamberlin, "Schley's Unfought Battle," 116 (first quotation); Cook, "The 'Brooklyn' at Santiago," 100 (second quotation).
41. Evans, *A Sailor's Log*, 449 (first quotation); Goode, *With Sampson Through the War*, 211, 221; Concas, *The Squadron of Admiral Cervera*, 83; Young and Moore, *Reminiscences and Thrilling Stories*, 17 (second quotation).
42. Trask, *The War With Spain*, 265–266.
43. Eberle, "The 'Oregon' at Santiago," 111.
44. Eberle, "The 'Oregon' at Santiago," 111.
45. Eberle, "The 'Oregon' at Santiago," 110.
46. André Morton Proctor, "The 'Gloucester's' Fight," *Harper's Weekly* (August 6, 1898), 775.
47. Trask, *The War With Spain*, 266.
48. William R. Shafter, "The Capture of Santiago de Cuba," *The Century Magazine*, February 1899, 624.
49. Trask, *War with Spain*, 287.
50. Shafter, "Capture of Santiago," 625–626.
51. Trask, *War with Spain*, 301; Young and Moore, *Reminiscences and Thrilling Stories*, 440 (quotation).
52. Caspar Whitney, "The Santiago Campaign." *Harper's* 97, no. 581 (October 1898), 816; J. C. Pendergrass to R. Anderson, July 1898, as published in the Springfield *Illinois Record*, September 3, 1898, in Willard B. Gatewood, Jr., *"Smoked Yankees" and the Struggle for Empire: Letters from Negro Soldiers, 1898–1902* (Urbana: University of Illinois Press, 1971), 52 (quotation).
53. Curtis V. Hard, *Banners in the Air: The Eighth Ohio Volunteers and the Spanish-American War*, edited by Robert H. Ferrell (Kent, Ohio, and London: Kent State University Press, 1988), 43 (first quotation); A. B. Feuer, *The Santiago Campaign of 1898: A Soldier's View of the Spanish-American War* (Westport, Conn., and London: Praeger, 1993), 105 (second quotation), 35 (third quotation).
54. Major Philip Reade's inspection report to the Inspector General in Washington, July 23, 1898, in U.S. Senate, *Report of the Commission Appointed by the President to Investigate the Conduct of the War Department in the War with Spain*, 8 vols. 56th Cong., 1st Sess., Sen. Doc. No. 221 (Washington, D.C.: Government Printing Office, 1900), I, 376–377; *Report of the Commission Appointed by the President*, I, 443.
55. Shafter, "Capture of Santiago," 627.
56. Trask, *War with Spain*, 313.
57. John D. Miley, *In Cuba with Shafter* (New York: 1899), 176–177.
58. Shafter, "Capture of Santiago," 628.
59. Shafter, "Capture of Santiago," 628.
60. James F. J. Archibald, "The Day of the Surrender of Santiago," *Scribner's Magazine* 24, no. 4 (October 1898), 415.
61. Archibald, "Day of the Surrender," 413–416;

Shafter, "Capture of Santiago," 629; John Stronach, "The 34th Michigan Volunteer Infantry," *Michigan History* 30 (April–June 1946), 299 (quotation).

62. Trask, *War with Spain*, 325; Mary C. Gillett, *The Army Medical Department, 1865–1917* (Washington, D.C.: Center of Military History, United States Army, 1995), 150–151.

63. George F. Telfer to Family, November 22, 1898, in George F. Telfer, *Manila Envelopes: Oregon Volunteer Lt. George F. Telfer's Spanish-American War Letters*, Edited by Sara Bunnett (Oregon Historical Society Press, 1987), 86; Mercedes Graf, "Band of Angels: Sister Nurses in the Spanish-American War," *Prologue: The Journal of the National Archives* 34 (Fall 2002), 205.

64. C. D. Rhodes, "The Diary of a Lieutenant," Society of Santiago de Cuba, *The Santiago Campaign* (Richmond: Williams Printing Company, 1927), 393.

65. Cleveland Moffett, "Stories of Camp Wikoff," *Leslie's Weekly* (November 11, 1898), 342; Trask, *War with Spain*, 326.

66. A. D. Webb, "Arizonans in the Spanish-American War," *Arizona Historical Review* 1 (January 1929), 66.

67. Trask gives the exact number sick as 4,270. *War with Spain*, 330.

68. Trask, *War with Spain*, 331 (first and second quotations); William Shafter to Corbin, August 8, 1898, in U.S. Government, *Correspondence Relating to the War with Spain and Conditions Growing Out of Same including the Insurrection in the Philippine Islands and the China Relief Expedition, between the Adjutant General of the Army and Military Commanders in the United States, Cuba, Porto Rico, China, and the Philippine Islands, from April 15, 1898 to July 30, 1902*, 2 vols. (Washington, D. C.: Government Printing Office, 1902), I, 216.

8. Eighth Corps to Manila

1. David F. Trask, *The War with Spain in 1898*, The Macmillan Wars of the United States Series, Louis Morton, gen. ed. (New York: Macmillan, 1981), 383–384.

2. George F. Telfer to Lottie, May 22, 1898, in *Manila Envelopes: Oregon Volunteer Lt. George F. Telfer's Spanish-American War Letters*, edited by Sara Bunnett ([Portland, Oregon]: Oregon Historical Society Press, 1987), [6] (first quotation); Thomas D. Thiessen, "The Fighting First Nebraska: Nebraska's Imperial Adventure in the Philippines, 1898–1899," *Nebraska History* 70, no. 3 (Fall 1989), 216 (second quotation).

3. H. C. Thompson, "War Without Medals," *Oregon Historical Quarterly* 59 (December 1948), 300.

4. V. Edmund McDevitt, *The First California's Chaplain* (Fresno, California: Academy Library Guild, 1956), 63.

5. Oscar King Davis, "Off for Manila," *Harper's Weekly* (June 11, 1898), 562.

6. Frank L. Millet, *The Expedition to the Philippines* (New York and London: Harper and Brothers, 1899), 4–5.

7. [Huntington], "A Trooper's Diary: From the Presidio to Honolulu," *The Outlook* (September 3, 1898), 15; William Joe Webb, "The Spanish-American War and United States Army Shipping," *American Neptune* 40 (July 1980), 184.

8. Millet, *Expedition to the Philippines*, 8 (first quotation); Charles S. Foster to John Orchard, August 2, 1898, Scrapbook in North Dakota Institute for Regional Studies, North Dakota State University, hereafter *North Dakota Scrapbook* (second quotation); [Huntington], "From the Presidio to Honolulu," 16 (third quotation);

Frank H. Johnson to his parents, June 14, 1898, in Frank Henton Johnson papers, State Archives, Nebraska State Historical Society, as cited by Thiessen, "The Fighting First Nebraska," 218 (fourth quotation); G. E. Towl to *Nebraska State Journal* (publ.), July 11, 1898, as cited by J. R. Johnson, "The Saga of the First Nebraska in the Philippines," *Nebraska History* 30 (June 1949), 145 (fifth quotation).

9. Trask, *War with Spain*, 387.

10. John Gearey to his mother, July 7, 1898, *North Dakota Scrapbook*.

11. Douglas White, "On to Manila: A True and Concise History of the Philippine Campaigns, Secured while Afloat with Admiral Dewey's Fleet, and in the Field with the 8th Army Corps," *Pacific Historical Magazine* 1, no. 1 (June 30, 1899), [6].

12. Johnson, "Saga of the First Nebraska," 145 (first quotation); Huntington, "Presidio to Honolulu," 18 (second quotation).

13. Joseph G. Evans to his mother, June 2, 1898, Joseph G. Evans collection, Oregon Historical Society (first quotation); George F. Telfer to his family, June 3, 1898, in Telfer, *Manila Envelopes*, 13 (second quotation); Jay Weaver quoted in Thiessen, "Fighting First Nebraska," 219 (third quotation).

14. F. D. Millet, "With General Merritt," *Harper's Weekly* (September 10, 1898), 898; Johnson, "Saga of the First Nebraska," 146; [Huntington], "A Trooper's Diary: From Honolulu to Manila," *The Outlook* (October 29, 1898), 521 (first quotation); Charles G. Avery to Charles R. McDonough, July 26, 1898, in "Glimpses of the Spanish-American War on Board the Flag Ship 'China,'" *Colorado Magazine* 39, no. 3 (July 1962), 186 (second quotation).

15. Millet, "With Merritt," 898; Huntington, "Honolulu to Manila," 522–523.

16. White, "On to Manila," [7].

17. Huntington, "Honolulu to Manila," 523; H. A. Luxton to *The Tribune* (Minneapolis?), in *North Dakota Scrapbook*.

18. Oscar King Davis, "The Taking of Guam," *Harper's Weekly*, (August 20, 1898), 829.

19. Davis, "Taking of Guam," 829.

20. Frank Portusach, "History of the Capture of Guam by the United States Man-of-War *Charleston* and Its Transport," *United States Naval Institute Proceedings* 43 (April 1917), 708. A newspaper reporter who was aboard the *Charleston* that day insists that the Spaniards did not mistake the gunfire for a friendly salute. Douglas White, "The Capture of the Island of Guam: The True Story," *Overland Monthly: A Magazine of California and the Pacific West* (March 1900), 229.

21. Portusach, "Capture of Guam," 707. Davis identifies the governor as Jose Marina y Vega, "Taking of Guam," 829.

22. Thompson, "War Without Medals," 306 (first quotation); White, "On to Manila," [13] (second quotation).

23. Davis, "Taking of Guam," 830.

24. Davis, "Taking of Guam," 830.

25. Davis, "Taking of Guam," 830.

26. Davis, "Taking of Guam," 830.

27. Avery, "Glimpses of the Spanish American War," 187–188; John F. Bass, "How We Took Wake Island," *Harper's Weekly* (September 17, 1898), 915 (quotation); Avery, "Glimpses of the Spanish American War," 187–188; Millet, *Expedition to the Philippines*, 14.

28. Trask puts Eighth Corps manpower at 407 officers and 10,437 men for a total strength of 10,844, *War with Spain*, 386.

29. Letter from H. A. Luxton, *North Dakota Scrapbook*.

30. Millet, "With Merrit," 898; [Huntington], "Honolulu to Manila," 524; John Gearey to his mother, July 7, 1898, *North Dakota Scrapbook*; H. A. Luxton to the Minneapolis *Tribune*, ca. August 2, 1898, *North Dakota Scrapbook*; Corporal Edwards to *The Forum*, July 8, 1898, *North Dakota Scrapbook*; Diary of G. Angus Fraser, July 13, 1898, North Dakota Institute for Regional Studies, North Dakota State University (quotation).
31. Bass, "How We Took Wake Island," 915.
32. Huntington, "Presidio to Honolulu," 17 (first and second quotations); H. A. Luxton to *The* (Minneapolis) *Tribune*, in *North Dakota Scrapbook* (third quotation).
33. Huntington, "Presidio to Honolulu." 17; H. A. Luxton to the Minneapolis *Tribune*, ca. August 2, 1898, *North Dakota Scrapbook*; Fraser diary, July 18, 1898; Corporal Edwards to *The Forum*, July 18, 1898, *Scrapbook*; John Gearey to his mother, July 7, 1898, *North Dakota Scrapbook* (first quotation); H. A. Luxton to the Minneapolis *Tribune*, ca. August 2, 1898, *North Dakota Scrapbook* (second quotation).
34. H. A. Luxton to the Minneapolis *Tribune*, ca. August 2, 1898, *North Dakota Scrapbook*.
35. H. A. Luxton to the Minneapolis *Tribune*, ca. August 2, 1898, *North Dakota Scrapbook*.
36. Huntington, "Presidio to Honolulu," 17; Edwards to the *Forum*, July 8, 1898, in the *North Dakota Scrapbook*; Fraser diary, July 22, 1898; H. A. Luxton to Minneapolis *Tribune*, ca. August 2, 1898, *North Dakota Scrapbook* (quotation).
37. Fraser diary, July 12, 1898; John Gearey to his mother, July 7, 1898, in *North Dakota Scrapbook* (first quotation); *Regulations for the Army of the United States, 1895* (Washington, D.C.: Government Printing Office, 1900); 176; H. A. Luxton to the Minneapolis *Tribune*, ca. August 2, 1898, *North Dakota Scrapbook* (second quotation); John Bowe, *With the Thirteenth Minnesota* (Minneapolis: 1905), 25 (third quotation); Fraser diary, July 18, 1898.
38. Anonymous to the Jamestown *Alert*, ca. August 2, 1898, in *North Dakota Scrapbook*.
39. Diary of John Peterson, July 23, 1898, North Dakota Heritage Center, State Historical Society of North Dakota; Fraser diary, July 17–18, 1898; Corporal Edwards to the *Forum*, July 18, 1898, *North Dakota Scrapbook*; Edmund P. Neill to his parents, August 29, 1898, Minnesota Historical Society (quotation); Bowe, *Thirteenth Minnesota*, 25.
40. Huntington, "Presidio to Honolulu," 16–18 (first quotation); H. A. Luxton to the Minneapolis *Tribune*, in the *North Dakota Scrapbook* (second quotation).
41. Fraser diary, July 19, 1898.
42. H. A. Luxton to the Minneapolis *Tribune*, in *North Dakota Scrapbook*.
43. Bowe, *Thirteenth Minnesota*, 26; Huntington, "Presidio to Honolulu." 17.
44. Corporal Edwards to *The Forum*, July 22, 1898, *North Dakota Scrapbook*; Peterson diary, July 21, 1898; H. A. Luxton to the Minneapolis *Tribune*, ca. August 2, 1898, *North Dakota Scrapbook*; Millet, *Expedition to the Philippines*, 16 (quotation).
45. H. A. Luxton to the Minneapolis *Tribune*, ca. August 2, 1898 (first quotation), *North Dakota Scrapbook*; Melvin C. Henry to J. H. Worst, August 2, 1898, *North Dakota Scrapbook* (second quotation); Bowe, *Thirteenth Minnesota*, 27 (third quotation).
46. H. A. Luxton to the Minneapolis *Tribune*, in *North Dakota Scrapbook*; H. A. Luxton to the Minneapolis *Tribune*, in *North Dakota Scrapbook*; John Gearey to his mother, July 7, 1898, in *North Dakota Scrapbook*; M. A. Hildreth letter in *North Dakota Scrapbook*.

9. The Philippines Campaign

1. John T. McCutcheon, "A Day Off Blockaded Manila," *The Chicago Record's War Stories* (Chicago: The Chicago Record, 1898), 133–139.
2. John T. McCutcheon, "American Soldiers in Cavite," *The Chicago Record's War Stories*, 175–176.
3. Frank L. Millet, *Expedition to the Philippines* (New York, 1899), 40.
4. Millet, *Expedition to the Philippines*, 45, 103–104; Charles R. Mabey, *The Utah Batteries: A History* (Salt Lake City: *Daily Reporter*, 1900), 20.
5. Millet, *Expedition to the Philippines*, 75–76.
6. Mabey, *Utah Batteries*, 21.
7. Millet, *Expedition to the Philippines*, 40.
8. Billy Edwards to *The Forum*, August 6, 1898, in *North Dakota Scrapbook*; Millet, *Expedition to the Philippines*, 65–66 (quotation).
9. Millet, *Expedition to the Philippines*, 55–56.
10. Millet, *Expedition to the Philippines*, 83–84; Brig. Gen. F. V. Greene's report, August 23, 1898, *55th Congress, 3rd Session, House Document 2, Serial Set 3745* (hereinafter *Serial Set 3745*), 63.
11. David F. Trask, *The War with Spain in 1898*, The Macmillan Wars of the United States Series, Louis Morton, gen. ed. (New York: Macmillan, 1981), 412.
12. Millet, *Expedition to the Philippines*, 85–87; John T. McCutcheon, "A Battle in the Night," *The Chicago Record's War Stories*, 189.
13. McCutcheon, "Battle in the Night," 189.
14. Douglas White, *On to Manila: A True and Concise History of the Philippine Campaigns, Secured While Afloat with Admiral Dewey's Fleet, and in the Field with the 8th Army Corps*, Pacific Historical Magazine 1, no. 1 (June 30, 1899), [23].
15. White, *On to Manila*, [23].
16. Report of Captain James O'Hara, 3rd U.S. Artillery, August 1898, *Serial Set 3745*, 103 (quotation); Millet, *Expedition to the Philippines*, 98; Gen. Greene's report, August 23, 1898, *Serial Set 3745*, 64.
17. Alexander L. Hawkins, "Official History of the Operations of the Tenth Pennsylvania Infantry, U.S.V. in the Campaign in the Philippine Islands." as an appendix to Karl Irving Faust, *Campaigning in the Philippines* (San Francisco: The Hicks-Judd Company, 1899; reprint, New York: Arno, 1970), 6; Report of Captain Richard W. Young, Battery A, Utah Artillery, August 20, 1898, *Serial Set 3745*, 98; James Rankin Young and J. Hampton Moore, *Reminiscences and Thrilling Stories of the War by Returned Heroes...* (Philadelphia: Elliott Publishing Company, 1899), 328 (quotation).
18. McCutcheon, "Battle in the Night," 192; V. Edmund McDevitt, *The First California's Chaplain* (Fresno, California: Academy Library Guild, 1956), 90; Another source attributes this "friendly fire" to the men of the Third U.S. Heavy Artillery, Young and Moore, *Reminiscences and Thrilling Stories*, 334.
19. McCutcheon, "Battle in the Night," 191.
20. Report of Major Sam R. Jones, August 23, 1898, *Serial Set 3745*, 62.
21. I have used the casualty figures of Gen. Greene's report, but other sources give different numbers. McCutcheon lists nine killed and forty-two wounded. O'Toole and Trask each list ten killed and thirty-three wounded. Correspondent Douglas White listed seven killed and forty-six wounded, and Colonel Hawkins of the Tenth Pennsylvania estimated his losses as six killed and twenty-nine wounded (one fatally). Gen. Greene's report, *Serial Set 3745*, 64; McCutcheon, "Battle in the Night," 189; G. J. A. O'Toole, *The Spanish War: An Amer-*

ican Epic 1898 (New York and London: W.W. Norton, 1984), 369; Trask, *War with Spain*, 413; White *On to Manila*, 23–25; Colonel A. L. Hawkins' report, August 20, 1898, *Serial Set 3745*, 94; Mabey, *Utah Batteries*, 23 (quotation).
22. Trask, *War with Spain*, 416.
23. John T. McCutcheon, "The Taking of Manila," *The Chicago Record's War Stories* (Chicago: The Chicago Record, 1898), 201; Joseph L. Stickney, *War in the Philippines and Life and Glorious Deeds of Admiral Dewey* (Joseph Stickney, 1899), 98–99.
24. General Order #3, August 9, 1898, in Faust, *Campaigning in the Philippines*, 86.
25. McCutcheon, "The Taking of Manila," 202.
26. Millet, *Expedition to the Philippines*, 142 (first quotation); John Bowe, *With the 13th Minnesota in the Philippines* (Minneapolis: A. B. Farnham, 1905), 33 (second quotation).
27. Millet, *Expedition to the Philippines*, 131–132; Brig. Gen. Thomas M. Anderson's report, August 29, 1898, *Serial Set 3745*, 56; Second Lieutenant William D. Connor's report, August 18, 1898, *Serial Set 3745*, 96–97.
28. Diary of Angus Fraser, August 12–14, 1898, Company B, 1st North Dakota Volunteer Infantry, G. Angus Fraser papers, North Dakota Institute for Regional Studies, North Dakota State University Library.
29. Millet, *Expedition to the Philippines*, 153–154; Sidney May, "Assault and Capture of Manila," *Hero Tales of the American Soldier and Sailor as Told by the Heroes Themselves* (Philadelphia: Century Manufacturing Company), 71.
30. Bowe identifies the captain as a Captain McQuaide in *Thirteenth Minnesota*, 34; Lieutenant Carl Stone, in a letter to his parents, identifies him as Captain McWade. Carl Stone, Jr., to his parents, August 16, 1898, in Carl L. Stone and Emma Elnora Stone Collection, Minnesota State Archives.
31. Millet, *Expedition to the Philippines*, 153–154; May, "Assault and Capture of Manila," 72.
32. Frank H. Johnson to his parents, August 16, 1898, in Frank Henton Johnson Papers, State Archives, Nebraska State Historical Society, as cited in Thomas D. Thiessen, "The Fighting First Nebraska: Nebraska's Imperial Adventure in the Philippines, 1898–1899," *Nebraska History* 70, no. 3 (Fall 1989), 227.
33. McCutcheon, "The Taking of Manila," 206–207.
34. White, *On to Manila*, [34].
35. Gen. Anderson's report, August 29, 1898, *Serial Set 3745*, 58–59; Francis V. Greene, "The Capture of Manila," *The Century Magazine* 57, no. 6 (April 1899), 931.
36. Report of Colonel James C. Smith, First California, August 18, 1898, *Serial Set 3745*, 95–96; Report of Captain William E. Birkhimer, Third U.S. Artillery, August 17, 1898, *Serial Set 3745*, 102.
37. Report of Colonel Irving Hale, First Colorado, August 18, 1898, *Serial Set 3745*, 78.

10. The Puerto Rico Campaign

1. Secretary Alger to General Miles, June 26, 1898, in *U.S. Government Correspondence*, I, 268–269.
2. John Metzger, 3rd Illinois Volunteers, to his sister, July 29, 1898, John W. Metzger Collection, Chicago Historical Society.
3. Col. A. Lowden Snowden to Alger, July 25, 1898, in *Correspondence*, I, 315; W. H. Eustis to Alger, August 2, 1898, in *Correspondence*, I, 347 (first quotation); C. F. Wright to T. C. Platt, July 21, 1898, in *Correspondence*, I, 302 (second quotation).

4. Charles W. Fairbanks to Alger, July 26, 1898, in *Correspondence*, I, 320; Corbin to Brigadier General James F. Wade, July 26, 1898, in *Correspondence*, I, 320; Ex-Governor Richard Yates to McKinley, July 28, 1898, in *Correspondence*, I, 329; Corbin to Tanner, July 30, 1898, in *Correspondence* I, 337; S. M. Cullom to Alger, July 30, 1898, in *Correspondence*, I, 336; Tanner to Corwin, August 6, 1898, in *Correspondence*, I, 365.
5. Charles E. Creager, *The Fourteenth Ohio National Guard, The Fourth Ohio Volunteer Infantry* (Columbus, Ohio: The Landon Printing and Publishing Company, 1899), 124; James Rankin Young and J. Hampton Moore, *Reminiscences and Thrilling Stories of the War by Returned Heroes...* (Philadelphia: Elliott Publishing Co., 1899), 305 (first quotation), 308 (second quotation).
6. T. Dart Walker, "The Puerto Rico Expedition," *Harper's Weekly*, August 20, 1898, 827.
7. Creager, *Fourteenth Ohio*, 124–126 (first four quotations); Karl Stephen Herrman, *A Recent Campaign in Puerto Rico: By the Independent Regular Brigade under the command of Brig. General Schwan* (Richard G. Badger & Co., 1899; reprint, Boston: E. H. Bacon & Co., 1907), 106–107; Creager, *Fourteenth Ohio*, 124–126; Frank E. Edwards, *The '98 Campaign of the 6th Massachusetts, U.S.V.* (Boston: Little, Brown and Company, 1899), 59 (fifth quotation), 62 (sixth quotation).
8. George G. King, *Letters of a Volunteer in the Spanish-American War* (Chicago: Hawkins and Loomis, 1929), 45.
9. Young and Moore, *Reminiscences and Thrilling Stories*, 305; "Extract From a Private Letter Received From a Member of Troop 'A.'" *Harper's Weekly* August 27, 1898, 850.
10. Edwards, *6th Massachusetts*, 79 (quotation); 86.
11. R. S. Bunzey, *History of Companies I and E, Sixth Regt., Illinois Volunteer Infantry from Whiteside County* (Morrison, Illinois: Rufus S. Bunzey, 1901), 220–223.
12. Edwards, *6th Massachusetts*, 86–87; Richard Harding Davis, "The Porto Rican Campaign," *Scribner's Magazine* 24, no. 5 (November 1898), 518.
13. Creager, *Fourteenth Ohio*, 191.
14. Davis, "Porto Rican Campaign," 519.
15. Davis, "Porto Rican Campaign," 519.
16. Herrman, *Campaign in Puerto Rico*, 32–33; Nelson A. Miles, *Serving the Republic: Memoir of the Civil and Military Life of Nelson A. Miles* (New York: Harper and Brothers, 1911), 301–302 (quotation).
17. Davis, "Porto Rican Campaign," 520.
18. Coppinger to Corbin, July 23, 1898, and Schwan to Corbin, July 23, 1898, in *Correspondence*, I, 309.
19. Carlton T. Chapman, "How the Stars and Stripes Came to Arroyo," *Harper's Weekly* (September 3, 1898), 874.
20. Herrman, *Campaign in Porto Rico*, 23.
21. Herrman, *Campaign in Porto Rico*, 25–26.
22. Herrman, *Campaign in Porto Rico*, 27–28 (first and second quotations); Bunzey, *Companies I and E*, 233 (third quotation).
23. Herrman, *Campaign in Porto Rico*, 59.
24. Herrman, *Campaign in Porto Rico*, 60.
25. General Schwan to General Miles, August 21, 1898, *Report of the Secretary of War, 55th Congress, 3rd Session, House Document 2, Serial Set 3745* (hereinafter *Serial Set 3745*), 249–253.
26. Young and Moore, *Reminiscences and Thrilling Stories* 298 (first quotation); Herrman, *Campaign in Porto Rico*, 61–62 (second quotation).
27. Herrman, *Campaign in Porto Rico*, 64.
28. Herrman, *Campaign in Porto Rico*, 18–19.
29. Report of General Schwan, August 22, 1898, *Serial Set 3745*, 256.

30. Bunzey, *Companies I and E*, 233; George G. King to his family, July 5, 1898, in King, *Letters of a Volunteer*, 38, 63 (quotation).
31. Bunzey, *Companies I and E*, 233–234; George G. King to his family, August 12, 1898, in King, *Letters of a Volunteer*, 69 (quotation).
32. James Harrison Wilson, *Under the Old Flag: Recollections of Military Operations in the War for the Union, the Spanish War, the Boxer Rebellion, Etc.* 2 vols. (New York and London: D. Appleton and Company, 1912), I, 440.
33. Wilson, *Under the Old Flag*, I, 442, 444–445.
34. Young and Moore, *Reminiscences and Thrilling Stories*, 287; Report of Lt. Col. John Biddle, August 18, 1898, *Serial Set 3745*, 238.
35. Report of Capt. H. L. Anderson, Battery F, 4th U.S. Artillery, August 18, 1898, *Serial Set 3745*, 235–236.
36. Richard Harding Davis, *Notes of a War Correspondent* (New York: Scribner's Sons, 1910), 103–111.
37. Report of Major General James H. Wilson, August 23, 1898, *Serial Set 3745*, 226–234.
38. Report of Second Lieutenant Edward P. O'Hern, 3rd U.S. Artillery, August 18, 1898, *Serial Set 3745*, 237.
39. Wilson, *Under the Old Flag*, 447–448.
40. Report of Maj. Gen. James H. Wilson, First Division, First Army Corps, *Serial Set 3745*, 231–232.
41. Creager, *Fourteenth Ohio*, 151.
42. J. D. Potter, 4th Ohio Volunteer Infantry, to A. B. Coit, August 7, 1898, *Serial Set 3745*, 143; General Peter C. Hains to Corbin, August 16, 1898, *Serial Set 3745*, 142; Creager, *Fourteenth Ohio*, 164.
43. David F. Trask, *The War with Spain in 1898*, The Macmillan Wars of the United State Series (New York: Macmillan, 1981), 362.
44. Creager, *Fourteenth Ohio*, 172–173.
45. Creager, *Fourteenth Ohio*, 174–177.
46. These were Troop E, Sixth U.S. Cavalry, the Philadelphia City Troop of Volunteer Cavalry, Light Battery B of Pennsylvania Artillery, the Twenty-Seventh Indiana Light Artillery Battery, Light Battery A of the Missouri Artillery, and Light Battery A of the Illinois Artillery.
47. James Rankin Young and S. Hampton Moore, *History of Our War With Spain* (Washington: 1898), 654–656.

11. Coming Home

1. Graham A. Cosmas, *An Army for Empire: The United States Army in the Spanish-American War* (Columbia, Missouri: University of Missouri Press, 1971; repr. College Station, Texas: Texas A & M University Press, 1994), 262.
2. Charles Johnson Post, *The Little War of Private Post* (Boston: Little Brown, 1960; New York: New American Library, 1961), 28–29
3. H. Irving Hancock, *What One Man Saw: Being the Personal Impressions of a War Correspondent in Cuba* (New York: Street and Smith, 1900), 176.
4. Attributed to John Sheehan of the Seventh U.S. Infantry in John Evangelist Walsh "Forgotten Angel: The Story of Janet Jennings and the *Seneca*," *Wisconsin Magazine of History* 81 (Summer 1998), 276; The story of the *Seneca*'s voyage is from Walsh, "Forgotten Angel," 267–293.
5. *Report of the Committee of the Massachusetts Reform Club Appointed to Collect Testimony in Relation to the Spanish-American War, 1898–1899* (Boston: George H. Ellis, 1899), 18, 20, 49.
6. Charles H. Brown, *The Correspondents' War: Journalists in the Spanish-American War* (New York: Charles Scribner's Sons, 1967), 435; Theodore Roosevelt, *The Rough Riders* (1899; reprint, New York: The New American Library of World Literature, 1961), 140 (quotation).

7. Royal A. Prentice, "The Rough Riders," *New Mexico Historical Review* 27 (January 1952), 44 (quotation); Roosevelt, *Rough Riders*, 137.
8. A. B. Feuer, *The Santiago Campaign of 1898: A Soldier's View of the Spanish-American War* (Westport, Conn., and London: Praeger, 1993), 127.
9. William Mayo Venable, *The Second Regiment of United States Volunteer Engineers* (Cincinnati: McDonald and Company, 1899), 25, 40–41.
10. James Rankin Young and J. Hampton Moore, *Reminiscences and Thrilling Stories of the War by Returned Heroes...* (Philadelphia: Elliott Publishing Company, 1899), 498–502.
11. Charles Herner, *The Arizona Rough Riders* (Tucson: University of Arizona Press, 1970), 201–202.
12. David F. Trask, *The War with Spain in 1898*, (New York: Macmillan, 1981), 334; Cosmas, *Army for Empire*, 265; G. J. A. O'Toole says that 126 died at Camp Wikoff, *The Spanish War: An American Epic 1898* (New York and London: W. W. Norton, 1984), 375.
13. "Organizations of Volunteers," *Correspondence Relating to the War with Spain* 2 vols. (U.S. Adjutant General's Office, 1902), I, 583–628.
14. H. E. Webber, *Twelve Months with the Eighth Massachusetts Infantry* (Salem, Mass.: 1908), 141–142: Franklin E. Pierce, *Reminiscences of the Experiences of Company L, Second Regiment Massachusetts Infantry, U.S.V., in the Spanish-American War* (Springfield, Mass.: 1900), 66; W. E. Biederwolf, *History of the One Hundred and Sixty-First Regiment, Indiana Volunteer Infantry* (Logansport, Indiana: 1899), 119 (quotation).
15. R. S. Bunzey, *History of Companies I and E, Sixth Regt., Illinois Volunteer Infantry from Whiteside County* (Morison, Illinois: 1901), 244; Curtis V. Hard, *Banners in the Air: The Eighth Ohio Volunteers and the Spanish-American War*, edited by Robert H. Ferrell (Kent: Kent State University Press, 1988), 38–39.
16. F. D. Millet, *The Expedition to the Philippines* (New York and London: Harper and Brothers, 1899), 47.
17. Webber, *Twelve Months with the Eighth Massachusetts*, 141 (first quotation); Pierce, *Reminiscences ... of Company L*, 66 (second quotation); Feuer, *The Santiago Campaign*, 117 (third quotation); Bunzey, *History of Companies I and E*, 245 (fourth quotation).
18. Preston Morrow, Havana, to his mother, Mrs. J.C.S. Morrow, December 31, 1898, published in a newspaper (probably the Quanah *Tribune-Chief*), Spanish American War Survey-First Texas Infantry Volunteers, U.S. Army Military History Institute, Carlisle, Pennsylvania.
19. Pierce, *Reminiscences ... of Company L*, 56 (first quote); Herner, *Arizona Rough Riders*, 166 (second quote).
20. Letter from Lieutenant Hildreth, published in unidentified newspaper, *North Dakota Scrapbook*; Wirt Williams to ?, August 18, 1898, in *North Dakota Scrapbook* (first quotation); George G. King, *Letters of a Volunteer in the Spanish-American War* (Chicago: Hawkins and Loomis, 1929), 55 (second quotation); Charles E. Creager, *The Fourteenth Ohio National Guard, The Fourth Ohio Volunteer Infantry* (Columbus, Ohio: The Landon Printing and Publishing Company, 1899), 212 (third quotation); Frank E. Edwards, *The '98 Campaign of the 6th Massachusetts, U.S.V.* (Boston: Little, Brown, and Company, 1899), 96 (fourth quotation), 250 (fifth quotation).
21. Bunzey, *Companies I and E*, 247 (first quotation); Cpl. Edwards to the *Forum*, in *North Dakota Scrapbook*; Charles S. Foster to E. C. Kinnear, August 11, 1898, in *North Dakota Scrapbook*; King, *Letters of a Volunteer*, 56; Bunzey, *Companies I and E*, 247; Creager, *The Fourteenth Ohio*, 213 (second quotation); Pierce, *Reminiscences ... of Company L*, 39.

22. Letter from Captain Carleton from Manila, dated August 11, 1898, published in an unknown newspaper, *North Dakota Scrapbook* (first and second quotations); George F. Telfer to Lottie, from Manila, December 7, 1898 in George F. Telfer, *Manila Envelopes: Oregon Volunteer Lt. George F. Telfer's Spanish-American War Letters*, edited by Sara Bunnett (Oregon Historical Society Press, 1987), 93 (third quotation); Letter from Quartermaster Sergeant Charles S. Foster to E. C. Kinnear from Manila, August 17, 1898, published in an unknown newspaper, *North Dakota Scrapbook* (fourth quotation).

23. Young and Moore, *Reminiscences and Thrilling Stories*, 265.

24. Hancock, *What One Man Saw*, 151–153.

25. Creager, *Fourteenth Ohio*, 185.

26. Edwards, *6th Massachusetts*, 154–155 (quotation), 166; Capt. Carleton letter, August 11, 1898, in *North Dakota Scrapbook*.

27. Charles R. Mabey, *The Utah Batteries: A History* (Salt Lake City: Daily Reporter, 1900), 31 (quotation); Edmund P. Neill to his brother, Victor, February 2, 1899, Edmund P. Neill Papers, Minnesota Historical Society, Minneapolis.

28. Webber, *Twelve Months with the Eighth Massachusetts*, 145–146.

29. Edmund P. Neill to his mother, November 22, 1898, Edmund P. Neill Papers, Oregon Historical Society.

30. Biederwolf, *One Hundred and Sixty-First Indiana*, 157, 159, 162.

31. Biederwolf, *One Hundred and Sixty-First Indiana*, 127; Post, *The Little War of Private Post*, 179; Young and Moore, *Reminiscences and Thrilling Stories*, 484–485, 494.

32. Pierce, *Reminiscences ... of Company L*, 30 (first quotation), 86; Edwards, *6th Massachusetts*, 166; King, *Letters of a Volunteer*, 86 (second quotation).

33. Preston Morrow, Havana, to his brother, Temple Houston Morrow, January 12, 1899, as published in the Quanah *Tribune-Chief*; Spanish American War Survey–First Texas Volunteer Infantry, U.S. Army Military History Institute, Carlisle, Pennsylvania; Webber, *Twelve Months With the Eighth Massachusetts*, 139.

34. Venable, *The Second Regiment of United States Volunteer Engineers*, 114; Bunzey, *Companies I and E*, 296 (quotation).

35. *The Nebraska Independent*, March 2, 1899, as cited by J. R. Johnson, "The Saga of the First Nebraska in the Philippines," *Nebraska History* 30 (June 1949), 150–151 (quotation).

36. Biederwolf, *One Hundred and Sixty-first Regiment Indiana*, 189, 191 (first and third quotations); John Black Atkins, *The War in Cuba: The Experiences of an Englishman With the United States Army* (London: Smith, Elder & Co., 1899), 210 (second quotation).

37. M. Koenigsberg, *Southern Martyrs: A History of Alabama's White Regiments During the Spanish-American War, Touching Incidentally on the Experiences of the Entire First Division of the Seventh Army Corps* (Montgomery, Alabama: Brown Printing Company, 1898), 203; Creager, *Fourteenth Ohio*, 299–300; Bunzey, *Companies I and E*, 321 (quotation), 326.

38. Mabey, *The Utah Batteries*, 92 (quotation); V. Edmund McDevitt, *The First California's Chaplain* (Fresno, California: Academy Library Guild, 1956), 133–135.

12. Epilogue

1. There seems to be no consensus on casualty figures. Cosmas says 281 battle deaths and "about 2,500" due to illness; Millis says 379 lost in combat and 5,462 lost to disease; O'Toole lists 385 combat deaths; and both "some 2,000" and the more precise 2,565 who perished from illness. Graham A. Cosmas, *An Army for Empire: The United States Army in the Spanish-American War*, 2d ed. (College Station: Texas A & M University Press, 1994), 244, 278; Walter Millis, *The Martial Spirit: A Study of Our War with Spain* (Boston and New York: 1931), 367; G. J. A. O'Toole, *The Spanish War: An American Epic 1898* (New York and London: W. W. Norton, 1984), 17, 375n.

2. Patrick McSherry, "Infanta Maria Teresa," *The Spanish-American War Centennial Website*, http://www.spanamwar.com/teresa.htm, accessed May 28, 2003; Mark Howells, "Pre-Dreadnought Preservation: The Infanta Maria Teresa," *Pre-Dreadnought Preservation*, http://www.oz.net/~markhow/pre-dred/index.htm, accessed May 28, 2003.

3. Patrick McSherry, "Reina Mercedes," *The Spanish-American War Centennial Website*, http://www.spanamwar.com/reinam.htm, accessed May 28, 2003.

4. Richard Sweeney, "A Gun from the Vizcaya at Lowell, Massachusetts," *The Spanish-American War Centennial Website*, http://www.spanamwar.com/vizcayagun.htm, accessed May 28, 2003; Mark Howells, The Almirante Oquendo, *Pre-Dreadnought Preservation*, http://www.oz.net/~markhow/pre-dred/index.htm, accessed May 28, 2003; Greg Youngstrom, "A Gun from the Almirante Oquendo," *The Spanish-American War Centennial Website*, http://www.spanamwar.com/Oquendogun.htm, accessed May 28, 2003.

5. Thomas B. Allen, "Remember the Maine?" *National Geographic* 193, no. 2 (February 1998), 108–109.

6. http://www.spanamwar.com, May 21, 2003.

7. Patrick McSherry, "The Monument to the Maine in Havana, Cuba," http://www.spanamwar.com, May 21, 2003; Tom Miller, "Remember the Maine," *Smithsonian* 28, no. 11 (February 1998), 55–56.

8. *Medal of Honor Recipients, 1863–1973*, 93d Cong., 1st Sess., Committee on Veterans' Affairs, Committee Print No. 15 (Washington, D.C.: Government Printing Office, 1973), 1–2, 355–373.

9. "Medal of Honor Awarded to Theodore Roosevelt," www.theodoreroosevelt.org/life/medalofhonor.htm, accessed July 15, 2003; Mitchell Yockelson, "'I Am Entitled to the Medal of Honor and I Want It': Theodore Roosevelt and His Quest for Glory," *Prologue* 30 (Spring 1998), 7 (first quotation), 16 (second quotation).

10. "Medal of Honor Awarded to Theodore Roosevelt," www.theodoreroosevelt.org/life/medalofhonor.htm, accessed July 15, 2003.

11. Yockelson, "'I Am Entitled to the Medal of Honor,'" 15.

12. Richard Melzer and Phyllis Ann Mingus, "Wild to Fight: The New Mexico Rough Riders in the Spanish-American War," *New Mexico Historical Review* 59 (April 1984), 127.

13. H. B. Bivins to a friend, July 8, 1898, published in the Southern Workman in August 1898, in Willard B. Gatewood, Jr., *"Smoked Yankees" and the Struggle for Empire: Letters From Negro Soldiers, 1898–1902* (Urbana: University of Illinois Press, 1971), 49–50 (first and second quotations); James Rankin Young and J. Hampton Moore, eds. *Reminiscences and Thrilling Stories of the War by Returned Heroes...* (Philadelphia: Elliott Publishing Company, 1899), 246–247 (third quotation and fourth quotations).

14. Arthur E. Gentzen diary entry for April 16, 1898, The Center for American History, University of Texas at Austin.

Bibliography

Archival Material

CHICAGO HISTORICAL SOCIETY

Sterling Johnston Collection: Diary and letters of Sterling Johnston, 1st Illinois Volunteers
Nicholas J. Budinger Collection: Reminiscences of Nicholas J. Budinger, Co. I, 1st Illinois Volunteers
John W. Metzger Collection: Letters of John W. Metzger, Co. G, 3rd Illinois Volunteers

FILSON CLUB, LOUISVILLE, KENTUCKY

Metzner Collection: Diary of Frederick George Benjamin, Co. D, 2nd Kentucky Infantry
Richard Hickman Menefee Collection: Letters of Richard H. Menefee, Battalion Adjutant, 1st Kentucky Infantry
Brown-Ewell Family Papers: Letter of Percy Brown
Enid Bland Yandell Collection: Letter of Lunsford Pitts Yandell, 1st Kentucky Infantry
Galt Family Papers: Letter of Pat
Harry Innes Todd and George Davidson Todd Papers: Letter of Chapman C. Todd, USS *Winslow*

FRANKLIN COLLEGE LIBRARY, FRANKLIN, INDIANA

David Demaree Banta Indiana Collection: Letters of Will R. Johnson, Company E, 158th Indiana Volunteer Infantry

INDIANA STATE LIBRARY, INDIANAPOLIS, INDIANA

Fred C. Hurt Collection: Letters of Fred C. Hurt, Hospital Corps
Lucius C. Embree Collection: Letters of O. M. Tichenor
Tipton County Collection: Letters of E. H. Phares and James W. Russell, Co. I, 160th Indiana (t/s)
Mrs. Charles W. Ballard Collection: Letters of John O'Connor and James A. Dineen, Co. M, 158th Indiana

Ezra Macy Collection: Letter of Charlie R. McGill, Co. L, 1st Illinois Infantry

KENDALL YOUNG LIBRARY, WEBSTER CITY, IOWA

F. A. Bonebright Collection: Letters of F. A. Bonebright, 52nd Iowa Volunteers

MINNESOTA HISTORICAL SOCIETY, ST. PAUL, MINNESOTA

Edmund P. Neill Papers: Letters of Edmund P. Neill, Co. G, 13th Minnesota Volunteers
Carl L. and Emma Elnora Stone Collection: Letters of Carl L. Stone, 13th Minnesota Volunteers
Sarah Gleason Papers: Letters of Carroll ?, Co. C, 15th Minnesota Volunteers

STATE HISTORICAL SOCIETY OF NORTH DAKOTA, BISMARCK, NORTH DAKOTA

John Peterson Collection: Diary of John Peterson, 1st North Dakota Volunteers
John Russater Collection: Diary of John Russater, 1st North Dakota Volunteers
Jesse E. Melton Collection: Scrapbook

NORTH DAKOTA INSTITUTE FOR REGIONAL STUDIES, NORTH DAKOTA STATE UNIVERSITY LIBRARY, FARGO, NORTH DAKOTA

G. Angus Fraser Papers: Diary of G. Angus Fraser, 1st North Dakota Volunteers
Spanish-American War Collection: Scrapbook of newspaper articles on North Dakota Volunteers

OREGON HISTORICAL SOCIETY

Willis Platts Collection: Diary of Sergeant W. A. Platts, Company M, 2nd Oregon Infantry

Joseph G. Evans Collections: Letters of Joseph G. Evans, Co. B, 2nd Oregon Volunteers
Lester P. Smith Collection: Letter of Lester P. Smith
Fred Ramsey Collection: Letter of Fred Ramsey, USN
Ira Minton Holsclow Collection: Letters of Ira Holsclow, Co. M, 1st South Dakota Volunteers

TOLEDO-LUCAS COUNTY PUBLIC LIBRARY, TOLEDO, OHIO

Park L. Myers Collection: Letters of Dr. Park L. Myers, 6th Ohio Volunteers

JOHN TYLER, AUSTIN, TEXAS

Letters of Lucius A. Tyler, 6th Massachusetts Volunteers

U.S. ARMY MILITARY HISTORY INSTITUTE, CARLISLE, PENNSYLVANIA

Spanish-American War Survey Collection
Preston Morrow, 1st Texas Volunteer Infantry
William B. Smith, 2nd Texas Volunteer Infantry
Julian H. Speedy, 2nd Texas Volunteer Infantry
Bascom Bishop Treadwell, 3rd Texas Volunteer Infantry
Howard H. Kilpatrick, 4th Texas Volunteer Infantry
Cyrus J. Holland, 1st Illinois Volunteer Infantry
Robert Briggs, 1st Illinois Volunteer Infantry
Irving G. King, 1st Illinois Volunteer Infantry
Cary T. Ray, 1st Illinois Volunteer Infantry
Casimir W. Sheppard, 1st Illinois Volunteer Infantry
George G. Tronjo, 3rd Illinois Volunteer Infantry
George W. Lord, 4th Illinois Volunteer Infantry
Charles Slade, 4th Illinois Volunteer Infantry
John E. Woodward, 16th U.S. Infantry
Adolph Wiener, 16th U.S. Infantry
William A. Longabaugh, 22nd U.S. Infantry
Oscar P. Ruth, 22nd U.S. Infantry
Sim Goddard, 3rd U.S. Volunteer Cavalry
Perry Law, 3rd U.S. Volunteer Cavalry
Rollo Roscoe Riegle, 157th Indiana Volunteer Infantry
Wheeler H. Martin, 1st Idaho Volunteer Infantry
Edward McConville, 1st Idaho Volunteer Infantry
James L. Swihart, 160th Indiana Volunteer Infantry
Joseph Choate King, 50th Iowa Volunteer Infantry
William W. Williams, 50th Iowa Volunteer Infantry
Charles W. Startsman, 50th Iowa Volunteer Infantry
Earle R. Clock, 52nd Iowa Volunteer Infantry
E. E. Wands, 52nd Iowa Volunteer Infantry
Evan L. Evans, 33rd Michigan Volunteer Infantry
John Geopfert, 33rd Michigan Volunteer Infantry
W. D. Parke, 33rd Michigan Volunteer Infantry
Frank Rawson, 33rd Michigan Volunteer Infantry
Charles F. Hiler, 33rd Michigan Volunteer Infantry
Albert Nelson Richardson, 33rd Michigan Volunteer Infantry
Claude W. Boyntan, 71st New York Volunteer Infantry
George Fern, 71st New York Volunteer Infantry
G. V. Kromer, 71st New York Volunteer Infantry
Alfred N. Foote, 1st Wisconsin Volunteer Infantry
Walter Charles Hintze, 1st Wisconsin Volunteer Infantry
John P. Stranberg, 2nd Wisconsin Volunteer Infantry
Maurice Peck, 2nd Wisconsin Volunteer Infantry
Walter A. Swope, 3rd Wisconsin Volunteer Infantry
Evander Noble, 3rd Wisconsin Volunteer Infantry
Charles C. Remington, 3rd Wisconsin Volunteer Infantry

Published Material

Abbott, Willis John. *Blue Jackets of '98* New York: Dodd, Mead and Company, 1899.
Agnew, James B. "Carromatos and Quinine: Private Longden and the Medical Corps of 1898." *Military Review* 59 (July 1979): 11–21.
Alger, Russell Alexander. "The Food of the Army during the Spanish War." *The North American Review* 172 (January 1901): 39–58.
All The World's Fighting Ships. London: Sampson Low, Marston and Company, 1898.
Allen, Francis J. "The Story of the USS Vesuvius and the Dynamite Gun." *Warship* 45 (January 1988): 10–15.
Allen, Thomas B. "Remember the *Maine*?" *National Geographic* 193, no. 2 (February 1998): 92–111.
_____, ed. "What Really Sank the *Maine*?" *Naval History* 12, no. 2 (March-April 1998): 30–39.
Aloe, Alfred. *Twelfth U.S. Infantry, 1798–1919*. New York: Knickerbocker Press, 1919.
Anderson, Sherwood. *Sherwood Anderson's Memoirs* New York: Harcourt, Brace and Company, 1942.
Archibald, James F. J. "The Day of the Surrender of Santiago." *Scribner's* 24, no. 4 (Oct 1898): 413–416.
_____. "The First Engagement of American Troops on Cuban Soil." *Scribner's* 24, no. 2 (Aug 1898): 177–182.
_____. "What I Saw in the War." *Leslie's Weekly* (October 20, 1898), 314; (November 3, 1898), 350; (November 17, 1898), 390; (December 1, 1898), 430; (December 8, 1898), 450; (December 29, 1898), 522.
Atkins, John Black. *The War in Cuba: The Experiences of an Englishman With the United States Army*. London: 1899.
Auxier, George W. "The Propaganda Activities of the Cuban *Junta* in Precipitating the Spanish-American War, 1895–1898." *Hispanic American Historical Review* 19, no. 3 (August 1939): 286–305.
Avery, Charles G. "Glimpses of the Spanish-American War: On Board the Flag Ship China." *Colorado Magazine* 39, no. 3 (July 1962): 185–194.
B., J. K. "The Stay-At-Home's Resolve." *Harper's Weekly* (September 24, 1898): 938.
Bache, Col. Dallas. "The Place of the Female Nurse in the Army." *Journal of the Military Service Institution of the United States* 25 (November 1899): 307–328.
Bacon, Alexander S. *The Seventy-First at San Juan*. New York: Cortlandt Press, 1900.
"A Balloon Plan." *Houston Post*, April 24, 1898.
"Barbarism at Montauk." *Harper's Weekly* 42 (September 10, 1898): 890.

Bass, John F. "Bound for Manila." *Harper's Weekly* (July 23, 1898): 722–724.
———. "How We Took Wake Island." *Harper's Weekly* (September 17, 1898): 915.
———. "A Night in the Insurgents' Trenches." *Harper's Weekly* (September 10, 1898): 898–899.
———. "Off for Manila." *Harper's Weekly* (July 2, 1898): 639.
Bates, Alfred E. "The Army — Its Staff and Supply Departments." *The Conservative Review* 3 (March 1900): 162–189.
Bayley, Frank Leslie. "A Yankee Jack-tar's Story." *Leslie's Weekly* (October 13, 1898), 294.
Beardslee, L. A. "The Trial of the Oregon." *Harper's New Monthly Magazine* 98, no. 587 (April 1899): 699–707.
Benjamin, Anna Northend. "Christian Work in Our Camps." *The Outlook* 59 (July 2, 1898): 566–569.
———. "The Truth About Army Rations." *Leslie's Weekly* (June 30, 1898); 426.
———. "A Woman's Visit to Santiago." *Leslie's Weekly* (August 25, 1898): 155.
Bernadou, J. B. "The *Winslow* at Cardenas." *The Century Magazine* 57, no. 5 (March 1899): 698–706.
Beyer, W. F., and O. F. Keydel, eds. *Deeds of Valor: How America's Heroes Won the Medal of Honor*. Detroit: The Perrien-Keydel Company, 1905.
Biennial Report of the Adjutant General of Illinois ... 1897–1898. Springfield: Phillips Bros., 1898.
Bierderwolf, W. E. *History of the One Hundred and Sixty-First Regiment, Indiana Volunteer Infantry*. Logansport, Indiana: 1899.
Bigelow, John. *Reminiscences of the Santiago Campaign*. New York and London: Harper Bros., 1899.
Bigelow, Poultney. "The Battle of Cabañas." *Harper's Weekly* (May 28, 1898): 525.
———. "In Camp at Tampa." *Harper's Weekly* (June 4, 1898): 550.
———. "A Yankee in Spain: With the Troops Bound for Cuba." *Harper's Weekly* (June 4, 1898): 542.
Bishop, J. B. "The Beef Verdict." *The Nation* 68 (May 11, 1899): 347–348.
———. "Get the Beef Contracts." *The Nation* 67 (March 23, 1899): 217–218.
Blow, Michael. *A Ship to Remember: The Maine and the Spanish-American War*. New York: William Morrow, 1992.
———. "One Learns Fast in a Fight." *MHQ: The Quarterly Journal of Military History* 7, no. 4 (Summer 1995): 20–29.
Bocock, John Paul. "Life on the 'Oregon.'" *Leslie's Weekly* (October 13, 1898), 294–295.
———. "The Spell-binding Rough Riders." *Leslie's Weekly* (November 3, 1898), 343.
Bonsal, Stephen. *The Fight for Santiago: The Story of the Soldier in the Cuban Campaign from Tampa to the Surrender*. New York: Doubleday and McClure, 1899.
Bowe, John. *With the Thirteenth Minnesota*. Minneapolis: 1905.
Bowers, George. *History of the 160th Indiana Volunteer Infantry*. Ft. Wayne, Ind.: 1900.

Bradford, James C., ed. *Crucible of Empire: The Spanish-American War and Its Aftermath*. Annapolis: Naval Institute Press, 1993.
Bradford, Richard H. "And *Oregon* Rushed Home." *American Neptune* 36 (October 1976): 257–265.
Britton, Ed E. "The Battles Around Santiago As Observed by a Swedish Officer." *Journal of the Military Service Institution of the United States* 26, no. 105 (May 1900): 388–398.
Brown, Charles H. *The Correspondents' War: Journalists in the Spanish-American War*. New York: Charles Scribner's Sons, 1967.
Brumby, Thomas M. "The Fall of Manila," edited by Willard E. Wright, *United States Naval Institute Proceedings*, August 1960.
Bullard, Robert Lee. "The Negro Volunteer: Some Characteristics." *Journal of the Military Service Institution of the United States* 29 (July 1901): 29–39.
Bunzey, R. S. *History of Companies I and E, Sixth Regt., Illinois Volunteer Infantry from Whiteside County*. Morison, Ill.: 1901.
Burton, James. "Photographing Under Fire." *Harper's Weekly* (August 6, 1898): 773–774.
Butcher, Alfred. "Close Shave of a Corporal." *Leslie's Weekly* (October 13, 1898), 294.
Calkins, Carlos G. "Historical and Professional Notes on the Naval Campaign of Manila Bay in 1898." *Proceedings of the United States Naval Institute*. 25, no. 2 (June 1899): 267–321.
Camp, Paul Eugen. "Army Life in Tampa During the Spanish-American War: A Photographic Essay." *Tampa Bay History* 9 (Fall-Winter 1987): 17–28.
Campbell, W. Joseph. "Not likely sent: The Remington-Hearst 'telegrams.'" *Journalism and Mass Communication Quarterly*, 77, no. 2 (Summer 2000): 405–422.
Carson, H. R. *Recollections of a Chaplain in the Volunteer Army: An address delivered before the Church Club of Louisiana at its annual meeting, January 25, 1899, by H. R. Carson, late Captain and Chaplain, Second Louisiana Volunteer Infantry*. Pamphlet. N.p., n.d.
Carter, William H. *From Yorktown to Santiago with the Sixth U.S. Cavalry*. Baltimore: The Lord Baltimore Press, 1900.
Cashin, Herschel V. et al. *Under Fire with the Tenth U.S. Cavalry*. New York: Arno, 1964.
Cassard, William G. "Rescuing the Enemy." *The Century Magazine* 58, no. 1 (May 1899): 116–118.
Cervera y Topete, Pascual. *The Spanish American War: A Collection of Documents Relative to the Squadron Operations in the West Indies*. Washington, D.C.: Government Printing Office, 1899. (Translation of *Guerra hispano-americana. Coleccion de documentos referentes a la escuadra de operaciones de las Antillas*, El Ferrol, 1899).
Chadwick, F. E. "The Navy in the War." *Scribner's* 24, no. 5 (November 1898): 529–539.
———. "The 'New York' at Santiago." *The Century Magazine* 58, no. 1 (May 1899): 111–114.
Chamberlin, Joseph E. "How the Spaniards Fought at Caney." *Scribner's* 24, no. 3 (September 1898): 278–282.

Chandler, Melbourne C. *Of Garryowen in Glory: The History of the Seventh United States Cavalry Regiment*. Annandale, Virginia: Turnpike Press, 1960.

Chapman, Carlton T. "After the Great Sea-Fight." *Harper's Weekly* (August 6, 1898): 774.

_____. "Cuba." *Harper's Weekly* (July 9, 1898): 673–675.

_____. "How the Stars and Stripes Came to Arroyo." *Harper's Weekly* (September 3, 1898): 874.

_____. "The Occupation of Ponce." *Harper's Weekly* (September 3, 1898): 863.

_____. "Off Santiago." *Harper's Weekly* (July 16, 1898): 701.

_____. "With Admiral Sampson's Fleet." *Harper's Weekly* (June 4, 1898): 538; (June 11, 1898): 578.

_____. "With the Fleet Off Santiago." *Harper's Weekly* (July 30, 1898): 740–741, 744.

Chapman, Gregory Dean. "Army Life at Camp Thomas, Georgia, During the Spanish-American War." *Georgia Historical Quarterly* 70 (Winter 1986): 633–656.

The Chicago Record's War Stories. Chicago: The Chicago Record, 1898.

Christy, Howard Chandler. "An Artist at El Poso." *Scribner's* 24, no. 3 (September 1898): 283–284.

_____. "Christy's Story of the War." *Leslie's Weekly* (August 18, 1898), 134.

Clarfield, Gerard. *United States Diplomatic History: From Revolution to Empire*. Englewood Cliffs, New Jersey: Prentice Hall, 1992.

Clark, C. S. "The Volunteer in War." *United Service Magazine* (London). Reprinted in *Journal of the Military Service Institution of the United States*. 24 (May 1899): 468–474.

Clark, Charles E. "Notes on Cervera's Strategy." *The Century Magazine* 58, no. 1 (May 1899): 103–111.

Clark, Edgar C. *My Fifty Years in the Navy*. Boston: 1917.

Clayton, Bertram T. "With General Miles in Porto Rico." *The Independent* (March 9, 1899): 679–682.

Coffman, Edward M. *The Old Army: A Portrait of the American Army in Peacetime, 1784–1898*. New York and Oxford: Oxford University Press, 1986.

Cohen, Stan. *The Spanish-American War, April–August 1898: A Pictorial History*. Missoula, Montana: Pictorial Histories, 1997.

Colston, W. Hilary. *The Spanish-American War Volunteer: Ninth United States Infantry....* Middletown, Pa.: Coston, 1899.

Combs, Jerald A. *The History of American Foreign Policy*. New York: Alfred A. Knopf, 1986.

Commander J. *Sketches From the Spanish-American War*. Washington, D.C.: Government Printing Office, 1899.

Concas y Palau, Victor M. *The Squadron of Admiral Cervera*. Washington, D.C.: Government Printing Office, 1900. (Translation of *La escuadra del Almirante Cervera*, Madrid, n.d.)

Cook, Francis A. "The 'Brooklyn' at Santiago." *The Century Magazine* 58, no. 1 (May 1899): 95–102.

Cook, Harry T. *"Remember the Maine,"* Winchester, Virginia: 1935.

Coolidge, Katharine. "Song of the Battle-Ship Stokers." *Harper's Weekly* (July 9, 1898): 670.

Coontz, Robert E. *From the Mississippi To The Sea*. Philadelphia: Dorrance and Company, 1930.

Cooper, Jerry M. "National Guard Reform, The Army, and The Spanish-American War: The View From Wisconsin." *Military Affairs* 42, no. 1 (February 1978): 20–23.

Cosmas, Graham A. *An Army for Empire: The United States Army in the Spanish-American War, 1898–1899*. Columbia: University of Missouri Press, 1971.

_____. "From Order to Chaos: The War Department, The National Guard, and Military Policy, 1898." *Military Affairs* 29, no. 3 (Fall 1965): 105–122.

_____. "Military Reform After the Spanish-American War: The Army Reorganization Fight of 1898–1899." *Military Affairs* 35 (February 1971): 12–17.

_____. "Securing the Fruits of Victory: The U.S. Army Occupies Cuba, 1898–1899." *Military Affairs* 38, no. 3 (October 1974): 85–91.

Crane, Capt. C. J. "The New Infantry Rifle." *Journal of the Military Service Institution of the United States* 19 (November 1896): 488–495.

Crane, Charles Judson. *The Experiences of a Colonel of Infantry*. New York: Knickerbocker, 1923.

Crane, Stephen. "War Memories." *Anglo-Saxon Review*. December 1899.

Creagher, Charles E. *The Fourteenth Ohio National Guard — the Fourth Ohio Volunteer Infantry*. Columbus: The Landon Printing and Publishing Co., 1899.

Creelman, James. "Battle Impressions." *The Cosmopolitan* (September 1898): 558.

Cumming, Wallace. "Life in Manila." *The Century Magazine* 56, no. 4 (August 1898): 563–572.

Cushing, A. B. "The Eighteenth United States Infantry," *The American Oldtimer* 8 no. 6 (April 1941): 46–51.

Davis, Oscar King. "Dewey's Capture of Manila." *McClure's Magazine* (February 1899): 171–183.

_____. "Fighting in the Philippines." *Harper's Weekly* (September 17, 1898): 918.

_____. "The Flying Squadron — Target Practice." *Harper's Weekly* (May 28, 1898): 515.

_____. "Off for Manila." *Harper's Weekly* (June 11, 1898): 562.

Davis, Richard Harding. "The Battle of San Juan." *Scribner's* 24, no. 4 (October 1898): 387–403.

_____. "The First Shot of the War." *Scribner's* 24, no. 1 (July 1898): 3–12.

_____. "In the Rifle Pits." *Scribner's* 24, no. 6 (December 1898); 644–658.

_____. "The Landing of the Army." *Scribner's* 24, no. 2 (August 1898): 184–186.

_____. "Our War Correspondents in Cuba and Porto Rico." *Harper's New Monthly Magazine* 98, no. 588 (May 1899): 938–948.

_____. "The Porto Rican Campaign." *Scribner's* 24, no. 5 (November 1898): 515–527.

_____. "The Rocking-Chair Period of the War." *Scribner's* 24, no. 2 (August 1898): 131–143.

_____. "The Rough Riders' Fight at Guasimas." *Scribner's* 24, no. 3 (September 1898): 259–273.

Dean, Teresa. "The Pitiful Side of War." *Leslie's Weekly* (August 25, 1898), 154–155.

DeBurgh, Joseph. "A Few Reminiscences of the First Expedition of American Troops to Manila." *The American Oldtimer* 6, no. 6 (April 1939): 23–29; and 7, no. 1 (November 1939): 26–30, 45–48.

DeConde, Alexander. *A History of American Foreign Policy*. 2d ed. New York: Charles Scribner's Sons, 1971.

Deignan, Osborn W. "The Sinking of the *Merrimac*." *Leslie's Monthly* (January 1899): 247–271.

Department of War. *Regulations for the Army of the United States, 1895*. Washington, D.C.: 1895.

Dewey, George. *Autobiography of George Dewey: Admiral of the Navy*. New York: Charles Scribner's Sons, 1913.

Dickman, I. T. *A Lecture on Balloons in War*. Washington, D.C.: United States Government Printing Office, 1896.

Dieuaide, T. M. "A Historic Scene on the 'Texas.'" *The Century Magazine* 58, no. 1 (May 1899): 118.

Dorwart, Jeffery Michael. "A Mongrel Fleet: America Buys a Navy to Fight Spain, 1898." *Warship International* 17, no. 2 (1980): 128–155.

Dunham, Dr. Carroll. "Medical and Sanitary Aspects of the War." *The Review of Reviews* 18 (October 1898): 415–427.

Eberle, Edward W. "The Bulldog of the Navy." *Leslie's Weekly* (September 8, 1898), 187.

———. "The 'Oregon's' Great Voyage." *The Century Magazine* 58, no. 6 (October 1899): 912–924.

———. "The 'Oregon' at Santiago." *The Century Magazine* 58, no. 1 (May 1899): 104–111.

Edwards, F. E. *The '98 Campaign of the 6th Massachusetts*. Boston: Little, Brown and Company, 1899.

Ellicott, John M. *Effect of Gun Fire of the United States Vessels in the Battle of Manila Bay (May 1, 1898)*. Washington, D.C.: 1899.

———. "The Defenses of Manila Bay." *United States Naval Institute Proceedings* 26 (1900): 279–287.

———. "The Naval Battle of Manila." *United States Naval Institute Proceedings* 26 (September 1900): 489–514.

Esteves, Herman Richard. "The United States, Spain, and the *Maine*, or the Diplomacy of Frustration." *Revista Interamericana Review* 2 (Winter 1973): 549–558.

Evans, Joel C. "The Battle of Manila Bay: Narrative of Joel C. Evans, Gunner of the 'Boston.'" *The Century Magazine* 56, no. 4 (August 1898): 624–627.

Evans, Robley D. *A Sailor's Log: Recollections of Forty Years of Naval Life*. New York and London: D. Appleton-Century Company, 1938.

———. "The 'Iowa' at Santiago." *The Century Magazine* 58, no. 1 (May 1899): 50–62.

"Extract From a Private Letter Received From a Member of Troops 'A.'" *Harper's Weekly* (August 27, 1898): 850.

Faust, Karl Irving. *Campaigning in the Philippines*. New York: Arno, 1970; reprint of 1899.

Ferrell, Robert H. *American Diplomacy: A History*. 3d ed. New York and London: W. W. Norton, 1975.

Feuer, A. B. *The Santiago Campaign of 1898: A Soldier's View of the Spanish-American War*. Westport, Conn., and London: Praeger, 1993.

———. "Battle Line Perfectly Formed." *Military History* 5 (Oct. 1989): 38–45.

Fiske, Bradley A. *From Midshipman to Rear-Admiral*. New York: The Century Company, 1919.

———. "Why We Won at Manila." *The Century Magazine* 57, no. 1 (November 1898): 127–135.

Fleming, Thomas J. "Pershing's Island War." *American Heritage* 19 (August 1968): 32–35, 101–104.

Fox, John, Jr. "Santiago and Caney." *Harper's Weekly* (July 23, 1898): 724; (July 30, 1898): 744; (August 6, 1898): 770.

———. "Volunteers in the Blue-Grass." *Harper's Weekly*. 42 (June 18, 1898): 591.

———. "With the Rough Riders at Las Guasimas." *Harper's Weekly* (July 30, 1898): 750–751.

———. "With the Troops for Santiago." *Harper's Weekly* (July 16, 1898): 698–701.

Franks, Kenny A. "The USS *Texas* and the Battle of Santiago." *Military History of Texas and the Southwest* 12, no. 1, 31–38.

Friend, Joseph A. "Another Notable Voyage." *Leslie's Weekly* (July 7, 1898), 7.

Freeman, Barbara M. "'An Impertinent Fly': Canadian Journalist Kathleen Blake Watkins Covers the Spanish-American War." *Journalism History* 15 (Winter 1988): 132–140.

Freidel, Frank. *The Splendid Little War*. Boston: Little, Brown and Company, 1958.

Fremont, J. C. "Torpedo-Boat Service." *Harper's New Monthly Magazine* 97, no. 583 (November 1898): 829–837.

Frye, James A. *The First Regiment Massachusetts Heavy Artillery United States Volunteers in the Spanish-American War of 1898*. Boston: The Colonial Company, 1899.

García Barrón, Carlos. "Enrique Dupuy de Lôme and the Spanish American War." *Americas* 36, no. 1 (July 1979): 39–58.

Gardner, Augustus Peabody. *Some Letters of Augustus Peabody Gardner*, edited by Constance Gardner. Boston and New York: Houghton Mifflin, 1920.

Gatewood, Willard B., Jr. *"Smoked Yankees" and the Struggle for Empire: Letters from Negro Soldiers, 1898–1902*. Urbana: University of Illinois Press, 1971.

———. "Alabama's 'Negro Soldier Experiment,' 1898–1899." *Journal of Negro History* 57 (October 1972): 333–351.

———. "Kansas Negroes in the Spanish-American War." *Kansas Historical Quarterly* 30 (Autumn 1971): 300–313.

———. "North Carolina's Negro Regiment in the Spanish-American War." *North Carolina Historical Review* 48 (Oct 1971): 370–387.

———. "Virginia's Negro Regiment in the Spanish-American War: The Sixth Virginia Volunteers." *Virginia Magazine of History and Biography* 80 (April 1972): 193–209.

———. "An Experiment in Color: The Eighth Illinois

Volunteers, 1898–1899." *Journal of the Illinois State Historical Society* 65 (Autumn 1972): 293–312.

Giddings, Maj. Howard A. "How to Improve the Condition and Efficiency of the National Guard." *Journal of the Military Service Institution of the United States* 21 (July 1897): 61–75.

_____. *Exploits of the Signal Corps in the War with Spain*. Kansas City: Hudson-Kimberly Publishing Company, 1900.

Gilchrist, Col. James G. "The Reorganization of Our State Troops." *Journal of the Military Service Institution of the United States* 23 (November 1898): 418–426.

Gillett, Mary C. *The Army Medical Department, 1865–1917*. Washington, D.C.: United States Army Center of Military History, 1995.

Gillette, Howard, Jr. "The Military Occupation of Cuba, 1899–1902: Workshop for American Progressivism." *American Quarterly* 25 (October 1973): 410–425.

"Give the Seventh a Chance." *Leslie's Weekly* (July 28, 1898), 62.

"Glimpses of Spanish-American War." *Colorado Magazine* 39, no. 3 (July 1962): 185–194.

Goode, W. A. M. *With Sampson Through the War: Being An Account of the Naval Operations of the North Atlantic Squadron During the Spanish American War of 1898*. New York: Doubleday and McClure, 1899.

Goodrich, Caspar F. "The *St. Louis*' Cable Cutting." *United States Naval Institute Proceedings* 26 (March 1900): 157–166.

Graf, Mercedes H. "Women Nurses in the Spanish-American War." *Minerva: Quarterly Report on Women and the Military* 19, no. 1 (Spring 2001): 3–38.

_____, "Band of Angels: Sister Nurses in the Spanish-American War." *Prologue: The Journal of the National Archives* 34 (Fall 2002): 196–209.

Graham, George Edward. "The Brave Yankee Tar!" *Leslie's Weekly* (July 21, 1898), 54.

_____. "Working the Thirteen-inch Gun." *Leslie's Weekly* (May 12, 1898), 299.

Grant, H. Roger. "The Fighting Firsts: The First South Dakota and Nebraska Volunteers in the Philippines, 1898–1899." *South Dakota History* 4 (Summer 1974): 320–332.

_____. "Letters From the Philippines: The 51st Iowa Volunteers at War, 1898–1899." *Palimpsest* 55 (1974): 162–177.

Greely, A. W. "Balloons in War." *Harper's New Monthly Magazine* 101, no. 601 (June 1900): 33–50.

Green, Michael Robert. "Houston Light Guard, 1873–1898." *Military History of Texas and the Southwest* 14, no. 2, 93–98.

Greene, Francis V. "The Capture of Manila." *The Century Magazine* 57, no. 5 (March 1899): 785–791; 57, no. 6 (April 1899): 915–932.

Grenville, John A. S. "American Naval Preparations for War with Spain, 1896–1898." *Journal of American Studies* 2 (April 1968): 33–48.

Guthrie, Joseph Alfred. "Preparing for Battle." *Leslie's Weekly* (September 22, 1898), 226.

Hancock, H. Irving. *What One Man Saw: Being the Personal Impressions of a War Correspondent in Cuba*. New York: Street and Smith, 1898.

Hansen, David M. "Zalinski's Dynamite Gun." *Technology and Culture: The International Quarterly of the Society for the History of Technology* 25, no. 2 (April 1984): 264–279.

Harbord, Lt. J. G. "The Necessity of a Well Organized and Trained Infantry at the Outbreak of War, and the Best Means to be Adopted by the United States for Obtaining Such a Force." *Journal of the Military Service Institution of the United States.* 21 (July 1897): 1–27.

Hard, Curtis V. *Banners in the Air: The Eighth Ohio Volunteers and the Spanish-American War*. Edited by Robert H. Ferrell. Kent, Ohio: Kent State University Press, 1988.

Harding, Priscilla M. "McKinley's Own: An Ohio Band Plays the 'Splendid Little War.'" *Timeline* 2 (October-November 1985): 10–21.

Harlowe, Jerry. "Dr. Gibbs, Stephen Crane & J. E. Hill." *Military Images*. 5, no. 2 (Sept.-Oct. 1983): 20–21.

Harper, Frank. "Fighting Far From Home: The First Colorado Regiment in the Spanish-American War." *Colorado Heritage: The Journal of the Colorado Historical Society* 1 (1988): 2–11.

Harris, H.S.T. "The Care of the Soldier in Camp, Garrison and the Field." *Journal of the Military Service Institution of the United States* 23, no. 94 (July 1898): 63–75.

Harris, Henry L., and Hilton, John T., eds. *A History of the Second Regiment, N.G.N.J. Second N.J. Volunteers Spanish War Fifth New Jersey Infantry*. Paterson, N.J.: 1908.

Haydock, Michael D. "'This Means War!'" *American History* 32, no. 6 (February 1998): 42–50, 62–63.

Heinl, Robert Debs, Jr. *Soldiers of the Sea: The United States Marine Corps, 1775–1962*. Annapolis: U.S. Naval Institute Press, 1962; Reprint, Baltimore: Nautical and Aviation Publishing Company, 1991.

_____. "How We Got Guantanamo." *American Heritage* 13, no. 2 (February 1962): 18–21, 94–97.

Henderson, W. J. "A War-Ship Community." *Scribner's* 24, no. 3 (September 1898): 285–295.

Herner, Charles. *The Arizona Rough Riders*. Tucson: University of Arizona Press, 1970.

Herrman, Karl Stephen. *A Recent Campaign in Puerto Rico: By the Independent Regular Brigade under the command of Brig. General Schwan*. Richard G. Badger & Co., 1899; reprint Boston: E. H. Bacon & Co., 1907.

Hero Tales of the American Soldier and Sailor as told by... Philadelphia: Century Manufacturing, 1899.

Herst, Herman, Jr. "The First U.S. Airman Shot Down in Combat." *Command: Military History, Strategy & Analysis* No. 16 (May-June 1992): 8–9.

Hines, Richard K. "'First to Respond to their Country's Call': The First Montana Infantry and the Spanish-American War and Philippine Insurrection, 1898–1899." *Montana: The Magazine of Western History* 52, no. 3 (Autumn 2002): 44–58.

Hitchman, James H. "The American Touch in Imperial Administration: Leonard Wood in Cuba, 1898–1902." *Americas* 24 (April 1968): 394–403.

Hobson, Richmond Pearson. *The Sinking of the "Merrimac": A Personal Narrative of the Adventure in the Harbor of Santiago de Cuba, June 3, 1898, and of the Subsequent Imprisonment of the Survivors*. New York: Century Company, 1899.

Holden-Rhodes, J. F. "'In Many a Strife...'" *United States Naval Institute Proceedings* 110 (November 1984): 78–83.

Horton, Corinne Stocker. "A Woman's Tale of the Wounded." *Leslie's Weekly* (September 15, 1898), 206–207.

Howard-Smith, Logan, and J. F. Reynolds-Scott. *The History of Battery A*.
Philadelphia: The John C. Winston Co., 1912.

Hull, John A. T. "The Hull Army Bill." *The Forum* 25 (June 1898): 396–402.

———. "The Organization of the Army." *The North American Review* 168 (April 1899): 385–398.

[Huntington]. "A Trooper's Diary." *Outlook* (July 30, 1898): 775–779; (September 3, 1898): 15–19; (October 29, 1898): 521–527.

Huse, Harry P. "On the 'Gloucester' After the Battle." *The Century Magazine* 58, no. 1 (May 1899): 115–116.

James, Leonard F. *American Foreign Policy*. New York: Scott, Foresman and Company, 1967.

Jamieson, Perry D. *Crossing the Deadly Ground: United States Army Tactics, 1865–1899*. Tuscaloosa: University of Alabama Press, 1994

Johnson, John R. "Nebraska's 'Rough Riders' in the Spanish-American War." *Nebraska History* 29 (June 1948): 105–112.

Johnson, John R. "The Saga of the First Nebraska in the Philippines." *Nebraska History* 30 (June 1949): 139–162.

———. "The Second Nebraska's 'Battle' at Chickamauga." *Nebraska History* 32 (June 1951):

Jones, Harry Wilmer. *A Chaplain's Experience Ashore and Afloat; the Texas Under Fire*. New York: A. G. Sherwood and Co., c.1901.

Jones, Howard. *The Course of American Diplomacy*. 2d ed. Chicago: The Dorsey Press, 1988.

Jones, V. C. "Before the Colors Fade: Last of the Rough Riders." *American Heritage* 20, no. 5 (Aug 1969): 42–43, 93–95.

Jones, Virgil Carrington. *Roosevelt's Rough Riders*. New York: Doubleday, 1971.

Kalisch, Philip A., "Heroines of '98: Female Army Nurses in the Spanish-American War." *Nursing Research* 24, no. 6 (November-December 1975): 411–429.

Keller, Peter. "The Rescue of Admiral Cervera." *Harper's New Monthly Magazine* 98, no. 587 (April 1899): 783–787.

Kelley, Donald Brooks. "Mississippi and 'The splendid little war' of 1898." *Journal of Mississippi History* 26, no. 2, (May 1964): 123–134.

Kelly, Edmond. "An American in Madrid During the War." *The Century Magazine* 57, no. 3 (January 1899): 450–457.

Kendrick, John F. *Thrilling Excerpts from the Rare Historical Record entitled "The Midsummer Picnic of '98."* Ca. 1954.

Kennan, George. *Campaigning in Cuba*. New York: The Century Co., 1899.

Kimball, William W. "Submarine Torpedo-Boats." *Harper's New Monthly Magazine* 101, no. 604 (September 1900): 557–569.

Kindleberger, Charles P. "The Battle of Manila Bay: Narrative of Dr. Charles P. Kindleberger, Junior Surgeon of the Flag-Ship 'Olympia.'" *The Century Magazine* 56, no. 4 (August 1898): 620–624.

King, Col. C. W. "United States Guard, Why Not?" *Journal of the Military Service Institution of the United States* 22 (May 1898): 642–651.

King, George C. *Letters of a Volunteer in the Spanish-American War*. Chicago: Hawkins and Loomis, 1929.

Kreidberg, Marvin A., and Merton G. Henry. *History of Military Mobilization in the United States Army 1775–1945*. Westport, Conn.: Greenwood Press, 1955.

Kuhns, Herman L. "Feeding an Army." *Hotel World* (7 parts) ca. 1898–1899.

Lacey, Edwin M. "The Cuban Diary of Edwin M. Lacey." Edited by Donald F. Tingley. *Journal of the Illinois State Historical Society* 56 (Spring 1963): 20–35.

Langellier, John Philip. "U.S. Infantry Field Uniforms, 1898–1902." *Military Illustrated* (Aug.-Sept. 1988): 34–38.

Lanier, Robert A., Jr. "Memphis Greets War With Spain." *Western Tennessee Historical Society Papers* 18 (1964): 39–58.

Lee, Arthur H. "The Regulars at El Caney." *Scribner's* 24, no. 4 (October 1898): 403–413.

Leffler, John J. "The Paradox of Patriotism: Texans in the Spanish-American War." *Hayes Historical Journal* 8 (Spring 1989): 24–48.

Legrand, Jean. "The Landing at Baiquiri [sic]." *United States Naval Institute Proceedings* 26 (March 1900): 117–126.

Lemons, J. Stanley. "The Cuban Crisis of 1895–1898: Newspapers and Nativism." *Missouri Historical Review* 60, no. 1 (1965).

Linderman, Gerald F. *The Mirror of War: American Society and the Spanish-American War*. Ann Arbor, Mich.: 1974.

Loud, George A. "The Battle of Manila Bay: Colonel George A. Loud's Diary, Written During the Battle." *The Century Magazine* 56, no. 4 (August 1898): 618–620.

———. "The Battle of Manila Bay: Narrative of Colonel George A. Loud." *The Century Magazine* 56, no. 4 (August 1898): 611–618.

Low, A. Maurice. "Amateurs in War." *The Forum* 26 (October 1898): 157–166.

Lumpkin, Ben Gray. "Marching to Cuba." *Colorado Magazine* 42, no. 1 (Winter 1965): 55–59.

Mabey, Charles R. *The Utah Batteries: A History*. Salt Lake City: Daily Reporter, 1900.

Mander, Mary S. "Pen and Sword: Problems of Reporting the Spanish-American War." *Journalism History* 9 (Spring 1982): 2–9, 28.

Marshall, Edward. *The Story of the Rough Riders: First United States Volunteer Cavalry, The Regiment in Camp and on the Battlefield.* New York: 1899.

———. "How It Feels To Be Shot." *The Cosmopolitan* (September 1898): 557–558.

———. "The Santiago Campaign: Some Episodes: A Wounded Correspondent's Recollections of Guasimas." *Scribner's* 24, no. 3 (September 1898): 273–277.

Martin, Harold. "Bombardment of San Juan." *Harper's Weekly* (May 28, 1898): 507.

———. "Santiago: The American Occupation." *Harper's Weekly* (September 17, 1898): 921–923.

Mason, Victor L. "New Weapons of the United States Army." *The Century Magazine* 49, New Series, No. 4 (February 1895): 570–583.

Mattson, Robert Lee. "Politics is Up!— Grigsby's Cowboys and Roosevelt's Rough Riders, 1898." *South Dakota History* 9 (Fall 1979): 303–315.

Mawson, Harry P. "Clothing an Army." *Leslie's Weekly* (September 1, 1898), 175.

———. "The Rough Riders in New York." *Leslie's Weekly* (October 13, 1898), 287.

———. "Tales from the 'Texas.'" *Leslie's Weekly* (September 15, 1898), 215.

McCaffrey, James M. "Texans in the Spanish-American War." *Southwestern Historical Quarterly* 106, no. 2 (October 2002): 255–279.

McCoy, John J. "The Irish Element in the Second Massachusetts Volunteers in the Recent War (with Spain)." *American Irish Historical Society Journal* 2 (1899): 85–88.

McCutcheon, John T. "The Surrender of Manila: As Seen From Admiral Dewey's Flagship." *The Century Magazine* 57, no. 6 (April 1899): 935–942.

McDevitt, V. Edmund. *The First California's Chaplain.* Fresno, California: Academy Library Guild, 1956.

Melzer, Richard, and Phyllis Ann Mingus. "Wild to Fight: The New Mexico Rough Riders in the Spanish-American War." *New Mexico Historical Review* 59 (April 1984): 109–136.

Mickelson, Peter. "Nationalism in Minnesota During the Spanish-American War." *Minnesota History* 41, no. 1 (1968) 1–12.

Miles, Nelson A. *Serving the Republic.* New York and London: 1911.

———. "The War with Spain." *North American Review* 168 (May 1899): 513–529; (June 1899): 749–760; 169 (July 1899): 125–137.

Miley, John D. *In Cuba with Shafter.* New York: 1899.

Miller, William G. *The Twenty Fourth Infantry Past and Present.* reprint Ft. Collins, Colorado: Old Army Press, 1972.

Millet, Frank L. *The Expedition to the Philippines.* New York: 1899.

Millet, F. D. "With General Merritt." *Harper's Weekly* (September 10, 1898): 898.

Millett, Allan R. *Semper Fidelis: The History of the United States Marine Corps.* The Macmillan Wars of the United States Series, Louis Morton, general editor. New York: Macmillan, 1980.

Millis, Walter. *The Martial Spirit: A Study of Our War with Spain.* Boston and New York: 1931.

Moffett, Cleveland. "Sending Our Sick Soldiers Home." *Leslie's Weekly* (September 29, 1898), 249, 252.

———. "Soldiers' Tales of Camp and Field." *Leslie's Weekly* (November 24, 1898), 402–403; (December 1, 1898), 422–423; (December 8, 1898), 442–443; (December 15, 1898), 470–471, (December 22, 1898), 494–495; (December 29, 1898), 520, 522.

———. "Stories of Camp Wikoff." *Leslie's Weekly* (October 6, 1898), 266–267; (October 13, 1898), 286–287; (October 20, 1898), 306–307; (October 27, 1898), 325–326; (November 3, 1898), 342–343; (November 10, 1898), 362; (November 17, 1898), 382–383.

———. "Stories of the Wounded." *Leslie's Weekly* (September 1, 1898), 166; (September 8, 1898), 186; (September 15, 1898), 206; (September 22, 1898), 226.

Mormino, Gary R. "Tampa's Splendid Little War: A Photo Essay." *Tampa Bay History* 4 (Fall-Winter 1982): 45–60.

Moskin, J. Robert. *The U.S. Marine Corps Story.* New York: McGraw-Hill, 1977.

Moss, James A. *Memories of the Campaign of Santiago.* San Francisco: Mysell-Rollins, 1899.

Mott, T. Bentley. "The Fall of Manila." *Scribner's* 24, no. 6 (December 1898): 681–687.

Mount, Graeme S. "Nuevo Mexicanos and the War of 1898." *New Mexico Historical Review* 58 (October 1983): 381–396.

Müller y Tejeiro, Jose. *Battles and Capitulation of Santiago de Cuba.* Washington, D.C.: Government Printing Office, 1899. (Translation of *Combates y capitulacion de Santiago de Cuba*, Madrid, 1898.)

Murray, Ray. "Lest We Forget." *Palimpsest* 29 (June 1948): 174–181.

Nalty, Bernard R. *The United States Marines in the War With Spain.* Washington, D.C.: 1959.

Nelson, Christian G. "Rebirth, Growth, and Expansion of the Texas Militia, 1868–1898." *Texas Military History* 2, no. 1 (February 1962), 1–16.

———. "Organization and Training of the Texas Militia, 1870–1897." *Texas Military History* 2, no. 2 (May 1962): 17–48.

———. "Texas Militia in the Spanish-American War." *Texas Military History* 2, no. 3 (August 1962): 193–209.

"New Interpretation Throws Open the Question of Cause." *National Geographic* 193, no. 2 (February 1998): 102–107.

New York Adjutant General's Office. *New York in the Spanish-American War, 1898.* 3 vols. Albany, 1900.

New York State Historian. *New York and the War with Spain.* Albany, 1903.

Niemeyer, Harry H. *Yarns of Battery A: With the Artillerymen at Chickamauga and Porto Rico.* [n.p., n.d.]

Norris, Frank. "With Lawton at El Caney." *The Century Magazine* 56, no. 2 (June 1898): 304–309.

O'Connor, Richard. "'Black Jack' of the 10th." *American Heritage* 18, no. 2 (Feb. 1967): 14–15, 102–107.

Offley, C. N. "The Oregon's Long Voyage." In *The Great Republic*, vol. 4. New York: Lippincott, 1901.

Offner, John L. *An Unwanted War: The Diplomacy of the United States and Spain Over Cuba, 1895–1898*. Chapel Hill and London: University of North Carolina Press, 1992.

O'Toole, G.J.A. *The Spanish War: An American Epic 1898*. New York and London: W. W. Norton, 1984.

Parker, John H. *History of the Gatling Gun Detachment, Fifth Army Corps, at Santiago, With a Few Unvarnished Truths Concerning that Expedition*. Kansas City: Hudson-Kimberly Publishing Company, 1898.

Parkinson, Russell J. "United States Signal Corps Balloons, 1871–1902." *Military Affairs* 24, no. 4 (Winter 1960–1961): 189–202.

Paterson, Thomas G., J. Garry Clifford, and Kenneth J. Hagan. *American Foreign Policy: A History*. 3d ed. Lexington, Massachusetts and Toronto: D. C. Heath, 1988.

Patrick, Jeff L. "Nothing But Slaves: The Second Kentucky Volunteer Infantry and the Spanish-American War." *Register of the Kentucky Historical Society* 89 (1991) 287–299.

Payne, James E. *History of the Fifth Missouri Volunteer Infantry*. James E. Payne, 1899.

Payne, Robert Bruce. "The Philippine War: The Diary of Robert Bruce Payne, 1899." Edited by John Hall. *Nebraska History* (Winter 1988): 193–198.

Pierce, Franklin E. *Reminiscences of the Experiences of Company L, Second Regiment Massachusetts Infantry, U.S.V., in the Spanish-American War*. Springfield, Mass.: 1900.

Post, Charles Johnson. *The Little War of Private Post*. Boston: Little Brown, 1960; New York: New American Library, 1961.

Prioli, Carmine. "The Second Sinking of the 'Maine.'" *American Heritage* 41, no. 8 (December 1990): 94–101.

Proctor, André Morton. "The 'Gloucester's' Fight." *Harper's Weekly* (August 6, 1898): 774–775.

Ralli, Pandia. "Campaigning in the Philippines, with Co. I of the First California Volunteers." *Overland Monthly* 33 (1899): 154–167; 220–232.

Ranson, E. "British Military and Naval Observers in the Spanish-American War." *Journal of American Studies* 3, no. 1 (July 1969): 33–56.

Ranson, Edward. "The Endicott Board of 1885–86 and the Coast Defenses." *Military Affairs* (Summer 1967): 74–84.

———. "The Investigation of the War Department, 1898–1899." *Historian* 34 (November 1971): 78–99.

Reilly, Margaret Inglehart. "Andrew Wadsworth, A Nebraska Soldier in the Philippines, 1898–1899." *Nebraska History* 68 (Winter 1987): 183–199.

Remington, Frederic. "With the Fifth Corps." *Harper's New Monthly Magazine* 97, no. 582 (November 1898).

Report of the Committee of the Massachusetts Reform Club Appointed to Collect Testimony in Relation to the Spanish-American War. Boston: George H. Ellis, 1899.

Rickover, H. G. *How the Battleship Maine Was Destroyed*. Washington, D.C.: Naval History Division, Department of the Navy, 1976.

Risch, Erna. *Quartermaster Support of the Army: A History of the Corps 1775–1939*. Washington: Quartermaster Historian's Office, Office of the Quartermaster General, 1962.

Roberts, William Ransom. "Under Fire in Cuba: A Volunteer's Eyewitness Account of the War with Spain." *American Heritage* 29, no. 1 (Dec 1977), 78–91.

Robertshaw, James Malcolm. "History of Company C Second Mississippi Regiment, Spanish-American War." In Dunbar Rowland, ed., *Publications of the Mississippi Historical Society: Centenary Series*. 1: 429–441. Jackson: 1916.

Rogers, W. A. "Camp Wikoff." *Harper's Weekly* 42 (September 10, 1898): 890.

Roosevelt, Theodore. *The Rough Riders*. New York: 1899.

Rosenberg, Morton M., and Thomas P. Ruff. *Indiana and the Coming of the Spanish-American War*. Muncie: Ball State University Press, 1976.

Russell, Walter. "An Artist With Admiral Sampson's Fleet." *The Century Magazine* 56, no. 4 (August 1898): 573–577

———. "Incidents of the Cuban Blockade." *The Century Magazine* 56, no. 5 (September 1898): 655–661.

Sampson, William T. "The Atlantic Fleet in the Spanish War." *The Century Magazine* 57, no. 6 (April 1899): 886–913.

———. "Destruction of Admiral Cervera's Fleet" (Copy of Sampson's report of the battle to the Secretary of the Navy, July 15, 1898), 55–64. In *The Great Republic*, vol. 4. New York: Lippincott, 1901.

Sargent, Herbert H. *The Campaign of Santiago de Cuba*. 3 vols. Chicago: A. C. McClurg & Co., 1907.

Sargent, Nathan. *Admiral Dewey and the Manila Campaign* Washington, D.C.: Naval Historical Foundation, 1947.

Saum, Lewis O. "The Western Volunteer and 'The New Empire.'" *Pacific Northwest Quarterly* 57 (January 1966): 18–27.

Schellings, William J. "The Advent of the Spanish-American War in Florida, 1898." *Florida Historical Quarterly* 29 (April 1961): 311–329.

———. "Florida Volunteers in the War with Spain, 1898." *Florida Historical Quarterly* 41 (July 1962): 47–58.

Schuster, Carl O. "Aerial Reconnaissance Before Airplanes." *Command: Military History, Strategy & Analysis* No. 43 (May 1997): 6–7.

Scurry, Thomas. *Report of the Adjutant-General of the State of Texas for 1899–1900*. Austin: Von Boeckman, Schutze & Co., 1899.

Seaman, Louis Livingston. "The United States Army Ration in the Tropics: A Suggestion from Experience." *The Century Magazine* 57, no. 4 (February 1899): 633–634.

Senn, Nicholas. *War Correspondence (Hispano-American War): Letters From Dr. Nicholas Senn*. Chicago: American Medical Association Press, 1899.

———. "Recent Experiences in Military Surgery After the Battle of Santiago." *Journal of the Military Service Institution of the United States* 23, no. 95 (September 1898): 309–323.

Shaffer, Ralph E. "The Race of the *Oregon*." *Oregon Historical Quarterly* 76 (1975): 269–298.

Shafter, William R. "The Capture of Santiago de Cuba." *The Century Magazine* 57, no. 4 (February 1899): 612–630.

———. "The Land Fight at Santiago," 71–82. In *The Great Republic*, vol. 4. New York: Lippincott, 1901.

Sheppard, William B. "How the Seventy-First Fought Like Tigers at El Caney." *Leslie's Weekly* (October 13, 1898), 294.

Shulimson, Jack, Wanda J. Renfrow, David E. Kelly, and Evelyn A. Englander, compilers and editors. *Marines in the Spanish-American War, 1895–1899: Anthology and Annotated Bibliography*. Washington, D.C.: History and Museums Division, Headquarters, U.S. Marine Corps, 1998.

Smythe, Donald. "Pershing in the Spanish-American War." *Military Affairs* 29 (Spring 1965): 25–33.

Society of Santiago de Cuba. *The Santiago Campaign*. Richmond: Williams Printing Co., 1927.

Snow, Richard F. "American Characters: Winfield Scott Schley." *American Heritage* 34, no. 1 (December 1982): 92–93.

The Spanish-American War: the Events of the War Described by Eye-witnesses. Chicago: Herbert S. Stone and Company, 1899.

Spears, John R. *Our Navy in the War with Spain*. New York: 1898.

———. "The Affair of the Winslow." *Scribner's* 24, no.2 (August 1898): 182–184.

———. "Afloat for News in War Times." *Scribner's* 24, no.4 (October 1898): 501–504.

———. "The Chase of Cervera." *Scribner's* 24, no. 2 (August 1898): 144–152.

———. "Torpedo Boats in the War with Spain." *Scribner's* 24, no. 5 (November 1898): 614–619.

Staunton, S. A. "The Naval Campaign of 1898 in the West Indies." *Harper's New Monthly Magazine* 98, no. 584 (January 1899): 175–193.

Steelman, Joseph F. *North Carolina's Role in the Spanish-American War*. Raleigh: North Carolina Department of Cultural Resources, Division of Archives and History, 1975.

Stelck, W. Ardell. "Sgt. Guy Gillette and Cherokee's 'Gallant Co. M' in the Spanish American War." *Annals of Iowa* 40, no. 8 (Spring 1971): 561–576.

Sternlicht, Sanford. *McKinley's Bulldog: The Battleship Oregon*. Chicago: Nelson-Hall, 1977.

Stevens, Michael E., ed. *Letters From the Front, 1898–1945*. Madison: Center for Documentary History, State Historical Society of Wisconsin, 1992.

Steward, Theophilus Gould. *The Colored Regulars in the United States Army*. 1904; reprint, New York: Arno, 1969.

Stewart, Merch Bradt. *The N'th Foot in War*. Kansas City, Missouri: Hudson Press, 1906.

Stickney, Joseph L. *War in the Philippines*. Springfield, Mass.: 1899.

———. "With Dewey at Manila." *Harper's New Monthly Magazine* 98, no. 585 (February 1899): 475–484.

St. Louis, Private. *Forty Years After*. Boston: Chapman and Grimes, 1939.

Stone, J. Hamilton. "Our Troops in the Tropics—From a Surgeon's Standpoint." *Journal of the Military Service Institution of the United States* 26 (May 1900): 358–369.

Stronach, John. "The 34th Michigan Volunteer Infantry." *Michigan History* 30 (April-June 1946): 289–304.

Strong, Putnam Bradlee. "Six Weeks on a Transport." *Leslie's Weekly* (November 3, 1898), 354.

———. "Manila Just as It Is." *Leslie's Weekly* (December 8, 1898), 443.

Taylor, Henry C. "The 'Indiana' at Santiago." *The Century Magazine* 58, no. 1 (May 1899): 62–75.

Telfer, George F. *Manila Envelopes: Oregon Volunteer Lt. George F. Telfer's Spanish-American War Letters*. Edited by Sara Bunnett. Portland: Oregon Historical Society Press, 1989.

Terrill, Tom Edward. "An Economic Aspect of the Spanish-American War." *Ohio History* 76 (Winter-Spring 1967): 73–75.

Thiessen, Thomas D. "The Fighting First Nebraska: Nebraska's Imperial Adventure in the Philippines, 1898–1899." *Nebraska History* 70, no. 3 (Fall 1989): 210–272.

Thomas, Donna. "'Camp Hell': Miami During the Spanish-American War." *Florida Historical Quarterly* 57 (October 1978): 141–156.

Thompson, H. C. "Oregon Volunteer Reminiscences of the War with Spain." *Oregon Historical Quarterly* 49 (1948) 192–204.

———. "War Without Medals." *Oregon Historical Quarterly* 59 (Dec 1948): 293–325.

Thompson, Winfield M. "Our Spanish Prisoners of War." *Harper's Weekly* (July 30, 1898): 754.

Tisdale, G. T. *Three Years Behind the Guns*. New York: Grosset and Dunlap, 1908.

Titherington, Richard H. "Our Spanish Prisoners at Portsmouth." *Harper's Weekly* (August 20, 1898): 826–828.

———. "The Truce." *Harper's Weekly* (August 13, 1898): 802–803.

Trask, David F. *The War with Spain in 1898*. New York: Macmillan, 1981.

Turner, T. A. *Story of the Fifteenth Minnesota Volunteer Infantry*. Minneapolis: 1899.

Ullman, Bruce L. "The War Balloon *Santiago*." *Aerospace Historian* 32 (June 1985): 117–129.

Upton, Emory. *The Military Policy of the United States*; 1904, reprint New York: Greenwood Press, 1968.

U.S. Senate. *Report of the Commission Appointed by the President to Investigate the Conduct of the War Department in the War with Spain*. 8 vols. 56th Cong., 1st Sess., Sen. Doc. No. 221. Washington, D.C.: 1900.

Vardaman, James K. "The Spanish-American War as revealed through the letters of Major James K. Vardaman." *Journal of Mississippi History*. 9, no. 2 (April 1947), 108–120.

Venable, William Mayo. *The Second Regiment of United States Volunteer Engineers.* Cincinnati: McDonald and Company, 1899.

Vivian, Thomas J., ed. *With Dewey at Manila.* New York: 1898.

W.C.E. "The Trip to Manila With Merritt." *Leslie's Weekly* (September 29, 1898), 247.

Wainwright, Richard. "The 'Gloucester' at Santiago." *The Century Magazine* 58, no. 1 (May 1899): 76–86.

Waldeck, Ruby Weedell. "Missouri in the Spanish-American War." *The Missouri Historical Review* 30 (1935–36): 365–400.

Walker, Dale L. "Bucky O'Neill and the Rough Riders." *Montana: Magazine of Western History* 21 (January 1971): 60–71.

Walker, T. Dart. "Dynamite-Guns in Puerto Rico." *Harper's Weekly* (September 10, 1898): 897.

———. "The Puerto Rico Expedition." *Harper's Weekly* (August 20, 1898): 827–828.

Wall, Barbara Mann. "Courage to Care: The Sisters of the Holy Cross in the Spanish-American War." *Nursing History Review* 3 (1995): 55–77.

Walsh, Henry Collins. "With the Blockading Fleet." *Harper's Weekly* (July 30, 1898): 754.

"War Ballooning in Cuba." *The Aeronautical Journal* (October 1899): 83–86.

"War History in Private Letters." *Outlook* (August 13, 1898): 919–923; (August 20, 1898): 968–973; (August 27, 1898): 1016–1021.

Webb, A. D. "Arizonans in the Spanish-American War." *Arizona Historical Review* 1 (January 1929): 50–68.

Webb, William Joe. "The Spanish-American War and United States Army Shipping." *American Neptune* 40 (July 1980): 167–191.

Webber, H. E. *Twelve Months with the Eighth Massachusetts Infantry.* Salem, Mass.: Newcomb and Gauss, 1908.

"West Meets East: The Philippines Through the Eyes of the Colorado Volunteers." *Colorado Heritage: The Journal of the Colorado Historical Society* 1 (1988): 12–32.

Wheeler, Joseph. *The Santiago Campaign, 1898.* Philadelphia: 1899.

White, Douglas. *On to Manila: A True and Concise History of the Philippine Campaigns, Secured While Afloat With Admiral Dewey's Fleet, and in the Field With the 8th U.S. Army Corps. Pacific Historical Magazine* 1, no. 1 (June 30, 1899): [1]-[54].

———. "The Capture of the Island of Guam, the True Story." *Overland Monthly*, March 1900.

White, William Allen. "When Johnny Went Marching Out." *McClure's Magazine* 11 (June 1898): 198–205.

Whitney, Caspar. "The Santiago Campaign." *Harper's New Monthly Magazine* 97, no. 581 (October 1898): 795–818.

Wilcox, Marion. "Diary of the War." *Harper's Weekly* (August 20, 1898): 811, 828.

Williams, Arthur. "Readiness for War." *Journal of the Military Service Institution of the United States* 21 (September 1897): 225–256.

Williams, Dion. "The Naval Battle of Manila," *United States Naval Institute Proceedings* (May 1928): 345–353.

Williams, Leonard. "The Army of Spain: Its Present Qualities and Modern Virtues." *United Service Magazine (London)* Reprinted in *Journal of the Military Service Institution of the United States* 21 (September 1897): 349–353.

Wilson, James Harrison. *Under the Old Flag: Recollections of Military Operations in the War for the Union, the Boxer Rebellion, etc.* 2 vols. New York and London: 1912.

Winslow, Cameron McR. "Cable-Cutting at Cienfuegos." *The Century Magazine* 57, no. 5 (March 1899): 708–717.

Winter, John G., Jr. "How It Feels to be Under Fire." *Leslie's Weekly* (September 22, 1898), 226.

Wintermuth, Peter. "Story of a Naval Electrician." *Leslie's Weekly* (August 11, 1898), 114.

Wood, E. P. "The Battle of Manila Bay." *The Century Magazine* 57, no. 6 (April 1899): 957–958.

Wood, Elmer Ellsworth. "Louisiana in the Spanish-American War, 1898–1899, As Recorded by Colonel Elmer Ellsworth Wood, Commander of the Second Regiment of Louisiana Volunteer Infantry." Edited by Walter Prichard. *Louisiana Historical Quarterly* 26 (July 1943).

Wozencraft, A. P. *Report of the Adjutant General of the State of Texas for 1897–98.* Austin: 1899.

Young, James Rankin, and J. Hampton Moore. *Reminiscences and Thrilling Stories of the War by Returned Heroes...* Philadelphia: Elliott Publishing Company, 1899.

Zogbaum, R. F. "The Blockading Fleet." *Harper's Weekly* (May 21, 1898): 501–502.

Unpublished Material

Delgado, Octavio A. "The Spanish Army in Cuba, 1868–1898: An Institutional Study." Ph.D. diss., Columbia University, 1980.

Leffler, John Joseph. "From the Shadows into the Sun: Americans in the Spanish-American War." Ph.D. diss., University of Texas, 1991.

Werner, Sister Maria Assunta, C.S.C. "The Sisters of the Holy Cross during the Spanish-American War, 1898–1899." 1986 Conference on the History of the Congregations of Holy Cross, Austin, Texas.

Internet Material

Booth, Harold. "Letter from Private Harold Booth, Co. K, First New York Volunteer Infantry," contributed by Robert Brockway, http://www.spanamwar.com, accessed October 29, 2002.

Cripps, George Edgar. "The Diary of George Edgar Cripps of the 34th Michigan Volunteer Infantry," contributed by Joe Riley, http://www.spanamwar.com, accessed October 29, 2002.

Crouse, William. "William Crouse, of the USS Concord Writes Home," contributed by Randolph Flood, transcribed by Jack L. McSherry, Jr., http://www.spanamwar.com, accessed October 29, 2002.

Edwards, Bertram Willard. "The Diary of Bertram Willard Edwards, Ordinary Seaman, USS Oregon," contributed by Susan Abbe, transcribed by Jack L. McSherry, Jr., http://www.spanamwar.com, accessed October 29, 2002.

Kuchmeister, Hermann W. "Private Hermann W. Kuchmeister's Account of the Cienfuegos Cable Cutting Expedition," contributed by William D. Furey, http://www.spanamwar.com, accessed October 29, 2002.

"Letters from the 34th Michigan Volunteer Infantry," contributed by Kevin Gilfether, http://www.spanamwar.com, accessed October 29, 2002.

Lewis, Morgan James. "Morgan James Lewis Writes Home About the Cruise to Cuba on the Transport Orizaba," http://www.spanamwar.com, accessed October 29, 2002.

Moore, J. House. "J. House Moore Writes Home About the Assault on El Caney," contributed by Robert Coley Thomas, http://www.spanamwar.com, accessed October 29, 2002.

Mullin, Burt O. "Burt O. Mullin of the 49th Iowa Volunteer Infantry, Company C, Writes Home," contributed by Charlotte Huckstead, http://www.spanamwar.com, accessed October 29, 2002.

Reese, William A., Jr. "William A. Reese Jr. of the 11th U.S. Infantry Writes Home," contributed by Clarke Reese, http://www.spanamwar.com, accessed October 29, 2002.

Robinson, George W. "The Diary of George W. Robinson, Fireman 2nd Division, No. 1 Fire Room, USS Oregon," contributed by Sean Cox, http://www.spanamwar.com, accessed October 29, 2002.

Schuster, M. A. J., Jr. "M. A. J. Schuster Jr.'s 'The Spanish-American War,'" contributed by Patricia Meis, http://www.spanamwar.com, accessed October 29, 2002.

Smith, William Burdette. "William Burdette Smith of the 13th Minnesota Volunteer Infantry, Co. F., Writes Home from California," contributed by the family of William Burdette Smith, http://www.spanamwar.com, accessed October 29, 2002.

Turley, Robert. "Diary of the war went through by Robert Turley," contributed by Bob Turley, http://www.spanamwar.com, accessed October 29, 2002.

True, Herbert Hyde, "The 71st New York at San Juan Hill," http://www.spanamwar.com, accessed October 29, 2002.

Werling, John. "Letters from Camp Cuba Libre or Letters from Corp. John Werling, Company D, 2nd New Jersey Volunteer Infantry," contributed by Mary Andrews, http://www.spanamwar.com, accessed October 29, 2002.

Wyre, Sherman. "Sherman Wyre of the 8th Ohio Volunteer Infantry, Co. H. Writes Home," contributed by Steven Wyre, transcribed by Jack L. McSherry, Jr., http://www.spanamwar.com, accessed October 29, 2002.

Index

Adula 62
African-Americans 22, 28–30, 34, 44, 77, 85–87, 90, 98–99, 102–103, 105, 123, 127, 159, 179, 189–190
Aguinaldo y Famy, Emilio 19, 145, 148, 149, 150, 152, 156
Alabama volunteers 27, 32, 40–41, 44, 184
Alcohol 35–36, 43, 76, 131, 136, 175–176, 183
Alfonso XII 5, 53
Alfonso XIII, King 190
Alger, Secretary of War Russell 22, 23, 28, 32, 77, 108, 124, 128, 158, 174, 177,
Almirante Oquendo 111, 113–115, 187
Alvardo 111, 119
American Red Cross 36, 45, 163, 175
Amphitrite 59–61
Anderson, Lt. E.A. 55–56
Anderson, Brig. Gen. Thomas M. 130, 142, 150, 153
Anducar, Pedro Duarte 134
Anthony, Maj. Frank 162
Archibald, James F. J. 54
Arizona volunteers 34, 103
Astor, John Jacob 28–29
Astor Battery 28–29, 143, 151, 153–154
Augustín, Basilio 18, 145, 151
Auñón y Villalón, Minister of Marine Ramón 63, 110
Australia 130, 134–135

Bagley, Ens. Worth 58
Balloons 58–59, 79, 92–93, 100–101
Baltimore 8–13, 15–17, 152, 188
Bates, Brig. Gen. John C. 83, 97, 108
Bernadou, Lt. John B. 58
Biddle, Lt. Col. John 168
Blanco y Erenas, Gov.-Gen. Ramón 110
Bliss, Lt. Col. Tasker 170, 190

Boston 8, 10, 12–15, 152
Boston Herald 176
Boynton, Brig. Gen. Henry V. 23, 45, 46
Braunersreuther, Lt. William 135–136
Brodie, Maj. Alexander 87
Brooke, Maj. Gen. John R. 158, 163, 171–173
Brooklyn 61, 64, 73, 111, 113, 118–121, 123, 182
Brown, Chaplain Henry A. 90
Brumby, Lt. Thomas M. 154–155
Buenaventura 53
Burroughs, Edgar Rice 191
Burt, Col. Andrew 22

Cable-cutting 54–57, 189
Cadarso, Don Luis 16
California volunteers 130, 132, 143, 148–150, 156, 182, 185
Callao 19, 152–154
Cámara, RAdm Manuel 63
Camps: Alva Adams 38; Alvin Saunders 31; Dewey 143–144, 146, 148, 152; George Thomas 22–23, 32, 34–36, 39–40, 42–46, 48, 76, 130; Hamilton 36; "Hell" (Miami) 35; McCalla 70–73; Merriam 129; Merritt 129–130; Russell Alger 23, 32, 35, 40, 43, 46, 76, 130; Wikoff 174, 177
Capron, Capt. Allyn, Jr. 86–88, 90, 94
Capron, Capt. Allyn, Sr. 94, 97
Cárdenas, bombardment of 57–58
Cardinal Cisneros 120
Castilla 12, 15, 17, 18, 187
Castillo Duany, Gen. Demetrio 93
Cervera, Lt. Angel 117
Cervera y Topete, Adm. Pascual 49, 50, 54, 58, 59, 60, 61, 62, 63, 64, 68, 80, 93, 109, 110, 111, 112, 113, 114, 115, 117, 119, 122, 145, 158, 186, 190
Chafee, Brig. Gen. Adna 89, 92–93, 97, 190
Charleston 131–136, 142, 152, 190

China 136–137
Christy, Howard Chandler 99–100
Cincinnati 53, 164
City of Chester 160
City of Para 137, 139, 148
City of Peking 130, 132
City of Sydney 130, 135
City of Washington 5
Clark, Capt. Charles E. 50–53, 115, 120, 121
Clinton, Pres. William 189–190
Clough, Gov. David M. 24
Cody, William "Buffalo Bill" 21
Coit, Col. A. B. 172
Colon 136
Colorado volunteers 21, 136, 145, 147–148, 153–154, 156
Columbia 161
Concord 8, 10, 12–15, 152
Cook, Capt. Francis 120–121
Concas y Palau, Capt. Victor 111–112, 114, 117
Converse, Capt. G.A. 62
Corbin, Adj. Gen. Henry 124, 159
Coreo 18
Crane, Stephen 70, 86
Creelman, James 98
Cristóbal Colón 49, 63, 64
Cuban revolution 3–4
Curtin, Ens. Roland I. 163
Cuthbertson, Maj. H. C. 148–149

Daiquirí, landings at 81–84
Daughters of the American Revolution (DAR) 47–48
Davis, Brig. Gen. Benjamin O. 190
Davis, Cmdr. Charles H. 163
Davis, Richard Harding 80, 82–83, 85–86, 88, 169, 186
Day, Secretary of State William 173
Dayton, Cmdr. J.H. 60
Derby, Lt. Col. George M. 93, 100–102
Detroit 60
Dewey, Cmdre./RAdm. George 1, 8–19, 49, 53, 54, 60, 121, 129, 136, 142, 145, 150–155, 188, 190

221

Index

Díaz, Gen. Pedro 54
Dickinson, Lt. Walter M. 96
District of Columbia volunteers 123
Dole, Pres. Sanford 133
Dolphin 69, 72
Don Antonio de Ulloa 12, 17
Don Juan de Austria 18
Dorst, Capt. Joseph H. 54
Drinking water 34–35, 45–46, 50, 81, 140, 160, 175
Duffield, Brig. Gen. Henry M. 92–94
Dynamite gun 123, 171–173

Eagle 55
Edison, Thomas 31
Edson, Ens. John T. 116–117
El Caney, Battle of 92–99, 104, 189
Elliott, Capt. George 72
Ellis, Yeoman George H. 118, 121
Emperador Carlos V. 63, 74, 120
Erickson, Gunner John 61
Ericsson 111, 119
Ernst, Brig. Gen. Oswald H. 168–170
Escario, Col. Federico 122
Eulate, Capt. Antonio 118–120
Evans, Capt. Robley D. 61, 66, 113, 119–121
Ewers, Lt. Col. E.P. 103

Fairbanks, Sen. Charles W. 159
Fish, Sgt. Hamilton 79, 87
Flagler, Henry 35
Florida volunteers 24, 42
Folger, Capt. W. 63
Food 37–39, 42, 132–133, 139–140, 160, 182, 184–185
Furor 111, 116–117

Garcia, Gen. Calixto 81, 125
Garretson, George 161–162, 164, 167
Gatling guns 83, 104, 123, 137, 165
Gen. Lezo 18
Georgia volunteers 77, 177
Gibbs, Ens. John B. 70–71
Glass, Capt. Henry 133–135
Gloucester 111, 116–117, 119, 122, 161, 163–164
Godkin, E.L. 6
Goodrich, B.F. 190
Goodrich, Capt. Caspar 57
Gould, Jay 177
Greene, Brig. Gen. Francis V. 136–137, 145, 147–148, 151, 153–154
Greenleaf, Col. Charles R. 127
Gridley, Capt. Charles 15, 16
Grimes, Capt. George 99–100
Guam, capture of 133–136, 186, 188
Guantánamo, capture of 69–73
Gussie 54

Haims, Lt. J.P. 170
Harvard 64, 120
Haskell, Col. J.T. 96
Hawaii 131–133, 136, 188
Hawkins, Col. Alexander 148

Hawkins, Brig. Gen. Hamilton S. 102, 104
Hearst, William Randolph 3, 6, 98
Henry, Brig. Gen. Guy V. 162–164
Hist 111, 119
Hobbs, Capt. Charles W. 149
Hobson, Lt. Richmond 65–68, 73, 123, 189, 191
Horn, Tom 191
Hotchkiss guns 29, 55, 87, 100, 153
Hughes, Lt. Edward M. 17–18
Hull, Cordell 190
Huntington, Lt. Col. Robert W. 69–73
Hudson 58, 175
Hugh McCulloch 10, 13–15, 18, 188
Hygiene 42–43, 45–46, 138–139, 176

Idaho volunteers 137
Illinois volunteers 26, 29, 39–40, 44, 123, 159, 161–162, 165, 167, 173, 177–179, 183–184, 191
Immortalite 152
Indiana 59–60, 68, 111–112, 119, 123, 148, 188
Indiana volunteers 27, 36, 39, 43, 46, 159, 177, 182, 184
Infanta María Teresa 111–114, 186–187
Iowa 59–61, 63–64, 66, 68, 73, 111, 113–114, 118–121, 188
Iowa volunteers 24, 33, 36, 40, 46
Isla de Cuba 16, 18
Isla de Luzon 18
Isla de Mindinao 10
Itrich, Chief Carpenter's Mate Franz 189

James McKee 132
Jáudenes y Alvarez, Gen. Fermín 151, 154, 157
Jennings, Janet 175
Jones, Chaplain Harry 71
Jones, Sam Maj. 149

Kansas volunteers 44
Kent, Brig. Gen. Jacob F. 82–83, 99, 102, 108
Kentucky volunteers 36
King, Chief of Staff Ernest J. 190
Knickerbocker 80, 83
Knights of Pythias 24
Knox, Secretary of the Navy William F. "Frank" 190
Krayenbuhl, Lt. Col. Maurice G. 149
Kwonghoi 155

Lamberton, Cmdr. B.P. 8–9, 12
Lancaster, Maj. J.M. 170
Las Guasimas, Battle of 85–90, 94, 105
Lawton, Brig. Gen. Henry W. 83, 85, 89, 92–94, 97, 100, 108
Leahy, Ens. William 190
Lebanon 182
Lee, Capt. Arthur 93
Linares Pomba, Gen. Arsenio 81, 91–92, 107, 110

Liscum, Lt. Col. Emerson 103
Lodge, Sen. Henry Cabot 189
Long, Secretary of the Navy John 62, 177
Louisiana volunteers 26, 30, 39
Ludlow, Brig. Gen. William 94

MacArthur, Brig. Gen. Arthur 137, 150–151, 153–154, 157
Magill, Second Lt. Louis J. 72
Maine 4–6, 14, 20–21, 31, 50, 51, 116, 152, 182, 184, 187–188
Manila, Battle for 147–155
Manilla Bay, Battle of 13–18, 121, 129, 136, 142, 189
Manning 54
Marblehead 53, 55–57, 64, 69–70, 73
March, First Lt. Peyton 28–29
Maria Theresa 121
Marietta 52
Marina, Gov. Juan 134–135
Marines, U.S. 4, 51–53, 55–57, 61, 69–73, 90, 118, 129, 135, 142, 182, 187, 189
Marqués del Duero 18
Marshall, Edward 86, 88–89
Martí, José 3
Mascots 21, 34, 74, 122
Massachusetts 61, 64, 66, 68, 73, 111, 123, 188
Massachusetts volunteers 21, 27, 30, 32–34, 40, 42, 80, 94–95, 99, 123, 160–162, 167, 176, 178–179, 181
Matanzas, bombardment of 53–54
Maxfield, Maj. J.E. 79–80, 92–93, 100–101, 191
Maynard, Washburn 57
McCalla, Cmdr. B.H. 55, 69, 71–72
McClernand, Lt. Col. Edward J. 100, 122
McGee, Dr. Anita Newcomb 47–48
McIntosh, Burr 84
McKinley, Pres. William 4, 6–7, 18–19, 23, 29, 44, 58, 63, 108, 177, 183, 191
McKittrick, Capt. William H. 125
Medal of Honor 188–190
Merrimac 63–68, 73, 109–110, 123, 187, 189, 191; scuttling 64–68, 123
Merritt, Maj. Gen. Wesley 129, 137, 145, 150–152, 190
Meteoro 63
Miami 175
Michigan volunteers 92, 94, 123, 126
Miles, Col. Evan 94
Miles, Maj. Gen. Nelson 124, 127, 129, 158, 161–164, 171, 173, 190
Miley, Lt. John D. 103, 105, 123, 125
Miller, Cmdr. J. M. 65
Minneapolis 62
Minnesota 43
Minnesota volunteers 24–25, 30, 37, 137–140, 144, 152, 154, 159, 179, 182
Mississippi volunteers 20, 24–25, 28, 36–37

Missouri volunteers 21, 27–28, 34, 39, 42
Mitchell, Billy 191
Mix, Tom 191
Mobile 175
Moffett, Ens. William 190–191
Mohican 8
Monocacy 8
Monterey 150
Montgomery 63
Montojo y Pasarón, Adm. Patricio 11–18, 129, 190
Morgan City 133, 141, 148
Movies 31, 102

Nanshan 8, 10
Nashville 53, 55–57
National Guard 20–21, 23, 24, 25
Neptune, King 50–51
Nebraska volunteers 25, 28, 31, 33–34, 42, 131–132, 136, 147, 154
Neville, 1st Lt. Wendall C. 70–71
New Jersey volunteers 31, 77
New Orleans 63–64, 73, 111
New Orleans Times Democrat 6
New York 53–54, 59–61, 64, 66–67, 73, 109, 116, 119, 123
New York Journal 3, 5–6
New York Tribune 6
New York volunteers 21, 24–26, 28, 32, 36, 38, 44, 46, 78, 81, 101–102, 106, 123. 159, 168, 175, 178
New York World 3, 5
Newark 111
Newport 131
North Carolina volunteers 24, 26, 40
North Dakota volunteers 131, 137, 139, 144, 153, 179–180
Nuns, Roman Catholic 48
Nurses 46–48

O'Hern, Lt. Edward P. 170
Ohio 141, 148
Ohio volunteers 31, 34, 35, 38, 40, 46, 77, 123, 159–160, 162, 171–173, 177–179, 184, 191
Olympia 8–10, 12–17, 151–153, 155, 188
O'Neill, Capt. William "Bucky" 83, 103
Ord, Lt. Jules 104
Oregon 49–54, 64, 68–70, 73, 111, 114–115, 118–123, 188, 190
Oregon volunteers 21, 32, 129, 132, 135, 144, 155

Panther 69
Parker, Lt. John H. 104
Patriota 63
Pelayo 120
Pennsylvania volunteers 34, 37, 136, 148–149, 159–160, 168–169, 173, 182
Pershing, Lt. John J. 89, 122, 190
Peru 132, 138
Petrel 8–10, 14–15, 17–18, 152–153, 189
Philip, Capt. John W. "Jack" 65, 71, 73, 111–115, 119

Physical examinations 26–27
Plutón 111, 116–117
Poetry 28, 38, 41–42, 112, 160, 183–184
Porter 61, 64, 69
Portusach, Frank 134
Potter, Capt. J.D. 171
Proctor, Asst. Engineer André 122
Puerto Rico, campaigning in 161–173
Pulitzer, Joseph 3, 6
Puritan 53–54

Quick, Sergeant John H. 72–73

Radford, Lt. Cyrus 71
Raleigh 8–10, 13, 15, 17, 152–153
Randall, Chief Engineer Frank B. 14
Rápido 63
Rea, George Bronson 5
Reconcentration camps 3
Reina Cristina 15–16, 18
Reina Mercedes 74, 119, 187
Reiter, G.C. 69
Relief 175
Remington, Frederic 79
Resolute 182
Richter, Capt. Reinhold 148
Rio Grande 79
Roosevelt, Pres. Franklin 190
Roosevelt, Lt. Col./Col./Pres. Theodore 4, 34, 70, 78–80, 84–89, 92, 100, 104–105, 114, 126, 128, 174–176, 189–191
Roosevelt, Tweed 189
Rough Riders 34, 36, 38–39, 43, 76–78, 80, 83–90, 92, 105–106, 175–177, 179, 189, 191

St. Louis 57, 159–160, 164
St. Paul 62, 159–160, 164
Sampson, RAdm William T. 53, 57, 59–66, 68–69, 73, 79–81, 91, 108–109, 111, 113, 119–122, 125, 190
San Antonio de Abad, Fort 145, 147–148, 151–154
Sandburg, Carl 191
Sandoval 69
San Francisco Post 54
San Juan, Puerto Rico, naval bombardment of 59–61
San Juan Heights, Battle of 92–94, 99–106, 110, 186, 189
San Marcos 188
Santa Fe New Mexican 24
Santiago, Naval Battle of 109–121, 158
Saturn 55
Schley, Commodore Winfield S. 61–64, 113, 118, 120–122, 188
Schwan, Brig. Gen. Theodore 158, 163–164, 166–167
Scorpion 61
Segurança 81–83, 91
Seneca 175
Shafter, Maj. Gen. William R. 1, 63–64, 75, 77, 79–85, 91–92, 97, 99–100, 102–103, 107–109, 111, 122–128, 158, 174, 190

Shaw, 2nd Lt. Melville J. 70
Siboney, landings at 85–86
Sickness 44–48, 92, 108, 126–128, 131, 141, 174, 176–177, 184, 186
Sightseeing 43–44
Sigsbee, Capt. Charles D. 4–5, 187
Solace 61
South Carolina volunteers 29
South Dakota volunteers 31
Souvenirs 43, 182, 187
Spicer, Capt. William F. 72
Sterling 64
Sterling, William 148
Sternberg, Surgeon Gen. George 128
Student volunteers 27–28
Sumner, Brig. Gen. Samuel S. 92, 105, 189
Suwanee 73
Swearing in 32–33

Talbot 79
Tanner, Gov. John 29, 44, 48, 159
Tarzan 191
Temerario 51, 53
Tennessee volunteers 190
Terror 59–60
Texas 56, 61, 64–65, 67–68, 73–74, 111–115, 118–119, 121, 188
Texas volunteers 25, 28, 32–33, 38, 177–178, 192
Todd, Cmdr. Chapman 57–58
Toral, Gen. José 107, 122–125, 158
Torrey, Jay 23
Training and drill 37, 39–42, 130, 143, 181
Tyler, Gov. J. Hoge 30

Uniforms 21, 27–29, 84, 124, 138, 161
United States Army: Artillery Regiments 137, 148, 153, 165–166, 168, 170, 191; Balloon troops 79; Cavalry 29–30, 34, 36, 38–39, 43, 54, 76–78, 80, 83–90, 105–106, 123, 125, 165, 175–177, 179, 189, 190, 191; Engineers 76; Infantry 22, 30, 54, 77, 78, 94–96, 97–99, 102–103, 105, 124, 125, 127, 130, 136–137, 145, 153, 154, 165–166, 189, 192
Utah volunteers 136–137, 144–145, 148–151, 153–154, 181, 184

Valencia 137, 139, 148
Vara del Rey, Gen. Joaquín 94, 99, 125
Virginia volunteers 28, 30, 44
Vizcaya 49, 111, 113, 115, 118–119, 187
Vulcan 186

Wainwright, Lt. Cmdr. Richard 116–117
Wake Island 136
Warren, Sen. Francis E. 23
Wasp 54, 163–164
Weather 42, 91, 123, 129, 138, 143–144, 148, 150
Weyler y Nicolau, Gov. Gen. Valeriano 3–4, 190

Wheeler, Maj. Gen. Joseph 85–87, 89, 92, 99, 106–108, 125, 189–190
Wheeler, Lt. Joseph, Jr. 125
Whittier, Lt. Col. Charles A. 154
Widemark, Seaman Frank 61
Wikoff, Col. Charles A. 102–103
Wildes, Capt. Frank 8
Williams, Consul O. F. 9–10, 13
Wilmington 57–58
Winder, Lt. William 13
Windom 55, 57
Winslow 58
Winslow, Lt. Cameron 55–57
Wisconsin volunteers 162, 168–170, 191
Women's Christian Temperance Union 36
Wompatuck 57, 60
Wood, Col./Brig. Gen. Leonard 78, 86–87, 89, 92, 105, 189–190
Wyoming volunteers 23, 137

Yankee 69, 73, 79
Yosemite 69
Young, Brig. Gen. Samuel B. M. 86–87, 92
Young Ladies' Soldiers Relief Society 36
Yucatan 78, 80, 84

Zafiro 8, 10, 13, 18
Zealandia 136

www.ingramcontent.com/pod-product-compliance
Ingram Content Group UK Ltd.
Pitfield, Milton Keynes, MK11 3LW, UK
UKHW050530150426
5217IPUK00026B/1872